# PRINCIPLES OF STATISTICS

For B.A., B.Com., M.A., M.Com.,
C.A., I.C.W.A., C.S. Examinations

VOLUME – I

**DR. DARYAB SINGH**
Reader, Department of Commerce,
Shivaji College,
(Delhi University), Delhi



ATLANTIC

ATLANTIC PUBLISHERS AND DISTRIBUTORS

*Published by*
**ATLANTIC PUBLISHERS AND DISTRIBUTORS**
B-2, Vishal Enclave, Opp. Rajouri Garden, New Delhi-27
Phones : 5413460, 5429987

*Sales Office*
4215/1, Ansari Road, Darya Ganj, New Delhi-110 002
Phones : 3273880, 3285873, 3280451
Fax : 91-11-3285873
e-mail : info@atlanticbooks.com
web : www.atlanticbooks.com



First Edition, 2001



*Typeset at*
APD Computer Graphics, Delhi

*Printed in India at*
Mehra Offset Press, Delhi

# PREFACE

In modern time, Statistics is used almost in every field of life. Keeping in view the universal use of Statistics, all Indian Universities and Professional Examination Boards have included Statistics as a subject in various courses. This book is written to meet the requirements of the students who are preparing for B.Com., B.A., C.A., I.C.W.A., and C.S., examinations.

Following are some important features of this book :

(1) The book is written in simple language and lucid manner so as to make it more comprehendable for the students.

(2) Theoretical and practical aspects of the subject are described in detail.

(3) Sufficient number of numerical problems with solutions are given. A large number of unsolved numerical problems are given at the end of each chapter for practice.

(4) In each chapter various formulae used are given as 'Formulae At a Glance'.

(5) The various symbols used are given with clear explanations.

(6) Latest questions asked in various Universities and Professional Examination Boards are included in this book.

I am thankful to all friends and colleagues specially Mr. Mahesh Singh Baghel, Lecturer, Apex Institute of Management and Science, Jaipur for their help and co-operation. I thank the Publishers, in particular Dr. K.R. Gupta, Managing Director of M/s Atlantic Publishers and Distributors, New Delhi for taking keen interest in publishing this book expeditiously in a neat and attractive style. I am also thankful to my wife Mrs. Swaran Lata for her co-operation.

**DARYAB SINGH**

# CONTENTS

## VOLUME I



## VOLUME II

# 1

# Statistics — Meaning, Definition and Characteristics

The present age is an era of science and technology. In modern times if any fact is to be presented whether it is social, political, economic, natural or connected with any other phenomenon, it should be expressed with clarity and brevity. If any aspect of a problem is presented and described in a vague language with ambiguous meaning, the correct comprehension of the problem is difficult to achieve. For instance, to say that India's population has been increasing perpetually is quite a vague expression lacking all precision. This description gives no idea of the extent of increase in the population saying that way makes the fact unconvincing and of no practical significance and utility. But if this very fact is presented by saying that in 1951 India's population was 36.1 crores which rose to 54.7 crores in 1971 and has gone to almost 100 crores in 2000; then one can get a clear and correct picture of the problem. That is why we find that in modern age people and institutions make use of figures (data) in their statements while quoting facts. A political leader substantiates his arguments with figures; when we read the Annual Reports of a commercial institution we come across a profuse use of data to establish its annual progress. In fact, the main reason of universal abundant use of figures or data is that they can present the facts in an exact, brief and convincing manner. In any description the use of data is of that paramount importance that if some one does not make use of them his description makes no sense. In this regard, Lord Kelvin has rightly said, "*When you can measure what you are speaking about and express it in numbers, you know something about it, but when you cannot measure it, when you cannot express it in numbers, your knowledge is of a meagre and unsatisfactory kind. It may be the beginning of knowledge, but you have scarcely in your thought advanced to the stage of a science.*" Facts expressed in figures about any phenomenon are called 'STATISTICS'. 'Statistics' relates to detailed and useful study of figures.

## Origin and Growth of Statistics

'Statistics' is not a new subject. The use of data has been very common in different disciplines of man's life in most of the countries since the earliest times. That is a different thing that in olden times there have been different terms used for the subject instead of 'Statistics'. The history of 'Statistics' is as old as man's living in an organised way; *i.e.* the use of data in relation to different problems faced by man traces its history to the period of his having started living in an organised state. First of all, the science of statistics was used by the agents of government for governmental purposes — the major purposes were the census, measurement of land, calculation of national wealth and estimate of the country's military strength. Regarding the application of the science of statistics if we scan the pages of history of different countries, we come to know that its use has been in vogue in almost all the countries since long time. Records show that the use of data in ancient Egypt was made in 2050 B.C. for building pyramids, calculating national wealth and census of population. In ancient Judea the census taken in 2030 B.C. estimated its population at 38,00,000. The Roman census was taken in 435 B.C. After the fifteenth century, publication of statistical handbooks also came into being. But it was Capt. John Graunt who, for the first time in the 17th century contributed to the scientific development of statistics. His first work *Observation on the London Bills Mortality* was published in 1662. During the 17th century in some western countries the gamblers started using the science of statistics. With the assistance of mathematicians, the gamblers of western nations used this science to throw light on the probability of uncertainty. And this gave an impetus to the growth of the 'Theory of Probability'.

Innumerable instances about the use of statistics are found in the history of ancient India. On studying very ancient Indian books like 'Manu-Niti', 'Shukra-Niti', 'The Ramayana', 'The Mahabharta' etc. we find that the writers of these books have taken the help of statistics in depicting the administration, population, military force, resources etc. of the erstwhile kingdoms. A similar use of statistical data has been made to indicate the number of the followers of Buddhism and Jainism. Kautilya's 'Arthshashtra' bears a testimony to the use of statistics in the description of facts during the regime of Chandragupta Maurya. A cursory glance on the history of the Mughal Period shows the use of the science of statistics in estimating census, military force, national wealth, revenue, measurement of land, price of goods etc. 'Ain-i-Akbari' — The mirror of Akbar's regime, can be quoted as an instance of the use of statistics. During Akbar's regime, his Finance Minister Raja Todermal used statistics for the first time for getting the land measured to ensure proper Revenue Administration. After the Mughals, during the British Rule in India, many fields came into the fold of the science of statistics. Nowadays, the application of statistics in almost every sphere of life has become very common.

Among the prominent people who have contributed a great deal to the development of statistics, the names worth mentioning are of — Captain John Graunt, Pastel, Cardeno, Farmet, Galilio, Karl Pearson, Galton, R.A. Fisher and A.L. Bowley. In India, Prof. P.C. Mahalnobis and Dr. V.K.R.V. Rao are regarded as the pioneers of statistics.

**Meaning and Definition of Statistics**

To understand 'Statistics' well we shall have to probe into the deep details of the word. The word 'Statistics' is synonymous with the German word STATISTIK and the Latin word STATUS. As a matter of fact, the word STATISTICS is derived from the Latin word STATUS. The German word Statistik and the Latin word Status mean — a political state. Since in the beginning the subject was used by the government only, it being similar to the word state was termed as statistics. In this context, statistics stands for the science used for governmental purposes. Later on its use was spread to the affairs of the people other than those of the government. In present context the word 'Statistics' pervades all subject-matter. With its present meaning 'Statistics' is used in two ways :

(a) *Statistics as Data* : in plural sense.

(b) *Statistics as a Science* : in singular sense.

**Meaning and Definition of Data**

In the plural sense, the meaning of statistics is expressed in the form of data. In this sense statistics means 'Descriptive Statistics'. In the form of data 'Statistics' means the aggregate of facts numerically expressed, like saying that the monthly incomes of Mr. A. and Mr. B are Rupees 15,000 and Rs. 10,000 respectively. But it should be effectively planted in our mind that all plural numerical facts are not statistics. It is, therefore, rightly said that "*All statistics are numerical facts, but all numercial facts are not statistics.*" Only those numerical facts that possess certain characteristics can be called statistics. A study of definitions given by different scholars from time to time will enable us to understand well those characteristics. Some definitions have been analysed below :

I. **Dr. A.L. Bowley** has defined statistics as, "*statistics are numerical statements of facts in any department of enquiry* *placed in relation to each other.*" This definition brings to light the following characteristics of numerical data :

(i) Statistics are numerically expressed.

(ii) Statistics are related to some department of enquiry.

(iii) Statistics should be placed in relation to each other.

These characteristics convey the impression that only those facts are statistical facts which are :

(a) numerically expressed,

(b) in aggregate

(c) related to a department of enquiry, and

(d) placed in relation to each other.

II. **Yule & Candall** defined statistics as, "*By statistics we mean quantitative data affected to a marked extent by multiplicity of causes.*"

The above definition expresses one more characteristic of statistics (data) *i.e.* they are much affected by multiplicity of causes. But this definition also is not quite comprehensive because it describes only two characteristics of statistics.

III. **Webster** defined statistics as, "*The classified facts representing the conditions of the people in a state; specially those facts which can be stated in numbers or in a table of numbers or in any tabular or classified arrangement.*"

This is an old definition of statistics — given during the time when statistics was used by states only. But in modern age, as we know, statistics pervades all walks of life. There is hardly any field where its tools are not applicable. Therefore this definition is too narrow to cover the modern meaning and application of statistics. Moreover, it throws no light on other characteristics of statistics than their being numerical facts and their presentation.

IV. **L.R. Conner** has defined statistics as, "*Measurements, enumerations or estimates of natural or social phenomena systematically arranged so as to exhibit their interrelations.*"

This definition although, throws light on many characteristics of statistics yet this too does not describe all the characteristics of the subject.

V. Giving definition of Statistics, **Prof. H. Secrist** has said, "*By statistics we mean aggregates of facts affected to a marked extent by multiplicity of causes, numerically expressed, enumerated or estimated to a reasonable standard of accuracy,* *collected in a systematic manner for a predetermined purpose and placed in relation to each other."*

The aforesaid definition describes all the characteristics of statistics. So this can be taken as a compact and most comprehensive definition of statistics.

**Characteristics of Statistics as Data**

Horace Secrist's definition points out the following characteristics of statistics as data :

**(1) Data are numerically expressed**

Statements of facts are generally of two types : qualitative statements of facts and numerical statements of facts. For instance, to state that 'Mr. X is an honest man' is a qualitative statement, but to say that Mr. X's age is 20 years is a numerical statement. All statistics are numerical statements of facts. Qualitative statements cannot be termed as statistics. Hence, the first characteristics of data is that they are numerically expressed.

**(2) Data are aggregates of facts**

A fact, being only a numerical fact does not constitute statistics. Besides their being numerical the facts should be in aggregates also, *i.e.* aggregates of numerical facts constitute statistics. Single, personal or isolated figures of facts are not statistics. For example only stating that Mr. X's age is 20 years won't constitute statistics because the fact is unrelated, uncomparable and thus has no significance. But to say that the ages of Mr. X and Mr. Y are 20 years and 50 years respectively, comes under the purview of statistics because of the figures comparability and aggregate. Similarly no single unit of a fact can be called statistics.

**(3) Data are affected by a multiplicity of causes**

One more characteristic of statistics is that they are affected to a marked extent by a multiplicity of causes. This characteristic of statistics is to be borne in mind while interpreting any phenomenon statistically. All forces having their effect on a fact must be studied well failing which the results will be erroneous. To illustrate, if it is stated that the price of wheat in 1991 was Rs. 600 per quintal which in 2000 rose to Rs. 900 per quintal, there may be many reasons for this increase — like increase in demand for wheat, decrease in its production, its export or the state of money circulation in the country etc. Therefore while commenting on this increase the fact to be given weightage is that the phenomenon is affected by a multiplicity of causes.

### (4) Data are enumerated or estimated according to reasonable standards of accuracy

This characteristic indicates two ways of collecting statistics *viz.*, (i) by actual counting and measurements or (2) by estimate. That is, statistics about any phenomenon can be collected either by actual counting or by estimate. If the field of enquiry is limited with not many units to be counted, then the statistics can be derived by enumerating them. But sometimes the area of enquiry is very large with innumerable units; in that case the collection of statistics can be had by estimate also. However, in that case the estimate should be reasonably proper. There should not be wide difference between the actual and the estimated statistics. If the estimate is not with reasonable standards of accuracy, the precise aspect of the problem will not come to light. To illustrate, if we are to estimate the income of middle class people in India, then the difference between the actual and the estimated facts and figures should be quite negligible — say to the extent of 100 to 200 rupees. A difference in thousands of rupees would distort the facts. Similarly, if we are to estimate the length and breadth of a house, the difference between the actual and estimated to the extent of a fraction of a metre is understandable, if the difference is very large, the estimate is totally erroneous and fails to throw any light on the actual problem. The enumeration or estimation of phenomenon depends upon its nature in actuality and the requisite accuracy therein. If perfect accuracy is a must in regard to the problem, the collection of the statistics should be done by the principle of counting; if perfect accuracy is not a dire requirement, the collection of data by estimate is also plausible. But while estimating the data, the reasonable standard of accuracy should be maintained. It should not be absolute inaccurate.

### (5) Data are collected in a systematic manner for a predetermined purpose

If statistics are desired to lead to right conclusion, then a systematic manner of data collection is quite essential. Data collected in a haphazard manner would lead to fallacious results, because the collection of data made unsystematically will provide many statistics unwanted for the purpose of enquiry, and many essential statistics will be missing from the links of collection. By this way of the collection of data, the results will be incomplete and misguiding. The purpose of collecting data should be well defined and specific and must be preplanned. In short, the statistics should be collected in a systematic manner and for a predetermined purpose.

### (6) Data should be placed in relation to each other

All statistics collected for some enquiry are arranged in different categories in relation with the similarity of phenomenon or subject. Likes should be arranged with likes only, because only likes are compared with likes. To illustrate, if statistics have been collected about the income, age and weight of different persons, the same should be arranged categorywise *i.e.* those of age with age, income with income and weight with weight. Then and then only their incomes, ages and weights can be compared. If the statistics of one's income are placed in relation to those of the age of the second and weight of the third they would lead to no conclusion and any derived result would be fallacious.

Facts can be called statistics only when they possess the aforesaid characteristics. Hence, statistics as data in plural sense would mean the statistics possessing these characteristics.

### Meaning of Statistics in Singular sense as Science

In singular form statistics is defined as a Science. In this sense the study of statistics is done with statistical methods. Looking from this angle statistics is defined with reference to its functions. In other words, statistics in that branch of science which involves the application of various methods to obtain numerical facts derive results and finally use them for drawing conclusion for getting inferences and devising steps for action. With this point of view also different authors have given different definitions of statistics that throw light on various characteristics of statistics as a branch of science. Those compact and comprehensive definitions are examined below :

(1) "*Statistics is the science of counting.*"

— *Dr. A.L. Bowley*

This defintion is narrow and incomplete because it covers only one aspect of this science. The science of statistics is the science not only of counting but has an unconfined scope. Besides, this definition tells nothing about the method of counting. Realizing the narrowness of this definition by him, Dr. Bowley himself has subsequently said as follows :

(2) "*Statistics may rightly be called the science of averages.*"

— *Dr. Bowley*

This defintion, though shows one more characteristic of the science of Statistics, yet it is unsatisfactory because statistics has more characteristics which are described at subsequent pages of this book.

(3) "*Statistics is the science of estimates and probabilities.*"

— *Boddington*

This definition is also not complete because statistics demands the study of many factors other than the estimates and probabilities.

(4) "*The Science of statistics is the method of judging collective, natural or social phenomenon from the results obtained by the analysis or enumeration or collection of estimates.*"

— *W.I. King*

Although this definition covers many characteristics of statistics yet this fails to throw light on all the characteristics of the subject under study here. This definition stresses upon the importance of estimates in obtaining results about a phenomenon. It tells nothing about the methods of deducing inferences from the collected data.

(5) "*Statistics or statistical method may be defined as the collection, presentation, analysis and interpretation of numerical data.*"

— *Croxton and Cowden*

It is a comprehensive definition of statistics. It points different stages in a statistical investigation. Croxton and Cowden are of the opinion that statistics, instead of being a science, is more precisely a scientific method. Hence, their definition covers four stages — viz. collection, presentation, analysis and interpretation of data.

(6) "*Statistics is the science which deals with collection, classification and tabulation of numerical facts as the basis for explanation, description and comparison of phenomenon.*"

— *Lovitt*

Lovitt considers statistics as a science and, therefore, has made a mention of many functions of this science in his definition. Almost a similar definition has been put forward by Seligman, which is as follows :

(7) "*Statistics is the science which deals with the methods of collecting, classifying, presenting, comparing and interpreting numerical data collected to throw some light on any sphere of enquiry.*"

— *Seligman*

This definition, like that of Lovitt's treats statistics as a science and throws light on some characteristics of it.

After examining all the above mention definitions this becomes amply clear that in singular form statistics is science that involves different stages of statistics in the light of above examined definitions, it can be stated that statistics is that science which deals with the methods of collecting, organising, editing, classifying, tabulating, presenting data through statistical tables diagrams and graphs, analysing and interpreting the numerical data collected to throw some light on social, political, natural or of any type of phenomenon as the basis of their explanation, description and comparison.

**Characteristics of Statistics as Science**

They are as follows :

(1) **Statistics is a Science :** In statistics as science we make a systematic study of data collected regarding some phenomenon and on their basis we study cause and effect relations and make attempts to generalize the scientific principles or laws. But statistics as a science is not similar to (natural) exact sciences like physics, zoology, chemistry etc. Its principles are not so exact and accurate as those of other natural sciences because its phenomena are affected to a marked extent by multiplicity of causes. Not taking it as an exact science, it can more appropriately be regarded as a scientific method.

(2) **Use of different stages in statistical investigation :** With the help of science of statistics the numerical facts of social, political, natural or any other sphere of enquiry are studied and this study involves many stages of investigation which are detailed below :

(a) *Collection of Data*. Collection of data is made for statistical investigation of a problem under study. The science of statistics describes those statistical methods which help in the collection of data. That is, the science of statistics refers to those methods by which data are to be collected. This science guides about the types of statistical data and those essential for handling the problem at hand.

(b) *Editing of Data*. The data collected should be generally in an organized form in order to be edited. The collected data should be rectified, modified and edited so carefully that they can be used to finalize the aspect of investigation. Data collected by different methods and from different sources may have among them some statistics which may be unwanted for the scope of investigation. In such circumstances, editing of collected data becomes essential. That would enable in segregating the unwanted figures. The science of statistics describes the technique of editing of data; this makes fair editing of data possible.

(c) *Classification and Tabulation of Data*. By editing the unwanted items are discarded. Then the remaining data are arranged according to their common characteristics, by way of classification and tabulation. Unclassified and untabulated data are of no use. Explaining the difference between classified and unarranged facts, J.R. Hicks has rightly said, "*Classified and arranged facts speak themselves, unarranged — they are as dead as mutton*".

— *J.R. Hicks*

After classification, the data are arranged, by tabulation in columns and rows so that the presented data have all clarity. The science of statistics tells the art of applying these methods.

(d) *Presentation of Data through Diagrams and Graphs.* To avoid the complexities of data, the collected figures are presented through diagrams and graphs. This function is also a characteristic of the science of statistics. A mere look at the diagrams and graphs of the data makes them easily understandable. To illustrate, if the statistical data about the population of different countries of the world during different years are given, only a keen and analytical reading of the same enable judge to use the descending order of the population of those countries. But this complicated phenomenon can be made easy to understand by showing figures through diagrams or graphs.

(e) *Analysis through averages and other statistical methods.* After collecting the data about a phenomenon their average is taken which will be representative value of a group of items. It will depict the characteristic of the universe. Measures of central value, by condensing the mass of data in one single value, enable us to get a bird's eye view of the entire data. Besides this with the help of dispersion and skewness the variability of data and the nature of data may be known. In statistics describes the process and techniques of these measurements.

(f) *Establishment of relationship and comparison.* One more characteristics of the science of statistics is that through this a relationship between two and more facts or a comparison between them can be established. That is, the methods of establishing relationship or of making comparison are described in the science of statistics.

(g) *Interpretation and Forecasing*. The last characteristic of the science of statistics is that with its help interpretation of the existing phenomenon can be made. That is, the characteristic of the problem can be assessed and its forecasting is made.

Hence, the science which provides knowledge about the aforesaid scientific methods is called the science of statistics.

## Is Statistics a Science or an Art or Both?

Before deciding the debatable subject whether statistics is a science or an art or both, it would be better to have a clear idea about the meaning of Science and Art, and then to decide whether statistics satisfies the characteristics of science or that of Art or of both.

### Meaning of Science

Ordinarily science means a systematized body of knowledge. In fact, if we analyses different definitions of science, we shall observe the following characteristics of science :

(i) Science is a systematic study of a subject.

(ii) Science establishes relationship between causes and their effects.

(iii) Science, after establishing a relationship between causes and effects generalizes scientific principles and laws.

If statistics is tested in the light of above charactertics, we find it satisfying them all. In statistics the facts related to any phenomenon are studied in a systematic manner. In regard to the phenomenon, the methods, from collecting the data to their interpretation and forecasting, are taken in an organized and well arranged way. By statistical investigation a relationship is established between the causes and their effect. And under this very process different principles and laws like — 'Law of Intertia of Large Numbers' and 'Law of Statistical Regularity' etc. are evolved.

So it can be inferred that statistics is a science but by its nature it is less exact than the natural sciences. Its laws are not so exact and accurate as those of physics, chemistry and zoology, etc. This is because the statistical phenomenon are affected by a multiplicity of causes. Still statistics is a science but only in limited sense. It is a specialised branch of knowledge. It is a body of methods for obtaining knowledge and deriving laws.

**Meaning of Art**

Science describes facts objectively. Scientific methods tell about the subject matter of a fact but does not have the skill of handling facts. Art, on the other hand enables us to handle facts for fulfilling a given objective. Art is the way of putting a knowledge to practice. It refers to ways and means of presenting and handling data. Art is action involving the application of given methods to obtain facts, make inferences logically and derive conclusions leading to devising action. This quality of art is a kind to that of statistics. That way statistics is an art.

From the above it may be concluded that Statistics is both — Science and Art.

**Types of Statistics**

Looking at from different angles, statistics falls into following types :

(a) **Statistical Methods.** Under this type of statistics, the different statistical methods are described. As we have already learnt, by statistical methods a phenomenon is judged on the basis of numerical data. So the study of those different methods by which numerical facts serve this purpose is essential. Statistical methods give knowledge in this regard. Statistical methods constitute data, collection of data, editing of data, classification, tabulation, presentation through diagrams and graphs, use of averages, co-relation, interpretation etc.

(b) **Applied Statistics.** The study of applied statistics tells how the different statistical methods are put to use in analysing and interpreting the facts about a phenomenon. It is applied statistics that guides about the category of data to be collected in regard to statistical investigation of a particular phenomenon; it also teaches about — the sources of data and the method of collecting them, *i.e.* by census method or sampling method, their presentation *i.e.* by diagram or graph, and what average is to be used and hence what conclusions can be derived. Applied statistics deals with collection of data and their interpretation mainly in regard to the phenomenon like census, production, prices, export-import etc.

**Relationship of Statistics with other Sciences**

Statistics pervades all subject matter. It has a deeply existing relationship with other sciences. Statistical methods are used to handle almost all types of phenomenon, *viz*. economic, social natural, physical, political etc. Hence statistical tools are applicable to all sciences which are indispensable for research, judgement and investigation in the above-mentioned fields. Statistics helps some sciences to test the accuracy of their laws, while some other sciences seek the assistance of statistics to generalize and postulate their principles and laws. The relationship of statistics with other sciences is discussed below in details :

(i) **Statistics and Mathematics.** While studying the definitions of statistics, we observed that its subject matter is numerical facts, *i.e.* it involves figures or numerals; but the right use of numerals is possible only with proper knowledge of mathematics without which the statistical conclusion are likely to be erroneous. So, Mathematics is treated to be the base of statistics. R.A. Fisher has treated statistics as a branch of applied mathematics. The famous mathematicians also have contributed a lot to the development of statistics. Much of the development and improvement in the statistical techniques is attributed to mathematicians — the names worth mentioning are of De Mere, Farmet, Cardeno etc. The use of averages, diagrams and graphs in statistics are nothing but mathematical processes. Besides, many statistical principles are based on mathematical theories. But statistics lacks the mathematical accuracy; it can lead to inferences even by estimates whereas mathematics leads to results through exact facts.

(ii) **Statistics and Physics.** Both these sciences are quite interrelated. In modern age, the principles are derived after the collection of data and these principles help in the experiments of physics. Even the accuracy of physical laws is tested by the use of statistical methods. Statistics finds its ample use in the research work of physics.

**(3) Statistics and Biology**

Like its use in physics, statistical techniques have proved to be of great use in Biology. To derive some results in regard to different animals, persons and plants the data are collected by statistical methods. Factual data collected by statistical methods help in estimating the correct position of some ailments. To illustrate, statistical investigation helps in assessing the mode of spreading of a disease, the extent of check of the disease, type of treatment, the effects, of disease on family life etc.

### (4) Statistics and Economics

"Statistics are the straw out of which I like every other economist, have to make bricks", has been observed by Prof. Alfred Marshall. The above quotation about statistics is by a renowned economist. This observation reveals the relationship between statistics and economics. Problems of economics also are analysed by statistics. Data are of immense help in the proper understanding of the economic problems — may be of consumption, production, exchange, distribution or revenue. Statistics is the key to economic planning. Estimate of resources available in the country, devising the methods of collecting them, judging the extent of desired economic progress, planning of incomes and expenditure — all this is very essential for economic planning. These steps are too complicated to be taken without the help of statistics. And this makes the use of statistics in economic planning quite significant. The development of econometrics as a separate branch within the field of economics is directly attributed to the importance of the use of statistics in economics. Statistics is greatly used in econometrics. This relationship is well proved by the fact that all economic policies are formulated on the basis of statistical methods. To illustrate this point the glaring examples are of — law of diminishing utility, law of consumer's surplus, law of marginal utility, law of demand and supply, principle of family budget etc.

### (5) Statistics and other Social Sciences

There does exist a relationship between statistics and other social sciences — like History, Political Science, Sociology, Geography, Psychology etc. All these sciences make use of data. The relation between statistics and Political Science is obviously proved by the fact that in ancient times statistics was evolved for politics. During those times statistics was called Science of State. Many phenomenon of Political Science are revealed by statistics. Similarly, historical facts are also analyzed by statistical data. Then those facts provide correct knowledge of the subject of history. The commendable work done by statistics in the field of Geography to collect data about resources from country to country, minerals, production, census of population, area etc. With the help of statistics, we can calculate the mental inclinations of the people of different sections of society, with different incomes, ages and mental conditions. This helps in psychological analysis, and proves an evident relationship of statistics with Psychology. Ultimately it can be easily said that statistics has a relationship with all social sciences.

## QUESTIONS

1. Write an essay on origin and history of Statistics.
2. What do you mean by Statistics? Explain the characteristics of Statistics.
3. "Statistics are aggregate of facts, affected to a marked extent by multiplicity of causes, numerically expressed, enumerated or estimated according to a reasonable standard of accuracy, collected in a systematic manner for a predetermined purpose and placed in relation to each other."

   — *H. Secrist*

   Explain the above definition.
4. What is the relationship of statistics with other sciences. Write in detail.
5. "Statistics are the straw out of which I like other economist, have to make bricks."

   Discuss this statement.

   — *Alfred Marshall*
6. Comment on the following statements —

   (a) "Statistics is the science of counting."

   (b) "Statistics is the science of estimates and probabilities."

   (c) "Statistics is the science of averages."
7. "Science without statistics bear no fruit, Statistics without Science have no root." Explain this statement.
8. Statistics is said to be both a science and an art. Why? What relation, if any, has statistics with other sciences?
9. "Statistics affects everybody and life at many points. It is both a science and an art."

   Explain the above statement with suitable example.
10. Discuss the scope of the science of statistics and show its relation to social and natural sciences.
11. "Statistics is not a science it is a scientific method." Explain the above statement.

    (*B. Com. Agra,* 1975)
12. What is statistics? How far do you think the knowledge of statistics is essential in the study of economics.
13. "Statistical methods include all devices of analysis and synthesis by means of which statistics are scientifically collected and used

to explain or discuss phenomena, either in their individual or related capacities." Explain this statement.

— *H. Secrist*

14. Define the term statistics and discuss its functions.
[*B. Com. (Pass), Delhi,* 1978]
15. "Statistics are not mere mass of figures." Explain critically.
[*C.S., June* 1995]
16. Define 'statistics' and discuss its limitations.
[*C.S., Dec.* 1995]
17. Define 'statistics' and state its functions.
[*C.S., June* 1996]
18. "All numerical statements are not statistics". Comment.
[*C.S., Dec.* 1996]

# 2

# Functions, Objects, Importance, Limitations and Distrust of Statistics

## FUNCTIONS OF STATISTICS

Statistics helps in studying numerical facts and attaining conclusions. With its help it becomes easy to gauge the precise position of many complicated phenomena. Statistics enables us to assess the mutual relationship between the facts of different categories, which can further compared with like ones. In the same way, statistics presents the facts briefly and easily. Inferences arrived at through statistics make prediction or forecasting possible and help in formulating and testing hypothesis. The various functions of statistics may be described as follows :

**(1) Presentation of facts in figures.** The foremost and significant function of statistics is the presentation of facts, relating to different problems and phenomena, in figures. It assures the definiteness and precision in the presentation of facts. It gives a clear picture of the phenomenon. If the statements of facts are not conveyed in precise and quantitative terms, but mere through wordly utterances, they lack definiteness and are not convincing. Then the idea is a vague one, and can be interpreted in different ways by different persons. So vague utterances carry no significance. To illustrate, mere stating that 'Mr. A's income is quite meagre' — conveys nothing precise; nothing definite, — it is a vague utterance. It tells nothing concrete about Mr. A's income and its being meagre or much. Different people will have different angles in interpreting this vague statement. On the other hand if this statement is quantified as "Mr. A's monthly income is Rs. 1250 and the average monthly income of the community he lived in is Rs. 5000" — it conveys definite impression that Mr. A's income is meagre. Hence, vague utterances, when expressed in numerical dimensions, carry a worthwhile information and can give a clear picture of the phenomenon.

**(2) Easy and brief Presentation of Facts.** Some facts are too large to remember and comprehend. Statistics helps in condensing mass of facts into a few significant figures. This easy and brief presentation of facts makes them easy to understand and remember. The overall information gained by statistical methods is meaningful. Many statistical methods like — averages, graphs, diagrams, placing in relation to each other etc. are such as can present the facts very briefly, concisely and precisely. As it is impossible to remember the statements of facts about the per capita income of various countries of the world, and to conclude from them the less or more per capita income of a particular country in relation to that of another is equally a difficult task. But by diagrams this can be well illustrated. Similarly it is difficult to remember the figures of expenditure of 100 persons of a group or community. But its average expenditure can be easily assessed by the statistical methods.

**(3) Establishment of Relationship.** Statistics helps in establishing a relationship between two or more co-related facts, and it can indicate if the relation is there or not; and if it is there — whether it is positive or negative, it also guides about the degree of the relation. This is with the help of Correlation-Analysis. The study of Co-relation of different facts reveals many significant points. If a relationship is established between the demand and price of an object, this may lead to many important and valuable conclusions.

**(4) Comparison.** Statistics enables a better appreciation of the significance of series of figures through its devices for comparison of data. With the help of statistics various averages, rates and coefficients are obtained which help in the comparison of different aspects of a problem. Comparison of figures makes the things meaningful. To illustrate, if we want to assess the better state of health of the citizens of two cities. We can do the same by comparing their death rates. The city having higher mortality rate will be of bad health conditions. It would imply that its citizens, in comparison with those of the other city are less healthy.

**(5) Interpretation of the Problem.** The application of statistical methods clarifies the real picture of a phenomenon. This can be done by the interpretation of the problem. For instance, if we want to study the position of unemployment in a country, whether all types of people there have employment or not; we are to collect the data in this regard then by interpreting them we can state with authenticity whether the country suffers from unemployment or not; — its rise or fall in comparison with the previous corresponding periods. If the statistics collected about this phenomenon indicate that five year back the number of unemployed people was five lacs which, by now has risen to eight lac, it can obviously be interpreted that the unemployment in that country is on the increase. Knowledge of the clear picture of the problem obliges the concerned personnel to devise methods and means to cope with the problem.

**(6) Forecasting.** Statistical methods not only interpret the present phase of a problem, but also they provide helpful means of forecasting future events. The study of previous statistical data give a knowledge of future tendencies leading to a meaningful present estimate. Census figures of previous years can help in calculating the rate of rise in population and thus, in estimating the future increase in it. A knowledge of future tendencies is very helpful in framing suitable policies and plans to improve the situation in facing the existing problem.

**(7) Help to other sciences in forming and testing the laws and principles.** Different social and natural sciences formulate laws and principles by studying events and facts. Statistics help those sciences in this task. The other sciences use statistics in collecting data about co-related eventualities and then formulate laws and principles. For instance, 'The law of demand' in Economics is derived from the data of demand and prices. Statistics also helps the other sciences in testing the truth of their formulated laws and principles.

**(8) Helpful in deciding the Policy.** By statistical study and interpretation the real picture of a problem becomes clear. Statistics, thus provides the basic material for framing suitable policies. To illustrate, if the statistical investigation gives an impression of continuous soaring prices, the government of the country can devise some policy to curb the price-rise. If in the society major part of the income is wasted on liquors, and basic requirements are not fulfilled; the government can adopt the policy of prohibition.

The above discussed functions of statistics amply show that it can express facts in a simple and definite way to take the picture of the problem glaringly clear. This increases the domain of personal knowledge and makes the decision of policies easy and essential. Summing up the functions of Statistics, *Robert W. Burgess* has beautifully remarked;

"*The fundamental gospel of Statistics is to push back the domain of ignorance, prejudice, rule of thumb, arbitrary and premature decisions, traditions and dogmatism, and to increase the domain in which decisions are made and principles are formulated on the basis of analysed quantitative facts.*"

## FUNCTIONS OF A STATISTICIAN

A Statistician analyses a phenomenon by statistical investigation. In other words, a statistician is a person who collects data, analyses them and interprets the problem. He adopts the following stages in his statistical investigation :

**1. Planning of Statistical Investigation.** A statistician, while taking an investigation in his hand plans it well. While planning, he takes decisive steps in regard to research methods, resources, research organisations, field or scope, extents of limits and units. Pre-planning of investigation reduces the chances of omissions and commissions, and the resources are also not misused.

**2. Collection ot Data.** After the proper planning, the statistician, or the investigator collects data; or administers the collection of data. The collection of data constitutes a potent step of the success of statistical investigation because, in other words, data are the raw-material of a statistical investigation. Therefore utmost care must be exercised in collecting data. It is the duty of the statistician to decide the nature of data to be used in the investigation — *i.e.* to see if they are primary or secondary data. He is also to decide the source of the data to be collected and the methods to be employed for the purpose.

**3. Analysis of Data.** A statistician analyses the collected data in accordance with the purpose of his investigation. For this purpose of analysis the statistician takes the steps like classification of data, preparation of summary tables from counts and totals, calculation of sampling errors and presentation. Then he compares them and establishes the mutual relations.

**4. Preparation of the Report of Investigation.** After applying the different methods of analysing the collected data, the statistician adopts the task of interpretation; *i.e.* he declares the picture of the problem as seen through the testing statistical methods. After interpretation, the statistician prepares his report of investigation containing all points and steps relating to the investigation.

**5. Forecasting.** A statistician predicts the future estimate of a problem after analysing and comparing the past and present statistical data. He throws a flood of light on the future aspect of the phenomenon as observed by his knowledge of future tendencies.

## OBJECTS OF STATISTICS

The principal object of statistics is to assess the existing position of a problem and to predict future events. By this science comparisons about the situation of problem at different intervals can be studied. The following are the main objects of statistics :

(i) To collect various numberical figures relating to a problem and to explain their correct meaning.

(ii) To cast light upon the reasons that are revealed by comparisons.

(iii) To draw a comparison between the existing and past data.

(iv) To investigate into unknown events.

(v) To cast light upon the situation of the problem.

(vi) To forecast the future tendencies of the problem.

The remarks of *Johnson* and *Jackson* are significant to expound the objects of statistics : "*The real purpose of statistical methods is to make sense out of facts and figures to prove the unknown, and to cast light upon the situation.*"

## IMPORTANCE OF STATISTICS

In modern times statistics has become an indispensable tool of research in almost every field to express the difficult and divergent facts and figures concisely and precisely. We have discovered the useful application of statistics by state, business organisations and other institutions and persons for their every problem. Statistics helps in studying all phenomena — political, economic, social, natural etc. Statistics not only studies the situation but also it helps in devising the methods and resources to tackle the problem. Commenting upon the importance of statistics, *Dr. A.L. Bowley* has remarked : "*A Knowledge of statistics is like a knowledge of foreign language or of Algebra. It may prove of use at any time under any circumstances.*"

Below given are the fields of importance of statistics :

(1) Importance in the political field.

(2) Importance in the social field.

(3) Importance in the economic field.

(4) Importance in the field of science.

**(1) Importance in the Political field.** As a matter of fact, political problems have been mainly responsible for origin of statistics. First of all it was used by the agents of the government for governmental purposes; for tackling different problems of the state. Importance of statistics in the realm of state is an old one. Any political problem can be weighed in the pans of statistics and methods of its solution can be traced. In modern times, the state and the political parties fall under the purview of statistics. Both these organisations or parties derive benefits from statistics. Government gets an awareness about its many important affairs with the aid of statistics; for instance : sources of income and expenditure of the state, tax-paying capacity of its citizens, population, national income, production etc. Political parties can assess their standing in the politics of the country during a particular period — *i.e.* number of the citizens in support of their policies; which part of the country voted them to victory; number of votes required by them in a particular region of the country; to what extent their policies were successful in the past etc. Thus it can be said that statistics is of great significance in the political field.

**(2) Importance in the Social field.** Statistics carries valuable significance for its use with regard to social problems. With its aid any social reformer can assess well — The real position of a society — underdeveloped and backward communities of the society, the evils prevalent in the society, the problems and tendencies of the citizens, the methods of eradicating the evils, solving the social problems etc. To illustrate the importance of statistics in the social field, we may consider instance and estimating the basic needs of people — food, clothing and shelter — the extent of their fulfilment *i.e.* how many people are not getting the bare necessities of life fulfilled and why, whether their income is small or they don't make a proper spending of it or they waste it on evil habits; *e.g.* if the people spend their income on liquors, the social reformers can give a call for prohibition, and suggest the methods of implementing it.

**(3) Importance in the Economic field.** The role of statistics in the field of economics is of vital significance. The proper understanding of economic problems and the ways of their handling is possible with the help of statistical data and methods; the problems may be connected with consumption, production, distribution, exchange or saving and investment of income. In the field of consumption, statistics guides the balancing the income and expenditure. To get desired satisfaction from income, the law of equi-marginal utility is kept in view; this law has been formulated with the help of statistics. Statistics guides and helps in adjusting the sources of production, production has been formulated with the help of statistics. In the field of exchange the demand and supply of a particular commodity is studied and its price is decided with the help of statistics. Statistics is helpful in devising the different sources of production, *i.e.* statistics enables us to gauge the productivity of a particular source. The economic policies of national income and distribution are formulated with the help of statistics. For the scope of revenue, statistics helps in knowing the taxable capacity of the people of the different strata of society. It can help in determining the taxable goods and people; the rate of taxing, the utility of taxes in different, works of development etc. When efforts are made in the realm of economic organisation we take shelter of statistics. As a matter of fact the questions regarding the estimation of the numerous resources, policies of their utilisation cannot be answered without statistics. Wide use of statistical methods and their application to the theoretical economic methods has led to the growth of 'Econometrics' which studies, with statistical data every economic problem or phenomenon.

In the economic field statistics is used by all persons or organisations connected with economics. It is used by all in business, commerce, trade, banking, transport, insurance, markets etc. Traders judge commercial cost, sale, production, loss, gain etc. with the help of statistics. Statistics is put to immense use in Banking — to ascertain credit instruments. The Insurance companies, with the statistical data of birth and mortality, estimate death-probability of the insured people, so that the rate of premium can be determined. Correct determination of Insurance premium is impossible without statistics. The same technique of applying statistical data is adopted in determining the premium in marine insurance and Fire-Insurance. People are observed generally making use of data in the stock-exchanges for quotation of shares and other securities.

**(4) Importance in the field of Science.** Statistics is synonymous to the scientific methods. It has proved to be of immense use in the study of physical and natural sciences. Statistics has proved to be indispensable in the scientific research work and in testing the hypothesis obtained from the research. In fact, in the realm of science, statistics is of two fold utility — in formulating and testing the scientific principles and laws. It is with the help of statistics that the scientists have tabulated a healthy person's pulse rate, blood pressure, heart-beating and his temperature. Any variation in these standard readings declares the man unhealthy. All this has been attained by the scientists by relying on factual data arranged with the help of statistics.

Thus we notice that statistics today has risen from the sciences of statecraft to the science of universal applicability.

## LIMITATIONS OF STATISTICS

Functions of statistics speak highly of its utility. This brings to facts the precision and clarity. But proper benefits from statistics can be derived only when its limitations are borne in mind. If the limitations of statistics are ignored, there is great likelihood of drawing wrong conclusions. The following are the limitations of statistics :

**(1) It studies only numerical facts.** Facts are generally of three types : (i) Qualitative facts like honesty, truth, character etc; (ii) Quantitative facts like income, production, cost etc; (iii) The facts that can be expressed in numerals indirectly like studying a student's intelligence on the basis of the marks obtained by him in an examination. Statistics does not deal with the first of the above mentioned types of facts. That is, qualitative facts are beyond the scope of statistics. In statistics only those facts can be studied that are capable of being numerically expressed. Therefore, while studying a problem statistically, it should be borne in mind that this analysis can provide us knowledge about only those aspects of the problem which are quantitative. Some other methods will have to be used to study the qualitative facts.

**(2) Statistical results give wrong information, if they are studied without references.** While interpreting statistical results, it is essential to bear in mind the references of the data; and the interpretation of the results should be based on these references. If the references are not kept in view, the interpretation is likely to be erroneous. For instance, if a statistical investigation shows that three business enterprises A,B,C have an average income of Rs. 1,000 lakhs each for the last three years. Without studying the references of data, this investigation can be interpreted to mean that the three business enterprises have the same capacity to earn profits. But a glance at the references of the three business enterprises would bring the following facts to light :

| Business Enter-prises | Profits (In Lakh Rs.) | | | |
|---|---|---|---|---|
| | First Year Rs. | Second Year Rs. | Third Year Rs. | Average Profits Rs. |
| A | 1,000 | 1,000 | 1,000 | 1,000 |
| B | 500 | 1,000 | 1,500 | 1,000 |
| C | 2,000 | 1,500 | –500 | 1,000 |

A perusal of the above table reveals that the capacity of earning profits of the three firms varies widely although the average profits of the three are identical. The first firm is earning equal profits every year; whereas the profits of the second firm are increasing every time, but the condition of profits of the third firm is not sound. Thus the statistical results should be interpreted in the light of the reference.

**(3) Statistical Results represent an average position of a problem which is related to a group.** The statistical results represent only the average position of a problem related to a group, *i.e.* statistical results show only an average tendency of a group. Therefore, while using its result for some purpose it must be borne in mind that some individual unit of the universe may be different from the conclusions arrived at. For instance if the statistical investigation shows that the average income of a group of Indian individuals is Rs. 4,500 per annum, this fact is true only in average form. There may be some people in that group having Rs. 10,000 as their annual income, and some earning only Rs. 2,000 annually, on this impression to declare the statistical result as erroneous is not correct because the income of majority persons is around Rs. 4,500 annually.

**(4) Statistical Results are not perfectly correct.** During a statistical investigation, the collection of data is done on the basis of estimate and some units of the universe may be ignored. That is, for statistical investigation, it is not essential to include all the units of the universe. Investigation can be done on the basis of samples also. Investigating that way, it is but natural that the results may not be fully correct. In such conditions, the statistical conclusions are correct on an average.

**(5) It discloses the problem and not the solution of the problem.** Statistics is a tool to indicate the real situation of the problem and not its solution. For instance, it can be assured with the help of statistics that the average per head income of group of individuals is say rupees 4,000 per annum. This indicates that the people are poor. But the solution of this problem (poverty) cannot be attained by means of statistics. That is, statistical conclusions indicate only the situation of the problem and not its solution.

**(6) There is a possibility of misuse of statistics.** Data can also lead to an erroneous form of a problem. If an investigator is already biased to a phenomenon of a problem, and is predetermined about the mode of presenting the problem before investigation, then he will use only those statistics that are related to the pre-planned aspect of the problem. For example, if some body makes a statistical investigation regarding the economic condition of a group of persons with a predetermination of showing the group well off, obviously he will collect data only of those persons who are rich. Such an investigation would indicate economic soundness of the group. While the actual position may be otherwise. So while using statistical results, it should be ensured that the data have not been misused.

**(7) Statistics may be used correctly only by experts.** Statistics being a technical subject is beyond the comprehension of common persons. Its proper use can be made only by those persons who know and understand its technicalities. The correct analysis of its conclusions can be made only by an expert in this subject. That is why it is remarked, "Statistics is a most dangerous tool in the hands of in experts." Statistics is wrongly used by inexperts. So it should be handled only by the experts.

## DISTRUST OF STATISTICS

By studying the characteristics, advantages, importance of Statistics it becomes evident that this science is very useful. But sometimes it is observed that by statistical analysis wrong conclusions are drawn instead of getting the correct picture of the aspect of the problem. This leads to distrust of statistics in the minds of people. Evincing their distrust of statistics various scholars have expressed their different opinions. Worth quoting from them are as under:

1. "*There are three kinds of lies — lies, damned lies and statistics.*"
2. "*Statistics can prove anything.*"
3. "*Statistics is a rainbow of lies.*"
4. "*Statistics are like clay of which you can make God or Devil as you please.*"

From the aforesaid opinions we get a glimpse of distrust of statistics. These views declare statistics as false. Anything can be proved (right or wrong) by using statistics as a tool suiting the whims of an investigator.

If we probe seriously into the distrusts of statistics, we find the arguments therein as lacking sound reasons. As a matter of fact statistics is neither a false science nor it prove every thing. It only presents the true phase of the phenomenon. As statistics is a technical and difficult subject, every body cannot use it properly. Moreover, data are used by biased people intentionally to prove some conclusions as erroneous. So the fault lies with the biased and incompetent investigators, and not with statistics.

### Causes of Distrust of Statistics

Following are causes for distrust of Statistics :

1. **Statistics is a complicated technique.** This subject is too technically complicated to be used by incompetent persons but sometimes it is used by inexperts and results drawn by them are obviously incorrect for which they start expressing distrust in statistics. That is why it is said that "*Statistics is a dangerous tool in the hands of inexperts.*" So only experts can use it correctly.

2. **Violation of the limitations of statistics.** Statistics has certain limitations. When these limitations are not borne in mind for investigation, the results are bound to be defective. This leads to distrust of statistics.
3. **Availability of conflicting data.** There arises the distrust of statistics when conflicting figures about the same problem are available. To illustrate, if data are collected regarding income of persons of a particular locality by two different investigators — one concluding Rs. 2,000 as average monthly income of the concerned people, and the other as Rs. 8,000 per month, on the basis of their data collected obviously these conflicting figures will lead to distrust of statistics in the minds of persons.
4. **Misuse by biased persons.** When the collection of data is biased, the conclusions will be wrong that will lead the people to distrust of statistics.
5. **Studying data without references.** If the statistical conclusions are studied without reference the results arrived at will be erroneous. Therefore before studying the statistical results, the study of connected references is a must. It is rightly said that "*Statistics should not be used as a blind-man does a lamp post for support not for illuminations*".

Distrust of Statistics arises from aforesaid reasons. In the light of this it is that if statistics is used by experts and unbiased persons, this branch of science will prove to be of great utility and without any fault.

## QUESTIONS

1. Explain the various functions of statistics.
2. What are the limitations of statistics? Write in detail.
3. "The science of statistics is a most useful servant, but only of great value to those who understand its proper use."
4. Elucidate the following statements :
   (a) "All its best science is statistical."
   — *Smith*
   (b) "The successful businessman is the one whose estimates closely approaches accuracy."
   — *Boddington*
5. Write a note on the misuse, limitations and distrust of statistics.

6. "Statistics should not be used as a blindman does a lamp post for support instead of for illumination." Comment on the above remark.
7. What are the functions of a statistician?
8. Comment on the following statements :
   (a) "Statistics are not worth the cost and labour involved in their collection and maintenance in ordinary business."
   (b) "Figures do not lie."
   (c) "Statistics should be handled only by experts."
9. Comment on the following :

   "There are three degrees of comparison in lying. There are lies, there are damned lies and there are statistics." How far do you agree with the above statement.
10. "Knowledge of statistics is like a knowledge of foreign language or of algebra. It may prove of use at any time under any circumstances." Comment on this statement.

    —*Dr. Bowley*
11. "Statistics are like clay of which you can make God or Devil as you please." Comment on this statement.
12. "Statistics can prove anything". Comment.

    (*C.S. June 1995*)

# 3

# Planning of Statistical Investigation

Stastistical investigation is rather technical and quite difficult. Proper planning therefore should be done before starting any statistical investigation. Pre-planning renders investigation easy and accurate. While planning out investigation, its objectives, format, period, sources, organisation, type and other important aspects are well thought out. The following factors are generally important regarding statistical investigation :

1. Objective of Investigation.
2. Scope of Investigation
3. Period of Investigation.
4. Sources and organization of Investigation.
5. Type of Investigation.
6. Unit of Investigation.
7. Collection of Data for Investigation.
8. Editing, Classification and Tabulation of Data.
9. Presentation and Analysis of Data.
10. Interpretation of Data.
11. Preparing Report.

**1. Objective of Investigation.** Before commencing any investigation it is very important to know as to why the present investigation is being taken up? What is the objective of the investigation? Any investigation would not be fruitful unless problems related to the investigation and its objectives are fully known. For in the absence of any definite scope and objective of a problem it is likely that many irrelevant information are collected and many relevant and significant information remains uncollected. For instance, if an index of wages of the labourers engaged in the leather industry in Kanpur is to be prepared then its objective being determined, only data regarding those prices will be collected which are paid by these labourers to consume goods. If the objective was not predetermined, it could be likely that the prices of those commodities could have been collected which were not used by the labourers or the wholesale prices could also possibly be collected. Known or predetermined objective helps in collecting the correct information. Hence, the objective of the investigation must be known.

**2. Scope of Investigation.** After fixing the objective of investigation it becomes necessary to know about its scope. the scope of investigation may be different according to the sources of investigators. In case of limited means, an investigator is advised to limit the scope of investigation, for a wide scope requires ample means. For example census and counting of national income are stupendous tasks. The advantage of fixing precisely the scope of investigation is that the enumerators collect only those data which are relevant for the work. As in the cited example above, only the retail prices of commodities prevailing in Kanpur will be collected which are consumed by the labourers in the Leather Industry there. In this instance, the scope of investigation is confined to Kanpur only.

**3. Period of Investigation.** Regarding the planning of investigation, its period is also very significant for the collected information should confirm to a definite period of time. The period of investigation is predetermined by some responsible officer so that other workers complete the work within that period. The period of investigation is generally fixed weekly, monthly, quarterly, half-yearly and yearly etc.

**4. Sources and Organization of Investigation.** While making plan of Statistical investigation it is also considered that from where the relevant information and data will be obtained. What will be sources of their information? The collection of data is either primarily done by the investigator or the concerned data have already been collected by some institution or person which are being used for the present investigation. Data may be obtained from the government statistical department and also from the Journals and magazines. While considering the sources of investigation the officers and workers to be engaged in the investigation are also taken into consideration at the very out set of investigation, in other words, it is necessary to take decision about how many persons are to be engaged in the investigation, what will be their responsibilities and interpersonal relationship? The success of any statistical investigation remains doubtful if there is no proper co-ordination.

**5. Type of Investigation.** The nature and scope of investigation should also be decided while planning for it. Because different methods are adopted for different types of investigation. On the criteria of nature and type, the investigation can be divided into the following :

A. *Primary or Secondary*. If the problem of investigation is such that it has never been inquired into and its study is being taken up for the first time by the investigator or an investigator is making a statistical interpretation after himself collecting the data about a problem from the very beginning then it is known as primary investigation. While making primary investigation, the investigator himself collects the data or gets them collected. Though difficult, such investigation is more reliable and correct. Secondary investigations are those which are done on the basis of data already collected by somebody else for some others investigators for such investigations, the investigator does not himself collect the data and information but interprets a statistical problem by using pre-collected data. This kind of investigation is easier to do but contains the possibility of several mistakes. While doing this kind of investigation, the investigator should keep well in his mind that the pre-collected data fit well with his problem and are not out dated. He should also try to test the correctness of such data by his own resources through sample checking.

B. *Census or Sample Investigation*. The statistical investigation which is done on the basis of data collected on all the units pertaining to the problem is known as census method investigation. This method becomes all the more necessary when the results are to be obtained most correctly. As each unit is studied under this, the real position becomes clear and the probability of mistake is also reduced to nil. Contrary to this, if information is not collected on each unit of the universe and the whole universe is interpreted on the basis of information collected in relation to a few sample units only, it is called sample method. This method is useful in the situations when most of the units of the universe are of similar nature or are uniform. This method of investigation saves time and expenditure. But in such an investigation it should be borne in mind that the units selected as samples represent other units also. Better it is that the samples should be taken through random sample method because in this method all the units have equal chance to be included and there is no bias of any kind also.

C. *Regular or Ad-hoc Investigation*. If the subject of investigation is such that is regularly investigated that is called regular investigation. This type of investigation is regularly done by a permanent organization. Several such investigations are regularly done by the economics or statistical departments of central or state governments which have a permanent organization under these departments. If the investigation is being done for some special reason and not regularly that is called ad-hoc investigation. There is only a temporary organization for such investigation and both are co-terminous.

D. *Postal or Personal or Both Types of Investigation*. If data for investigation are collected by post, it is known as postal investigation. The questionnaires are sent to the informants by post which are sent back by them to the investigator after filling them and the latter interprets the problem on the basis of this information. This method can be used only when the informants are educated and can send back the answers of the questionnaires. Besides posts, data can also collected by personally visiting the informants. This is called personal investigation. The investigation based on this method can throw more light on the problem and so many facts can be known which cannot be known through the postal medium. For example, an estimate of income of the low class people can be had by post, but through personal investigation, along with the assessment of their income, a close look at the pitiable condition of the people of that class can also be had. This type of investigation is conducted in limited area only.

E. *Confidential or Public Investigation*. From the point of view of secrecy the investigation can be of two types — confidential or public investigation. Some times investigations are conducted by government or commercial organizations on such topics or subjects as are kept confidential such as investigation pertaining to army. For such investigations reliable men of confidence are engaged and generally the findings of such investigations are not brought to light for general public but, on the other hand, there are investigations which are not kept secret and their findings are made public. This type of investigations are called public investigations.

F. *Investigation by Government or Others*. If a governments gets an investigation conducted for its own purpose then that is called government investigation. Information are generally easily available about the investigations conducted by government. But if an investigation is conducted by a commercial or industrial institution or an individual then that is called private investigation. Sometime it is difficult to collect information about such an investigation because the informants are less interested in imparting information and resources also of an individual or an institution are comparatively less than that of the government. Therefore, investigation covering a vast area cannot easily be done by this method.

Thus, according to the nature, investigations can be of different types mentioned above.

**6. Unit of Investigation.** 'Unit' is a very significant concept for statistical investigation. In statistics, facts are collected in terms of figures and then they are analysed and interpreted. So by what standard of the numerical facts should be collected becomes very significant. For example, the income of people should be collected in terms of rupees or in terms of pound-sterling or according to any other standard. The measure adopted for collecting, analysing and presenting data is known as statistical unit. It is not enough to determine unit while deciding about it, it is important to know its complete definition also. For example if data pertaining to students result of an examination of different universities are collected for comparison and they are classified as Ist division, IInd division and IIIrd division, it should also be defined that at what percentage these divisions will be awarded, because some universities awards IInd division at 50%, some at 48% and others at 45%. While determing unit, the following should be borne in mind :

A. *The Unit should be stable*. The unit to be adopted should be such as remains stable. If a unit goes on changing from time to time, the new unit will entail difficulty while comparing it with the previous one.

B. *The Unit should be Standard One*. The Unit to be used for investigation should not be local but should be standard and widely used. It becomes feasible to compare then at international level by adopting such a unit.

C. *The Unit should be simple, clear and definite*. The unit should be easily comprehensible to investigator. It should also contain the quality of clarity and definiteness along with that of simplicity. If it is not clear it is likely to be wrongly used.

D. *The Unit should be suitable for Investigation*. Units can be of different types, but from amongst there, the investigator should use only that unit which is suitable for his investigation. For example, centimetre, metre, kilometre etc. are the units of measuring length, but for measuring the height of men, only the unit of 'centimetre' will be suitable. And if Kilometre is used as a unit of measurement in this context it will be totally unsuitable and full of errors, consequently, the result based on this unit will also be confusing and inaccurate.

E. *The Units should be Similar*. All the units used in the investigation should be similar in nature and the measurement of all the units should also be identical.

**Types of Units.** In Statistics different types of units are used. Based on the uses and nature of units, they can be classified in the following manner :

(i) Units of Measurement of Collection
 (a) Simple Unit
 (b) Composite Unit
(ii) Units of Analysis and Interpretation
 (a) Rate
 (b) Ratio
 (c) Percentage
 (d) Coefficient

**(i) Units of Measurement of Collection.** By these units are meant those which are used to measure the form or character of a problem. The facts pertaining to the problem are collected in the form of data in these units. In other words, these are the units in which the facts related to the problem are collected in the form of data. This is the reason for calling these units as the units of collection. For example, if rupee be used to know the income of people of any place and it is told in terms of rupees only that the income of different people of that place is so and so in terms of rupee then this unit will be called as the unit of measurement of collection. The units of measurement and collection are also of two types :

A. *Simple Unit*. When a problem is measured on the basis of one measurement only as in yards, Kilograms, Pounds etc. it is called simple unit. They are very simple units and normally these are the units used in investigation.

B. *Composite Unit*. When for collection of data more than one determinants are used, that is called composite unit such as per passenger Km. meaning thereby one Km. journey by a passenger.

**(ii) Units of Analysis and Interpretation.** Under statistical investigations, it is not only to collect facts pertaining to a problem, but it is also to statistically analyse and interpret the collected facts. Therefore, in order to know the character of a problem, the collected facts are analysed and interpreted. In statistics, for analysis and interpretation different types of units are used. These are known as the units of analysis and interpretation. There can be more than one unit for the analysis and interpretation of a problem. They are of the following types :

A. *Rate*. Rates are used to compare different 'Variables' amongst them. The meaning of rate is determined by knowing the common relationship obtaining amongst the individual units at a fixed value. The fixed value can be 100; 1,000 or 1,00,000. For instance, if the interest of Rs. 50 on Rs. 500 for a year and Rs. 30 on Rs. 200 for a year was received, then, in order to know on which of the two principals the interest was more, it is necessary to find out the rate of interest per hundred. In the first case, the rate of interest is 10% per year and in that of the second it is 15% per year. It can be said on this basis that the second principal money has received more interest. Leaving the rate of interest, birth-rate, death-rate etc. are calculated per 1,000.

B. *Ratio*. Under this the mutual relationship between two related data are determined in the form of ratio. For example the ratio of income and expenditure, the ratio of educated and uneducated and the ratio of male and female etc.

C. *Percentage*. Sometime a particular fact may be having various elements and investigator may be interested to know the portion of each element separately to analyse the problem. In this situation percentage is an useful unit. For example the total cost of certain article consists the elements of raw material, wages and other expenses. In this case to analyse the cost usefully, the percentage of each element on total cost should be shown separately, *i.e.* portion of that element in total cost in relation to 100. If the total cost of a television set is Rs. 4000 and raw material cost is Rs. 2400, the percentage of raw material cost on total cost will be $2400/4000 \times 100 = 60\%$. This percentage is a unit of analysis in relation to 100.

D. *Coefficient*. When change in two values is known by comparing their dividend and divisor, it is called the coefficient.

For example, if there are 100 educated persons in 1000 in one city and 150 educated persons in 3,000 in another city then the coefficients of the educated persons will be in order of 100/1000 = .10 and 150/3000 = 0.5 respectively. Coefficient are generally used to compare the two or more facts.

**7. Collection of Data for Investigation.** Collection of appropriate data is necessary for the success of investigation. Therefore, the investigator should beforehand decide how the data will be collected. What will be the standard of accuracy in the collected data? Prior determination of many significant factors regarding data is very important. What kind of data will be used in the investigation — primary or secondary or both? Who will be the persons to collect data? What methods of collecting data will be adopted? Getting questionnaires prepared etc. are included in the planning of an investigation.

**8. Editing, Classification and Tabulation of Data.** After collecting data the job of their edition, classification and tabulation begins. Planning regarding these therefore, should be done beforehand. The selection of right type of person for editing the data is important. It is very necessary to decide as to what principles will be adopted for approximation, rectification etc. of data, how the data will be classified on the basis of the principle of homogeneity and what tables will be used to present them effectively.

**9. Presentation and Analysis of Data.** After editing, the problem is analysed by different mediums and other statistical methods. Therefore, the statistical methods to be adopted for the presentation and analysis of data should be determined. What method of presenting the data through pictures and diagrams will be adopted should be decided.

**10. Interpretation of Data.** After analysing the problem by statistical method, it becomes important to reveal its character and form. It should therefore made clear in the very beginning as to who will act as interpreter. Interpretation work is generally done by the investigator himself.

**11. Preparation of Report.** After completing all the aforementioned things, a report is prepared about the statistical investigation which is done by the interpreter himself. The report should be simple, clear and be able to reveal the actual character of the problem. It is always proper to indicate the future form of the problem in the report.

## QUESTIONS

1. What is the utility of planning of statistical investigations? Describe those factors which should be kept in mind for statistical investigation.
2. What is a 'statistical investigation'? Describe the preliminary steps you would take in planning a statistical investigation.
3. What do you mean by statistical units? What are the characteristics of a good unit.
4. Supposing you are appointed as a statistician by the Rajasthan Government to conduct a survey to study the pattern of consumption of the rural population of the state. Outline the procedure you will adopt in the conduct of the survey.
5. What do you mean by statistical investigation? Mention the points that should be looked into before starting an investigation.
6. "Planning is essential for statistical investigation". Comment on this statement.
7. Describe the preliminary steps which should be taken before commencing the work of collection of data.
8. How would you conduct an enquiry about 'payment of wages' in an industry? On what points would it be necessary for you to be clear before actually beginning investigation work.
9. What is a statistical unit? Is it necessary that data be homogeneous?

# 4

# Collection of Data

When an investigation is started in statistics data relating to a subject are used and on the basis of data the problem is interpreted. Therefore, in statistical investigation data have great importance. It is necessary that, in order to throw accurate facts of the problem, the data pertaining to that are properly collected. Therefore, it is necessary to follow correct methodologies for collecting statistical facts. There are various methods in Statistics to collect data. Before using different methods of data-collection the study of the types of data becomes an imperative because different methods are used for different types of data. The following are the types of data :

## TYPES OF DATA

1. Primary Data
2. Secondary Data

**1. Primary Data.** When the investigator himself originally collects or gets collected the data related to the problem that is called primary data. This type of data are originally collected by the investigator. In the words of H. Secrist, "*By primary data are meant those which are original, that is those in which little or no grouping has been made, the instance being recorded or itemized as encounted. They are necessary raw materials*". For example if the collection of marks in Statistics obtained by B.Com. students of Delhi University is done by the investigator by asking the students themselves, then that will be called primary data.

**2. Secondary Data.** By secondary data are meant those the collection of which has been done by someone else but the investigator is making use of them for his own investigation. According to M.M. Blair, "*Secondary data are those already in existence and which have been collected for some other purpose than the answering of the question in hand.*" Secondary data are generally obtained from newspapers and magazines, various publications, persons and institutions.

When primary data are used for the second time, they become secondary data. In the above instance if the collection of marks of the B.Com. Students in Statistics is done from the records of Delhi University by the investigator then these data will be called secondary data.

Making clear the difference between primary and secondary data Wessel, Willet and Simone have written, "*Data originally collected in the process of the investigation are known as primary data, those collected by other persons are called secondary data.*"

There are different processes for collecting both the types of primary and secondary data which are described below :

## METHODS OF COLLECTION OF PRIMARY DATA

1. Direct Personal Investigation
2. Indirect Oral Investigation
3. Information from Local Sources and Correspondents
4. Information through Schedules and Questionnaires
   - A. Filled up by Informants
   - B. Filled up by Enumerators.

**1. Direct Personal Investigation.** According to this method the investigator personally contacts persons about whom he is collecting information. That is why this is called direct personal investigation. For example, if someone wants to investigate about the monthly wages of the workers of a factory and if he collects data about their monthly wages by personally talking to them then this method of data collection will be called 'direct personal investigation' method. The person making investigation by this method should be educated, skillful and tactful. It is also necessary in this method for the investigator to know the language that the informants converse in. This method is useful for serious study of any subject, but the scope of investigation through this method is rather limited because the investigator being a single person cannot contact the informants spread over a wide area.

Following are the merits and demerits of this methods :

**Merits**

1. **Personal Contact.** Because the investigator himself has to personally collect data by contacting the informants therefore personal relationship is established between the informants and the investigator which helps in maintaining goodwill and co-operation between them.

2. **Secrecy.** This method is extremely useful when investigation deals with secret topics. The topic remains absolutely secret.
3. **Serious Study of Problem.** The problem gets seriously studied when data are collected by this method. By this method, even those matters which are indirectly related to the problem come to be known which is not possible by any other method. For example the working conditions of workers which have bearing upon their efficiency is also known while collecting data about their wages.
4. **Reliable Test.** No scope of distrust and doubt is left anywhere in this method as the investigator himself collects data by contacting the concerned persons.
5. **Uniformity among Data.** There is uniformity among all data as they are collected by the same person in this method.

Alongwith the aforementioned merits, there are certain demerits also of this method which are given below :

**Demerits**

1. **Limited Scope.** Investigation in this method is possible only of a limited area. Problems having wider scope cannot be tackled by this method.
2. **Partiality.** Data are collected by the investigator himself there is every chance of the feeling of partiality having entered into their collection.
3. **Difficulties in Collecting Data.** There are certain topics which the concerned persons do not personally like to divulge anything about. In such situations there is difficulty in collecting data.
4. **Wrong Collection by Unqualified Investigator.** If the investigator does not know statistical methods then wrong data will be collected by this method and conclusions drawn from this would also be wrong.
5. **Deprived of the services of Trained and Specialized persons.** This method deprives the investigation of the services of skilled persons in collecting data.

**2. Indirect Oral Investigation.** On collecting data by this method the investigator contacts such persons as have knowledge about the persons related to that particular problem. Hence, this is called indirect oral investigation. At times it so happens that the persons related to the problem show hesitancy in imparting information or are unable to understand and answer the questions of the investigator or there is language gap between the investigator and the informant. In situations like these the direct personal investigation method is rendered to of no use and the collection of data by indirect oral method becomes useful. In practice also it is observed that investigators take profuse recourse to this method. The success of this method depends upon the persons who are imparting indirect information. Therefore the representative persons should be selected properly and after due consideration. The following points should be kept in mind while selecting representative persons :

1. The representative person should be educated and qualified.
2. The persons should be such as have direct relationship with the actual people and have complete knowledge about the facts concerning the problem.
3. The representative person should be impartial.

This method has the following merits and demerits :

**Merits**

1. **Investigation of a Vast area.** Study of vast area can be made by this method because information about many people can be gathered from one representative person. For example, information about wages of thousands of factory workers can be gathered by talking to say 50 factory owners.
2. **Less Expensive.** It is less expensive because a lot of information can be gathered by contacting a few individuals only.
3. **Information from Qualified and Specialized persons.** Under this, information are collected from persons who are qualified and experts in that field. Hence, accurate data are gathered.
4. **Impartiality.** The chances of being partial by the investigator get diminished in this method.

**Demerits**

1. **Indirect knowledge.** Many significant aspects do not come to light in this method of indirect collection of data.
2. **Harm by selecting wrong representatives.** In case of a wrong selection of the representative the results are bound to be wrong. In other words, if the person selected does not

have any knowledge or he adopts a partial attitude then wrong data will be collected.

In the end, it can be said that the success and usefulness of this method lies in the selection of a right representative.

**3. Information from local sources and correspondents.** There are many an investigation dealing with such topics the detailed information about which can be obtained from local associations. Hence, in order to save time and expenditure, the investigator collects such information from local associations themselves. This method is known as 'Collection of Data from local sources'. For example, data pertaining to any market-price are got from the trade association of that market. Besides local information, sometimes the investigator appoints his correspondents at different places who go on collecting the necessary data. Correspondents are appointed when information is to be gathered regularly. For example, the newspapers appoint their correspondents at different places for collecting market-rate and other information who collect and send the concerned data to the newspapers from each places.

**Merits and Demerits**

The greatest advantage of this method is that data pertaining to a very vast area can be collected on nominal expenditure. But then collecting quite correct data by this method cannot be guaranteed.

**4. Information through Schedules and Questionnaires.** This is frequently used method for collecting data. This is a written and scientific method of data-collection. Data by this method are collected with the help of schedules and questionnaires. Questions are prepared regarding those aspects of the problem about which data are to be collected and it is on the basis of the answers of those questions that the concerned data are collected. There are two ways of collecting data by questionnaires and schedules :

**A. Schedules and Questionnaires filled up by Informants.** In order to collect data based on this method, the schedules and questionnaires are filled up by informants themselves. In order to get the questionnaires filled by such persons, the investigator goes to them and request them to answer the questions contained in the questionnaires or such schedules and questionnaires are sent to the concerned persons by post along with a letter of request to the informants to co-operate and fill-up the questionnaires. Generally, questionnaires are got filled by sending it through the post. The following should be kept in view while investigating by this method —

1. Letter of request for co-operation must be sent along with the questionnaires.
2. Informants must be assured of keeping their answers confidential.
3. If possible, the persons answering the questionnaires should be offered gifts and presents by way of encouragement for answering the questions.
4. If the questionnaire is got filled up by sending it through the post then addressed envelops affixed with postal stamps should also be sent to get the answers back.
5. The informants must be informed as far as possible about the objective of the investigation.
6. The questions included in the questionnaires should also be appropriate. In other words, the prepared questionnaire should possess some specific qualities.

**Points worth keeping in view while preparing Questionnaires.** The success of an investigation depends entirely on the questions which are included in the questionnaire. The following points therefore should be considered while making a questionnaire :

1. **Questions must be clear.** The questions included in the questionnaire should be clear and without any ambiguity.
2. **The language of the questions should be simple and correct.** The investigator should not frame difficult questions for the questionnaire. There is no scope of showing one's scholarship by using difficult language in forming the questions. The language of the question should be that of daily use and correct from grammatical point of view.
3. **The Questions should be such as elicit short answers.** The questions should not elicit descriptive answers such as how inflation in India can be prevented etc. On the other hand, the questions should elicit short answers such as 'what is your educational qualification'? More appropriately the answer should be in 'Yes' or 'No'! For example, 'are you a graduate?' It would be better to write below all the possible answers of a question if it involves multiple answers and the informant should be asked to tick the correct answer only. This will be made clear by the illustration that follows :

*Example.* What is your educational qualification? Tick the correct answer in the Square provided against.

| | | | |
|---|---|---|---|
| Uneducated | ☐ | Higher Secondary Education | ☐ |
| Primary Education | ☐ | Graduate | ☐ |
| Middle Education | ☐ | Post Graduate | ☐ |
| Any Special qualification | ☐ | | ☐ |

If true is someone post Graduate, he will tick the square given against it. The questions therefore should be simple and brief and should not entail difficulty for the informant.

4. **The questions should not hurt the personal feelings.** The questionnaire should not contain any such question as hurts the feelings of the informants. For example, if you ask some one how many thefts have you committed? or how many lies have you told? then he will perhaps never answer these questions.
5. **Care of personal secrecy.** The questions should not be such as tend to leakout one's personal secrecy.
6. **Use of respectful language.** The language used in the questionnaire should be respectful.
7. **Proper number of questions in the questionnaire.** By proper number is meant that neither a large number of questions are included in the questionnaire nor the number of questions is so small that they fail to throw sufficient light on the facts of the problem. There should be appropriate number of questions in the questionnaire in order to throw light on the related facts of an investigation.
8. **Questions should suit to the purpose.** Only those questions should be enlisted in the questionnaire which help accomplish the objective of the investigation.
9. **Questions should not involve technical answers.** The questions that require any kind of technical knowledge should be excluded from the questionnaire. They should, on the other hand, be such as can be answered by the informant on the basis of his general knowledge.
10. **Questions should not be repeated.** The same question should not be put time and again in the questionnaire.
11. **Questions should supplement each other.** There should be included some questions in the questionnaire which can test the correctness of the answers of the earlier questions.

**12. Mentioning the Act pertaining to the Investigation.** If the investigation conducted is under any Act, then that Act must be referred to in the questionnaire and mention must also be made of punishment resulting from the violation of that Act.

**13. Assurance of confidentiality in the questionnaire.** The questionnaire should contain the assurance of confidentiality and the informant must also be assured that the answers will be used for the purposes of investigation only and not for any other purpose.

**14. Continuity in the questions.** The questions in the questionnaire should be orderly and attractive.

All the above mentioned qualities must be present in a model questionnaire used for an investigation

Here below are given some samples of model questionnaires :

**Questionnaire 1**

**Purpose :** The purpose of this investigation is to collect data pertaining to the monthly expenditure of students. The furnished information will be strictly kept secret and will be used for the purpose of the present investigation only.

1. Name of the Student.........
2. Class......... Department......................
3. Name of the College and Address........
4. Do you reside in Hostel....... Yes ☐ No ☐
5. Home Address...................................
6. Age of the Student...........................
7. Name of the father/guardian..............
8. Occupation of the father/guardian.......
   a. Agriculture ☐
   b. Commerce and Business ☐
   c. Service ☐
   d. Other ☐
9. Monthly income of the father/guardian
   i. Less than Rs. 3,000 ☐
   ii. From Rs. 3,000 and to Rs. 5,000 ☐
   iii. From Rs. 5,000 to Rs. 10,000 ☐
   iv. From Rs. 10,000 to 20,000 ☐
   v. Above Rs. 20,000 ☐

10. Income of other Members of the family (if any)
    i. Less than Rs. 3,000
    ii. From Rs. 3,000 to Rs. 5,000
    iii. From Rs. 5,000 to Rs. 10,000
    iv. From Rs. 10,000 to Rs. 20,000
    v. Above Rs. 20,000.
11. Student's own monthly income (if any)?
    i. Source of income ..................
    ii. Amount of income .................
12. Total Income of the family ...........
13. Monthly amount of money meant for the student's expenditure ........
    i. From the family .....................................
    ii. From personal income .............................
    iii. From scholarship or other educational grant........
14. The amount of money spent by the student per month and items of expenditure.

| *Items of expenditure* | *Expenditure incurred per month* |
|---|---|
| i. College fees | ........ |
| ii. Books and Stationery | ........ |
| iii. Hostel Expenditure | ........ |
| a. Food ........ | |
| b. Rent ....... | |
| iv. Travelling expenses | ........ |
| v. Entertainment expenses | ........ |
| vi. Expenditure on other items (specify the items clearly) | ........ |
| Total Expenditure | ........ |

16. Do you spend the entire amount of money that you get per month?

    Yes ☐ No ☐
17. How much money do you save if you don't spend the entire amount? ☐
18. Do you get the full amount of money according to your need?

    Yes ☐ No ☐

19. How much less do you get if you don't get the full amount.? ☐

20. Can you reduce some expenses on some of the items mentioned above? Yes ☐ No ☐

21. If you can reduce to what extent? ☐

**Questionnaire 2**

A Cosmetics company is thinking about introducing a new product (Hair Spray) in the market. The company wants to make a consumer survey in this connection. Make a suitable questionnaire by which the survey can be properly conducted.

**Consumer Survey conducted by Datta Cosmetic Co.**

**Questionnaire**

1. Name ......... 2. Address ...........
3. Age ........... 4. Occupation ........
   - i. Agriculture ☐
   - ii. Trade & Business ☐
   - iii. Service ☐
   - iv. Any other (mention clearly) ☐
   - v. Unemployed ☐
5. Sex
   - i. Male ☐
   - ii. Female ☐
6. Income per month
   - i. NIL ☐
   - ii. Less than Rs. 3,000 ☐
   - iii. From Rs. 3,000 to Rs. 5,000 ☐
   - iv. From Rs. 5,000 to Rs. 10,000 ☐
   - v. From Rs. 10,000 to Rs. 15,000 ☐
   - vi. From Rs. 15,000 to Rs. 20,000 ☐
   - vii. More than Rs. 20,000. ☐
7. Which make-up aids do you use?
   - i. Only Hair oil ☐
   - ii. Powder ☐
   - iii. Cream ☐

iv. Lipstick ☐
v. Kum-Kum Bindi ☐
vi. Hair Spray ☐

8. Which company's cosmetic do you generally purchase?
   i. ... ... ...
   ii. ... ... ...
   iii. ... ... ...
   iv. ... ... ...
9. Which of our beauty aids do you purchase?
   i. Hair oil ☐
   ii. Powder ☐
   iii. Lipstick ☐
   iv. Bindi ☐
   v. Hair Spray ☐
10. Why do you purchase cosmetics from our or from any other company?
   i. They are cheap ☐
   ii. Easily available ☐
   iii. Like the fragrance ☐
   iv. Like the packing ☐
   v. To brighten up beauty ☐
11. What defects do you find in our cosmetic?
   i. Price is not proper ☐
   ii. Packing is not attractive ☐
   iii. Not easily available ☐
   iv. Don't like its scent ☐
   v. Don't brighten up beauty ☐
12. Do you think it necessary to use cosmetics for making your personality attractive?
   i. Yes ☐ ii. No ☐
13. How much money do you spend per month on cosmetics?
   i. Less than Rs. 300 ☐ ii. From Rs. 300 to Rs. 500 ☐
   iii. From Rs. 500 or Rs. 1,000 ☐ iv. From Rs. 1,000 to Rs. 2,000 ☐
   v. From Rs. 2,000 to Rs. 5,000 ☐ vi. More than Rs. 5,000 ☐

14. Do you talk to your friends about cosmetics?
    i. Yes ☐ ii. No. ☐
15. Which medium of advertisement attracts you most to use cosmetics?
    i. Radio ☐ ii. Television ☐
    iii. Newspapers & Magazines ☐ iv. Neon Sign Board ☐
    v. Any other
16. Have you ever visited the show-room of our company?
    i. Yes ☐ ii. No ☐
    iii. If you have visited, how did you find it?
    Attractive ☐ Not attractive ☐
17. Would you like to use our new product (Hair Spray)?
    i. Yes ☐ ii. No. ☐ iii. Uncertain ☐
18. What special qualities would you expect in a good Hair Spray?
    i. Fragrance ☐ ii. Cheapness ☐
    iii. Attractive in packing ☐ iv. Useful for the Hair ☐

Following are the merits and demerits when questionnaires and schedules are filled up by informants :

**Merits**

1. **Investigation of a vast area.** Investigation of a vast area can be conducted by this method because the filled up answers of the questionnaires by informants can be received by post even from outside countries.
2. **Economical.** This is an inexpensive method. It involves expenditure only for preparing, sending and getting back the questionnaires. No expenditure is incurred for travelling.
3. **Original Investigation.** Original data are collected by this method because the information are got directly filled up by the informants.
4. **Written Method.** This is a written method of collecting data which helps in maintaining a permanent record of the data.
5. **Unbiased.** As the informants themselves answer the questions therefore the investigation becomes impartial.
6. **Correct Result.** Results based on the data collected by this method are correct because unadulterated information is used in this method.

**Demerits**

1. **Answers to the questions not received.** Generally answers of many a questionnaire are not received back. Only those interested in some aspect of the problem send the answers after filling them. Neutral persons generally do not send the answers of the questionnaires back.
2. **Suitable for educated class only.** Data under this method is collected only from that class of people which is educated. It is not possible to collect data from uneducated people by this method, because they are unable to provide written answers to the questions.
3. **Incorrect Answers.** While answering the questionnaires most informants generally do not take much interest nor do they be very careful as a result of which there are greater possibilities for the answers being incorrect.
4. **Incomplete Answers.** Sometimes many an informant either don't answer some of the questions at all or give incomplete answers. In such a situation correct result is not possible to be derived from such data.

**B. Schedules and Questionnaires Filled up by Enumerators.** This method is similar to the one mentioned above. In this also the collection of data is based on the answers of the questionnaires and schedules. This method is different from the first one in the sense that under this the informants themselves don't fill up the questions, but the answers in the questionnaires are filled up by the enumerators by gathering information from the informants. The success of investigation by this method also depends upon the questionnaires. Therefore, care should be taken of all the points referred to above in the context of preparing model questionnaire in preparing a questionnaire under this method also. The investigator while appointing enumerators should make sure that they are skillful, acquainted with the subject of investigation and also with the informants. They must have a thorough knowledge of the language, nature, customs and habits of the informants because the information have to be filled up by the enumerators by asking the informants only.

The merits and demerits of this method are generally those of the method that has been described previously. The special merits and demerits of this method are the following :

**Merits**

1. Information from uneducated class can also be collected by this method.

2. Answers of difficult questions can also be obtained.
3. Enumerators take interest in the work because they are the paid employees of the investigator.
4. The possibility of the answers not being received gets reduced because the enumerator personally collects data by making request to the informants.

**Demerits**

1. This method is more expensive in comparison to the first method.
2. There is possibility of partiality in it because the enumerators fill up the questionnaires by asking the informants, therefore they can twist the information according to their will and write down them accordingly.
3. The results will be incorrect if the investigation is conducted by unqualified enumerators.

**Suitable Method of Collection of Primary Data**

After studying different methods referred to above the question comes up to mind as to what method should be adopted for collecting primary data?

There is not only one or any definite answer to this question. Adopting a method depends upon the nature and objective of investigation, ability of the investigator, sources and scope of investigation etc. Different methods should be adopted in different situations for collecting data. The following points should be borne in mind when selecting any one method :

1. **The Nature and objective of the Investigation.** The first thing to be seen is the nature and the objective of the investigation. If the investigation involves vast knowledge and accuracy as necessary ingredients, the direct personal investigation method will be useful and the investigation where purity and accuracy are not the absolutely desirable elements and where investigation is a continuous phenomenon, the collection of data there by local resources and correspondents will be more appropriate.
2. **Qualification of the Investigator.** If the investigator is a very qualified person, then he himself can collect data. But if he is not fit to collect data himself, then data can be collected with the help of enumerators.
3. **Means of the Investigator.** If the investigator has only limited resources then the method that involves minimum

expenditure should be adopted. But if the investigator is a man of vast resources, he can have recourse to methods involving more money and therefore more advantages.

4. **The Scope of Investigation.** The scope of investigation also much affects the method to be used for the investigation. In a limited scope of investigation, direct personal method of investigation is more suitable with a slightly wider scope, the indirect oral method of investigation can be used for collecting data. But in case of the scope being very vast, the collection of data can be done by questionnaire and schedule method of collecting data.

Thus it becomes quite apparent that different methods are rendered suitable in different circumstances and for different requirements.

**Method of Collection of Secondary Data**

When an investigator uses for his own purposes the data collected and used by other person or institution then that is called secondary data. The investigator should look into whether the data related to his own investigation have already been collected by any other person or institution. If such data are already available, the investigator may use the same data for his own investigation. This renders the investigation less expensive and the work gets easier also. The methods of collection of secondary data are different depending upon the publication of data. From this point of view, these data are of the following types :

(a) **Published Data.** These are the data which have been published in a newspaper, magazine or in any other form. In order to collect such data the concerned publication are consulted. Following are the kinds of published data :

1. *International Publications.* These are data that are published by international institutions such as International Labour Organization (ILO), International Monetary Fund etc.

2. *Government Publications.* Every country and state collect data on various subjects and get them published. The investigator collects these data from these publications. The Government of India has set up many such institutions whose function is to collect and publish data such as C.S.O. and N.S.S. etc.

3. *Semi-Government Publications.* Many significant data are collected by some semi-Government agencies such

as governmental committees, commissions and publications from local bodies etc.

4. *Publications from Universities and other Educational Institutions*. Generally, all the Universities and colleges conduct research work. The related data are collected and the institutions publish those data.
5. *Publications in Newspapers and Magazines*. Many Magazines and newspapers publish data which can be collected from them. Commerce, Eastern Economist and Taxation are some of the prominent publications of this type in India.
6. *Publications from Business Concerns*. Data are collected by big business concerns also and they publish these data.
7. *Personal Publications*. Researchers also collect and publish data.
8. *Publications from Trade and other Organizations*. Different Trade organizations and organizations established for other purposes get some very significant data published.

The investigator can collect data for his use from any of the different publications described above.

**(b) Unpublished Data.** When the data that are collected but remain unpublished and when any other person uses them for his purpose, such unpublished data are called unpublished secondary data. These data can be obtained on request from the concerned persons or institutions. These data are generally available from researchers and institutions involved in research work.

## Points Worth Keeping In Mind When Using Secondary Data

Many points should be taken into consideration while using secondary data. As secondary data are collected by some other persons therefore it is necessary to examine their reliability and accuracy. If they are not used with care, the possibility of mistake enhances. About the use of published data Dr. A.L. Bowley has said, "*It is never safe to take published statistics at their face value, without knowing their meaning and limitations, and it is always necessary to criticise arguments that can be based on them.*"

Similarly, hinting at the defects of secondary data Prof. Corner also has said, "*Statistics, especially other people's statistics are full of pitfalls for the user.*"

Hence, while using secondary data it should be looked into whether they are reliable, suitable to purpose and are sufficient and if they are so, then only they should be used. In order to test the reliability, suitability and sufficiency, the following things should be inquired into :

1. **The purpose of the collection of data.** First of all it should be seen that what was the purpose of collecting these data?

   If the purpose confirm to our investigation, then only we should use them not otherwise.

2. **Qualification of the data-collector.** Who was the person to primarily collect the Data? Was he qualified for collecting data? What method did he follow in collecting data? All these questions should be well considered. The use of these data will be fruitful if the answers to the questions are satisfactory otherwise not.

3. **Correctness of data collection.** What was the standard of correctness at the initial stage when the data were collected. Whether standard of correctness was lower than the one fixed for our investigation or not. If the standard was not lower than our own standard of correctness, only then its use will be appropriate.

4. **Time of data collection.** If there has been no change in the character of the problem from when the data were first collected and now, then the use of these data will be appropriate.

5. **Meaning of Unit.** What is the meaning of unit used for collecting data first time? If that meaning conforms to the unit fixed by us, then these data should be used. But if both differ from each other, the data should not be used.

6. **Tallying the data obtained from various means.** If the same type of data have been collected by more than one person and institution then we should see whether there is uniformity among them or not. If there is substantial variation among them than the correctness of these data is rather doubtful.

7. **Comparison between Secondary and Primary data.** Some statistics should be collected by way of primary collection and the primary data should be compared with that of the secondary one. If on comparison, they are found correct then the remaining data can be assumed as correct but if

these data differ from the primary data then they should in no case be used.

Secondary data should be used by taking care of the points mentioned above otherwise the results will be wrong and doubtful.

## QUESTIONS

1. What are the different types of data? What are the methods of collection of data?
2. Explain the various methods in the collection of statistical data, of these which would you prefer? Give reasons.
3. "In collection of statistical data, common sense is the chief requisite and experience the chief teacher." Discuss this statement with comments.
4. Discuss in brief the methods generally used in the collection of primary data.
5. What are the factors which should be kept in mind while selecting a method of collection of primary data.
6. Distinguish between primary and secondary data? Explain the various methods of collecting primary data and point out their relative merits and demerits.
7. What are the essentials of a good questionnaire? What points should be taken into consideration while selecting the enumerators?
8. What do you know about secondary data? What are the things which should be kept in mind while using the secondary data?
9. "Secondary data should never be accepted without careful inquiry." Enumerate and explain the pitfalls that otherwise await the user.
10. Define 'secondary data'. State their chief sources and point out the dangers involved in their use and what precautions are necessary before using them.
11. What are the chief requirements of a good questionnaire for use in statistical inquiry? Explain them giving illustrations.
12. "It is never safe to take published statistics at their face value without knowing their meaning and limitations." Comment on this statement.
13. "Statistics, especially other people's statistics are full of pitfalls for the user unless used with caution." Elucidate the above statement and mention what are the sources of secondary data.

14. You are the Sales Promotion Officer of Delta Cosmetic Co. Ltd. Your company is about to market a new product. Design a suitable questionnaire to conduct a consumer survey before the product is launched. State the various types of persons that may be approached for replying to the questionnaire.

[*B. Com. (Pass) Delhi, 1974*]

15. Discuss the various methods of collecting 'Primary data'. State the methods you would employ to collect information about utilisation of plant capacity in small-scale sector in the Union Territory of Delhi.

[*B. Com. (Pass) Delhi, 1976*]

16. Distinguish between 'Primary Data' and 'Secondary Data'. State the chief sources of Secondary Data. What precautions are to be observed when such data are to be used for any investigation?

[*B. Com. (Pass) Delhi, 1977*]

17. Explain the various methods of collecting Primary Data.

[*B. Com. (Pass) Delhi, 1977*]

18. Distinguish between 'primary data' and 'secondary data'.

(*C.S. June 1995*)

19. Briefly explain the methods of collecting primary data.

(*C.S. Dec. 1995*)

20. You are working as an investigator in a company. You are asked to collect primary data. What methods of primary data collection would you adopt and why?

(*C.S. Dec. 1996*)

# 5

# Types of Statistical Investigation — Census and Sample Methods

In Statistical investigation, statistical facts are collected about the concerned problem. The collection of statistical facts is either of all the units related to the problem or the conclusions are drawn for the 'Universe' by collecting statistics about only a few representative units connected with the problem. The investigator has to decide in advance about the method of investigation to be adopted for the purpose. Following are the two methods of Statistical Investigation :

1. Census Method; and
2. Sample Method

Let us first of all know what is the meaning of 'Universe' before taking-up a detailed discussion about the above mentioned two methods.

## MEANING OF UNIVERSE OF POPULATION

All the units collectively related with the subject-matter about which an investigation is being conducted are called 'Universe'. In otherwords, by 'Universe' is meant that group of units which is being studied for the purpose of investigation. For example, if an investigation is to be conducted on the marks obtained in statistics by the students of a class then all the students of that class in that subject will be the 'Universe'. If that class consists of 50 students, the same 50 students will form the 'Universe'. The 'Universe' may be real or imaginary. In the above example, the group of students is the real universe. But there are investigation wherein the universe is not real but imaginary. Imaginary groups, for instance, are formed in order to find out 'probability'. On tossing up a coin, the probabilities are that it will fall either head or tail. Therefore it will be an imaginary 'Universe'. Universe has been defined by different scholars in the following manners :

1. "*A universe or population may be defined as an aggregate of items possessing a common trait or traits.*"

*— Simpson & Kafka*

"*A population is the totality of objects under consideration.*"

*— A.C. Rosander*

## CENSUS METHOD

When the conclusions are drawn on the basis of the statistical facts collected for each unit of the universe, it is known as census method. When the investigation is conducted by this method, not a single unit is left out about which data are not collected. For example if a class consists of 50 students and the marks of each student are collected then it will be called census method. This method is useful in the investigations where the standard of accuracy has to be kept very high.

Following are the advantages and defects of the census method :

**Advantages**

1. In any investigation conducted by this method the problem receives right attention because all the units of universe are studied under this.
2. On adopting census method for investigation the possibility of partiality on the part of the investigator finishes. Under this method the investigator is not free to collect only those units which he thinks are fit to be collected as his own bias.
3. A detailed knowledge about the problem is possible by this method.
4. If the scope of investigation is limited one or if there are only a few units in the universe, this method is extremely useful.
5. If most of the units in universe are different from each other then using any other method than this will be wrong.

**Defects**

1. This method involves a lot of time and money. This is not useful therefore for those who have limited resources.
2. It is difficult to adopt this method for investigations involving vast areas because information about many unit of the universe is hard to get.
3. The investigator has sometimes to face many a problem on adopting this method. Where some units of the universe

have been destroyed, their data cannot be collected. For example if certain articles in a factory have been destroyed due to fire outbreak, then any estimate about them cannot be made by the remains of either the burnt or half-burnt articles. In this situation, therefore, the census method can not be adopted.

4. If the units of the universe are of the type that get exhausted if investigated by the census method then this method is of no significance. Such units could be either eatables or living creatures. If, for example, it is to find out by tasting it whether a Kilo of meat is fresh or not. On using census method, then the whole meat will vanish by doing so. In this situation the proper course should be to taste only a small portion of 1 Kg. meat and then find out whether the meat is fresh or otherwise.

## SAMPLING METHOD

Sometimes it is difficult to adopt census method due to its being complex and expensive and investigation is conducted for vast area. Statistics about all the units of the universe is not collected when the investigation is conducted by sample method. Only a few representative units of the universe are selected in this method and conclusions are drawn for the whole universe on the basis of the data collected for those units. The sample method is a scientific method of investigation. The conclusions drawn from this method are as reliable and accurate as these drawn from the census method. The validity of this method is this that if some units of the universe are similar in form, colour, quality, shape and nature then why the conclusions be not drawn about all the units on the basis of a few of each type. This method is generally used in practice.

Following are the merits and demerits of the sample method :

**Merits**

1. This is easier than the census method.
2. Investigation conducted by this method does not involve either a lot of time or money nor does it requires any extensive organisation.
3. Investigation about vast fields can also be conducted by this method.
4. This is useful even in those situations wherein using census method is harmful and impractical.

**Demerits**

1. There is possibility of partiality on the part of the investigator in this method because he can draw the desired result on the basis of only biased units selected as the samples.
2. If wrong samples have been selected then the results will be incorrect and illusive.
3. As the investigation in this method is conducted by means of representative units the investigator has to decide beforehand as to which units should be regarded representatives for the concerned universe and this in fact is a difficult job.
4. There are many a sub-method also of the sample system and the investigator has to select those sub-methods.
5. If the universe is too small to have sufficient units in it, the investigation of that universe by means of this method would be of no avail.
6. If all the units of the universe are different from each other or there is no unit which can be regarded as the representative unit then using this method for investigating such a 'Universe' will not prove fruitful.
7. In order to use this method, it is necessary to have the knowledge and skill of collecting samples which is a technical kind of job. Therefore everyone cannot use this method with requisite success.

On careful consideration of the defects of sample method described above, it can be said that if the sample units and the sample method have been correctly selected then these defects automatically disappear.

If sample method has been adopted for any investigation, the representative units and samples should not be selected by closing the eyes. Many factors should be taken into consideration while selecting samples. The most important factors for selecting proper samples are described below :

**Selection of Proper Samples.** While selecting the samples, the concerned person is faced with the problem as to which and how many units should be selected as samples.

They should be decided on the basis of following criteria :

1. **Representative Unit.** It should be remembered while chosing samples that the units selected as samples represent others. No unit in the universe should be left out which is not represented by the sample unit or else the results would be

inaccurate. But then the selection of the representative units is possible only when the investigator does not follow a biased course.

2. **Number of Sample Units.** Generally question comes up while adopting the sample method as to what should be the number of units selected as samples. The answer to this question is not definite. The only thing to be remembered is that the number of units should be sufficient or the results will be inaccurate if the number of sample-units is too small. Because it is likely then that some of the units of the universe are entirely left out without being represented by any sample. But the number of units selected as samples should not be too many either because that will involve a lot of expenditure of time and money and the investigator will be deprived of the fundamental advantage of the sample method. Therefore the number of sample-units should neitiner be too many nor too few but should be sufficient enough.

3. **Difference in the Nature of Sample Units.** The units selected as samples should be different in nature from each other, that is, they should be independent units. For example, if a study of the examination results of the students of a class is to be done by the sample-method then such students should be selected as represent the failures, third class, second class, first class and distinction-categories etc.

The above facts if taken into consideration while selecting samples give correct results.

## METHODS OF SAMPLING

There are various methods for selecting samples. The selection of samples can be made by the investigator after considering about their relevance. The following are the methods of selecting samples :

1. Deliberative or Purposive Sample Method.
2. Random Sample Method.
3. Quasi-Random Sample Method.
4. Stratified Sample Method.
5. Multi-stage Sample Method.

**1. Deliberative or Purposive Sample Method.** No definite methodology is adopted when samples are selected following this method. The investigator under this method selects on his own, those units of the universe as samples which he deems to be representatives.

Therefore, different units are selected as samples in this method by different investigators. The basis for selecting units as samples in this method is the will, nature and experience of the investigator alone. But the samples selected based on this method are normally inaccurate because personal feelings greatly affect the selection. Following are the main defects of this method :

1. Owing to greater influence of personal feelings and bias in selecting samples, biased samples are selected. Therefore, representative units don't get selected as samples.
2. The conclusions drawn on the basis of this method are not quite accurate.
3. There is no equal opportunity for each unit to be selected as samples. On the contrary, there is no chance at all for some units to get selected as samples.

It is better therefore not to use this method for choosing samples due to the defects described above.

**2. Random Sample Method.** This is regarded as the best method for selecting samples. In this method the investigator cannot select units as samples as he likes. On the other hand, every unit has equal chance to be selected as sample. Different authors have given the following definitions of random sampling method :

1. "*Random samples are characterised by the way in which they are selected. 'Random' is not used in the sense of 'hap-hazard' or 'hit or miss'. A random sample is a sample where each item in the universe has an equal or known opportunity of being selected — providing chance and only chance determines which items are to be included in the sample chosen.*"

— *Simpson & Kafka*

In the above definition the word 'random' has been very well explained. It should always be borne in mind in this connection that by 'random' is not meant hap-hazard' selection. By this are meant those samples wherein chance for each unit of the universe for getting selected are equal.

2. "*Random sampling is the form applied when the method of selection assures each individual element in the universe an equal chance of being chosen.*"

— *Parten*

3. "*A random sample is a sample selected in such a way that every item in the population has an equal chance of being included.*"

— *W.M. Harper*

After studying all the definitions above, it may be said that by random sampling method is meant that method which includes equal chance for each unit of the universe to be chosen as sample.

The following methods are applied for choosing samples under random sampling method :

(1) **By Draw of Lot.** Lottery system is used for choosing samples under this method, that is, samples are drawn on the lottery pattern. A desired number of slips are got drawn from the whole lot by an impartial person after getting his eyes closed. The units bearing the numbers of the slips drawn are taken as samples. For example, in order to choose 20 mill-workers as samples from a lot of 100, one hundred slips in number will be made bearing number of all the workers and then mixed in a box by shaking that off. Thereafter 20 slips will be picked up from the box by an impartial person closing his eyes. Data will then be collected about those workers whose slips have been drawn out. In practice, this method is very simple and much less expensive.

(2) **By rotating Drum.** This is similar to the lottery method. In this, numbers are written on some pieces of metal or cardboard which are put in a drum and mixed by rotating the drum well. Then these pieces are taken out one by one either by hand or by machine corresponding to as many numbers as are required to be selected as sample-units. The units corresponding to these numbers only written on the pieces are selected as samples. This method is also simple as well as less expensive.

(3) **By using Tippet's Table.** In order to select units as samples, a scholar named Tippet prepared a table containing 10,400 figures of 4 digits each. To take samples with the help of this table any point in the table is ascertained blindfoldly. Thereafter the required number of samples will be picked up from the table in succession.

This method is slightly arduous.

Random samples can be selected by using any one of the methods mentioned above.

**Merits**

Following are the merits of this method :

1. This method offers equal chances for all units to be selected as samples and therefore there is no room for partiality.

2. Results based on the data collected by this method are correct.
3. This is a scientific method of collecting data. Samples in this method are not subservient to any one's will or whim.

**3. Quasi-Random Sample Method.** In this first of all the whole universe is classified on some basis and the first unit is randomly selected as a sample. Subsequently other units of sample are selected one by one in order from the remaining categories already classified. Thus, this method is called quasi-random sample method because in this only the initial unit is selected on the basis of random sample method and the rest of the required units get automatically selected in order. To illustrate, if a universe consists of 100 persons out of which 10 persons are to be selected, the whole universe will be classified into 100/10 = 10 divisions on the numerical principle. The first unit will then be chosen randomly. Thereupon, for each next unit 10 will be added. Suppose the first person selected as sample has serial number 9, the rest of the persons selected will have serial numbers 19, 29, 39, 49, 59, 69, 79, 89 and 99 respectively, which are obtained by adding 10 to each of the subsequent number after the initial number 9.

**4. Stratified Sample Method.** Under this method all the units of the universe are divided into various strata on the basis of their different properties and then from among the units of various strata, the sample units will be selected proportionately. For instance, in making a study of the total population of a township, the population will first be divided into two classes of male and female and samples from each of the two groups will be taken proportionately. If the 10,000 population of the township consists of 60 per cent male and 40 per cent female and if, 1,000 persons are to be chosen as samples, then 600 males and 400 females will be selected as samples which are 60 per cent and 40 per cent respectively of the total number of samples of the selected. This method, is used in situations where units are different in natures and properties.

This method is quite useful and advantageous. As the units of the universe in this method are already divided according to their properties and samples of the units of different properties are taken, therefore there is every chance to get the representative units.

**5. Multi-stage Sample Method.** When the universe is so vast that its study becomes formidable at one stretch, it is divided into many groups and then data are collected for each group. For instance having to study about a country as a whole, it has to be divided into states first, the states into districts, districts into tehsils and the last into towns and villages. And the results arrived at by selecting towns and villages as sample units. This sample method will be called multi-stage sample method. The method accords great importance even to each unit how-so-ever small as sample.

There are certain principles regarding the reliability of sample method which confirm and clarify the correctness of results of investigation conducted by this method. They are as following :

**Theory of Probability and Sampling Method**

The theory of probability offers an estimate of a phenomenon as either being or not. This theory is of immense practical importance because everyone wants to and is interested in knowing the future-events. To know this logically is possible only by the theory of probability. Theory of probability has been defined variously; some of which are here below :

1. "*Probability is a measure of our expectations that an event will (or will not) happen.*"

— *Conner*

2. "*Probability is the ratio of favourable events to the total numbers of equally likely events.*"

— *Laplace*

Thus, probability theory tells us what are the chances of an event to happen. For instance, a coin being tossed has always an equal chance of falling either head or tail which in the language of mathematics is said that a tossed up coin has 50 per cent or ½ and ½ chance of being head or tail. The theory of probability is shown in a formula form given below :

$$p = \frac{m}{m + n}$$

$$q = \frac{n}{m + n}$$

p = Probability of the success of the event

q = Probability of the failure of the event

m = Number of favourable events

n = Number of unfavourable events.

If the happening of an event is definite, the probability of its not happening will be nil then.

The significance of the theory of probability in applying it to the method of sampling lies in the sense that it tells that if some units are selected as samples from the universe then there is probability for various units to be selected samples in the same proportion as they actually form the part of the universe. Thus the results derived from the samples will be the same as they would be from the census of universe.

**Law of Statistical Regularity**

This is based on the theory of probability. This law tells that articles or units selected from a large group by random sample method contain on the average all the characteristics of that group. In the words of Prof. I.W. King, "*The law of statistical regularity formulated in mathematical theory of probability lays down that a moderately large number of items chosen at random from a very large group are almost sure on the average, to have the characteristics of the large group.*"

It becomes clear thus that the sample-units so selected are the representative units of the universe and sample method therefore can be relied upon.

**Law of Inertia of Large Numbers**

This law is the corollary of the law of statistical regularity. This law tells us that greater numbers are more constant in comparison with smaller numbers, that is, there are few changes in bigger numbers. This law makes it apparent that the more the number of samples, the lesser are the possibilities of inaccuracy. As there is more possibility of balance between positive and negative differences when more units are taken as samples, results derived from the investigation based on sample method, will come out as accurate. The sample method owes its utility to the law of inertia of large numbers only. In the words of Dr. A.L. Bowley, "*Great number have great inertia. It is consistency of great numbers that makes statistical measurement possible.*"

Changes in greater numbers occur in a long period and with less frequency whereas changes in lesser numbers often occur. It is owing to the inertia of greater numbers that make future estimates possible, not otherwise.

All the laws referred to above disclose that if the samples have been properly selected then theoretically results derived from them will be as true and reliable as the results derived from the investigation conducted by census method.

## QUESTIONS

1. What are the different types of statistical investigations?
2. What do you mean by census method? Discuss the merits and demerits of census method.
3. Compare the merits of a census enumeration and a random sample survey. Can a census be verified through sampling. If so can you discuss any such plan used in India?
4. Define sample method of investigation. What are the different types of sample method?
5. Compare the relative advantages and disadvantages of the methods of complete enumeration (census) and the method of random sampling in social and economic enquiries.
6. What do you understand by random sample method? Explain the various methods of taking random sample.
7. Briefly describe the methods of random sampling and comment on its uses in social investigations.
8. What is sampling? What are the essentials of a good sample? Name the various methods of sampling and explain them in brief.
9. What is stratified sample? Discuss its merits.
10. "A sample may be large yet worthless, because it is not random; or it may be random but unreliable, because it is small." Comment upon the above statement and explain the importance of sampling in our daily life.
11. Distinguish between sample method and census method of collection of data. Explain the various techniques of sampling. [*B.Com.* (*Pass*), *Delhi, 1972, 1978, 1979*]
12. Write a brief note on :
    (i) Census method
    (ii) Theory of Probability
    (iii) Law of Statistical Regularity
    (iv) Law of inertia of large numbers.
13. Explain the following :
    (i) The law of statistical regularity.
    (ii) The law of inertia of large numbers.
    (*C.S. June 1997*)

# 6

# Editing of Data

The act of systematically arranging and rendering the collected data fit to be used and come in handy is called editing. The collected data are huge accumulation of numerical facts. They are collected by various enumerators each having more or less different way of doing this job; many facts not relevant to the present investigation are also collected at the time of data-collection and some data having been collected in haste and without care come out to be incorrect. Therefore, in such cases as there it becomes necessary to arrange data collected by various enumerators and rectify them by putting them to accuracy tests. Data are edited in order to perform this action. Editing is immensely important because no conclusions can be drawn from the mere heap of collected data. Editing in statistical investigation is as important as it is for newspapers, just as a newspaper or magazine editor decides as to which information should be given at what place in the newspaper by pruning and trimming them, like wise, for statistical work also, the editor prunes and trims the collected data, corrects them and renders them adaptable and befitting to the aims of the investigation.

Incorrect data get collected owing to shortage of enumerators in data collection, prevailing prejudice and indifference to work and at times informants too furnish insufficient, incomplete and wrong information. In such situations the editor has to see that data collected are not incorrect. Efforts should be made to get the incomplete information completed. But if they remain incomplete still they will not be in the interest of the investigation to use them.

The following facts are significant in regard to editing of data :

**1. Accuracy.** Correct analysis of any problem calls for correct data collected about it for if data are not accurate results will be wrong and confusing. The editor therefore is duly bound to examine about the correctness of data and if they are incorrect, make arrangement to rectify them. Here by 'accuracy' is not meant the absolute accuracy of data. In statistics, as we know, the collection of data is done either through enumeration or estimation and at times it is not possible to measure the actual state of things. For example, it is likely that a man's height is actually 5 feet 7 inches when he is estimated to be 5 feet 6 inches tall. The estimation here is 1 inch less. But this kind of difference is acceptable in statistics. The editor has to see about the accuracy that in collecting data proper standard has been maintained. He should not be meticulously exact about absolute accuracy of data because this involves a lot of expenditure and result or conclusion will also not be substantially different even without absolute accuracy. In this connection the thinking of the following scholars are notable :

1. "*Attempt to obtain the greatest possible degree of accuracy are frequently merely wastes of time.*"

*— I.W. King*

2. "*In common use only a certain conventional accuracy is needed.*"

*— Dr. A.L. Bowley*

3. "*The statistician must be careful not to discard any accuracy that can be justified.*"

*— C.T. Clark & L.L. Schkade*

The standard of accuracy will be different for different types of problems. But while determining the standard of accuracy it should be taken care of that the actual state of a thing does not lose its perspective and its form remains intact. For example, the difference of an inch or so is acceptable regarding a man's height but if this difference extents into feet or metres, the actual state of fact will not be known at all.

The standard of accuracy is more accurately adhered to in physical sciences where even the slightest deviation leads to very serious consequences. In the case of social sciences greater degree of accuracy is not absolutely necessary.

**2. Approximation.** The actual statistics accumulated on collecting data is sometimes so vast that it is difficult to remember and compare. Such a vast statistics is abridged in order to make it comparable. This operation is known as the act of approximation of statistics. For example, in 1999 the total amount of actual profit of a firm was Rs. 92,521. This is too big amount to remember and any comparison based on this is difficult. Therefore after approximating it, it can be said that the amount of profit of that firm in 1999 was Rs. 92,500. While approximating, the place value of approximation is to be done beginning from unit to ten, hundred, thousand and lac etc. This depends upon the vastness and correctness of statistical information. The following methods are used for approximation.

(A) *Approximation to the Nearest Whole Number* : This method is frequently used for approximation. According to this method of approximation, the value which is less than half of the place value of approximation is ignored and if the value is half or more than half then that is approximated to the nearest whole number. For example, for the approximation of the unit, place value less than .5 will be ignored and value which is .5 or more than .5 will be included as a unit. Like this, for the approximation of the place value of ten, hundred, thousand and lac, the values less than 5; 50; 500, and 50,000 will be ignored.

The following can clarify the above statement :

**Example**

| | | Production in Tons | | | |
|---|---|---|---|---|---|
| Year | Actual Figures | Approximated Figures | | | |
| | | Unit | Ten | Hundred | Thousand |
| 1990 | 25,95,833.5 | 25,95,834 | 25,95,830 | 25,95,800 | 25,96,000 |
| 1991 | 28,18,331.4 | 28,18,331 | 28,18,330 | 28,18,300 | 28,18,000 |
| 1992 | 29,25,245.8 | 29,25,246 | 29,25,250 | 29,25,300 | 29,25,000 |
| 1993 | 32,84,386.1 | 32,84,386 | 32,84,390 | 32,84,400 | 32,84,000 |
| 1994 | 33,18,471.6 | 33,18,472 | 33,18,470 | 33,18,500 | 33,19,000 |
| 1995 | 35,19,672.2 | 35,19,672 | 35,19,670 | 35,19,700 | 35,20,000 |
| 1996 | 39,26,232.7 | 39,26,233 | 39,26,230 | 9,26,200 | 39,26,000 |

(B) *By discarding some Figures* : According to this method, all the numbers coming after the place upto which the approximation is to be done are ignored whether the numbers are more than half, half or less than half. The total value of statistics thus approximated becomes far less than that of the actual statistics. Hence approximation of statistics by this method is not right.

The data given in the earlier illustration will be approximated by this method in the following manner :

**Example**

| | | Production in Tons | | | |
|---|---|---|---|---|---|
| Year | Actual Figures | Approximated Figures | | | |
| | | Unit | Ten | Hundred | Thousand |
| 1990 | 25,95,833.5 | 25,95,833 | 25,95,830 | 25,95,800 | 25,95,000 |
| 1991 | 28,18,331.4 | 28,18,331 | 28,18,330 | 28,18,300 | 28,18,000 |
| 1992 | 29,25,245.8 | 29,25,245 | 29,25,240 | 29,25,200 | 29,25,000 |
| 1993 | 32,84,386.1 | 32,84,386 | 32,84,380 | 32,84,300 | 32,84,000 |
| 1994 | 33,18,471.6 | 33,18,471 | 33,18,470 | 33,18,400 | 33,18,000 |
| 1995 | 35,19,672.2 | 35,19,672 | 35,19,670 | 35,19,600 | 35,19,000 |
| 1996 | 39,26,232.7 | 39,26,232 | 39,26,230 | 39,26,200 | 39,26,000 |

(C) *By raising the figures to next higher figure* : This method is just opposite to the one mentioned above. By approximating data by this method number '1' is added to the place-value upto which the data are to be approximated. Though this method is quite easy in practice, yet approximations are full of statistical errors because the value of each item under this is increased. Hence this is also a less desired method to be used for approximation.

The explanation of approximation by this method in the context of the above example can be done in the following manner :

**Example**

| | | Production in Tons | | | |
|---|---|---|---|---|---|
| Year | Actual Figures | Approximated Figures | | | |
| | | Unit | Ten | Hundred | Thousand |
| 1990 | 25,95,833.5 | 25,95,834 | 25,95,840 | 25,95,900 | 25,96,000 |
| 1991 | 28,18,331.4 | 28,18,332 | 28,18,340 | 28,18,400 | 28,19,000 |
| 1992 | 29,25,245.8 | 29,25,246 | 29,25,250 | 29,25,300 | 29,26,000 |
| 1993 | 32,84,386.1 | 32,84,387 | 32,84,390 | 32,84,400 | 32,85,000 |
| 1994 | 33,18,471.6 | 33,18,472 | 33,18,480 | 33,18,500 | 33,19,000 |
| 1995 | 35,19,672.2 | 35,19,673 | 35,19,680 | 35,19,700 | 35,20,000 |
| 1996 | 39,26,232.7 | 39,26,233 | 39,26,240 | 39,26,300 | 39,27,000 |

On comparing the three methods of approximation described above, it must have become clear that the first one (approximation to the nearest whole number) is superior to the rest because not much gap is left between the actual and the approximated data in this method. In this, lesser and greater values of various items get adjusted among them and the difference as a whole comes out to be negligible. Whereas according to the second method (By discarding some figures) the actual data are far greater than the approximated data and hence the difference between them comes out to be far too much. This is owing to the reason that the value of each item in this method is reduced. In the same way difference comes out to be far enough by the third method (By raising the figure to next higher figure) because in this some value is added to each of the items. Therefore, only the first method should be used for approximation.

The difference between actual values and approximated values in various methods of approximation can be explained by the following illustration :

**Example**

| | | | | Expenses (in Rs.) |
|---|---|---|---|---|
| Family | Actual Figures | Approximation in '000 | | |
| | | Ist Method | IInd Method | IIIrd Method |
| A | 15,232 | 15,000 | 15,000 | 16,000 |
| B | 18,431 | 18,000 | 18,000 | 19,000 |
| C | 19,530 | 20,000 | 19,000 | 20,000 |
| D | 20,640 | 21,000 | 20,000 | 21,000 |
| Total | 73,833 | 74,000 | 72,000 | 76,000 |
| | | 73,833 | 73,833 | 73,833 |
| Difference | | 167 | –1,833 | +2,167 |

It becomes clear from the above example that difference is the least when approximated by the first method. Hence only this method is useful for making approximation.

**3. Statistical Errors.** The data procured by approximation are generally different from the actual ones. That is, there is noticeable gap between the actual and the approximated or estimated values. This difference in data is called 'Statistical error'. It should be remembered in regard to statistical error that this is different from common error or mistake. This error is unavoidable despite having all the precautions whereas common error results from carelessness, deliberate attempt or sheer ignorance of someone. It is necessary to therefore, to probe accurately the statistical error and the causes thereof.

**Causes of Statistical Errors.** Following are the causes of statistical errors :

1. *Errors of Origin*. By errors of origin is meant those errors that originate in collecting data. They are born of the method of collecting data having some defects. These defects in collecting data persist due to many reasons which are give below :
   1. Selecting wrong samples.
   2. Prejudiced attitude of enumerators.
   3. Wrong information furnished by the informants.
   4. Collection of data through guess.
   5. Incompetence of enumerators.
   6. Selection of unsuitable unit.
2. *Errors of Inadequacy*. There will be sufficient difference between the actual and the estimated values if the investigation has been conducted by sample method and very few units have been selected as samples from the universe. In order to avoid the recurrence of such errors, enough units should be chosen as samples.
3. *Errors of Manipulation*. These errors occurs from careless analysis of data. These errors may be due to adopting wrong methods of approximation, classification, enumeration and measurement. Therefore correct methods in relation to the above factors should be used in order to avoid such errors.

## TYPES OF STATISTICAL ERRORS

Statistical errors are of two types :

1. Biased Error
2. Unbiased Error

**1. Biased Errors.** These errors originate from the biased attitudes of the informants and enumerators. If at any stage of investigation, the personnels connected with it adopt a biased conduct, there will be difference between the actual state of things and information collected about them. Such consequences are dangerously serious. These are of constant and accumulative nature. An optimistic person would collect such data as reveal less than actual or real shape of the problem whereas a man of pessimistic disposition would tend to collect data that present the problem in a bigger form. For example, if an estimate of income of Indian people is made not by unbiased persons but by two such men out of whom one represents capitalistic thinking and the other communistic thinking, then the man with capitalistic leaning will collect data about income of those people who have higher income whereas the man with communistic inclination will collect data about the income of people of low income group. Thus, owing to biased ideological inclinations, there will be difference between the collected data and the actual data. Biased errors are born of the following reasons :

1. Biased attitude adopted by the investigator.
2. Partiality committed by enumerators in collecting data.
3. Deliberate furnishing of wrong information by informants.
4. Selecting wrong samples.
5. Defective method of filling different items.

**2. Unbiased Errors.** These are different from the errors described above. These are due to the nature of the statistics. In statistics information are collected on the basis of estimation as well as by samples, as a result of which difference between the actual data and the estimated data is quite natural. Errors resulting from this reason only are called unbiased error. These errors are not damaging and are of compensatory nature because if one item has been estimated less, the other can be estimated more also. Therefore the total sum of such errors is quite negligible.

## METHODS OF MEASUREMENTS OF STATISTICAL ERRORS

Statistical errors can be measured in two ways :

1. Absolute Error.
2. Relative Error.

**1. Absolute Error.** Absolute error is the difference between the actual value and the estimated value. In other words, estimated value is deducted from the actual value, the remainder is called absolute error. This can be presented in a formula form as shown below :

Absolute Error = Actual value – Estimated value

**Example.** If a person's monthly income of Rs. 5000 has been estimated at Rs. 4800 per month, than, in this case, 5000 – 4800 = Rs. 200 is the absolute error.

**2. Relative Error.** Such errors are determined for comparing two or more than two information. That is why this is called relative error. Errors of this type are known by finding the proportion of the values of absolute errors with the collected values. They can be found out by the formula given below :

$$\text{Relative error} = \frac{\text{Absolute error}}{\text{Collected value}}$$

In the example given above the relative error will be as the following :

$$\text{Relative error} = \frac{5000 - 4800}{4800}$$

$$= \frac{200}{4800}$$

$$= .042$$

Relative errors can be shown in percentage form also using the following formula :

$$\text{Percentage error} = \frac{\text{Absolute error}}{\text{Collected value}} \times 100$$

$$= \frac{5000 - 4800}{4800} \times 100$$

$$= \frac{200}{4800} \times 100$$

$$= 4.2\%$$

**Estimation of Statistical Errors.** When data are collected about a problem it is more generally the case that actual data are not known. In this situation, statistical errors are only estimated. The following formulae are used to estimate the kinds of various statistical errors.

**1. Formula propounded by Prof. Boddington —**

A. *Biased Error (Estimated)*

i. Absolute Error = Average Absolute Error × Number of items

$$\text{ii. Relative Error} = \frac{\text{Average Error} \times \text{Number of items}}{\text{Total of Estimated Data}}$$

B. *Unbiased Error (Estimated)*

i. Absolute Error = Average Absolute Error × $\sqrt{\text{Number of items}}$

$$\text{ii. Relative Error} = \frac{\text{Average Absolute Error} \times \sqrt{\text{Number of items}}}{\text{Total of estimated data}}$$

**2. Formula propounded by Dr. Bowley —**

Unbiased Absolute Error (Estimated) :

$$= \frac{2}{3} \times \frac{\text{Average Absolute Error}}{\sqrt{\text{Number of items}}}$$

**Average Absolute Error.** The average of the maximum and the minimum of the probable difference at the time of approximating different units of the universe is called "Average Absolute Error". For instance, if the statistics of different items of the universe have been estimated on the basis of the place-value of ten following, "*approximation to the nearest whole number*" method, then, on approximation, the maximum difference will be 5 and the minimum will be zero, for 5 or more will be taken as 10 (Following Approximation to the nearest whole Number-method) and less than 5 will be left out or ignored.

$$\text{Its average absolute value will be} = \frac{5 - 0}{2} = 2.5$$

**Illustration 1.** Calculate the Estimated (i) Biased, and (ii) Unbiased Statistical Errors from the following information :

Number of items = 16

Total of Estimated Data = (i) 1800 (Approximated to the nearest whole number)

(ii) 1900 (Approximated by raising the figure to next whole number)

(iii) 1700 (Approximated by discarding some figures)

Place of Approximation = Two digits

**Solution**

Calculation of different Errors by the formulae given by Prof. Boddington.

**Biased Error**

$$\begin{aligned} \text{Absolute error} &= \text{Average Absolute Error} \times \text{Number of items} \\ &= 50 \times 16 \\ &= 800 \end{aligned}$$

$$\text{Relative Error} = \frac{\text{Average Absolute Error} \times \text{Numer of items}}{\text{Total of Estimated Data}}$$

$$= \frac{50 \times 16}{1900} = .42 \qquad \text{(in second case)}$$

$$= \frac{50 \times 16}{1700} \qquad \text{(in third case)}$$

$$= .47$$

**Unbiased Error**

$$\text{Absolute Error} = \text{Average Absolute Error} \times \sqrt{\text{Number of items}}$$

$$= 25 \times \sqrt{16}$$

$$= 25 \times 4$$

$$= 100$$

$$\text{Relative Error} = \frac{\text{Average Absolute Error} \times \sqrt{\text{Number of Items}}}{\text{Total of Estimated Data}}$$

$$= \frac{25 \times 4}{1800}$$

$$= \frac{100}{1800}$$

$$= .056$$

**Note.** Three situations have been given in the above illustration :

(i) Wherein the total of estimated data is 1800 which has been obtained from approximation to the nearest whole number. This is an unbiased method because here less than one half has been left out and one half or more than half has been assumed as one and has been added. Here the average absolute error will be $\frac{50 - 0}{2} = 25$ because approximation upto two digits has been made.

In case of (ii) and (iii), the approximation is biased for in the second the figure has been raised to the next whole number and in the third one the figure has been left out. In both of these the average absolute error will be $\frac{100 - 0}{2} = 50$

## QUESTIONS

1. What do you mean by editing of data? Why editing of data is essential?
2. Write a note on the editing of primary and secondary data for purposes of analysis and interpretation.
3. What do you mean by a reasonable standard of accuracy? Is it necessary to keep the perfect accuracy in statistics? Comment.
4. In what way does a statistical error differ from a mistake? What classes of errors are there and how may they be measured.
5. What is approximation of data? What are the different methods of approximation of data?
6. Describe the various methods of approximation. Which is the best method of approximation and why?
7. What is a statistical error? How does it differ from a mistake? How would you measure it?
8. (a) Discuss the main sources of errors in statistics and their effects.

   (b) State the various methods of approximation and their utility in statistics.
9. "Of the biased errors, the statistician should have none; but of the unbiased ones, the more the merrier, notwithstanding that they are also error." Elucidate.
10. What do you mean by biased error and unbiased error? What are the causes of these errors?
11. "Perfect accuracy is very seldom obtained in statistics." Explain this statement critically.
12. What standard of accuracy is needed in statistical investigation? State the various methods of approximation and their utility in statistics.
13. What are absolute and relative errors? How would you calculate these errors?
14. Discuss the main sources of errors in statistics. What classes of errors are known to you? How would you measure them?
15. What do you mean by estimation of statistical errors? How would you estimate the various errors?
16. What are statistical errors?

    [*B.Com.* (*Pass*), *Delhi*]

# 7

# Classification and Tabulation of Data

In order to render the collected data suitable to be used for investigation, they are classified on the basis of likeness of their nature and properties and the classified data are shown in the form of tables in order to present them precisely. Many a unit from the total units of the universe are homogeneous and they are classified into different groups on the basis of homogeneity and the total information of the universe are presented in an arranged and precise manner by placing different groups in table-forms. The process of classification and tabulation is of great importance for statistical operations because from a mere heap of collected information no results can be arrived at. For example, in an investigation pertaining to the population of a place, data in the beginning about male, female adult, child, educated, uneducated, employed and unemployed persons of each family will be collected through schedules and questionnaires. But in order to get result from these data it will be necessary that data about all the categories mentioned above of all the families are placed in different groups. It is only then that the number of men, women, major and minor persons of that place can be known. Like wise, educated, uneducated, employed and unemployed constituting the population can also be known. These various groups can be put in a table which gives a clear picture of the whole universe. Therefore, facts not classified and properly arranged don't serve any purpose. In this connection J.R. Hicks says, "Classified and arranged facts speak themselves, unarranged they are as dead as mutton."

**Meaning of Classification of Data.** Classification of data is grouping of the collected data in various classes on the basis of likeness or similarity of their property, nature and tendency. Some units are alike despite there being diversity among the units of the universe and to group or classify all the units on the basis of this likeness from the prevailing diversity into some classes is called classification. For example, a class consists of students of different mental calibres and yet in this diversity there must be some students of equal calibre also. There are 20 students in that class, let us suppose, out of which 4 are first class students, 10 second class and 6 third class. This example makes it clear that the universe consists of different standards (first, second and third class) of students and yet there are some similarities among some of them on the basis of which students have been divided into different groups of 4, 10 and 6 students. Some of the definitions propounded by scholars are given below :

1. "*Classification is the process of arranging data into sequences and groups according to their common characteristics of separating them into different but related parts.*"

   — *H. Secrist*

2. "*Classification is the grouping of facts into classes that are distinguished by some significant characteristics.*"

   — *Spur and Bonini*

3. "*Classification is the process of arranging things (either actually or notionally) into groups or classes according to their resemblances and affinities and give expression to the unity of attributes that may subsist amongst a diversity of individuals.*"

   — *L.R. Connor*

**Things Essential for Classification.** The following things must be taken care of in order to classify data into different groups and classes :

1. *Inclusion of Every Fact.* While classifying, it must be seen that the method adopted is such as includes all the facts in various groups. That method will be defective if it fails to include all the facts in classification. Sometimes in classification a class named 'miscellaneous facts' is also created wherein the remaining facts not classified under any group are put down. But it is better not to include such a class while classifying the data.
2. *Clarity.* The groups in which the facts have been divided must be very clear with a definite connotation.
3. *Homogeneity.* The facts should be classified into separate groups or classes according to homogeneity criteria *i.e.*, each group should have data of similar properties and nature.
4. *Sufficient Classes.* Classification should have sufficient number of groups. The entire information of the universe should not be divided into far many groups nor in so few a group that

the very aim of the classification itself is not achieved. The number of classes and groups should therefore be only sufficient.

5. *Stability*. A steady policy should be adhered to in regard to classification. If some facts bearing common characteristics have been included in a particular group, all the facts bearing that characteristics should be included in that very class.
6. *Flexibility*. The method of classification should be such as allows flexibility and can be changed according to the requirements of the problems of investigator at different times. With the change of time, the nature of units also undergo changes. Thus, there should be provision to accommodate changes in the method of classifications.

**Objects of Classification.** Data are divided into different groups due to the following reasons :

1. Classification is done in order to abridge vast data so that they become easily comprehensible.
2. Data are also classified with a view to comparing two or more than two sets of data among them.
3. The collected data being only a heap of disorganized stuff are necessary to be re-arranged and organized which is done through classification.
4. Classification is necessary to make the collected data easier.
5. Classification is done to know separately all the units of the universe based on homogeneity principle.

**Methods of Classification.** Following are the methods of classification of data from different points of view :

1. According to Attributes or Qualities :

A. Simple Classification.

B. Multiple Classification.

2. *According to Variables or Quantity :*

**1. According to Attributes.** In this method the entire information of the universe is divided into classes according to their attributes such as educated, uneducated, healthy-unhealthy etc. Such a classification applies to those facts which cannot be measured in terms of figures.

This classification is of two types :

(a) *Simple Classification*. Facts under this are classified according to the presence or absence of a particular quality *i.e.* the entire fact is divided into two parts such as dividing the population into urban and rural section. This method of classification is very simple.

(b) *Multiple Classification*. As indicated by its name, under multiple classification the entire universe is divided into many sections. This method is slightly tedious but these days generally this type of classification is in use. The following illustration may explain this classification.

**Example.** There are 500 workers in a factory out of which 300 are male and 200 are female; 280 males and 150 females are trained. From the trained male workers 250, from the untrained 15, from trained female workers 130 and that of untrained female 40 are adults. Their classification is shown below :

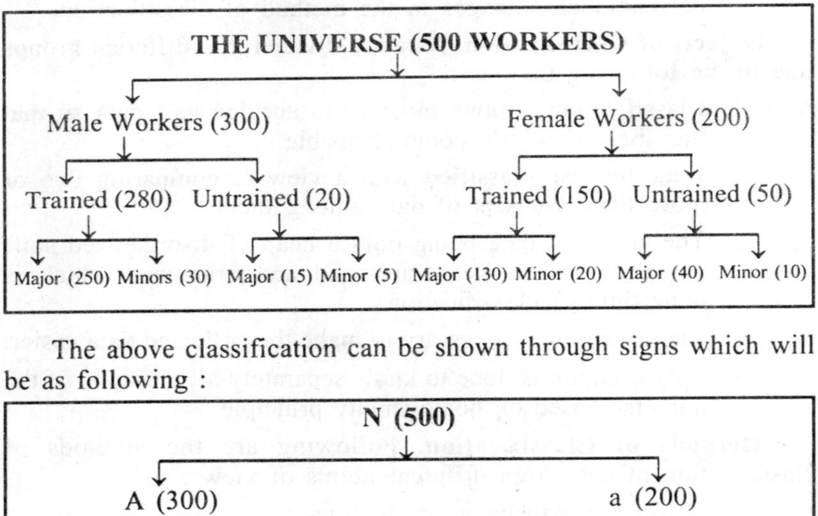


The above classification can be shown through signs which will be as following :

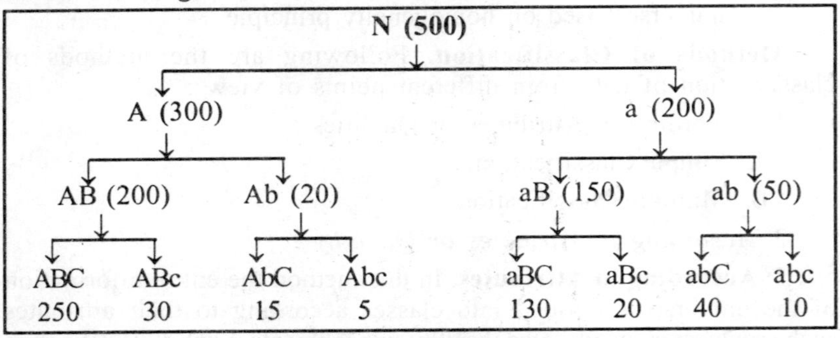


Different signs in the above illustration have been used to represent the following facts :

N = Total number of Workers.

A = Male Workers

a = Female Workers
B = Trained Labours
b = Untrained Labours
C = Adults
c = Minors

**2. Classification According to Variables or Quantity.** Facts measurable in terms of figures are classified numerically. Statistics classified according to size or time are called variables. For example, the measurement of income, expenditures, import, export is done in numerals. Under this kind of classification facts are divided according to the uniformly of numerical values. For instance, in order to divide statistics pertaining to income, the universe can be classified into various income-groups such as persons having income upto Rs. 100, persons with Rs. 100 to Rs. 200 income, persons with Rs. 200 to Rs. 500 income and persons with more than Rs. 500 income etc. This kind of classification is known as classification according to variables.

Statistical facts are classified into various statistical series.

**Statistical Series :** When facts or variables are listed sequentially and in order on the basis of similarity of numerical measurement, that is called 'Statistical series'. Put differently, Statistical series are in a classified and sequential list of equal or similar measures. Prof. Horace Secrist has said, "*A series as used statistically may be defined as things or attributes of things arranged according to some logical order.*" Statistical series are of different types according to their nature and composition. They are as following :

1. *According to Nature*
(A) Time Series
(B) Spatial Series
(C) Series according to Conditions
2. *According to Construction*
(A) Individual Series
(B) Discrete Series
(C) Continuous Series

**1. According to Nature**

(A) *Time Series.* In series of this type, the entire facts of the universe are put into different classes according to time, hence these series are called as 'time series'.

**Example.** The Following series is an example of time series :

| Years | Production (in Quintals) |
|---|---|
| 1994 | 130 |
| 1995 | 154 |
| 1996 | 162 |
| 1997 | 182 |
| 1998 | 170 |
| 1999 | 194 |
| 2000 | 200 |

(B) *Spatial Series.* In the series of this type, facts organized according to different places are put in a list in order, hence these are called spatial series.

Following is the example of such series :

**Example.** Persons Selected in A Competitive Examination

| States | No. of Persons |
|---|---|
| Uttar Pradesh | 737 |
| Bihar | 464 |
| West Bengal | 349 |
| Maharashtra | 395 |
| Mysore | 235 |
| Madras | 336 |
| Punjab | 203 |
| Rajasthan | 205 |

(C) *Series according to Conditions.* When data are shown in categories to conditions, it is called series according to conditions.

**Example.** Monthly expenditure of a family

| Items | Expenditure (in Rs.) |
|---|---|
| Food | 180 |
| Clothes | 50 |
| House Rent | 80 |
| Education | 25 |
| Miscellaneous | 35 |
| Total | 370 |

**2. According to Construction.** The statistical series prepared according to construction are also called 'frequency distribution'. In such series, frequency of variables of various types are shown. According to construction, series are of the following three types :

(A) *Individual Series*. In the series of this type, all the units of the universe are measured separately. For example, if a universe consists of 10 persons and statistics of income of all of them are shown separately, this series will be called individual series. In this type of series, every measurement has one item or every variable has one frequency. Series of this type can be of all the three types *i.e.*, according to time or conditions or place.

Following is the example of this types of series :

**Example.** Following is the list of marks obtained by 10 students in an examination :

| Roll No. | 1 | 2 | 3 | 4 | 5 | 6 | 7 | 8 | 9 | 10 |
|---|---|---|---|---|---|---|---|---|---|---|
| Marks | 50 | 48 | 36 | 62 | 49 | 65 | 38 | 30 | 70 | 25 |

In the above example, the marks obtained by each roll number are written against them. Thus, this is an individual series. It is better to arrange individual series for statistical operations and it is necessary to put them in sequence for finding certain average values related to them. Series can be shown according to order in the following two ways :

(i) *In Ascending Order*. In this type of order, the smallest value are put first then the next higher value and so on in this order. The figures of above example are shown in ascending order as follows :

Marks obtained by 10 students in ascending order :

Marks : 25, 30, 36, 38, 48, 49, 50, 62, 65, 70

(ii) *In Descending Order*. Values in this type are shown just in the opposite order of the above type, that is, the highest value will be written first, then the value smaller than the first and so on in this order. The above example has been shown below in descending order :

Marks obtained by 10 students in ascending order :

Marks : 70, 65, 62, 52, 49, 40, 38, 36, 30, 25

(B) *Discrete Series*. Under discrete series, the frequency of each measurement is written *i.e.*, the measurement of each item is not written separately but the frequency related to each measure is shown against that measurement. The number of items is called frequency. Measurements in this series are in discontinuity. That is why this is known as discrete series.

**Example.** Marks obtained by some students are shown in the following order :

| Marks (X) | Number of Students (F) |
|---|---|
| 5 | 6 |
| 10 | 3 |
| 15 | 4 |
| 20 | 10 |
| 25 | 15 |
| 30 | 12 |
| 35 | 8 |
| 40 | 6 |

The above example indicates that there are 6 students obtaining 5 marks, 3 students obtaining 10 marks and so no. Discrete series can be made on the basis of individual series also. If the number of items is in plenty then the categories of data should be made like this.

**Method of constructing discrete series.** Various measures of the universe are written down in a sequence in order to form discrete series. Thereafter, against these measurements are written the number of items related to them. The following illustration may explain this process :

**Illustration 1.** You are given the figures of daily income of 50 workers :

Income in Rs. : 5, 3, 2, 4, 1, 1, 6, 2, 2, 5, 4, 5, 5, 3, 3, 6, 7, 1, 8, 7, 8, 10, 5, 5, 4, 4, 3, 3, 3, 1, 5, 2, 3, 8, 9, 7, 7, 2, 4, 6, 5, 1, 3, 4, 4, 5, 7, 2, 1, 4.

Construct a discrete series from the above data.

**Solution**

*Construction of discrete series* (In ascending order)

| Tally Sheet | | |
|---|---|---|
| Income (Rs.) | Tally income | Frequency |
| 1 | ~~IIII~~ I | 6 |
| 2 | ~~IIII~~ I | 6 |
| 3 | ~~IIII~~ III | 8 |
| 4 | ~~IIII~~ III | 8 |
| 5 | ~~IIII~~ IIII | 9 |
| 6 | III | 3 |
| 7 | ~~IIII~~ | 5 |
| 8 | II | 2 |
| 9 | II | 2 |
| 10 | I | 1 |
| | Total | 50 |

This table may be shown in descending order as follows :

| Income (Rs.) | Tally income | Frequency |
|---|---|---|
| 10 | I | 1 |
| 9 | II | 2 |
| 8 | II | 2 |
| 7 | ~~IIII~~ | 5 |
| 6 | III | 3 |
| 5 | ~~IIII~~ IIII | 9 |
| 4 | ~~IIII~~ III | 8 |
| 3 | ~~IIII~~ III | 8 |
| 2 | ~~IIII~~ I | 6 |
| 1 | ~~IIII~~ I | 6 |
| | Total | 50 |

**Illustration 2.** Prof. Marshall has defined Economics as follows :

*"Economics is a study of man's actions in the ordinary business of life. It enquires as to how he gets his income and how he spends it. Thus it is on the one hand a study of wealth and on the other and more important side a part of the study of man."*

Construct a series showing the frequencies with which words of different numbers of letters occur in the above definition treating as the variable the number of the letters in each word. Ignore marks of punctuation.

**Solution**

**Discrete Series**

| No. of Letters | Tally Sheet | No. of words (Frequency) |
|---|---|---|
| 1 | III | 3 |
| 2 | IIII IIII IIII II | 17 |
| 3 | IIII IIII II | 12 |
| 4 | IIII III | 8 |
| 5 | IIII | 4 |
| 6 | III | 3 |
| 7 | I | 1 |
| 8 | III | 3 |
| 9 | II | 2 |
| | Total | 53 |

(C) *Continuous Series.* Under this type of series, variables or measurements are written in classes or groups and measurements are continuous, there being no gap between one group and the other. That is the reason why the series of this type are called continuous series.

**Example**

| Marks | Number of Students |
|---|---|
| 0-10 | 12 |
| 10-20 | 16 |
| 20-30 | 25 |
| 30-40 | 35 |
| 40-50 | 20 |
| 50-60 | 8 |

The following are significant facts about continuous series :

i. *Class Intervals or Groups.* When classes are used to measure all the units of the universe, they are called class intervals or groups. For example '0-10' and '10-20' are classes.

ii. *Class Limits.* Two numerals of a class are called limits or boundaries. A fact is included in a class if it falls within these limits. The higher value of a class is called upper limit and the lower value is lower limit. For example, in the class 10-20, 20 is the upper limit and 10 is the lower limit.

iii. *Magnitude of Class Limits.* The interval between the upper limit and the lower limit is called the magnitude of class-intervals. In the class of 10-20, 20-10=10 is the magnitude of class interval.

iv. *Frequency.* The number of items of the value of any class in the universe is called frequency. In the above example 12, 16, 25 etc. are the frequencies of groups 0-10, 10-20, 20-30 respectively.

v. *Mid-value.* The average value of the upper and the lower limits of class is called mid-value or mid-point. In the class of '10-20' $\left(\frac{10 + 20}{2} = 15\right)$ is the mid-value.

**Various Types of Ways of presenting of Continuous Series**

Continuous series are of various types can be presented variously. Sometimes these series having been presented in a special manner and are difficult to make out as to what kind of series are they. Therefore one should try to understand well the following types :

**1. Continuous Series written in Ascending and Descending Order.** In series written in ascending order, classes are written starting from lower values to higher values, in descending order on the contrary the class of higher value is written down first followed by smaller classes in a sequence and at the end remains the lowest class. Series of this type are written in the following manner :

| (A) *Continuous Series in Ascending Order* | | (B) *Continuous Series in Descending Order* | |
|---|---|---|---|
| Class Intervals | Frequencies | Class Intervals | Frequencies |
| 0-10 | 16 | 50-60 | 13 |
| 10-20 | 12 | 40-50 | 15 |
| 20-30 | 18 | 30-40 | 20 |
| 30-40 | 20 | 20-30 | 18 |
| 40-50 | 15 | 10-20 | 12 |
| 50-60 | 13 | 0-10 | 16 |

**2. Exclusive and Inclusive Series.** If the classes are so formed that the upper limit of the first class and the lower limit of the second class is same, it is called as exclusive series. In Series of this type the items of upper limit values will not be included in that class, on the other hand they will be included in the next class. For example, if the data pertaining to income have been divided in to 50-100, 100-150 etc. class, a person with Rs. 100 income will be included in the frequency of second class and the man with Rs. 150 income will be included in the frequency of third class. In other words, the upper limit of a class is not included in the same class but is included in the immediate next higher class. Therefore this is called exclusive series.

In the inclusive series, the items of the upper limit values are included in the same class. Hence, it is called inclusive series. In the series of this type, the values of the upper limit of first class and that of the lower limit of the next class are different.

Both the above mentioned series are written in the following manner :

**Example**

| (A) *Exclusive Series* | | (B) *Inclusive Series* | |
|---|---|---|---|
| Monthly Income (Rs.) | No. of Persons | Monthly Income (Rs.) | No. of Persons |
| 50-100 | 6 | 50-99 | 62 |
| 100-150 | 8 | 100-149 | 81 |
| 150-200 | 12 | 150-199 | 120 |
| 200-250 | 9 | 200-249 | 93 |
| 250-300 | 7 | 250-299 | 17 |

Inclusive series are sometimes converted for some statistical operations into exclusive series. For such conversions, the average difference of the upper limit of the first class and the lower limit of the second class is added to the upper limit and deducted from the lower limit of the classes. In the above example, the average difference between the upper limit and the lower limit of the two classes is .5 which if added to the upper limit and deducted from the lower limit of these classes and it will yield the following exclusive series :

| (C) Variables | Frequency |
|---|---|
| 49.5-99.5 | 62 |
| 99.5-149.5 | 81 |
| 149.5-199.5 | 120 |
| 199.5-249.5 | 93 |
| 249.5-299.5 | 17 |

Exclusive series may be written in the following manner also :

| (D) Class | Frequencies |
|---|---|
| 50-99.99 | 6 |
| 100.149.99 | 8 |
| 150-199.99 | 12 |
| 200-249.99 | 9 |
| 250-299.99 | 7 |

The above series can be converted in the following way :

| | |
|---|---|
| (E) 50-100 | 6 |
| 100-150 | 8 |
| 150-200 | 12 |
| 200-250 | 9 |
| 250-300 | 7 |

Like wise, exclusive series can be written in the following manners also :

| Groups | Frequencies |
|---|---|
| (F) Exceeding 50 and not exceeding 100 | 6 |
| " 100 " " 150 | 8 |
| " 150 " " 200 | 12 |
| " 200 " " 250 | 9 |
| " 250 " " 300 | 7 |

OR

| Groups | Frequencies |
|---|---|
| (G) 50 and below 100 | 6 |
| 100 " " 150 | 8 |
| 150 " " 200 | 12 |
| 200 " " 250 | 9 |
| 250 " " 300 | 7 |

**Example**

(F) and (G) series are also exclusive series and generally they can also be written in the same way as the series in the example (E) have been written.

**3. Openend Frequency Distribution.** Sometimes the value of the lower limit of the first class and the upper limit of the last class is not given and in their places either blank (?-10) (50-?) is left or in place of lower limit words such as below or under and in place of upper limit words like more or above are written. Such series are called open-end series. But for statistical operations it is necessary to write numerals at such ends. In order to do so, the magnitude of the open-end class should to found out by having a look at the construction of the series, and this magnitude, in order to find out the value of lower limit, should be deducted from the upper limit of the class; and to find out the upper limit, this should be added to the lower limit of the class. This process may be better explained by the following example :

**Example**

| **Open-End Distributions** | | | |
|---|---|---|---|
| (a) Class-Intervals | f | (b) Classes | f |
| —10 | 18 | Below 10 | 15 |
| 10-20 | 15 | 10-20 | 18 |
| 20-30 | 12 | 20-50 | 12 |
| 30-40 | 16 | 50-100 | 6 |
| 40— | 8 | 100 & above | 8 |

In part (a) of the above example, the value of the lower limit of the first class will be 10-10 = 0 (zero) and the value of the upper limit of the last class will be 40 + 10 = 50. As in the proximate class intervals 10-20 and 30-40, the magnitude is 10, therefore the above values will emerge when 10 is deducted from the upper limit of the first class and is added to the lower limit of the last class. In part

(b) of the above example the lower limit of the first class of the given series will be 10-10 = 0 (zero) and the value of the upper limit of the last class will be 100 + 50 = 150 because the proximate classes are 10-20 and 50-100 respectively and the magnitude of these classes will be adjusted in the known limits of the classes in order to know the values of the unknown limits.

**Example.** The open-end series may be written in the following manner also :

| (a) Classes | f | (b) Classes | f | (c) Classes | f |
|---|---|---|---|---|---|
| 0-10 | 16 | 0 - | 6 | - 10 | 6 |
| - | 9 | 10 - | 9 | - 20 | 9 |
| - | 15 | 20 - | 15 | - 30 | 15 |
| - | 8 | 30 - | 8 | - 40 | 8 |
| - | 2 | 40 - | 2 | - 50 | 2 |
| 50-60 | 3 | 50 - | 3 | - 60 | 3 |

In the series given in part (a), (b) and (c), the values of many limits of class-intervals are not known. All these series will be converted for statistical operations in the following way :

| C.I. | f |
|---|---|
| 0-10 | 6 |
| 10-20 | 9 |
| 20-30 | 15 |
| 30-40 | 8 |
| 40-50 | 2 |
| 50-60 | 3 |

**4. Cumulative Frequency Distribution.** Sometimes series are given in the form of cumulative frequencies. Series of this type are converted into ordinary continuous series for the purpose of analysis of the problem.

Following are the examples of cumulative frequency series :

**Example**

| Cumulative Frequency Distribution (More than order) | | Conversion in Ordinary Series | |
|---|---|---|---|
| (a) No. of Persons | | (b) Income | No. of persons |
| Income more than 10 | 100 | 10-20 | 10 |
| " " " 20 | 90 | 20-30 | 25 |
| " " " 30 | 65 | 30-40 | 7 |
| " " " 40 | 58 | 40-50 | 28 |
| " " " 50 | 30 | 50-60 | 30 |

| Cumulative Frequency Distribution (Less than order) | | | | Conversion in ordinary Series | |
|---|---|---|---|---|---|
| (c) Marks Below | | | No. of Students | (d) Marks | No. of Students |
| " | " | 5 | 12 | 0-5 | 12 |
| " | " | 10 | 20 | 5-10 | 8 |
| " | " | 15 | 30 | 10-15 | 10 |
| " | " | 20 | 44 | 15-20 | 14 |
| " | " | 25 | 60 | 20-25 | 16 |
| " | " | 30 | 75 | 25-30 | 15 |
| " | " | 35 | 80 | 30-35 | 5 |

In the above Example, parts (a), (c) contain the examples of cumulative frequency distribution which will be converted according to (b) and (d) into ordinary frequency distribution for various statistica! purposes.

**5. Frequency Distribution containing Mid-values.** Some times the series do not contain class-intervals but only mid-values and frequencies are given. In such a situation, it should be remembered that the series are basically continuous. Therefore any operation is to be performed on the basis of the use of the limits of class-intervals then the given series, should, first of all, be converted into ordinary continuous series. For such a conversion two mid-values are added in order and their average is taken which is the upper limit of the first class and the lower limit of the second class.

**Example**

| (a) Mid-value | Frequency | (b) Class-interval | Frequency |
|---|---|---|---|
| 15 | 10 | 10-20 | 10 |
| 25 | 25 | 20-30 | 25 |
| 35 | 7 | 30-40 | 7 |
| 45 | 12 | 40-50 | 12 |
| 55 | 30 | 55-60 | 30 |

In part (a) of the above example has been given the mid-values. That can be converted into ordinary series as in part (b) of the example. This conversion has been done on the basis of the average of two limits which is $\frac{15+25}{2}$, $\frac{25+35}{2}$, $\frac{35+45}{2}$, and $\frac{45+55}{2}$, that is, 20, 30, 40 and 50 respectively 20 will be the upper limit of the first class and the lower limit of the second class, 30 the upper limit of the second class and the lower limit of the third class, 40 the upper limit of the third and the lower limit of the fourth class and 50 will be the upper limit of the fourth and the lower limit of the fifth class. The value of the lower and the upper limits of the first and the last class, found out according to open-end series method which will come out to be 10 and 60.

## METHOD OF CONSTRUCTION OF CONTINUOUS SERIES

The greatest difficulty that is faced by the person while constructing continuous series is how many class-intervals should be formed for the whole universe and what should be the magnitude of class intervals? There is no any definite solution to this problem. This depends upon the will of the investigator and the number of the units of the universe. In this connection the important thing to remember is that the number of class-intervals should be only sufficient, neither too many nor too few. In connection with the number of class-intervals Prof. H.A. Sturges has propounded a formula according to which the number of class interval suffices for all the types of universe howsoever big or small. This formula is as follows :

$$n = 1 + 3.322 \text{ Log N}$$

$n$ = Number of class intervals

$N$ = Total Number of Observations.

The above formula also can be used to find out the number of class-intervals, but the person constructing series can effect change as per requirement in the number of class-intervals derived by that formula mentioned above.

The magnitude of class intervals may be calculated by the following method :

$$\text{Class Magnitude} = \frac{\text{Largest Item} - \text{Lowest Item}}{\text{Number of Class Intervals}}$$

The magnitude of class-intervals can be known by approximating the number derived from the above method.

**Illustration 3.** Construct the continuous series within class intervals 0-10, 10-20 and so on from the following data :

18, 19, 8, 17, 6, 6, 5, 4, 3, 5, 5, 8, 9, 13, 25, 16, 22, 28, 30, 32, 31, 27, 26, 23, 35, 38, 40, 42, 41, 39, 37, 15, 27, 26, 29, 30, 32, 35, 44, 48, 49, 10, 15, 20, 40, 41, 46, 49, 43, 23.

**Solution**

**Construction of Continuous Series**

| Variables | Tally Sheet | Frequency |
|---|---|---|
| 0-10 | ꟷ̸ꟷ̸ꟷ̸ꟷ̸ ꟷ̸ꟷ̸ꟷ̸ꟷ̸ | 10 |
| 10-20 | ꟷ̸ꟷ̸ꟷ̸ꟷ̸ III | 8 |
| 20-30 | ꟷ̸ꟷ̸ꟷ̸ꟷ̸ ꟷ̸ꟷ̸ꟷ̸ꟷ̸ I | 11 |
| 30-40 | ꟷ̸ꟷ̸ꟷ̸ꟷ̸ ꟷ̸ꟷ̸ꟷ̸ꟷ̸ | 10 |
| 40-50 | ꟷ̸ꟷ̸ꟷ̸ꟷ̸ ꟷ̸ꟷ̸ꟷ̸ꟷ̸ I | 11 |
| | Total | 50 |

**Illustration 4.** Present the following data of the percentage marks of 60 students in the form of a frequency table with 10 classes of equal width. One class being 40-49.

| | | | | | | | | | |
|---|---|---|---|---|---|---|---|---|---|
| 41 | 17 | 83 | 63 | 54 | 92 | 60 | 58 | 70 | 06 |
| 67 | 82 | 33 | 44 | 57 | 49 | 34 | 73 | 54 | 63 |
| 36 | 52 | 32 | 75 | 60 | 33 | 09 | 78 | 28 | 30 |
| 42 | 93 | 43 | 80 | 03 | 32 | 57 | 67 | 24 | 64 |
| 63 | 11 | 35 | 82 | 10 | 23 | 0 | 41 | 60 | 32 |
| 72 | 53 | 92 | 88 | 62 | 55 | 60 | 33 | 40 | 37 |

**Solution**

**Construction of Continuous Series**

| Class Intervals | Tally Bars | Frequency |
|---|---|---|
| 0-9 | IIII | 4 |
| 10-19 | III | 3 |
| 20-29 | III | 3 |
| 30-39 | ꟷ̸ꟷ̸ꟷ̸ꟷ̸ ꟷ̸ꟷ̸ꟷ̸ꟷ̸ I | 11 |
| 40-49 | ꟷ̸ꟷ̸ꟷ̸ꟷ̸ II | 7 |
| 50-59 | ꟷ̸ꟷ̸ꟷ̸ꟷ̸ III | 8 |
| 60-69 | ꟷ̸ꟷ̸ꟷ̸ꟷ̸ ꟷ̸ꟷ̸ꟷ̸ꟷ̸ I | 11 |
| 70-79 | ꟷ̸ꟷ̸ꟷ̸ꟷ̸ | 5 |
| 80-89 | ꟷ̸ꟷ̸ꟷ̸ꟷ̸ | 5 |
| 90-99 | III | 3 |
| | Total | 60 |

**Illustration 5.** You are given the records of ages of some husbands and their wives as follows :

| S. No. | Age of husbands (Years) | Age of wives (Years) | S. No. | Age of husbands (Years) | Age of wives (Years) |
|---|---|---|---|---|---|
| 1 | 25 | 18 | 21 | 19 | 16 |
| 2 | 20 | 19 | 22 | 20 | 21 |
| 3 | 55 | 40 | 23 | 30 | 25 |
| 4 | 32 | 28 | 24 | 35 | 34 |
| 5 | 35 | 38 | 25 | 40 | 25 |
| 6 | 19 | 14 | 26 | 42 | 40 |
| 7 | 18 | 16 | 27 | 50 | 47 |
| 8 | 25 | 24 | 28 | 38 | 28 |
| 9 | 26 | 27 | 29 | 40 | 26 |
| 10 | 40 | 37 | 30 | 26 | 23 |
| 11 | 42 | 35 | 31 | 20 | 16 |
| 12 | 50 | 25 | 32 | 25 | 18 |
| 13 | 60 | 55 | 33 | 30 | 18 |
| 14 | 62 | 58 | 34 | 32 | 27 |
| 15 | 38 | 35 | 35 | 28 | 25 |
| 16 | 32 | 30 | 36 | 26 | 28 |
| 17 | 28 | 20 | 37 | 30 | 18 |
| 18 | 30 | 22 | 38 | 32 | 26 |
| 19 | 30 | 28 | 39 | 35 | 28 |
| 20 | 35 | 25 | 40 | 36 | 35 |

Construct two way frequency table taking class intervals 0-20, 20-40 and so on for the age of husbands and 0-15, 15-30 and so on for the age of wives.

**Solution**

| Age of Husbands (years) | Age of Wives (years) | | | | Total |
|---|---|---|---|---|---|
| | 0-15 | 15-30 | 30-45 | 45-60 | |
| 0-20 | I (1) | II (2) | | | 3 |
| 20-40 | | 𝍸 𝍸 𝍸 𝍸 II (22) | 𝍸 (5) | | 27 |
| 40-60 | | III (3) | IIII (4) | I (1) | 8 |
| 60-80 | | | | II (2) | 2 |
| Total | 1 | 27 | 9 | 3 | 40 |

**Illustration 6.** Prepare a frequency distribution from the following figures relating to bonus paid to factory workers :

**Bonus Paid to Workers (in Rupees)**

| | | | | | | | | | |
|---|---|---|---|---|---|---|---|---|---|
| 86 | 62 | 58 | 73 | 101 | 90 | 84 | 90 | 86 | 61 |
| 84 | 63 | 56 | 72 | 102 | 56 | 83 | 92 | 87 | 60 |
| 83 | 69 | 57 | 71 | 103 | 57 | 87 | 93 | 88 | 59 |
| 76 | 70 | 54 | 70 | 104 | 58 | 88 | 94 | 89 | 57 |
| 74 | 86 | 55 | 60 | 105 | 59 | 89 | 84 | 90 | 74 |
| 67 | 84 | 82 | 70 | 60 | 60 | 90 | 81 | 91 | 76 |
| 60 | 83 | 78 | 80 | 65 | 61 | 96 | 82 | 93 | 102 |
| 69 | 91 | 76 | 90 | 70 | 63 | 94 | 83 | 94 | 101 |
| 70 | 94 | 77 | 100 | 75 | 69 | 93 | 84 | 95 | 96 |
| 72 | 100 | 74 | 101 | 80 | 67 | 92 | 85 | 96 | 92 |

*Note* : Take a class-interval of 5.

[*B. Com.* (*Pass*) *Delhi*]

**Solution**

| Classes | Tally Bars | Frequency |
|---|---|---|
| 51-55 | II | 2 |
| 56-60 | 𝍸 𝍸 IIII | 14 |
| 61-65 | 𝍸 I | 6 |
| 66-70 | 𝍸 𝍸 | 10 |
| 71-75 | 𝍸 III | 8 |
| 76-80 | 𝍸 II | 7 |
| 81-85 | 𝍸 𝍸 III | 13 |
| 86-90 | 𝍸 𝍸 IIII | 14 |
| 91-95 | 𝍸 𝍸 III | 13 |
| 96-100 | 𝍸 | 5 |
| 101-105 | 𝍸 III | 8 |
| | Total | 100 |

**Illustration 7.** Form a frequency distribution from the following data by Inclusive Method taking 4 as the magnitude of class-intervals :

10, 17, 15, 22, 11, 16, 19, 24, 29, 18
25, 26, 32, 14, 17, 20, 23, 27, 30, 12
15, 18, 24, 36, 18, 15, 21, 28, 33, 38
34, 13, 10, 16, 20, 22, 29, 19, 23, 31

[*B. Com.* (*Pass*) *Delhi*]

**Solution**

| Class Intervals | Tally Table | Frequency |
|---|---|---|
| 10-13 | ~~IIII~~ | 5 |
| 14-17 | ~~IIII~~ III | 8 |
| 18-21 | ~~IIII~~ III | 8 |
| 22-25 | ~~IIII~~ II | 7 |
| 26-29 | ~~IIII~~ | 5 |
| 30-33 | IIII | 4 |
| 34-37 | II | 2 |
| 38-41 | I | 1 |
| | Total | 40 |

**Illustration 8.** Prepare a statistical table from the following data taking the class width as 7 by inclusive method :

| | | | | | | | | | | |
|---|---|---|---|---|---|---|---|---|---|---|
| 24 | 26 | 28 | 32 | 37 | 5 | 1 | 7 | 9 | 11 | 15 |
| 13 | 14 | 18 | 29 | 31 | 32 | 6 | 4 | 2 | 9 | 18 |
| 27 | 36 | 3 | 9 | 15 | 21 | 27 | 33 | 4 | 8 | 12 |
| 16 | 20 | 5 | 10 | 3 | 8 | 1 | 6 | 4 | 9 | 2 |
| 7 | 12 | 18 | 27 | 23 | 21 | 29 | 22 | 15 | 17 | 28 |

[*B. Com.* (*Pass*), *Delhi*]

**Solution**

| Class Intervals | Tally Bars | Frequency |
|---|---|---|
| 1-7 | ~~IIII~~ ~~IIII~~ ~~IIII~~ | 15 |
| 8-14 | ~~IIII~~ ~~IIII~~ II | 12 |
| 15-21 | ~~IIII~~ ~~IIII~~ I | 11 |
| 22-28 | ~~IIII~~ IIII | 9 |
| 29-35 | ~~IIII~~ I | 6 |
| 36-42 | II | 2 |
| | Total | 55 |

**Illustration 9.** From the following data construct a bivariate frequency distribution :

| | | | | | | | | |
|---|---|---|---|---|---|---|---|---|
| Age of Husbands (in years) : | 28 | 26 | 27 | 25 | 28 | 28 | 27 | 27 |
| Age of wives (in years) : | 22 | 21 | 21 | 20 | 22 | 21 | 21 | 20 |
| Age of Husbands (in years) : | 26 | 27 | 27 | 26 | 25 | 26 | 27 | |
| Age of Wives (in years) : | 20 | 19 | 21 | 19 | 19 | 20 | 20 | |

[*B. Com. (Pass), Delhi*]

**Solution**

| Age of Husbands (in years) | Age of Wives (in years) | | | | Total |
|---|---|---|---|---|---|
| | 19 | 20 | 21 | 22 | |
| 25 | I (1) | I (1) | — | — | 2 |
| 26 | I (1) | II (2) | I (1) | — | 4 |
| 27 | I (1) | II (2) | III (3) | — | 6 |
| 28 | — | — | I (1) | II (2) | 3 |
| Total | 3 | 5 | 5 | 2 | 15 |

**Illustration 10.** Prepare a bivariate frequency distribution for the following data :

| | | | | | | | | | | |
|---|---|---|---|---|---|---|---|---|---|---|
| Marks in Law | 10 | 11 | 10 | 11 | 11 | 14 | 12 | 12 | 12 | 13 |
| Marks in Statistics | 20 | 21 | 22 | 21 | 23 | 23 | 22 | 21 | 20 | 24 |
| Marks in Law | 13 | 10 | 13 | 12 | 11 | 12 | 10 | 14 | 14 | 10 |
| Marks in Statistics | 24 | 23 | 24 | 23 | 22 | 23 | 22 | 22 | 24 | 23 |

[*B. Com. (Pass), Delhi*]

**Solution**

| Bivariate Frequency Distribution | | | | | | |
|---|---|---|---|---|---|---|
| Marks in Statistics | Marks in Law | | | | | Total |
| | 10 | 11 | 12 | 13 | 14 | |
| 20 | I (1) | — | I (1) | — | — | 2 |
| 21 | — | II (2) | I (1) | — | | 3 |
| 22 | II (2) | I (1) | I (1) | — | I (1) | 5 |
| 23 | II (2) | I (1) | II (2) | — | I (1) | 6 |
| 24 | — | | | III (3) | I (1) | 4 |
| Total | 5 | 4 | 5 | 3 | 3 | 20 |

## TABULATION

Arranging classified data in columns and rows is called tabulation. In statistics, tabulation is of great significance. By tabulation the classified data can be shown precisely at one place. The knowledge of the whole universe is imparted by table in a very brief and quick manner.

Some scholars have given the following definitions of tabulation :

1. "*Tables are means of recording in permanent form the analysis that is made through classification and of placing in juxtaposition things that are similar and should be compared.*"

   *—H. Secrist*

2. "*Tabulation in its broadest sense is an orderly arrangement of data in columns and rows.*"

   *— Blair*

3. "*Tabulation involves the orderly and systematic presentation of numerical data in a form designed to elucidate the problem under consideration.*"

   *— L.R. Conner*

It becomes clear from the above definitions that for the success of a work it is necessary to present that in an orderly and well organized manner. Disorganized data have no meaning and on the basis of unarranged data the knowledge and comparison of homogeneous items is difficult. Tabulations fulfill and these requirements.

**Objects of Tabulation**

Following are the aims of tabulation :

1. Arranging data on the basis of homogeneity into rows and columns so that homogeneous items can be known apparently.
2. Tabulation is necessary to compare various items of the universe among themselves.
3. To present information in an arranged order and precise form is the function of tabulation.
4. Data can be understood by having a glance over the table.

**Important Factors regarding Tabulation.** Showing data in columns and rows is scientific and very technical. They are shown in tables in order to give them a definite meaning alongwith the fact that the entire data are presented in a precise and well-arranged manner. The following facts are important about tabulation :

1. **Heading of Tables.** Heading should be written above every table. They should be shown in the table in such a way that they give a correct meaning and knowledge about the data included in the tables. Their size must also be taken care of. The heading preferably should be short but not shortened to the extent that there is no meaning emerging out of it or gives wrong meaning. At the same time, they should not be so long as to give an idea of its being a summary and not a heading.
2. **Proper utilization of columns and rows.** Columns and rows should be intelligently and properly used. They should not exceed the required number nor fall too short of that. Every column and row on top of it have its sub-heading written. The size also of column and row must conform to the requirement. The lines drawn for each column and row should be thick or thin according to the seriousness of the subject.
3. **Homogeneity.** Homogeneous items must be sorted out and put in separate columns and rows.

4. **Note.** A note at the foot of the table may be given if the information contained in the rows and columns require further elucidation.
5. **Source.** Mention must also be made of the sources and means from where data used in the tables have been collected or taken at the foot of the table.
6. **Size.** The size of the table must be appropriate to the subject of investigation.
7. **Neatness.** While making tables, there should be no overwriting and mutilation of words and numerals. That is, one must be careful to see that any kind of impurity and untidiness does not enter in the tables.
8. **Approximation.** It is better to include the data in tables only after approximating them.
9. **Brevity.** If the figures in the table consist of many digits having too many zeroes to their right then in order to remove or reduce them, it should be noted on top of the tables that the figures given in the tables represent thousands, lacs or crores, whatever the case.
10. **Unit.** The unit used to measure the problem should also be mentioned in the table. For example, in which of these — rupees, pounds or dollars the income has been measured.

It is always useful to prepare any table by keeping in mind the above noted facts.

## KINDS OF TABLES

According to their construction, the tables may be divided into the following two parts :

1. Simple Table.

2. Complex Table.

(A) Double Table

(B) Triple Table

(C) Multiple Table.

**1. Simple Table.** From the point of view of construction, this is the most easy kind. Hence, it is called simple or easy table. In this kind of table only one quality of fact is shown. Following is an example of this type of table.

TABLE NO. 1

*Table showing population of a town in various years*

| Year | Population of Lakhs |
|---|---|
| 1991 | 8 |
| 1992 | 10 |
| 1993 | 11 |
| 1994 | 14 |
| 1995 | 15 |
| 1996 | 18 |
| 1997 | 20 |
| 1998 | 21 |
| 1999 | 24 |

**2. Complex Table.** This is a slightly difficult kind of table from the point of view of construction. Many facts related to investigation are shown in this type of table.

Following are the types of this kind of tables :

(A) *Double Table.* In this type, two facts related to a problem are shown, hence it is called double table. Following is an example of this type :

TABLE NO. 2

*Table showing population of a town according to sex*

| | Population (in Lakhs) | | |
|---|---|---|---|
| Year | Male | Female | Total |
| 1991 | 4.3 | 3.7 | 8 |
| 1992 | 5.2 | 4.8 | 10 |
| 1993 | 5.7 | 5.3 | 11 |
| 1994 | 7.8 | 6.2 | 14 |
| 1995 | 7.9 | 7.1 | 15 |
| 1996 | 9.2 | 8.8 | 18 |
| 1997 | 11.0 | 9.0 | 20 |
| 1998 | 11.3 | 9.7 | 21 |
| 1999 | 13.0 | 11.0 | 24 |

(B) *Triple Table.* In this type of tables, three facts related to the problem arr shown, hence it is called triple table. Its example is given below :

TABLE NO. 3

*Table showing population of a town according to sex and age*

| Sex / Age / Years | Population (in lakhs) | | | | | | | | | | |
|---|---|---|---|---|---|---|---|---|---|---|---|
| | Male | | | | | Female | | | | | Grand Total |
| | Below 15 | 15-30 | 30-45 | 45 & above | Total | Below 15 | 15-30 | 30-45 | 45 & above | Total | |
| 1991 | 0.8 | 1.2 | 1.7 | 0.6 | 4.3 | 0.6 | 1.0 | 1.4 | 0.7 | 3.7 | 8 |
| 1992 | 0.9 | 1.3 | 1.9 | 1.1 | 5.2 | 0.7 | 1.1 | 1.6 | 1.4 | 4.8 | 10 |
| 1993 | 1.1 | 1.5 | 2.2 | 0.9 | 5.7 | 0.9 | 1.2 | 2.0 | 1.2 | 5.3 | 11 |
| 1994 | 1.4 | 1.6 | 2.4 | 2.4 | 7.8 | 1.2 | 1.3 | 2.1 | 1.6 | 6.2 | 14 |
| 1995 | 1.5 | 1.8 | 2.6 | 2.0 | 7.9 | 1.3 | 1.5 | 2.3 | 2.0 | 7.1 | 15 |
| 1996 | 1.6 | 1.9 | 3.5 | 2.2 | 9.2 | 1.4 | 1.6 | 3.0 | 2.8 | 8.8 | 18 |
| 1997 | 1.8 | 2.0 | 4.2 | 3.0 | 11.0 | 1.5 | 1.8 | 4.0 | 1.7 | 9.0 | 20 |
| 1998 | 2.0 | 2.2 | 4.3 | 2.8 | 11.3 | 1.8 | 2.0 | 4.0 | 1.9 | 9.7 | 21 |
| 1999 | 2.1 | 3.5 | 4.5 | 2.9 | 13.0 | 1.9 | 3.0 | 4.1 | 2.0 | 11.0 | 24 |

(C) *Multiple Table.* In this type of tables, more than three facts related to investigation are shown in the table, hence it is called multiple table. Construction of this type of table is most difficult. The example of this type is given below :

TABLE NO. 4

*Table showing population of a town according to sex, age and employment*

| Years | Age / Sex | Population (in lakhs) | | | | | | | | | | |
|---|---|---|---|---|---|---|---|---|---|---|---|---|
| | | Employed | | | | | Unemployed | | | | | Grand Total |
| | | Below 15 | 15-30 | 30-45 | 45 & above | Total | Below 15 | 15-30 | 30-45 | 45 & above | Total | |
| 1998 | Male | 3 | 8 | 12 | 9 | 32 | 8 | 2 | 3 | 5 | 18 | 50 |
| | Female | 2 | 8 | 6 | 4 | 20 | 5 | 1 | 2 | 6 | 14 | 34 |
| | Total | 5 | 16 | 18 | 13 | 52 | 13 | 3 | 5 | 11 | 32 | 84 |
| 1999 | Male | 3 | 10 | 15 | 7 | 35 | 9 | 3 | 3 | 5 | 20 | 55 |
| | Female | 3 | 8 | 8 | 3 | 22 | 6 | 2 | 2 | 8 | 18 | 40 |
| | Total | 6 | 18 | 23 | 10 | 57 | 15 | 5 | 5 | 13 | 38 | 95 |
| 2000 | Male | 4 | 11 | 18 | 3 | 36 | 10 | 3 | 3 | 6 | 22 | 58 |
| | Female | 3 | 9 | 10 | 2 | 24 | 7 | 2 | 3 | 8 | 20 | 44 |
| | Total | 7 | 20 | 28 | 5 | 60 | 17 | 5 | 6 | 14 | 42 | 102 |

***Note.*** All figures in Table Nos. 1-4 are imaginary.

**Illustration 11.** The population of district 'A' was 20 lakhs, 22 lakhs, 25 lakhs, 28 lakhs and 30 lakhs in years 1994, 1995, 1996, 1997 and 1998 respectively. Represent the above data through a table.

**Solution**

TABLE NO. 5

**Population Distribution in District 'A' 1994-1998**

| Years | Population (in Lakhs) |
|---|---|
| 1994 | 20 |
| 1995 | 22 |
| 1996 | 25 |
| 1997 | 28 |
| 1998 | 30 |

**Illustration 12.** Various population surveys were made of district 'A' from 1994-1998 and it was found that there were 8 lakhs females and 12 lakhs males in 1994, in 1995 males were 13 lakhs and females were 9 lakhs, in 1996 males were 13 lakhs and females were 12 lakhs, in 1997 females were 13 lakhs and males were 15 lakhs and in 1998 the number of males were 16 lakhs and females were 14 lakhs.

Represent the above data through suitable table.

**Solution**

TABLE NO. 6

**Population in District 'A' 1994-1998**

| Years | Population (in Lakhs) | | Total |
|---|---|---|---|
| | Females | Males | |
| 1994 | 8 | 12 | 20 |
| 1995 | 9 | 13 | 22 |
| 1996 | 12 | 13 | 25 |
| 1997 | 13 | 15 | 28 |
| 1998 | 14 | 16 | 30 |

**Illustration 13.** If in addition to the information given above in 'Illustration 12' it was also discovered that the urban male population in 1994, 1995, 1996, 1997 and 1998 was 4 lakhs, 5 lakhs, 6 lakhs,

7 lakhs and 7 lakhs respectively; and the rural population of females in various years was 5 lakhs, 5 lakhs, 7 lakhs, 7 lakhs and 8 lakhs respectively. How will you represent these data through a suitable table.

**Solution**

TABLE NO. 7

**Population in District 'A' 1994-1998**

| Years | Population (in Lakhs) | | | | | | Grand Total |
|---|---|---|---|---|---|---|---|
| | Females | | | Males | | | |
| | Urban | Rural | Total | Urban | Rural | Total | |
| 1994 | 3 | 5 | 8 | 4 | 8 | 12 | 20 |
| 1995 | 4 | 5 | 9 | 5 | 8 | 13 | 22 |
| 1996 | 5 | 7 | 12 | 6 | 7 | 13 | 25 |
| 1997 | 6 | 7 | 13 | 7 | 8 | 15 | 28 |
| 1998 | 6 | 8 | 14 | 7 | 9 | 16 | 30 |

**Illustration 14.** If in addition to the information given in 'Illustration 12 and 13' it was also reported by the surveyors that the number of educated females in urban area was 2 lakhs, 2.5 lakhs, 3.5 lakhs, 4.5 lakhs and 5 lakhs in 1994, 1995, 1996, 1997 and 1998 respectively, while the number of uneducated females in rural areas was 1.5 lakhs, 2 lakhs, 3 lakhs, 2.5 lakhs and 2 lakhs respectively in various years. On the other hand the number of uneducated males in urban areas was reported as 1 lakh, 1.5 lakhs, 1 lakh, 1 lakh and .5 lakh in 1994, 1995, 1996, 1997 and 1998 respectively. The educated male in rural areas were 5 lakhs, 5.5 lakhs, 5.5 lakhs, 6 lakhs and 6.5 lakhs in various years.

Represent the above figures with the help of a suitable table.

(*For Solution : See Table No. 8 on page 108*)

**Illustration 15.** Of the 3,785 schools in Malaya in 1999; 210 used English as the language of instruction (2,646 teachers, 78,325 pupils), 1,321 were Malaya Schools (6,242 teachers, 1,99,579 pupils), 1,364 Chinese (5,337 teachers 1,89,230 pupils) and 890 Indian (1,267 teachers, 35,456 pupils). Prepare a table to provide information about the school population in Malaya in 1999 and about the number of pupils per teacher in different types of schools.

[*B.A.* (*Hons.*) *Eco.*, *Delhi*]

**Solution :** (Illustration 14)

TABLE No. 8

**Population in District 'A' 1994-1908**

| Year | Population (in lakhs) | | | | | | | | | | | | | | |
|---|---|---|---|---|---|---|---|---|---|---|---|---|---|---|---|
| | Females | | | | | | Total Female | Males | | | | | | Total Male | Grand Total |
| | Urban | | | Rural | | | | Urban | | | Rural | | | | |
| | Edu-cated | Un-edu-cated | Total | Edu-cated | Un-edu-Cated | Total | | Edu-cated | Un-edu-cated | Total | Edu-cated | Un-edu-cated | Total | | |
| 1994 | 2 | 1.0 | 3 | 3.5 | 1.5 | 5 | 8 | 3.0 | 1.0 | 4 | 5.0 | 3.0 | 8 | 12 | 20 |
| 1995 | 2.5 | 1.5 | 4 | 3.0 | 2.0 | 5 | 9 | 3.5 | 1.5 | 5 | 5.5 | 2.5 | 8 | 13 | 22 |
| 1996 | 3.5 | 1.5 | 5 | 4.0 | 3.0 | 7 | 12 | 5.0 | 1.0 | 6 | 5.5 | 1.5 | 7 | 13 | 25 |
| 1997 | 4.5 | 1.5 | 6 | 4.5 | 2.5 | 7 | 13 | 6.0 | 1.0 | 7 | 6.0 | 2.0 | 8 | 15 | 28 |
| 1998 | 5.0 | 1.0 | 6 | 6.0 | 2.0 | 8 | 14 | 6.5 | 0.5 | 7 | 6.5 | 2.5 | 9 | 16 | 30 |

**Solution**

TABLE NO. 9

**Schools in Malaya**

| Schools | No. of Schools | Students | Teachers | Students per Teacher |
|---|---|---|---|---|
| English | 210 | 78,325 | 2,646 | 30 |
| Malaya | 1,321 | 1,99,579 | 6,242 | 32 |
| Chinese | 1,364 | 1,89,230 | 5,337 | 35 |
| Indian | 890 | 35,456 | 1,267 | 28 |
| Total | 3,785 | 5,02,590 | 15,492 | 32 |

**Illustration 16.** Out of the total numbers of 1,807 women, who were interviewed for employment in a textile factory of Bombay, 512 were from textile areas, and the rest were from non-textile areas. Amongst the married women, who belonged to textile areas, 247 were experienced and 73 inexperienced; while for non-textile areas, the corresponding figures were 49 and 520. The total number, of inexperienced women was 1,341, of whom 111 resided in the textile areas. Of the total no. of women, 918 were unmarried; and of these, the no. of experienced women in the textile and non-textile areas was 154 and 16 respectively. Tabulate.

[*B.Com.* (*Hons.*), *Delhi*]

**Solution**

TABLE NO. 10

**Distribution of Employed Women in Bombay According to Area, Marital Status and Experience**

| Job Experience | Textile Areas | | | Non-Textile Areas | | | Grand Total |
|---|---|---|---|---|---|---|---|
| | Married | Unmarried | Total | Married | Unmarried | Total | |
| Experienced | 247 | 154 | 401 | 49 | 16 | 65 | 466 |
| Inexperienced | 73 | 38 | 111 | 520 | 710 | 1230 | 1341 |
| Total | 320 | 192 | 512 | 569 | 726 | 1295 | 1807 |

**Illustration 17.** In a sample study about coffee habit in two towns; the following information were received :

*Town A* : Females were 40%; total coffee drinkers were 45% : and males non-coffee drinkers were 20%.

*Town B* : Males were 55%; males non-coffee drinkers were 30%; and females coffee drinkers were 15%.

Represent the above data in a tabular form.

[*B.Com. (Hons.), Delhi; C.A., May 1997*]

**Solution**

TABLE NO. 11

**Distribution of Population According to Sex and Coffee Drinkers' Habit**

(In Percentage)

| Coffee Drinking Habit | Towns | | | | | |
|---|---|---|---|---|---|---|
| | A | | | B | | |
| | Male | Female | Total | Male | Female | Total |
| Coffee Drinkers | 40 | 5 | 45 | 25 | 15 | 40 |
| Non-Coffee Drinkers | 20 | 35 | 55 | 30 | 30 | 60 |
| Total | 60 | 40 | 100 | 55 | 45 | 100 |

**Illustration 18.** Represent the following statement in a suitable tabular form :

"The developmental outlay of the Central and State Governments amounted to Rs. 4,800 crores over the period of the Second Plan, as against Rs. 2,356 crores under the First Plan. The allocations in the Second Plan to the six major heads of development, namely, Agriculture and Community Development, Irrigation and Power, Industry and Mining, Transport and Communications, Social Services and Miscellaneous Heads were, in crores of rupees, 568, 913, 890, 1,385, 945 and 99 respectively. The corresponding amounts in the First Plan were in crores of rupees, 357, 661, 179, 557, 533 and 69, respectively. Thus there was a sizable increase in outlay, in 'absolute terms' under each head. But as a proportion of total outlay, there was a substantial increase under the head, Industry and Mining, from 7.6% in the First Plan to 18.5% in the Second Plan and a moderate increase under Transport and Communications, from 23.6% to 28.9%. The percentage increase in the outlay of the Second Plan relative to that of the First

Plan for the six major heads of development are 59.1, 38.1, 397.2, 148.7, 77.3 and 43.5 respectively. The proportion of total outlay decreased from 15.1% in the First Plan to 11.8% in the Second Plan in Agriculture and Community Development, from 28.1% to 19.0% in Irrigation and Power and from 22.6% to 19.7% in Social Services."

[*B.A.* (*Hons.*) *Eco.*, *Delhi*]

**Solution**

TABLE NO. 12

**Development Outlay of Central & State Governments**

(in Crores of Rupees)

| Categories | First Five-Year Plan | | Second Five-Year Plan | | | % Increase in II Plan compared to I Plan |
|---|---|---|---|---|---|---|
| | Outlay | % of Total outlay | Outlay | % of Total outlay | % change in outlay from First Plan to Second Plan | |
| (i) Agriculture and Community Development | 357 | 15.15% | 568 | 11.83% | –3.32% | 59.1% |
| (ii) Irrigation & Power | 661 | 28.06% | 913 | 19.03.% | -9.03% | 38.1% |
| (iii) Industry & Mining | 179 | 7.60% | 890 | 18.54% | +10.94% | 397.2% |
| (iv) Transport & Communications | 557 | 23.64% | 1,385 | 28.85% | +5.21% | 148.7% |
| (v) Social Services | 533 | 22.62% | 945 | 19.69% | –2.93% | 77.3% |
| (vi) Miscellaneous | 69 | 2.93% | 99 | 2.06% | –0.87% | 43.5% |
| Total | 2,356 | 100% | 4,800 | 100% | 0.00% | 103.8% |

## QUESTIONS

1. What do you mean by classification of data? What are the objects of classification of data?
2. What are the factors which should be kept in mind while classifying data? Describe.

3. Define classification, what part does it play in statistics? State the main bases or divisions by reference to which you will classify statistical observations.
4. What are the objects of classification of data? Discuss the different methods of classification.
5. What is the meaning of statistical series? What are the types of statistical series.
6. What are the requisites of a good statistical table?
   (*C.S. June 1996*)
7. What do you understand by 'classification of data'? State its objectives.
   (*C.S. June 1996*)
8. What is tabulation? What are its uses? Mention the items that a good statistical table should contain.
   (*C.A. Nov. 1996*)
9. What are the advantages of data classification? What primary rules ordinarily be followed for classification?
   (*C.A. Nov. 1997*)
10. Which important points should be kept in mind while preparing a good statistical table?
    (*C.A. May 1999*)
11. How will you construct discrete and continuous series from individual observation?
12. Define continuous series. Describe the essential elements of a continuous series.
13. What do you mean by tabulation? What are the advantages of tabulation?
14. Discuss the purpose, methods and importance of tabulation in any statistical investigation. Mention the kinds of tables generally used.
15. What are the types of tabulation? Give an imaginary specimen of each type of table.
16. What are the factors which should be kept in mind while preparing a table? Describe.
17. "Either for one's own use or for the use of others, the data must be presented in some suitable form." Comment on this statement and discuss the function and importance of tabulation in a scheme of investigation. What points should be taken into consideration in tabulating statistical data?

18. Distinguish between classification and tabulation. Discuss the purpose, methods and importance of classification.
19. Construct a continuous series from the following data :
    40, 48, 53, 69, 92, 50, 55, 49, 93, 95, 82, 76, 65, 55, 43, 63, 77, 80, 82, 62, 60, 53, 54, 70, 99, 77, 76, 88, 42, 66, 57, 75, 65, 56, 48, 94, 84, 74, 62, 53, 43, 41, 45, 48, 49, 50, 47, 62, 63, 70.
20. Compile a discrete series, showing the frequency with which words of different numbers of letters occur in the extract reproduced below (omitting punctuation marks) treating as the variable, *i.e.* the number of the letters in each word.
    "Success in the examination confers no absolute right to appointment, unless Government is satisfied, after such inquiry as may be considered necessary that the candidate is suitable in all respects for appointment to the public service."
21. You are given below the wages paid to some workers in a sugar factory, from a frequency distribution with class interval of 10 paise.

Wages in Rs.

| | | | | | | | | | |
|---|---|---|---|---|---|---|---|---|---|
| 1.10 | 1.36 | 1.44 | 1.55 | 1.98 | 1.67 | 1.27 | 1.39 | 1.51 | 1.75 |
| 1.03 | 1.37 | 1.40 | 1.52 | 1.31 | 1.81 | 1.04 | 1.38 | 1.60 | 1.28 |
| 1.49 | 1.46 | 1.50 | 1.42 | 1.29 | 1.47 | 1.87 | 1.47 | 1.15 | 1.56 |
| 1.65 | 1.44 | 1.41 | 1.17 | 1.69 | 1.30 | 1.45 | 1.73 | 1.26 | 1.42 |
| 1.53 | 1.46 | 1.19 | 1.62 | 1.32 | 1.33 | 1.47 | 1.20 | 1.76 | 1.09 |
| 1.46 | 1.95 | 1.16 | 1.42 | 1.68 | 1.38 | 1.35 | 1.77 | 1.66 | 1.07 |
| 1.13 | 1.67 | 1.27 | 1.22 | 1.36 | 1.34 | 1.24 | 1.25 | 1.12 | 1.57 |
| 1.58 | 1.59 | 1.21 | 1.56 | 1.55 | 1.40 | 1.48 | 1.62 | 1.70 | 1.92 |
| 1.86 | 1.35 | 1.82 | 1.78 | 1.54 | 1.37 | 1.41 | 1.43 | 1.57 | 1.48 |

22. In an inquiry to find out relation between age and monthly wages, the following data were collected from 40 mill workers :

| S. No. | Age (Years) | Wages (Rs.) | S. No. | Age (Years) | Wages (Rs.) | S. No. | Age (Years) | Wages (Rs.) | S. No. | Age (Years) | Wages (Rs.) |
|---|---|---|---|---|---|---|---|---|---|---|---|
| 1 | 37 | 80 | 11 | 45 | 135 | 21 | 41 | 89 | 31 | 35 | 120 |
| 2 | 21 | 100 | 12 | 33 | 101 | 22 | 38 | 92 | 32 | 42 | 113 |
| 3 | 49 | 101 | 13 | 28 | 99 | 23 | 41 | 81 | 33 | 40 | 119 |
| 4 | 36 | 109 | 14 | 41 | 113 | 24 | 37 | 140 | 34 | 45 | 90 |
| 5 | 37 | 102 | 15 | 31 | 100 | 25 | 45 | 94 | 35 | 50 | 76 |
| 6 | 34 | 104 | 16 | 30 | 99 | 26 | 46 | 119 | 36 | 24 | 158 |
| 7 | 23 | 81 | 17 | 35 | 130 | 27 | 28 | 99 | 37 | 21 | 76 |
| 8 | 34 | 110 | 18 | 30 | 139 | 28 | 43 | 109 | 38 | 22 | 76 |
| 9 | 31 | 100 | 19 | 29 | 80 | 29 | 41 | 92 | 39 | 21 | 94 |
| 10 | 41 | 89 | 20 | 21 | 79 | 30 | 31 | 110 | 40 | 38 | 82 |

Tabulate the above data in the following form :

| Wages Groups (Rs.) | No. of Mill Workers (Age Group) | | | Total |
|---|---|---|---|---|
| | 21-30 Yrs. | 31-40 Yrs. | 41-50 Yrs. | |
| 76-100<br>101-125<br>126-150<br>151-175 | | | | |
| Total | | | | |

23. In a newspaper column, describing the incidence of influenza among tuberculosis person living in the same family, the following paragraph appeared :

"Exactly a fifth of the 1,00,000 inhabitants showed signs of tuberculosis and no fewer than 5,000 among them had attack of influenza, but among them only 1,000 lived in uninfected houses. In contrast with this 1/15 of tuberculosis persons who did not have influenza were still exposed to infection. Altogether 21,000 were attacked by influenza and 41,000 were exposed to risk of infection, but the number who were having influenza but not tuberculosis lived in houses where no other cases of influenza occurred was only 2,000.

Redraft the information in a concise and elegant tabular form.

24. Prepare a blank table, showing the distribution of students of a college according to age, class, residence for arranging (a) physical training and (b) tutorial classes.

25. Following figures relate to weekly wages of workers of a factory :

Wages (in Rs.)

| | | | | | | | | | |
|---|---|---|---|---|---|---|---|---|---|
| 100 | 100 | 101 | 102 | 106 | 86 | 82 | 87 | 109 | 104 |
| 75 | 89 | 99 | 96 | 94 | 93 | 92 | 90 | 86 | 78 |
| 79 | 84 | 83 | 87 | 88 | 89 | 75 | 76 | 76 | 79 |
| 80 | 81 | 89 | 99 | 104 | 100 | 103 | 104 | 107 | 110 |
| 110 | 106 | 102 | 107 | 103 | 101 | 101 | 101 | 86 | 94 |
| 93 | 96 | 97 | 99 | 100 | 102 | 103 | 107 | 107 | 108 |
| 109 | 94 | 93 | 97 | 98 | 99 | 100 | 97 | 88 | 86 |
| 84 | 83 | 82 | 80 | 84 | 86 | 88 | 91 | 93 | 95 |
| 95 | 95 | 97 | 98 | 100 | 105 | 106 | 103 | 85 | 84 |
| 77 | 78 | 80 | 93 | 96 | 97 | 98 | 98 | 98 | 87 |

Prepare a frequency table by taking a class interval of 5.

[*B. Com.* (*Pass*) *Delhi*]

26. In a trip organised by a college, there were 100 persons; the average cost works out to Rs. 15.60 per head. There were 80 students each of whom paid Rs. 16. Members of the teaching staff were charged at a higher rate. The number of servants was 6 (all males) and they were not charged. The number of ladies was 20% of the total of which two were lady staff members. Tabulate the above information in proper tabular form.

(*C.A., Nov. 1998*)

27. What is frequency distribution? Prepare a suitable frequency distribution of the weights (in kgs) of 33 students of a class given below :

42, 74, 40, 60, 82, 115, 41, 61, 75, 83, 63, 53, 110, 76, 84, 50, 67, 65, 78, 77, 56, 95, 68, 69, 104, 80, 79, 79, 54, 53, 59, 81, 100.

(*C.A. Nov. 1991*)

28. Following are the marks (out of 100) obtained by 50 students in Statistics :

| | | | | |
|---|---|---|---|---|
| 70 | 55 | 51 | 42 | 57 |
| 45 | 60 | 47 | 63 | 53 |
| 33 | 65 | 39 | 82 | 55 |
| 64 | 58 | 61 | 65 | 42 |
| 50 | 52 | 53 | 45 | 45 |
| 25 | 36 | 59 | 63 | 39 |
| 65 | 45 | 49 | 54 | 64 |
| 75 | 42 | 41 | 52 | 35 |
| 30 | 35 | 15 | 48 | 26 |
| 20 | 40 | 55 | 46 | 18 |

Make a frequency distribution taking a class interval of 10 marks (Take the first class interval as 0-10)

[*B. Com. (Hons.), Delhi*]

29. Following figures give the ages of newly married husbands and their wives in years. Represent the data by a frequency distribution.

| | | | | | | | | | | |
|---|---|---|---|---|---|---|---|---|---|---|
| *Age of husband* | 24 | 26 | 27 | 25 | 28 | 24 | 27 | 28 | 25 | 26 |
| *Age of wife* | 17 | 18 | 19 | 17 | 10 | 18 | 18 | 19 | 18 | 19 |
| *Age of husband* | 25 | 26 | 27 | 25 | 27 | 26 | 25 | 26 | 26 | 26 |
| *Age of wife* | 17 | 18 | 19 | 19 | 20 | 19 | 17 | 20 | 17 | 18 |

[*B. Com. (Hons.), Delhi*]

30. Monthly wages (in Rs.) received by 30 workers in a factory are as follows :

| | | | | | | | | | |
|---|---|---|---|---|---|---|---|---|---|
| 310 | 320 | 325 | 375 | 397 | 335 | 354 | 331 | 300 | 370 |
| 315 | 390 | 350 | 327 | 323 | 360 | 386 | 342 | 380 | 359 |
| 305 | 318 | 337 | 393 | 385 | 340 | 367 | 367 | 363 | 392 |

Prepare a frequency distribution table classified on the basis of wages with class interval of 10. Also obtain the percentage frequency in each class interval.

(*ICWA, Dec. 1998*)

31. The following are the marks obtained by 30 boys in an examination. Construct a frequency table with class interval of 10 :

| | | | | | |
|---|---|---|---|---|---|
| 7 | 18 | 37 | 53 | 24 | 39 |
| 68 | 40 | 93 | 43 | 11 | 27 |
| 21 | 19 | 32 | 75 | 52 | 84 |
| 52 | 29 | 92 | 79 | 45 | 81 |
| 53 | 8 | 41 | 14 | 26 | 26 |

Also give cumulative frequency (less than) table.

(*ICWA, June 1998*)

32. Marks obtained by 44 candidates in statistics and Income tax are given below :

| Marks in Statistics | Marks in Income-tax | Marks in Statistics | Marks in Income-tax | Marks in Statistics | Marks in Income-tax | Marks in Statistics | Marks in Income-tax |
|---|---|---|---|---|---|---|---|
| 25 | 11 | 34 | 28 | 39 | 25 | 37 | 36 |
| 16 | 18 | 20 | 19 | 40 | 27 | 23 | 32 |
| 23 | 25 | 18 | 13 | 22 | 14 | 33 | 19 |
| 25 | 27 | 35 | 30 | 42 | 30 | 35 | 35 |
| 12 | 16 | 23 | 22 | 43 | 31 | 32 | 34 |
| 28 | 29 | 20 | 23 | 25 | 21 | 33 | 33 |
| 32 | 30 | 37 | 29 | 27 | 34 | 22 | 32 |
| 18 | 20 | 36 | 30 | 32 | 20 | 36 | 40 |
| 27 | 26 | 28 | 36 | 29 | 37 | 44 | 42 |
| 15 | 12 | 27 | 22 | 32 | 23 | 24 | 15 |
| 33 | 25 | 30 | 38 | 40 | 37 | 35 | 41 |

Prepare a bivariate frequency distribution table of the above data in the following form by choosing class intervals of 7 marks each, *viz.*, 10-17, 17-24 onwards till 38-45.

| Marks in Income-tax | Marks in Statistics | | | | | Total |
|---|---|---|---|---|---|---|
| | 10-17 | 17-24 | 24-31 | 31-38 | 38-45 | |
| 10-17 | | | | | | |
| 17-24 | | | | | | |
| 24-31 | | | | | | |
| 31-38 | | | | | | |
| 38-45 | | | | | | |
| Total | | | | | | |

***Note.*** Show the actual process of tabulation.

33. Present the information contained in the following text in a suitable tabular form, giving an appropriate title —

"The total rural population of India according to 1971 census was 2,948 lakhs of which 2,404 lakhs belonged to agricultural classes. Of the total urban population of 618 lakhs, 531 lakhs belonged to non-agricultural classes.

Of the rural agricultural classes, 687 lakhs were self-supporting persons, 1,414 lakhs were non-earning dependents and 303 lakhs were earning dependents. The rural non-agricultural population comprised 544 lakhs of which 170 lakhs were self-supporting persons, 326 lakhs were non-earning dependents and 48 lakhs were earning dependents. In the urban agricultural classes 23 lakhs were self-supporting, 56 lakhs were non-earning dependents, and 8 lakhs were earning dependents. The urban non-agricultural population comprised 531 lakhs of persons of whom 153 lakhs were non-earning dependents and 31 lakhs were earning dependents.

34. Out of total number of 2,807 women, who were interviewed for employment in a textile factory, 912 were from textile areas and the rest from non-textile areas. Amongst the married women, who belonged to textile areas, 347 were having some work experience and 173 did not have work experience, while for non-textile areas the corresponding figures were 199 and 670 respectively. The total number of women having no experience was 1,841 of

whom 311 resided in textile areas. Of the total number of women 1,418 were unmarried and of these the number of women having experience in the textile and non-textile areas was 254 and 166 respectively.

Tabulate the above information.

(*C.A., May 1998*)

35. Present in a tabular form with suitable captions etc. the information contained in the following :

In 1998 out of a total of 1750 workers of a factory 1200 workers were members of a trade union. The number of women employed was 200 of which 175 did not belong to a trade union. In 1999, the number of union workers increased to 1580 of which 1290 were men. On the other hand the number of non-union workers fell down to 208 of which 180 were men. In 2000, there were on the pay rolls of the factory, 1850 workers of whom 1,800 belonged to a trade union. Of all the employees in 2000; 300 were women of whom only 8 did not belong to a trade union.

36. Tabulate the following information —

In a trip organised by a college there were 80 persons each of whom paid Rs. 15.50 on an average. There were 60 students each of whom paid Rs. 16. Members of the teaching staff were charged at a higher rate. The number of servants was 6 (1 male) and they were not charged anything. The number of ladies was 20% of the total of which one was a lady staff member.

37. Represent the following information in suitable tabular form with proper rulings and headings;

The annual Report of the Ishapore Public Library reveals the following points regarding the reading habits of its members :

Out of the total 3,713 books issued to the members in the month of June 2000; 2,100 were fictions. There were 467 members of the library during the period and they were classified in five classes A, B, C, D and E. The number of members belonging to the first four classes were respectively 15; 176; 98 and 129; and the number of fictions issued to them were 103; 1,187; 647 and 58 respectively. Number of books, other than textbooks and fictions, issued to these four classes of members were respectively 4; 390; 217 and 341. The textbooks were issued only to members belonging to the classes C, D and E and the number of textbooks issued to them were 3; 317 and 160 respectively.

During the same period, 1,247 periodicals were issued. These included 396 technical journals of which 36 were issued to members of class B, 45 to class D and 315 to class E.

To members of the classes B, C, D and E the number of other journals issued were 419; 26; 231 and 99 respectively.

The report, however, showed an increase by 3.9% in the number of books issued over last month, though there was a corresponding decrease by 6.1% in the number of periodicals and journals issued to members.

*(I.C.W.A.)*

38. Present the following information in a tabular form and suggest a suitable title :

"The production of 10.95 lakh tonnes of rice in Maharashtra in 1962-63 was the lowest in the period since 1955-56. In 1963-64, however, it has shown a spectacular recovery and reached the level of 15.14 lakh tonnes. During 1963-64 wheat and bazri output decreased. The production of bazri which was 5.50 lakh tonnes in 1962-63 declined to 4.51 lakh tonnes in 1963-64. The production of wheat also decreased from 4.63 lakh tonnes in 1962-63 to 3.43 lakh tonnes in 1963-64. The area under pulses has shown a decreasing trend and the production was less by 22,000 tonnes in 1963-64 than the production of 8.89 lakh tonnes in 1962-63". (5 marks)

*(I.C.W.A., June 1997)*

# 8

# Presentation of Data Through Diagrams and Graphs

Facts when presented in numerical forms only are not easy for everyone to grasp, compare and commit to memory. It is difficult for some one to derive solution from a maze of lengthy numerical details. It requires intelligence, hardwork and knowledge to draw comparison and conclusion on the basis of numerical facts. Hence facts only numerically presented do not become useful to people in general. But these limitations of numerical facts can be removed by using diagrams and graphs, that is, if facts are presented through diagrams and graphs, they become very easy and comparable even at a glance. Generally, it is observed that facts of extensive numerical details are easily presented by diagrams and graphs. That is the reason why governmental, quasi-governmental and business institutions while presenting their annual reports and other information for general public, have recourse to diagrams and graphs.

## PRESENTATION OF DATA THROUGH DIAGRAMS

When the shape of any fact is delineated through diagrams, that is called presentation through diagrams. Diagrams are in the form of lines, squares, circles and rectangles. At times the shape of data is also delineated through maps and pictures. All these methods are included within the ambient of presentation, through diagrams. They are attractive to look at and are easily acceptable to common people. Figures given in lakhs, crores or given in decimal are difficult for a man of moderate understanding to grasp but when the same presented through diagrams, everyone understand them. The following are the merits and demerits of data presented through diagrams :

**Merits.** Presenting facts through diagrams has several advantages, facts become easier, comparable and easily comprehensible; vast and complex fact get shortened and they can be presented in a more attractive manner. Following are the advantages of presenting numerical facts through diagrams :

**1. Easy understanding of facts expressed in complicated numerals.** Facts or data shown in large figures can be easily understood when they are presented through diagrams. Complicated figures are usually very dry for common people, but presentation through diagrams removes dryness of facts and makes them comprehensible. In this connection Moroney's statement given below is quite significant :

"*Cold figures are uninspiring to most people. Diagrams help us to see the pattern and shape of any complex situation. Just as a map gives us a bird's eye view of a wide stretch of a country and diagrams help us to visualise the whole meaning of a numerical complex at a single glance.*"

**2. Knowledge of the nature of problem at a glance.** What is the nature or the shape of the problem may be known by diagrams by just taking a glance at them. No mathematical operation of any kind is necessary to find out the nature or shape of the problem.

**3. Help in comparison.** When two or more facts are to be compared among them or facts belonging to different period are to be compared, diagrams are very handy for the purpose.

**4. Diagrams present facts attractively.** Facts look attractive when they are presented through diagrams. Even those persons to whom numericals look cold, the actual state of things become apparent and clear by just a look at the diagrams.

**5. Minute display of the problem.** Vast subjects can be minutely shown by diagrams. Such facts as the population of the world can be easily shown in a small map.

**6. Economical in Times and labour.** In finding out about any fact through diagrams requires less labour and time that when the same is done through figures.

**Demerits.** Following are the demerits of presenting fact through diagrams :

**1. Approximate or estimated knowledge.** By this one can have only an estimated and not an accurate knowledge of any situation.

Hence this kind of presentation is useful only when one is to have a mere estimation of a problem.

**2. Limited use of diagrams.** These should be used only when numerals are either too many or too complicated. Presentation of this type when figures are too few does not serve any useful purpose. Diagrammatic presentations are not meant for experts but only for common people to have an estimate or comparative view of a problem.

**Rules regarding Preparation of Diagram.** The following rules for preparing diagrams should be followed :

**1. Suitable heading.** Every diagram should have a suitable heading above it giving information about the subject of the diagram.

**2. Attractive.** Diagram should be constructed in such a way that it might look attractive. With a view to make them attractive and beautiful, the diagrams are some time coloured also.

**3. Proper Size.** The size of the diagrams should confirm to the subject and the place or paper whereon it is to be shown.

**4. Fixed Scale.** Scale should be fixed for preparing a diagram and all the facts should be shown according to the measurement of that scale in order to bring uniformity among all the items.

**5. Use of approximated figures.** Figures to be presented through diagrams should be approximated and it is better to convert figures shown in decimals into whole numbers.

**6. Use of abbreviations and signs.** If in the diagram, facts having more than one attribute should be made clear by using signs and abbreviations as to how a fact has been shown.

Diagrams prepared by keeping in view the above points come out to be accurate, attractive, beautiful and useful.

## KINDS OF DIAGRAMS

Diagrams are of the following kinds :

1. One Dimensional Diagram
2. Two Dimensional Diagram
3. Three Dimensional Diagram

4. Pictograms or Pictures
5. Cartograms or Maps.

**1. One Dimensional Diagram.** Diagrams of this type are prepared on one measurement scale only, that is, the shape of the problem is shown by a single measurement. The measurement of the length of diagram shown the shape of the problem. Width and thickness have no significance, though at times they are added only to make the diagram a bit more attractive. Diagrams of this kind are divided into a few more types which are given below :

(a) Line Diagrams
(b) Simple Bar Diagrams
(c) Multi-bar Diagrams
(d) Sub-Divided Bar Diagrams
(e) Sub-Divided Percentage Bar Diagrams
(f) Horizontal Bar Diagram
(g) Broken Scale Bar Diagram
(h) Duo-Directional or Dialateral Bar Diagram
(i) Pyramid Diagram
(j) Deviation Bar Diagram

(a) *Line Diagrams.* When diagrams are made by drawing simple lines of different lengths showing different fact in preparation they are called line diagrams. This type of diagrams though very simple are not attractive. An idea of this type may be had from the following illustration.

**Illustration 1.** Represent the following data by line diagram :

| S. No. | 1 | 2 | 3 | 4 | 5 | 6 | 7 | 8 | 9 | 10 |
|---|---|---|---|---|---|---|---|---|---|---|
| Income (in Rs.) | 80 | 90 | 105 | 108 | 110 | 115 | 118 | 120 | 125 | 130 |

**Solution**

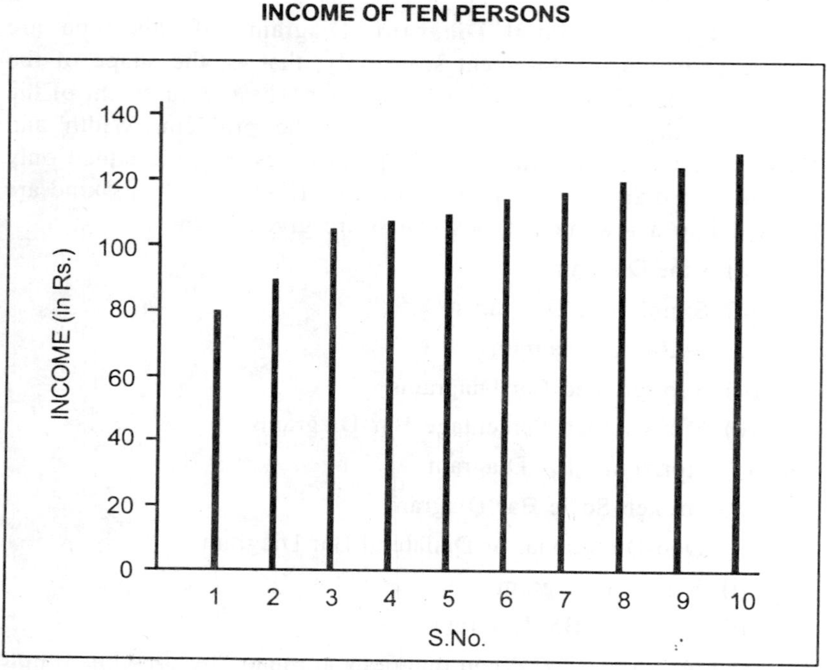


Diagram 1

(b) *Simple Bar Diagrams.* In diagrams of this type, vertical bars of different lengths are made according to the proportional values of facts. The width of all these bars is the same. Width is given with a view to make the bars more attractive or else width is of no significance. While making these bars the important thing to be kept in mind is that lengthwise the bars should be either in the increasing order or in decreasing order, because this order gives them symmetrical appearance and, therefore, the diagrams look attractive. The base of different items should be shown at equal spacing. The following is the illustration of this type of diagram.

**Illustration 2.** Following data are related to the population of a city of 7 years. Represent them through a suitable diagram.

| | | | | | | | |
|---|---|---|---|---|---|---|---|
| Years : | 1991 | 1992 | 1993 | 1994 | 1995 | 1996 | 1997 |
| Population (in thousands) : | 10.0 | 10.5 | 11.2 | 13.0 | 14.0 | 14.5 | 15.0 |

**Solution**

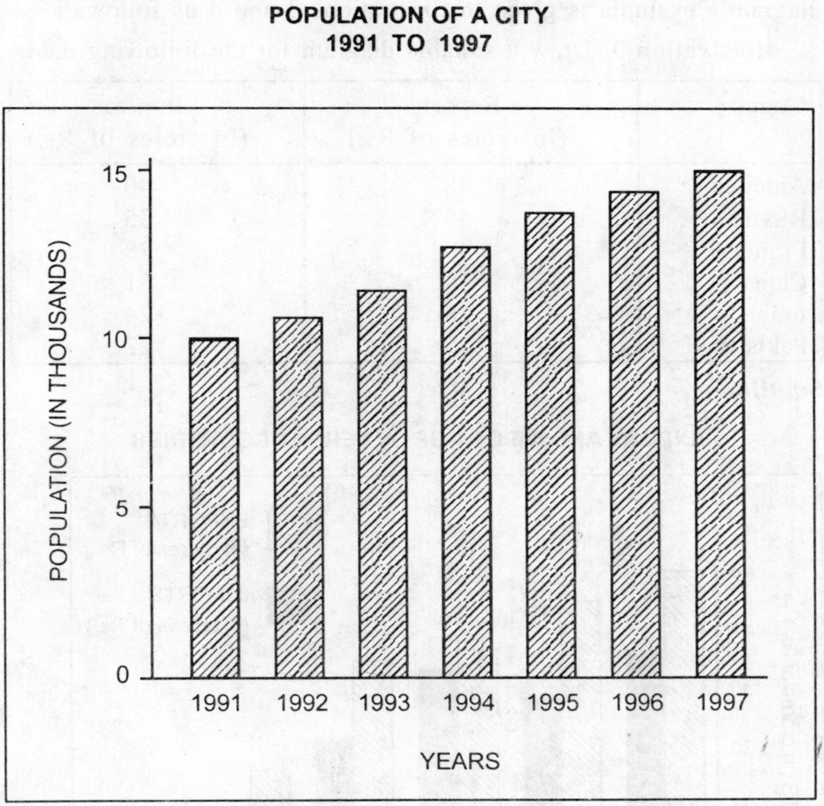


Diagram 2

(c) *Multi-bar Diagram.* When there are numerous facts related to the same place or time and when these facts are shown in a single diagram with the help of bars, that is called multi-bar diagram. In such diagrams bars for all the facts are made in the same way as described earlier and all the bars representing the facts pertaining to the same place or time are stuck close together. For another place or time bars for all the facts are made likewise and some gap is left after the first place or time-bars. Thus bars of different places and times are separately made leaving some blank space in between. Different bars are filled with different colours and designs in order to show and clarify how different fact have been presented in the diagram and signs, indicating thereof, are also given in the diagram. Multi-bar diagram's example is given in illustrations 3 and 4 as follows :

**Illustration 3.** Draw a suitable diagram for the following data :

| Country | Exports (In crores of Rs.) | Imports (In crores of Rs.) |
|---|---|---|
| America | 48 | 40 |
| Russia | 45 | 35 |
| France | 40 | 38 |
| China | 39 | 31 |
| India | 28 | 24 |
| Pakistan | 25 | 22 |

**Solution**

**EXPORT AND IMPORT OF DIFFERENT COUNTRIES**

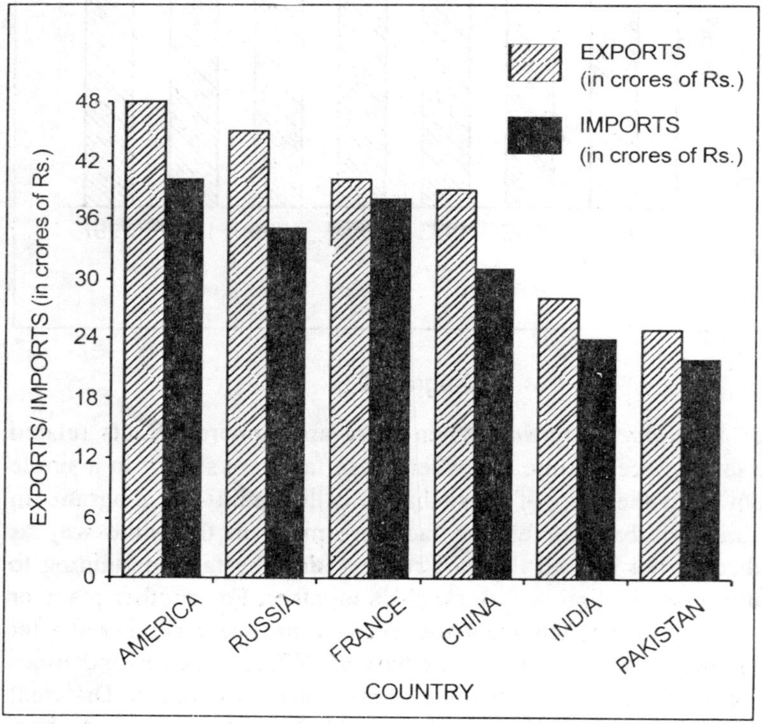


Diagram 3

**Illustration 4.** Industrial and agricultural outputs of some years are given as follows :

| Years | Industrial output (In lakhs of Rs.) | Agricultural output (In lakhs of Rs.) |
|---|---|---|
| 1996 | 25 | 18 |
| 1997 | 28 | 20 |
| 1998 | 35 | 25 |
| 1999 | 32 | 22 |
| 2000 | 42 | 30 |

Show the above data diagrammatically.

**Solution**

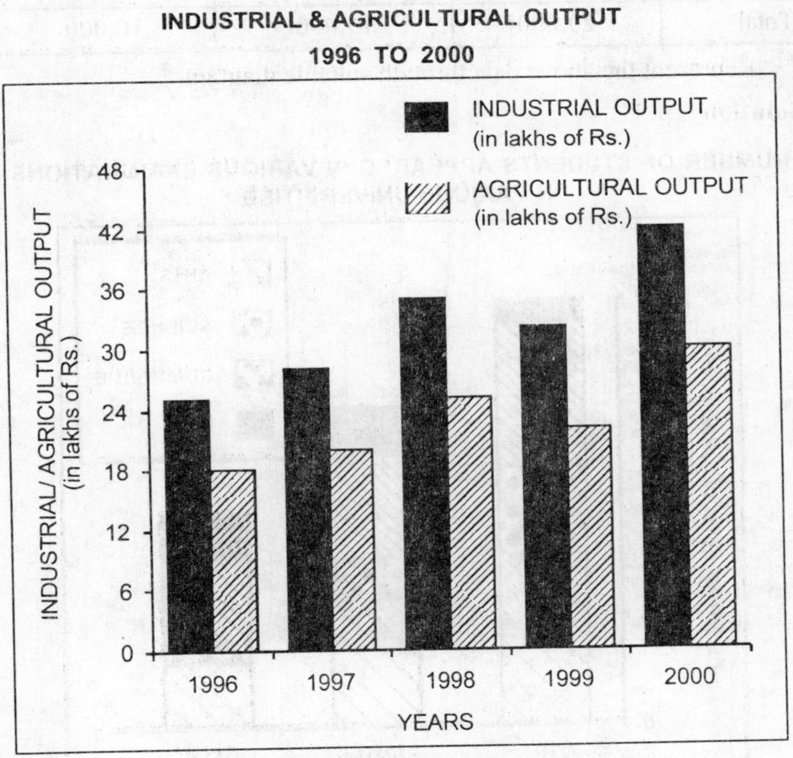


Diagram 4

(d) *Sub-divided Bar Diagram*. These diagrams are used in situations when facts have related sub-facts such as various sources of income and various items of expenditure etc. When such facts are shown by a single bar, the bar is divided on the basis of the proportion of sub-facts and the diagrams thus made is called sub-divided bar diagrams. In this type of diagrams only absolute figures are shown. The illustration of this diagram is given below :

**Illustration 5.** You are given the data of students who appeared in various examinations in various universities as follows :

| Subjects | No. of Students Appeared in Examination | | |
|---|---|---|---|
| | Agra University | Panjab University | Delhi University |
| Art | 8,000 | 6,000 | 3,000 |
| Science | 4,000 | 2,000 | 1,000 |
| Commerce | 7,000 | 5,000 | 4,000 |
| Law | 1,000 | 2,000 | 2,000 |
| Total | 20,000 | 15,000 | 10,000 |

Represent the above data through suitable diagram.

**Solution**

**NUMBER OF STUDENTS APPEARED IN VARIOUS EXAMINATIONS IN VARIOUS UNIVERSITIES**

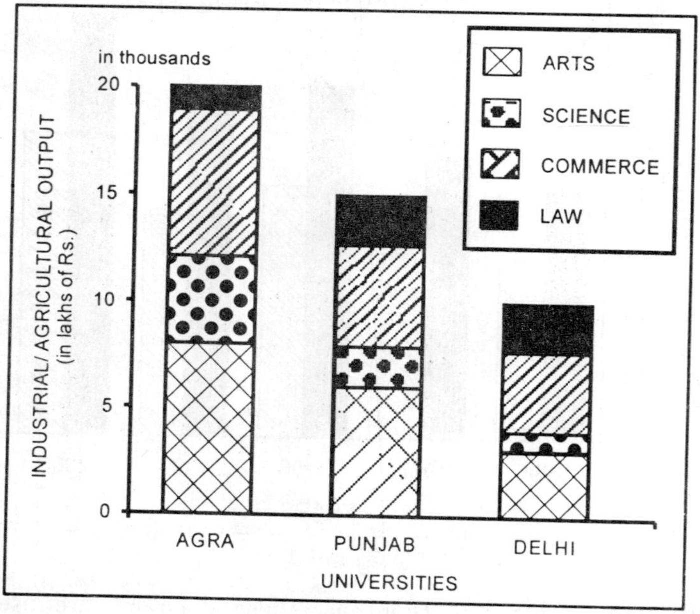


Diagram 5

(e) *Sub-divided Percentage Bar Diagram*. This type is also like the above described one and this is also used to delineate those facts which are divided into sub-facts. The difference between this type and the previous one is that in the above one, only absolute values are shown by the diagram and in this type the relative values (percentages) are shown by bar-diagrams. These are better than the sub-divided bar diagram because comparison becomes easier by this. In such diagrams various values are shown in percentages. Therefore, these are called as sub-divided-bar diagrams.

The following is the example of such diagrams :

**Illustration 6**

**Monthly Expenditure of Some Families**

| Items | Expenditure (in Rs.) | | | |
|---|---|---|---|---|
| | Family A | Family B | Family C | Family D |
| Food | 55 | 90 | 110 | 120 |
| House Rent | 10 | 30 | 66 | 80 |
| Clothes | 10 | 20 | 30 | 60 |
| Education | 10 | 15 | 30 | 40 |
| Entertainment | 5 | 10 | 16 | 40 |
| Miscellaneous | 10 | 35 | 48 | 60 |

Draw a sub-divided percentage bar diagram to represent the above expenditures of various families.

**Solution**

**Calculation of monthly Expenditure of Families in Percentage**

| Items | Expenditure (in Rs.) | | | | | | | |
|---|---|---|---|---|---|---|---|---|
| | Family A | | Family B | | Family C | | Family D | |
| | Actual | % | Actual | % | Actual | % | Actual | % |
| Food | 55 | 55% | 90 | 45% | 110 | 37% | 120 | 30% |
| House Rent | 10 | 10% | 30 | 15% | 66 | 22% | 80 | 20% |
| Clothes | 10 | 10% | 20 | 10% | 30 | 10% | 60 | 15% |
| Education | 10 | 10% | 15 | 7.5% | 30 | 10% | 40 | 10% |
| Entertainment | 5 | 5% | 10 | 5% | 16 | 5% | 40 | 10% |
| Miscellaneous | 10 | 10% | 35 | 17.5% | 48 | 16% | 60 | 15% |
| Total | 100 | 100% | 200 | 100% | 300 | 100% | 400 | 100% |

PERCENTAGE EXPENDITURE OF SOME FAMILIES

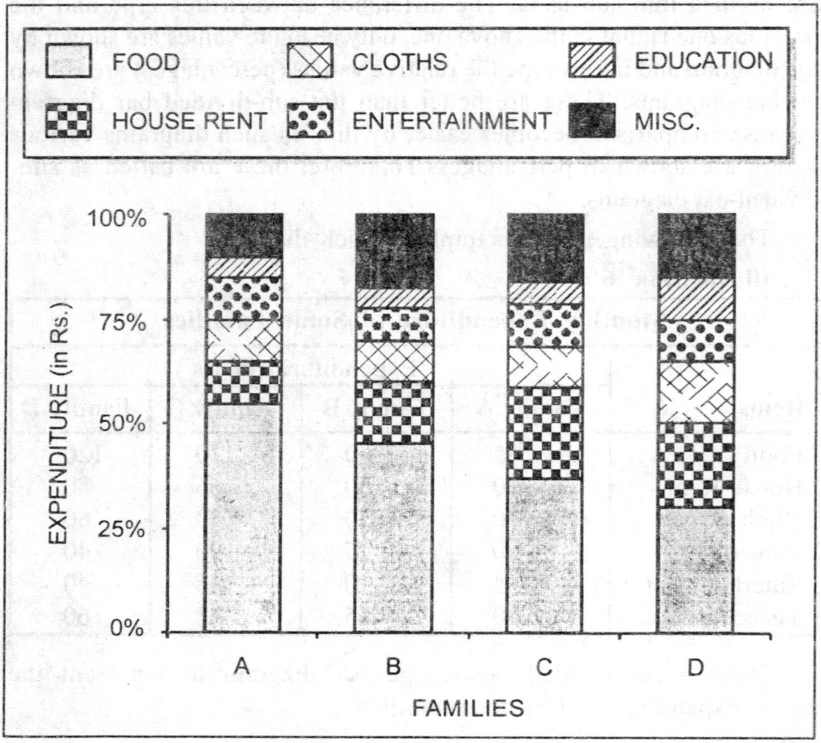


Diagram 6

**Illustration 7.** Show by suitable diagram the absolute as well as relatives change in the student population of the colleges A and B in the different departments from 1995 to 2000.

| Department | College A | | College B | |
|---|---|---|---|---|
| | 1995 | 2000 | 1995 | 2000 |
| Art | 300 | 350 | 100 | 200 |
| Science | 120 | 500 | 150 | 250 |
| Commerce | 200 | 650 | 130 | 150 |
| Law | 100 | 300 | 100 | 120 |

**Solution**

**Students' population in percentage of different departments in colleges A & B**

| Departments | College A | | | | College B | | | |
|---|---|---|---|---|---|---|---|---|
| | 1995 | | 2000 | | 1995 | | 2000 | |
| | Actual | % | Actual | % | Actual | % | Actual | % |
| Arts | 300 | 42% | 350 | 19% | 100 | 21% | 200 | 28% |
| Science | 120 | 16% | 500 | 28% | 150 | 31% | 250 | 35% |
| Commerce | 200 | 28% | 650 | 36% | 130 | 27% | 150 | 21% |
| Law | 100 | 14% | 300 | 17% | 100 | 21% | 120 | 16% |
| Total | 720 | 100% | 1800 | 100% | 480 | 100% | 720 | 100% |

**Solution**

**(A) Absolute —**

**POPULATION OF STUDENTS IN DIFFERENT DEPARTMENTS IN COLLEGE A AND B 1998 AND 2000**

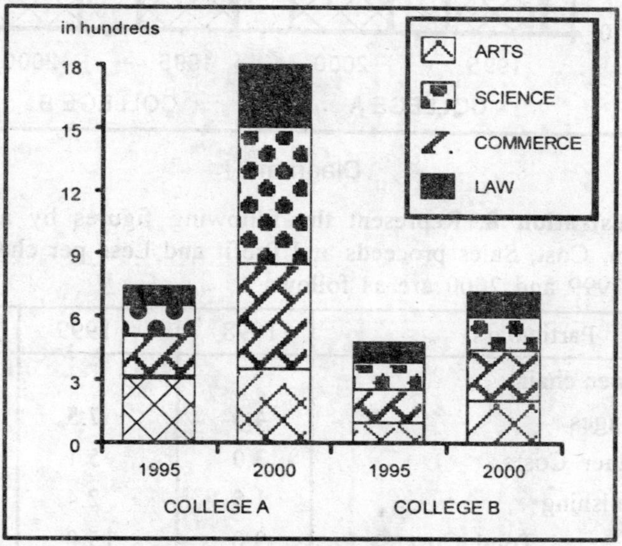


Diagram 7

Diagram 7

**(b) Relative —**

**POPULATION OF STUDENTS IN DIFFERENT DEPARTMENTS IN COLLEGE A AND B (PERCENTAGE) 1995 AND 2000**

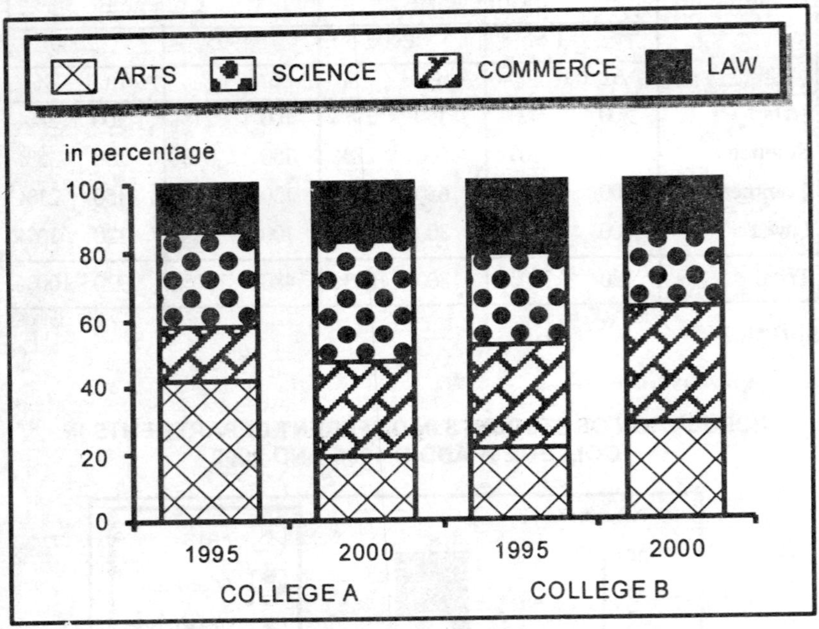


Diagram 8

**Illustration 8.** Represent the following figures by a suitable diagram. Cost, Sales proceeds and Profit and Loss per chair during 1998, 1999 and 2000 are as follows :

| Particulars | 1998 | 1999 | 2000 |
|---|---|---|---|
| Cost per chair : | | | |
| Wages | 4.5 | 7.5 | 10.5 |
| Other Costs | 3.0 | 5.1 | 7.0 |
| Polishing | 1.5 | 2.4 | 3.5 |
| Total Cost | 9.0 | 15.0 | 21.0 |
| Proceeds per Chair | 10.0 | 15.0 | 20.0 |
| Profit (+) Loss (–) per Chair | +1 | = | –1 |

(*B. Com. Agra, 1980*)

**Solution**

'Sub-divided percentage bar diagram' will be the suitable diagram to show the above data appropriately. Before making the diagram the given data will be converted into percentages in the following manner :

| Particulars | 1998 | | | 1999 | | | 2000 | | |
|---|---|---|---|---|---|---|---|---|---|
| | Rs. | Percentage | Cumulative percentage | Rs. | Percentage | Cumulative percentage | Rs. | Percentage | Cumulative percentage |
| Wages | 4.5 | 45 | 45 | 7.5 | 50 | 50 | 10.5 | 52.5 | 52.5 |
| Other Costs | 3.0 | 30 | 75 | 5.1 | 34 | 84 | 7.0 | 35.0 | 87.5 |
| Polishing | 1.5 | 15 | 90 | 2.4 | 16 | 100 | 3.5 | 17.5 | 105.0 |
| Total Cost | 9.0 | 90 | 90 | 15.0 | 100 | 100 | 21.0 | 105.0 | 105.0 |
| Profit/Loss + − | +1.0 | 10 | 10 | — | — | — | −1.0 | −5.0 | −5.0 |
| Proceeds | 10.0 | 100 | 100 | 15.0 | 100 | 100 | 20.0 | 100.0 | 100.0 |

COST, SALE, PROFIT & LOSS PER CHAIR IN PERCENTAGES

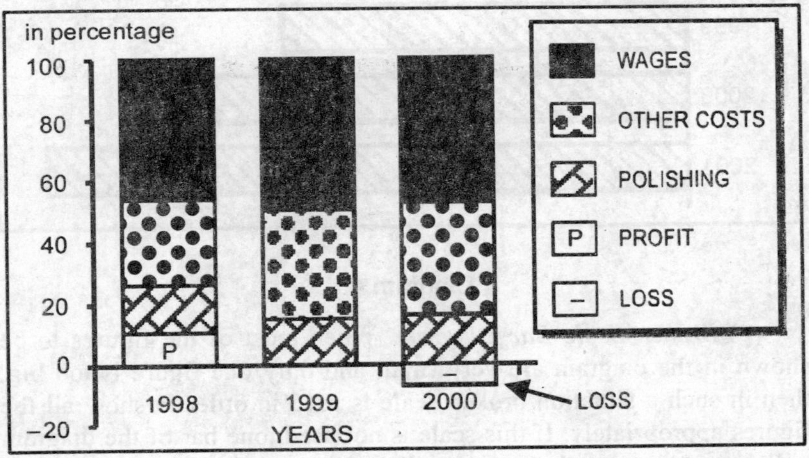


Diagram 9

(f) *Horizontal Bar Diagram*. This is like simple bar diagram with the only difference that bars instead of being vertical are in horizontal position. In these diagrams the bar-measurement is taken from above. The following illustration itself will explain this diagram.

**Illustration 9.** Construct a horizontal bar diagram from the following figures :

| | | | | | | |
|---|---|---|---|---|---|---|
| Years : | 1996 | 1997 | 1998 | 1999 | 2000 | 2001 |
| Production In Rupees (Lakhs) : | 15 | 18 | 20 | 25 | 30 | 40 |

**Solution**

**PRODUCTION 1996-2001**

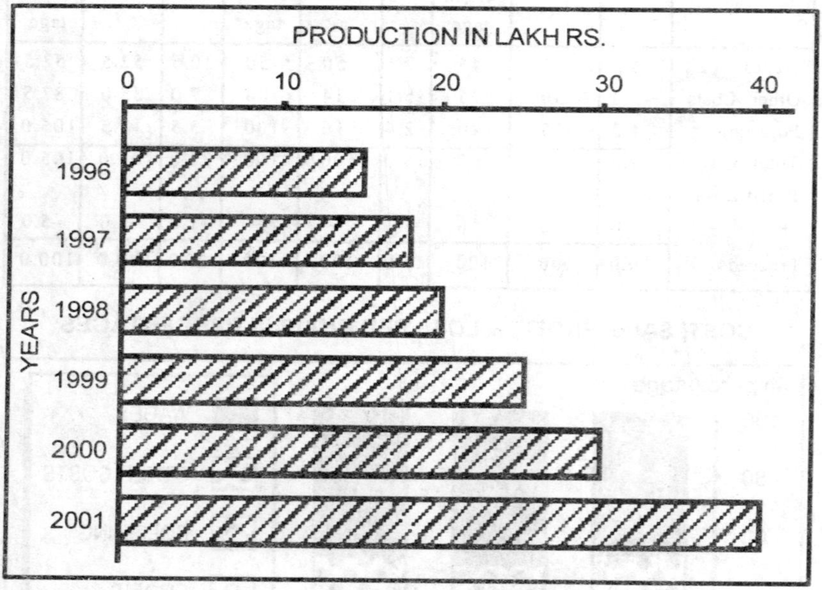


Diagram 10

(g) *Broken Scale Bar Diagram.* When most of the figures to be shown in the diagram are very small and only one figure is too big, then in such a situation broken scale is used in order to show all the figures appropriately. If this scale is not used, one bar of the diagram will be too long and the rest will be too small. Therefore to give proper shape to all the bars, this diagram is used. The following illustration will explain this diagram.

**Illustration 10.** Represent the following data with a suitable diagram :

| | | | | | | | | |
|---|---|---|---|---|---|---|---|---|
| Firms | : | A | B | C | D | E | F | G |
| Profits in ('000 Rs.) | : | 5 | 8 | 10 | 12 | 15 | 20 | 95 |

**Solution**

PROFITS OF FIRMS (IN '000 RUPEES)

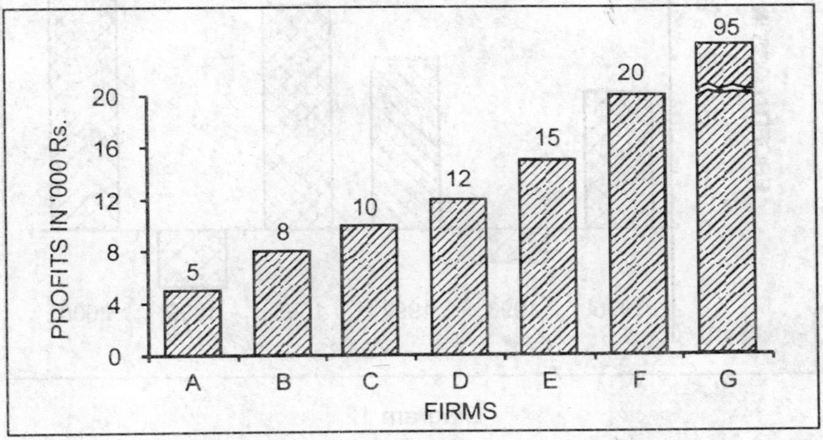


Diagram 11

(h) *Duo-Directionai or Dialateral Bar Diagram.* When the given data are of both positive and negative type dialateral bar diagrams are made in order to show them properly. In these diagrams, bars are made both above and below the zero point, hence they are called duo-directional bar diagrams. Bar above the zero point are positive figures and below are negative figures. The following illustration will explain this.

**Illustration 11.** Represent the following data by a suitable diagram :

| | | | | | | | |
|---|---|---|---|---|---|---|---|
| Years | : | 1995 | 1996 | 1997 | 1998 | 1999 | 2000 |
| Profit/Loss + – (in '000 Rs.) | : | 12 | –3 | 15 | 20 | –5 | 30 |

**Solution**

PROFIT/LOSS 1995-2000 (IN '000 Rs.)

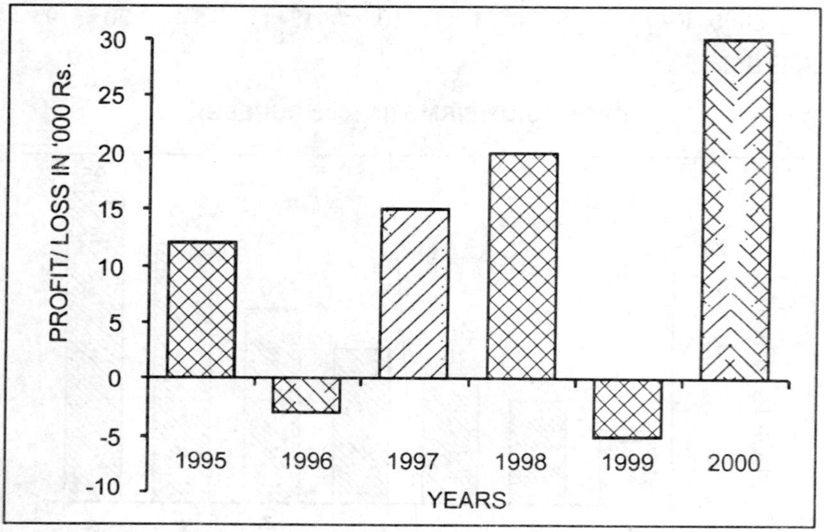


Diagram 12

(i) *Pyramid Diagram*. This diagram is used to show two related facts. The shape of this Diagram is like a pyramid. Hence it is called Pyramid Diagram. To make this diagram, a vertical line is drawn in the middle of the base line and on both the sides of the vertical line horizontal bars are made. This diagram is used to show facts about population-division, employment etc. This is good to look at. The following illustration will explain this.

**Illustration 12.** Following are the figures regarding student population in a college in last 5 years :

| Years | : | 1996 | 1997 | 1998 | 1999 | 2000 |
|---|---|---|---|---|---|---|
| Male Students | : | 250 | 320 | 400 | 450 | 500 |
| Female Students | : | 150 | 180 | 250 | 300 | 400 |
| Total | : | 400 | 500 | 650 | 750 | 900 |

Represent the above figures with a suitable diagram.

**Solution**

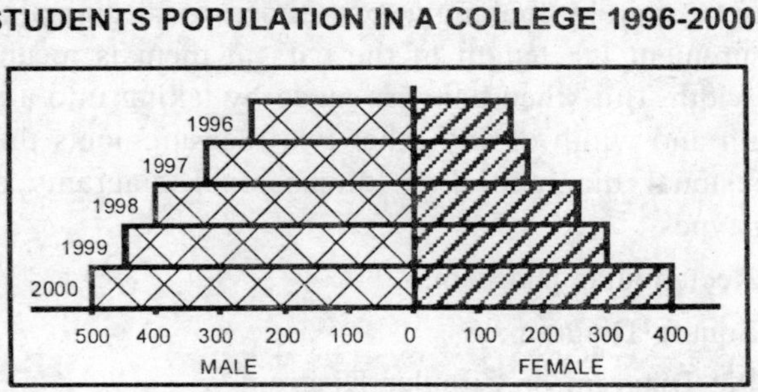


Diagram 13

(j) *Deviation Bar Diagram*. When the difference of two facts is shown in the diagram, that is called by this name. This diagram is used to show such facts as business payment, balance, income-expenditure cost-sale etc. Following is given a sample of this diagram.

**Illustration 13.** Represent the following data through a deviation bar diagram :

| | | | | | | | |
|---|---|---|---|---|---|---|---|
| Years | : | 1996 | 1997 | 1998 | 1999 | 2000 | 2001 |
| Budgeted Expenditures in lakh (Rs.) | : | 5 | 8 | 10 | 15 | 19 | 23 |
| Budgeted sources of Income in lakh (Rs.) | : | 4 | 6 | 13 | 20 | 15 | 30 |

**Solution**

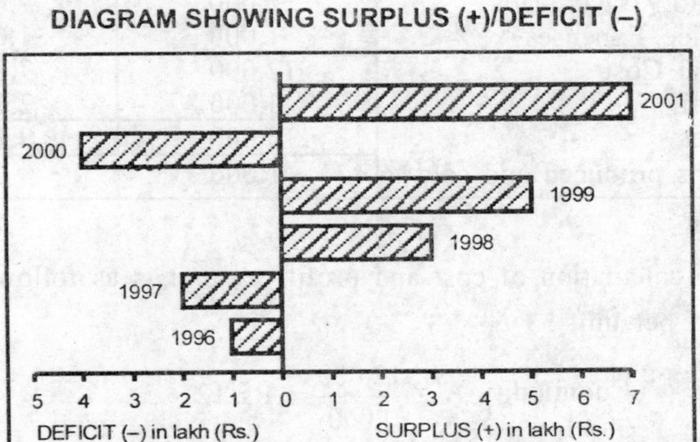


Diagram 14

## 2. Two-Dimensional Diagram

It may be seen by looking at one dimensional diagrams that only one measurement *i.e.* length of the bars in them is meaningful and not their width. But when bars are made by taking into account both their length and width or any other two measurements that is called two-dimensional diagram. Two dimensional diagrams are of the following types :

(a) Rectangular Diagram.

(b) Square Diagram.

(c) Pie Diagram or Circular Diagram.

(d) Angular Diagram.

**(a) Rectangular Diagram.** In this type of diagram bars of various length and width are made. The area of length and width differs in proportion to facts that are to be presented. This type is divided into two sub-types —

(i) *Absolute Diagram.* In absolute diagrams actual data are delineated by such rectangles as have different areas in proportion to various items. Following is the illustration of absolute diagram.

**Illustration 14.** Draw a diagram from the following data calculating the cost and profit per unit of each commodity :

| Cost/Sales | Commodity A Rs. | Commodity B Rs. |
|---|---|---|
| Material | 5,000 | 3,000 |
| Labour | 4,000 | 2,000 |
| Factory Overheads | 2,000 | 1,000 |
| Office Expenses | 1,000 | 1,000 |
| Total Cost | 12,000 | 7,000 |
| Profit | 3,000 | 2,100 |
| Sales | 15,000 | 9,100 |
| Units produced and sold | 1,000 | 700 |

**Solution**

The calculation of cost and profit per unit is as follows :

Cost per unit :

$$\text{Commodity A : } \frac{12,000}{1,000} = \text{Rs. } 12$$

$$\text{Commodity B : } \frac{7,000}{700} = \text{Rs. } 10$$

Profit per unit :

$$\text{Commodity A} : \frac{3{,}000}{1{,}000} = \text{Rs. } 3$$

$$\text{Commodity B} : \frac{2{,}100}{700} = \text{Rs. } 3$$

The above facts may be represented by diagram as follows :

**COST AND PROFIT PER UNIT OF COMMODITIES A AND B**

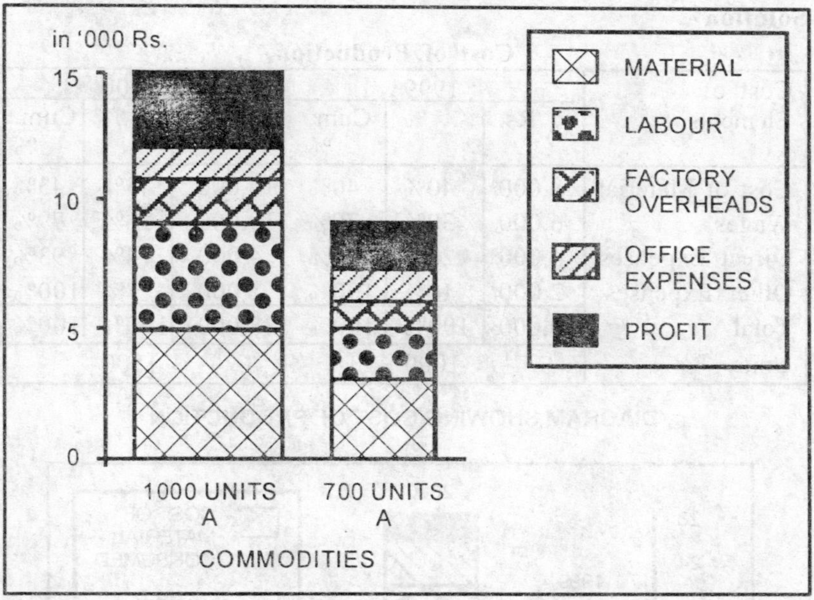


Diagram 15

(ii) *Relative Diagram.* Such diagrams are drawn to compare two or more facts. The percentage of items are shown in such diagrams. Following illustrations will make clear the form of such diagrams.

**Illustration 15.** Prepare a rectangular diagram for the following data :

Cost of production of a commodity :

| | 1999 Rs. | 2000 Rs. |
|---|---|---|
| (i) Cost of material consumed | 8,000 | 13,000 |
| (ii) Wages | 6,000 | 10,000 |
| (iii) Direct Expenses | 4,000 | 5,000 |
| (iv) Other Expenses | 2,000 | 2,000 |
| (v) The number of units produced | 1000 (units) | 1500 (units) |

**Solution**

**Cost of Production**

| Cost of Elements | 1999 | | | 2000 | | |
|---|---|---|---|---|---|---|
| | Rs. | % | Cum. % | Rs. | % | Cum. % |
| Cost of Material | 8,000 | 40% | 40% | 12,000 | 43% | 43% |
| Wages | 6,000 | 30% | 70% | 10,000 | 36% | 79% |
| Direct Expenses | 4,000 | 20% | 90% | 4,000 | 14% | 93% |
| Other Expenses | 2,000 | 10% | 100% | 2,000 | 7% | 100% |
| Total | 20,000 | 100% | 100% | 28,000 | 100% | 100% |
| Units | | 1000 | | | 1500 | |

**DIAGRAM SHOWING COST OF PRODUCTION**

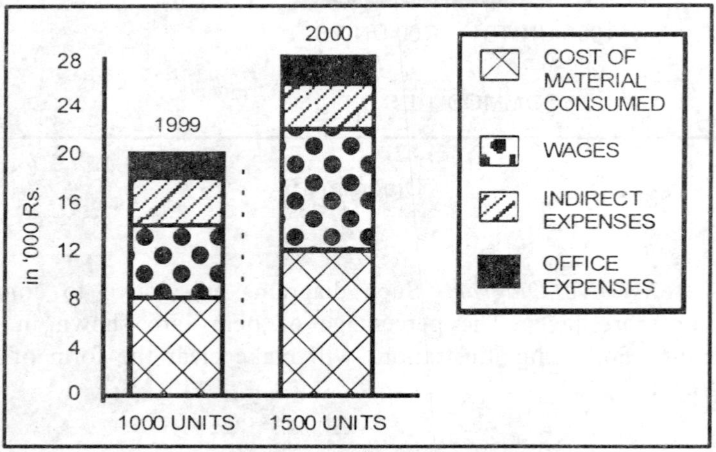


Diagram 16

**Illustration 16.** Show the details of monthly expenditure of two families given below by means of two-dimensional diagram.

| Items of Expenditure | Family A Income Rs. 500 P.M. Rs. | Family B Income Rs. 400 P.M. Rs. |
|---|---|---|
| Food | 140 | 120 |
| Clothing | 80 | 80 |
| House Rent | 100 | 60 |
| Education | 30 | 40 |
| Fuel & Lighting | 40 | 20 |
| Miscellaneous | 40 | 40 |

**Solution**

**Monthly expenditure in percentage**

| Items of Expenditure | Family A Income Rs. 500 P.M. | | Family B Income Rs. 400 P.M. | |
|---|---|---|---|---|
| | Actual Rs. | % | Actual Rs. | % |
| Food | 140 | 33% | 120 | 33% |
| Clothing | 80 | 19% | 80 | 22% |
| House Rent | 100 | 23% | 60 | 17% |
| Education | 30 | 7% | 40 | 11% |
| Fuel & Lighting | 40 | 9% | 20 | 6% |
| Miscellaneous | 40 | 9% | 40 | 11% |
| Total | 430 | 100% | 360 | 100% |

**PERCENTAGE EXPENDITURE OF TWO FAMILIES**

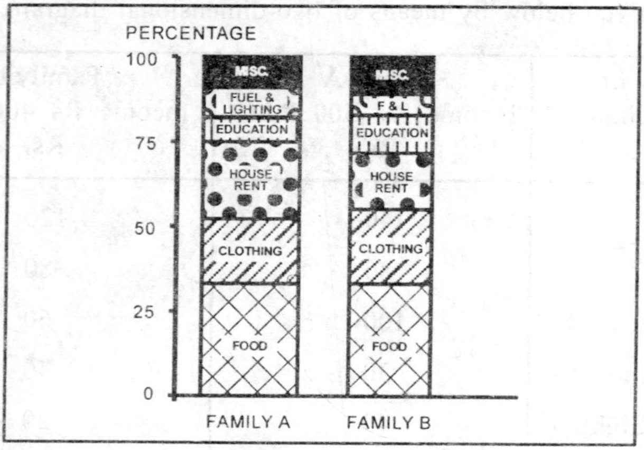


Diagram 17

**(b) Square Diagram :** When differences among various figures are too many, it is difficult to show them through rectangles because one rectangle of the diagram becomes too big and the others becomes too small. To avoid facing such difficulty, square diagrams are made. Under this type of diagram, square roots of facts or their mutual proportions are found which is the measurement of their length and breadth. Facts then are shown by making the squares of the same length and breadth. For example, in order to actually shown the incomes of two persons with Rs. 5 and Rs. 500, the bar or rectangle showing the income of the second person will be 100 times bigger than the first one's which will be rather inappropriate. Therefore, we have to find their proportion first which is 1 : 100 and then the square root of 1 and 100 which will be 1 : 10. This proportion will be presumed as the scale of one arm of the square diagram and on the basis of this the square-diagram will be completed. The following illustration contains a sample of square diagram.

**Illustration 17.** Draw a suitable diagram for the following data :

| City | A | B | C | D |
|---|---|---|---|---|
| Population | 16,00,000 | 4,00,000 | 1,44,000 | 64,000 |

**Solution**

There is very big difference between lowest value and highest value in the given data of population, therefore, square diagram is suitable for this problem.

**Calculation of Square Root**

| City | Population | Ratio | Square Root |
|---|---|---|---|
| A | 16,00,000 | 100 | 10 |
| B | 4,00,000 | 25 | 5 |
| C | 1,44,000 | 9 | 3 |
| D | 64,000 | 4 | 2 |

These square roots may be shown by a diagram as follows :

**POPULATION OF SOME CITIES**

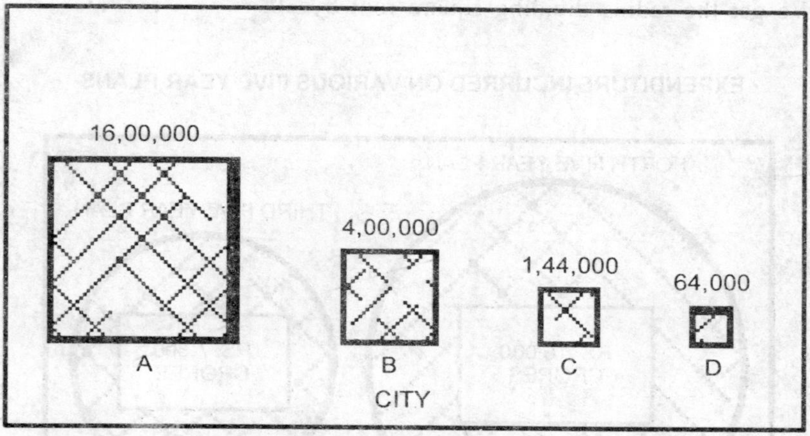


Diagram 18

**(c) Pie or Circular Diagram :** When figures are shown in circles that is called circular diagram. Circular diagrams look beautiful and attractive in appearance to construct such diagrams. Square roots of figures are found and the same square root becomes the radius of the circle. Following is an illustration of circular diagram.

**Illustration 18.** Represent the following data through pie diagram :

| Five Year Plan | Expenditure (in Crore Rs.) |
|---|---|
| First Five-Year Plan | 1,960 |
| Second Five-Year Plan | 4,600 |
| Third Five-Year Plan | 7,500 |
| Fourth Five-Year Plan | 16,000 |

**Solution**

**Calculation of Radius**

| Five Year Plans | Expenditure (in Crores) Rs. | Square root | Radius in cm. |
|---|---|---|---|
| First Plan | 1,960 | 44.27 | 1.5 |
| Second Plan | 4,600 | 67.82 | 2.26 |
| Third Plan | 7,500 | 86.60 | 2.9 |
| Fourth Plan | 16,000 | 126.49 | 4.2 |

We get the radius dividing square root by 30.

**EXPENDITURE INCURRED ON VARIOUS FIVE YEAR PLANS**

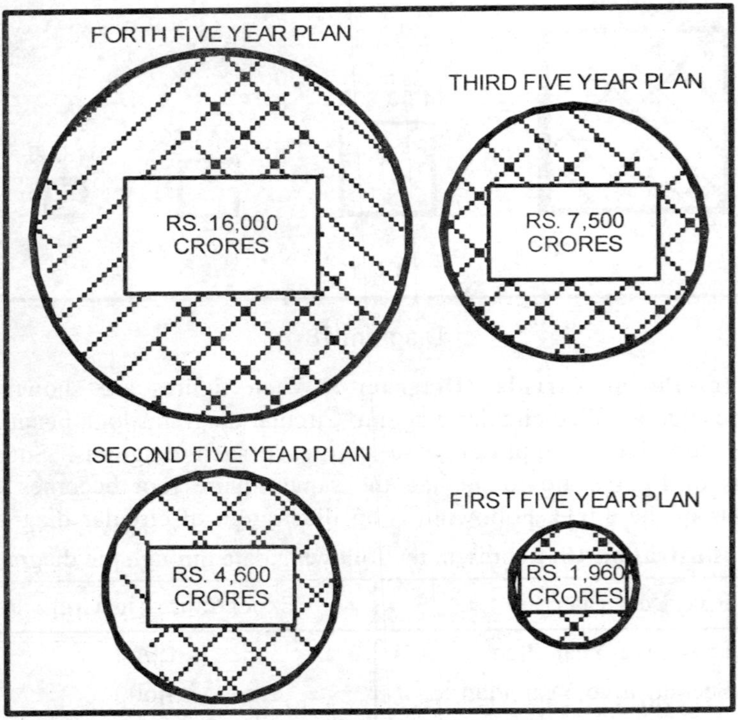


Diagram 19

**(d) Angular Diagram.** When circular diagram is divided proportionately according to various items that is called angular diagram. A circle consists of 360° in all and these degrees are angularly divided into various facts. The following formula is applied to divide the circle :

$$\frac{\text{Value of any Item}}{\text{Total Value of all}} \times 360°$$

This will give the degree of the angle of that item.

**Illustration 19.** Given below are the data relating to the expenditure of three families.

| Items of expenditure | Family A Rs. | Family B Rs. | Family C Rs. |
|---|---|---|---|
| Food | 12.0 | 30.0 | 90.0 |
| Clothing | 2.0 | 7.0 | 35.0 |
| Rent | 2.0 | 8.0 | 40.0 |
| Education | 1.50 | 3.0 | 12.0 |
| Litigation | 5.0 | 5.0 | 40.0 |
| Conventional necessaries | .50 | 3.0 | 60.0 |
| Miscellaneous | 1.00 | 4.0 | 23.0 |

Represent the above data by Angular Diagram.

**Solution**

**Calculation of radius of various circles and degrees of angles**

| Items of expenditure | Family A | | Family B | | Family C | |
|---|---|---|---|---|---|---|
| | Rs. | Degree of angles | Rs. | Degree of angles | Rs. | Degree of angles |
| Food | 12.0 | 180° | 30.0 | 180° | 90.0 | 108° |
| Clothing | 2.0 | 30° | 7.0 | 42° | 35.0 | 42° |
| Rent | 2.0 | 30° | 8.0 | 48° | 40.0 | 48° |
| Education | 1.50 | 22.5° | 3.0 | 18° | 12.0 | 14.4° |
| Litigation | 5.00 | 75° | 5.0 | 30° | 40.0 | 48° |
| Conventional necessaries | .50 | 7.5° | 3.0 | 18° | 60.0 | 72° |
| Miscellaneous | 1.00 | 15° | 4.0 | 24° | 23.0 | 27.6° |
| Total | 24.00 | 360° | 60.0 | 360° | 300.0 | ·360° |
| Square root | 4.9 | | 7.75 | | 17.32 | |
| Measurement of radius in cm. | 1.6 | | 2.6 | | 5.8 | |

**ITEMWISE EXPENDITURE OF THREE FAMILIES**

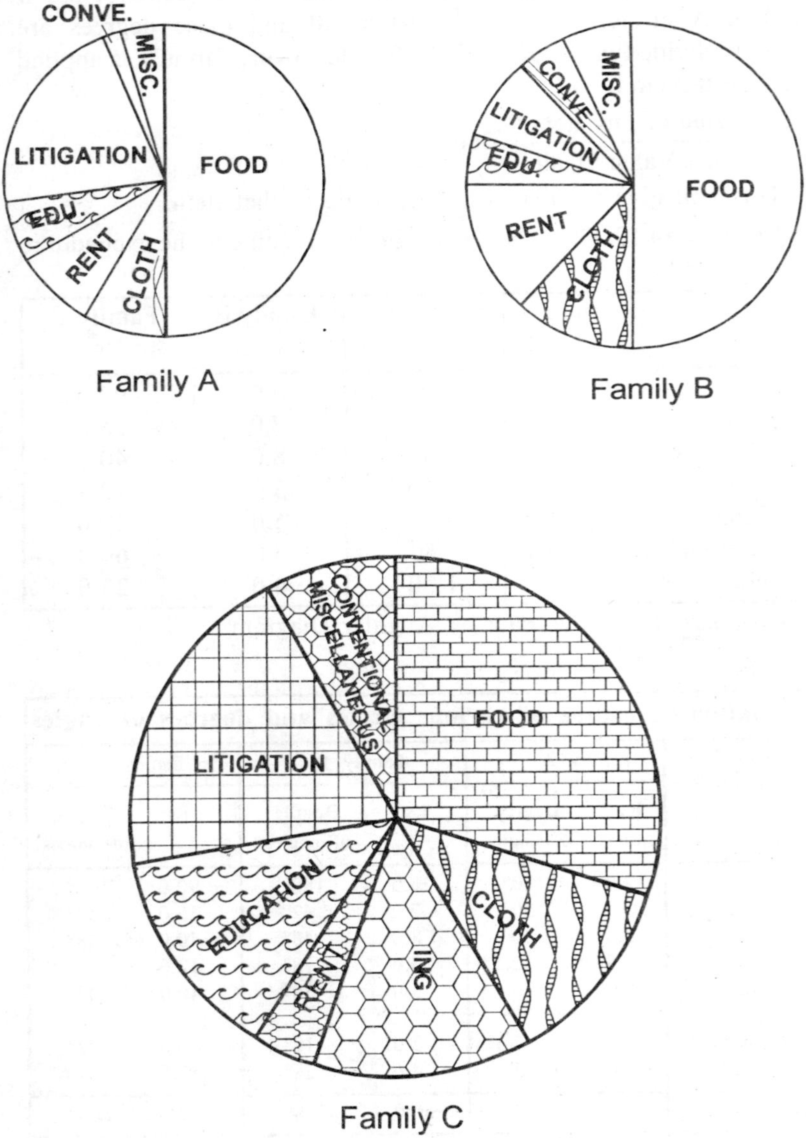


Diagram 20

**Illustration 20.** A, B, C and D are partners in a partnership firm sharing profits and losses in the ratio of 4 : 3 : 2 : 1 respectively. The firm earned a profit of Rs. 14,400 for the year ending 31st December, 2000. Draw a Pie Diagram to show the profits earned by different partners.

[*B. Com.* (*Pass*), *Delhi*]

**Solution**

SHARE IN PROFITS OF A FIRM OF
A, B, C, D (PARTNERS) IN RS.

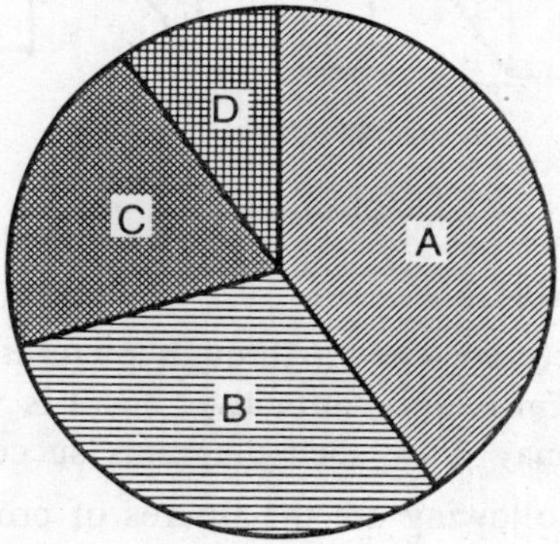


Diagram 21

### 3. Three Dimensional Diagrams

In this type of diagram all the three measurements of length, width and height taken into consideration. These diagrams are difficult to make. In order to make such diagram, the cube-root of figures is found first and then after taking suitable measurements of the cube-roots, diagrams are made.

**Illustration 21.** Draw a three-dimensional diagram for representing the following data :

| Companies : | A | B | C | D |
|---|---|---|---|---|
| Production (in thousand tons) : | 27 | 125 | 343 | 512 |

**Solution**

| Company | Production in (thousand tons) | Cube roots | Side of Cube |
|---|---|---|---|
| A | 27 | 3 | .3″ |
| B | 125 | 5 | .5″ |
| C | 343 | 7 | .7″ |
| D | 512 | 8 | .8″ |

**PRODUCTION OF FOUR COMPANIES**

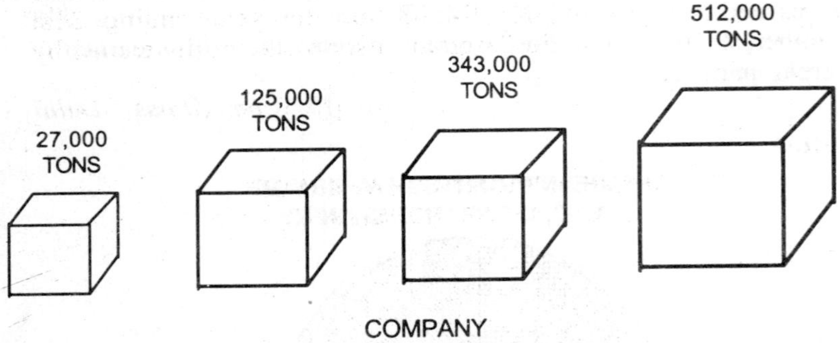


Diagram 22

**4. Pictograms or Pictures**

When various facts are shown through pictures, that is called pictogram. This diagram is quite attractive, but it is very difficult to draw. A good artist may draw such diagrams successfully.

**Illustration 22.** Following are the figures of production of cars in different years of a company :

| Years | : | 1996 | 1997 | 1998 | 1999 | 2000 |
|---|---|---|---|---|---|---|
| Production (in lakhs) | : | 2 | 3 | 5 | 6 | 7 |

**CARS PRODUCTION OF A Co. 1996-2000**

Diagram 23

## 5. Cartograms or Maps

When facts are presented through maps, that is called cartographic presentation. This is also a difficult type of diagram. Here, below is an example of cartographic presentation.

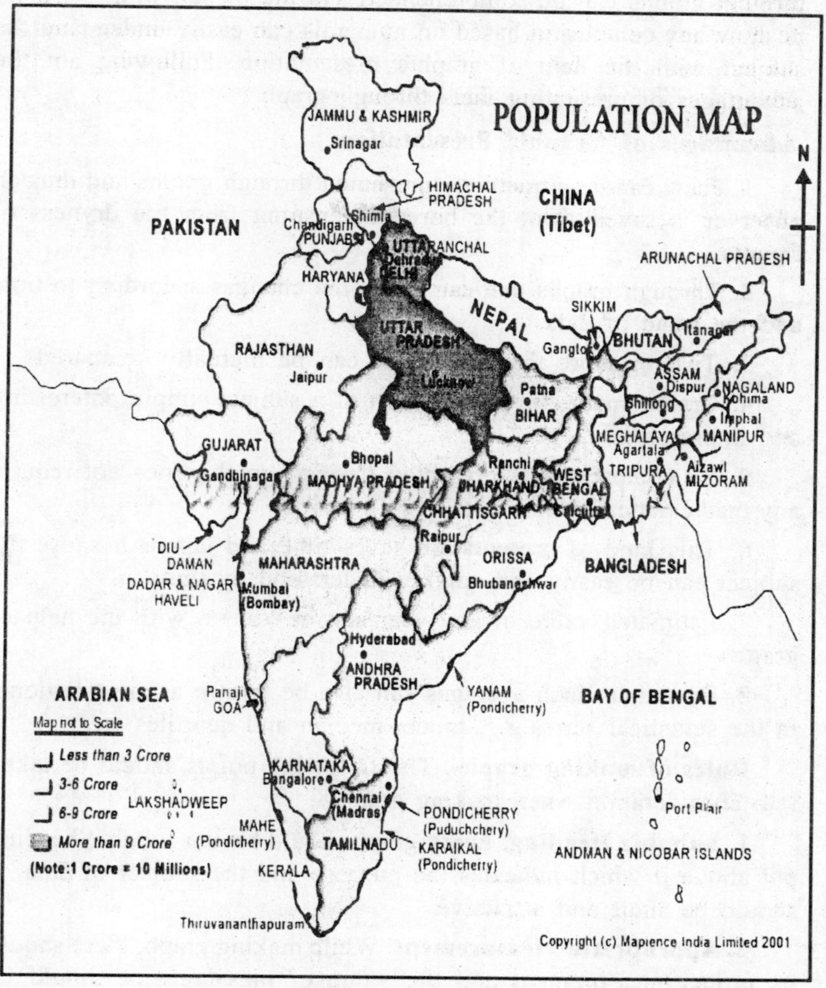


MAP

## PRESENTATION OF DATA THROUGH GRAPHS

Just as data are presented through diagrams, data can also be presented through graphs. When graph-sheets are used to make diagrams we call it 'Presentation through Graph'. Facts presented through graphs can be comprehended and the person who is unable to draw any conclusion based on numerals can easily understand the subject with the help of graphic presentation. Following are the advantages of presenting facts through graph :

**Advantages of Graphic Presentation**

1. Facts can be attractively presented through graphs and thus an observer is saved from the boredom ensuing from the dryness of figures.

2. Through graphs one can know the changes according to time and the trend of data.

3. Two or more than two facts can be mutually compared.

4. Graphs make the presentation of a subject simple, interesting and impressive.

5. To compare facts presented through graphs does not require any mathematical skill.

6. This kind of presentation saves time and labour because the subject can be easily and quickly understood by this.

7. Estimated value of any year can be known with the help of graphs.

8. By graphs such averages can also be known as are positional in the statistical series *e.g.* mode, median and quartiles etc.

**Rules of making graphs.** The following points should be taken into consideration when making graphs :

**1. Suitable Heading.** Every graph should have a suitable heading put above it which indicates the purpose and the subject of data. It should be short and attractive.

**2. Appropriate Measurement.** While making graph, there should be proper measurement and the value of measurement should be written in the graph.

**3. Attractive construction of graph.** Graphs should be made neat, beautiful and attractive. Lines should be drawn straight and clear.

**4. Use of false base line.** If the values of dependent variables are big than in such a situation false base line should be used.

**5. Signs :** In the graph, signs about various lines as to what line shows what fact should be given.

**Graph Paper.** Graphs are made on graph-paper. The graph-paper consists of small square columns which are generally 1/10″ or 1/10 centimeter in size. In making graphs on graph-paper independent variables are shown on the baseline. It is on the horizontal line and is also called X-axis. Dependent data are shown on the vertical line which is called ordinate or Y-axis. The point where the horizontal and the vertical line cut each other is called point of origin. Taking this point to be of 0 (zero) value, independent values are written toward right of X-axis and dependent values are written upward on the Y-axis. The point of origin divides the graph-paper in four parts which are called quadrants. Related facts in a graph paper are explained in graph number 1 as below :

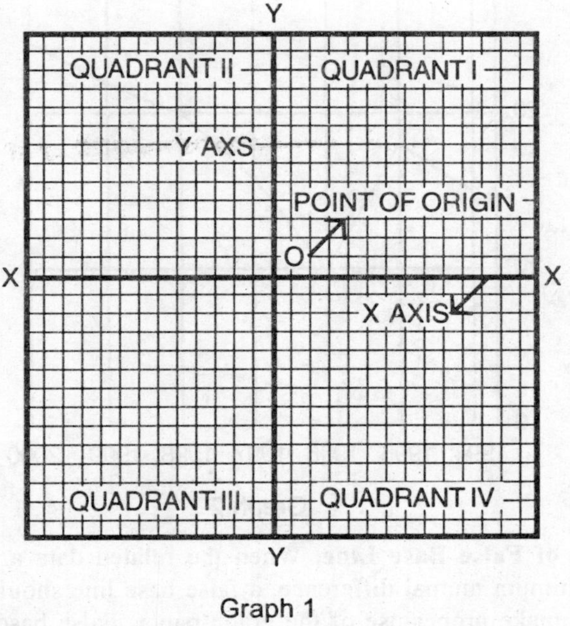


Graph 1

**Types of Graphs.** Graphs are of the following types :

1. Graphs of time-series or Historigram.
2. Graphs of Frequency Distribution

**1. Graphs of Time Series or Historigram.** Values based on time and shown by graphs are called graphs of time-series *e.g.* graph of prices, graphs of productions of various times etc. In making graphs of time series, time is shown on X-axis and values related to them are shown on Y-axis. Taking 0 (zero) on the point of origin values are taken upward on the Y-axis and to the right on the X-axis. The sample of this type of graphs is as follows.

**Illustration 23.** Represent the following data graphically :

| | | | | | | | |
|---|---|---|---|---|---|---|---|
| Years | 1999 | 1995 | 1996 | 1997 | 1998 | 1999 | 2000 |
| Expenditure (in thousands of Rs.) | 15 | 18 | 10 | 16 | 20 | 22 | 25 |

**Solution**

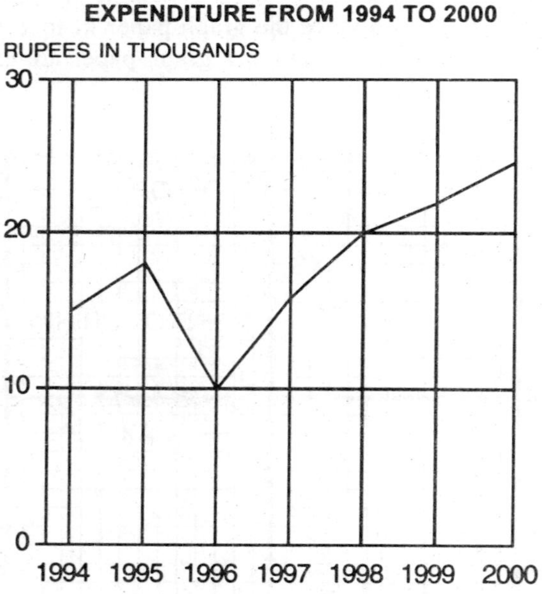


Graph 2

**Use of False Base Line.** When the related data are very large with minimum mutual difference, a false base line should be used in order to make proper use of the graph-paper. False base line can be made by drawing a zig-zag line and just above this line the smallest figure or any number nearer to it from among the given figures is written and then the values next to it are written. The whole graph-paper is divided for the value equal to the difference between the biggest and the smallest data. This makes the graph clear and correct. If false base line is not used, graphs of very big numbers will be very difficult to make and the graph will be made on the upper portion of graph-paper and most of the portion of lower region will remain empty. The advantages of the false base line will be explained by the following illustration.

**Illustration 24.** You are given the data of industrial output of some years.

| Years | : | 1990 | 1991 | 1992 | 1993 | 1994 | 1995 | 1996 | 1997 | 1998 | 1999 |
|---|---|---|---|---|---|---|---|---|---|---|---|
| Output (in thousand tons) | : | 55 | 58 | 56 | 55 | 60 | 58 | 59 | 57 | 55 | 60 |

**Solution**

INDUSTRIAL OUTPUT FROM 1990 TO 1999

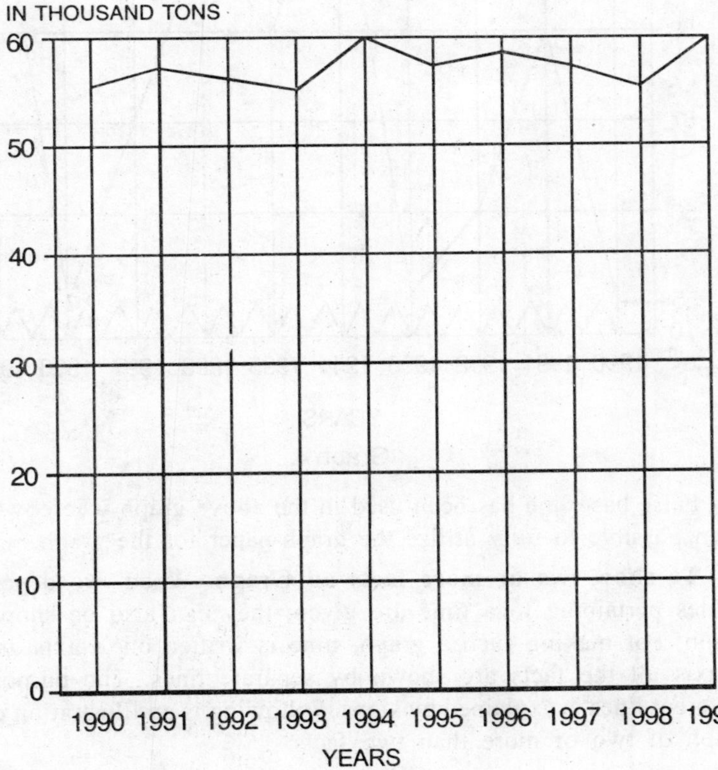


Graph 3

If the above data is recorded on the graph-paper without using the false base line the graph will be like the above graph 3. It is clear from this graph that the full graph sheet remains unutilized and the graph also looks unattractive. Because the values in this data are very large and the difference also between the smallest and the biggest is 60 – 65 = 5. Therefore, it is better to show such facts with the help of false base line by which the following graph will emerge :

**INDUSTRIAL OUTPUT FROM 1990 TO 1999**

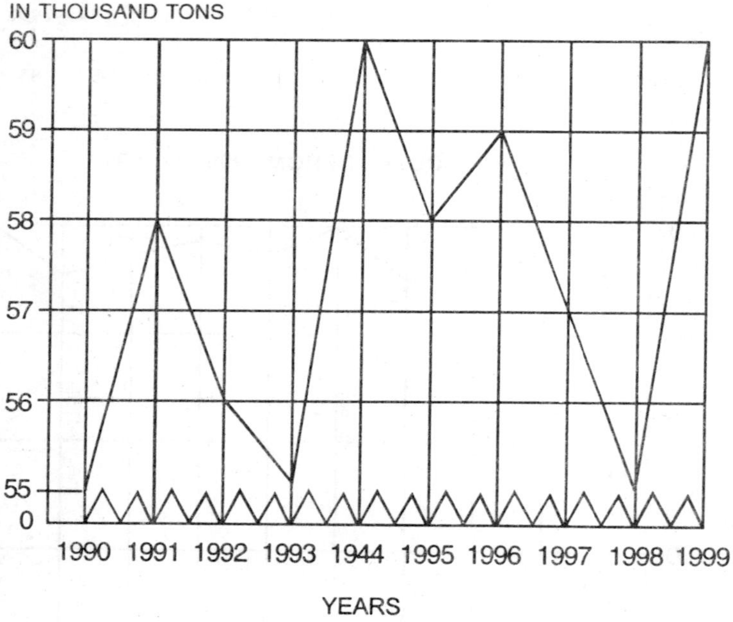


Graph 4

False base line has been used in the above graph whereby it has been possible to fully utilize the graph-paper for the graph.

**To show two or more facts on Graph.** When two dependent values pertaining to a time are given, they can also be shown by graph. For making such a graph, time is written on X-axis and on Y-axis all the facts are shown by separate lines. The purpose of different lines is explained by signs. Following is an illustration of the graph of two or more than two facts.

**Illustration 25.** Represent the following figures by a graph :

| Years : | 1990 | 1991 | 1992 | 1993 | 1994 | 1995 | 1996 | 1997 | 1998 | 1999 | 2000 |
|---|---|---|---|---|---|---|---|---|---|---|---|
| Demand : | 100 | 110 | 120 | 125 | 110 | 115 | 130 | 135 | 140 | 125 | 150 |
| Supply : | 100 | 108 | 102 | 105 | 108 | 110 | 125 | 135 | 150 | 130 | 160 |

**Solution**

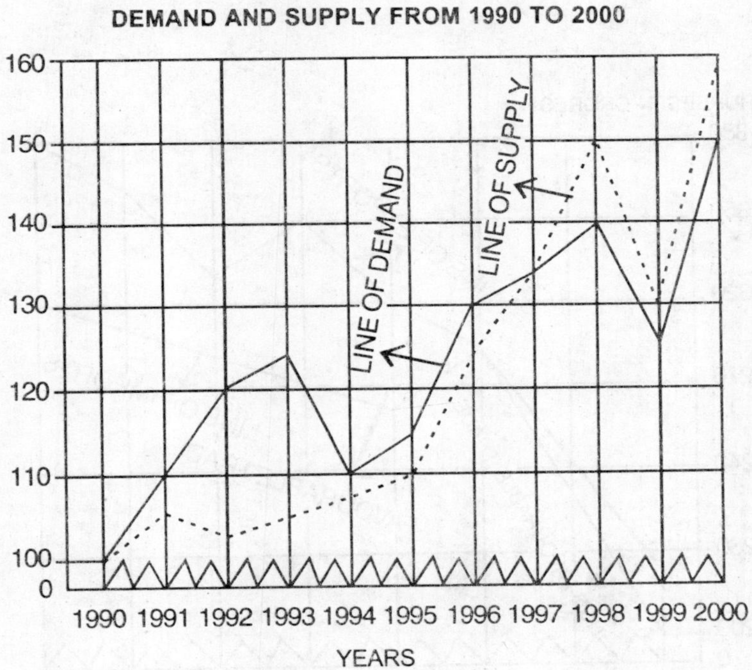


Graph 5

**Illustration 26.** Represent the following data graphically :

| Years | Export (in crores Rs.) | Import (in crores Rs.) | Balance of trade (in crores Rs.) |
|---|---|---|---|
| 1993 | 200 | 220 | –20 |
| 1994 | 250 | 260 | –10 |
| 1995 | 300 | 300 | 0 |
| 1996 | 320 | 280 | +40 |
| 1997 | 350 | 290 | +60 |
| 1998 | 330 | 300 | +30 |
| 1999 | 360 | 310 | +50 |
| 2000 | 380 | 320 | +60 |

**Solution**

### EXPORTS — IMPORTS AND BALANCE OF TRADE FROM 1993 TO 2000

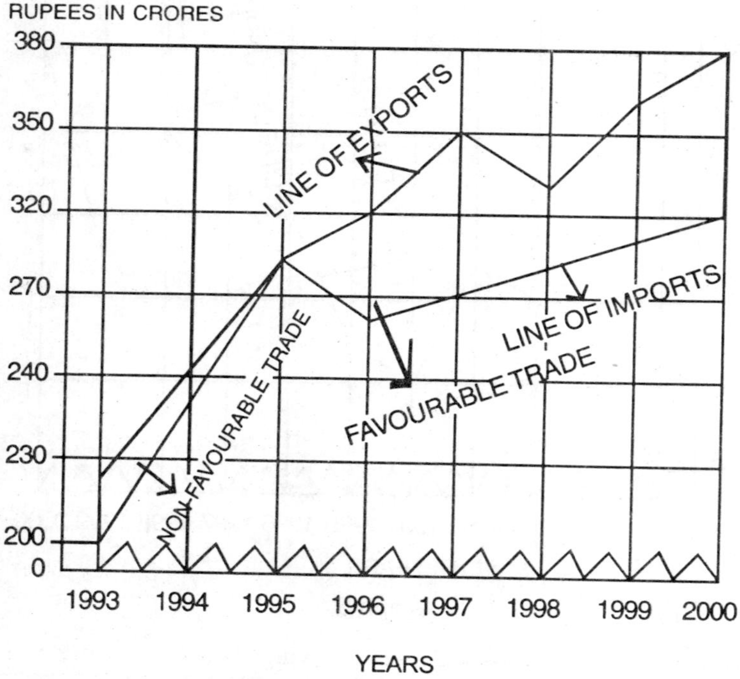


Graph 6

The example can be shown by the following graph also :

**EXPORTS-IMPORTS AND BALANCE OF TRADE FROM 1993 TO 2000**

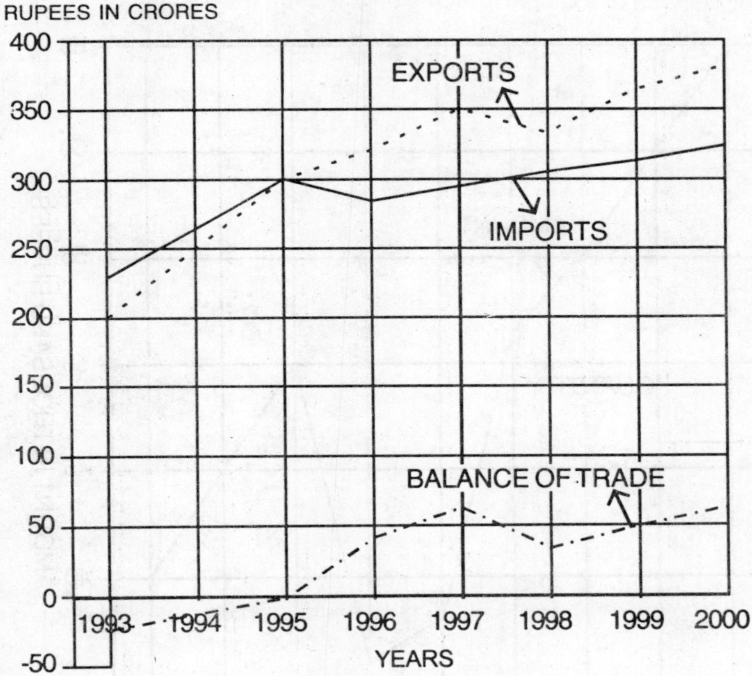


Graph 7

**Two-Dimensional Graphs.** Two variables pertaining to the same time given in different units can also be shown or presented by graph. Following is an example of this type of graphs :

**Illustration 27.** Draw a graph for the following data :

| Years | Production Quantity (Quintals) | Amount (Rs.) |
|---|---|---|
| 1992 | 320 | 40,000 |
| 1993 | 330 | 45,000 |
| 1994 | 350 | 50,000 |
| 1995 | 390 | 35,000 |
| 1996 | 310 | 38,000 |
| 1997 | 360 | 52,000 |
| 1998 | 370 | 55,000 |
| 1999 | 400 | 60,000 |
| 2000 | 420 | 65,000 |

**Solution**

**PRODUCTION FROM 1992 TO 2000 IN QUANTITY AND AMOUNT**

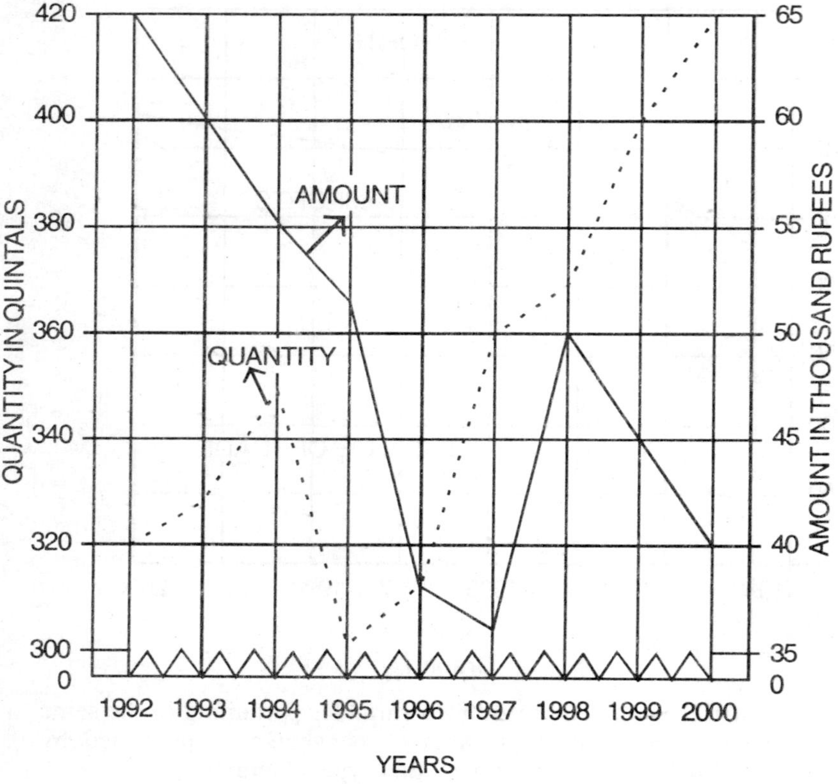


Graph 8

**Illustration 28.** Prepare a graph from the following data by using false base :

Consumer Price Index Numbers (1990 = 100)

| Year | 1995 | 1996 | 1997 | 1998 | 1999 | 2000 |
|---|---|---|---|---|---|---|
| All India | 177 | 186 | 192 | 207 | 250 | 360 |
| Delhi | 185 | 199 | 211 | 222 | 265 | 337 |

[*B. Com.* (*Pass*), *Delhi*]

**Solution**

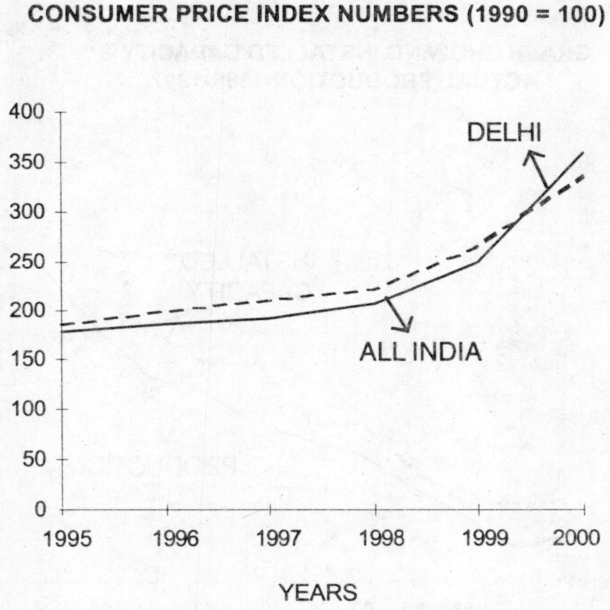


Graph 9

**Illustration 29.** Construct a suitable diagram from the following time series :

| Year | Installed Capacity (in Metric Tons) | Production (in Metric Tons) | Year | Installed Capacity (in Metric Tons) | Production (in Metric Tons) |
|---|---|---|---|---|---|
| 1985 | 10.500 | 10,000 | 1992 | 15,000 | 13,000 |
| 1986 | 10,500 | 9,500 | 1993 | 15,000 | 14,000 |
| 1987 | 10,500 | 9,000 | 1994 | 16,000 | 14,500 |
| 1988 | 10,500 | 10,000 | 1995 | 16,000 | 16,000 |
| 1989 | 11,500 | 11,000 | 1996 | 20,000 | 18,000 |
| 1990 | 13,000 | 12,000 | 1997 | 20,000 | 19,000 |
| 1991 | 13,000 | 12,500 | | | |

[*B. Com.* (*Pass*), *Delhi*]

**Solution**

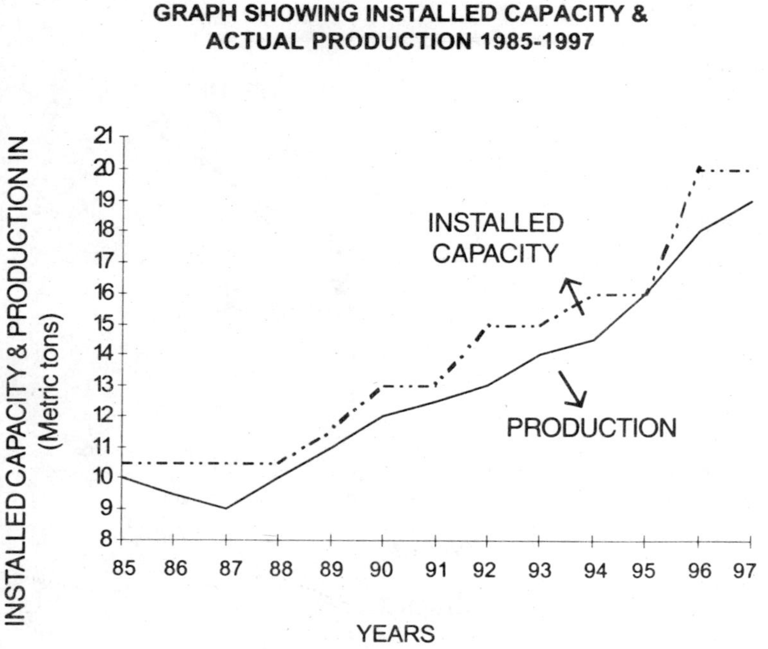


Graph 10

## Ratio Scale and Logarithmic Curve

This type of curves is used for the purpose of comparison, *i.e.* when in the graph, not the actual or absolute but relative values are shown, the scale taken in ratio, logarithms of the given values of the scale are found and the same (logarithms) are drawn on the graph. This gives a clear idea of charges having taken place at different times. This types of graph is also called Semi-Logarithmic Curve because on its X-axis the scale is actual and on Y-axis the scale is on the base of logarithms. The following example will explain this curve.

**Illustration 30.** A firm reported that it net worth in the years 1995-96 to 1999-2000 was as follows :

| Year : | 1995-96 | 96-97 | 97-98 | 98-99 | 99-2000 |
|---|---|---|---|---|---|
| Net Worth : | 100 | 112 | 120 | 133 | 147 |

Plot the above data in the form of a semi-logarithmic graph. Can you say anything about the approximate rate of growth of its net worth?

[*B.A.* (*Hons.*), *Eco. Delhi*]

**Solution**

| Years | Net Worth | Logs |
|---|---|---|
| 1995-96 | 100 | 2.0000 |
| 96-97 | 112 | 2.0492 |
| 97-98 | 120 | 2.0792 |
| 98-99 | 133 | 2.1239 |
| 99-2000 | 147 | 2.1673 |

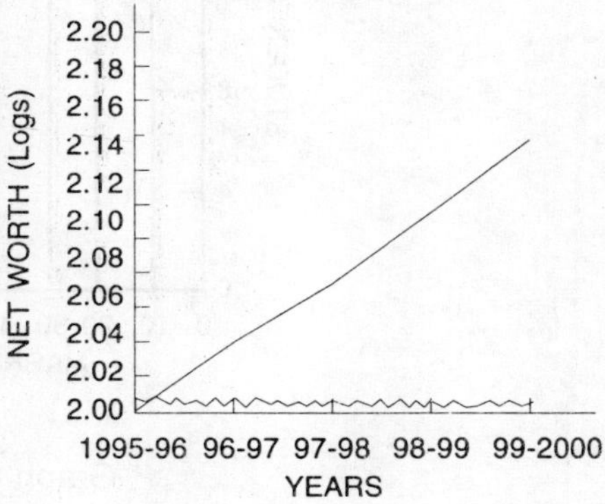


**2. Graphs of Frequency Distribution.** Statistical series can also be presented through graphs and their positional averages can be determined. Following graphs are made regarding statistical series :

1. Histogram;
2. Frequency Polygon;
3. Frequency Curve;
4. Cumulative Frequency Curve of OGIVE;
5. Galton Curve.

**1. Histogram.** This type of graphs are made to draw continuous series. For each class-interval a rectangle is made and the area of all these rectangles differs in proportion according to the frequency of various class-intervals. Rectangles of all class-intervals are made close to each other. Below is an example of this type of graph :

**Illustration 31.** Draw a histogram from the following series :

| Marks : | 0-10 | 10-20 | 20-30 | 30-40 | 40-50 | 50-60 | 60-70 |
|---|---|---|---|---|---|---|---|
| No. of Students : | 8 | 12 | 15 | 20 | 16 | 12 | 6 |

**Solution**

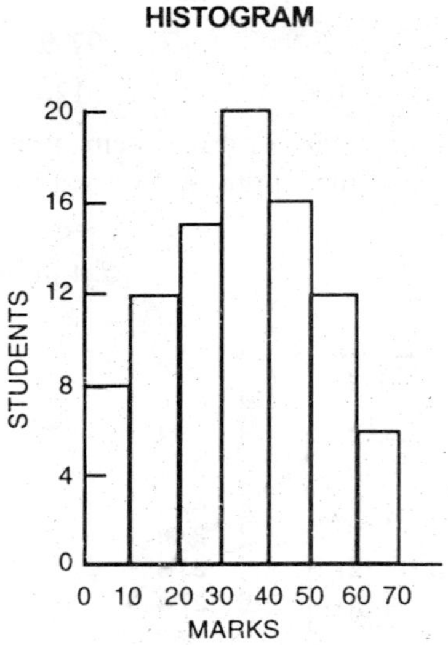


Graph 11

**Calculation of mode with the help of Histogram**

By histogram rectangles the value of mode can also be determined. In order to find out the value of mode, the upper edges of the tallest rectangle connected with the upper edges of the rectangles which are before and after the tallest one by two lines which cross each other. From the point where the two lines cross each other, a perpendicular is drawn on the base line and the value of the point of the base line where the perpendicular line meets is found and that is mode. The method of finding mode through histogram is explained in graph No. 12 below.

**Illustration 32.** Find mode from the following data with the help of histogram :

| | | | | | | |
|---|---|---|---|---|---|---|
| Groups : | 0-5 | 5-10 | 10-15 | 15-20 | 20-25 | 25-30 |
| Frequency : | 6 | 9 | 15 | 13 | 12 | 5 |

**Solution**

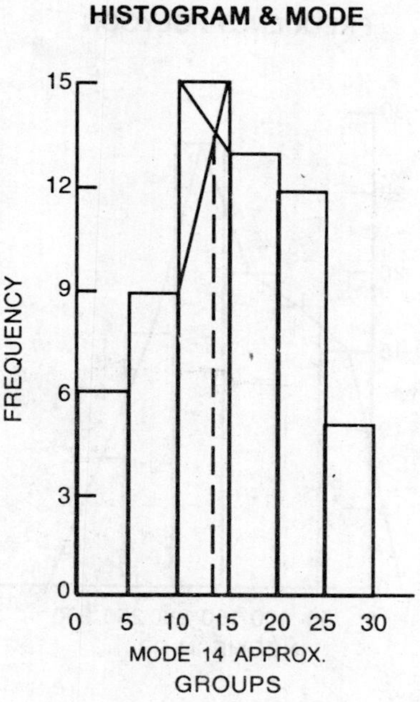


Graph 12

**2. Frequency Polygon.** Continuous series can also be presented on the graph by frequency polygon. Histogram are made first for making frequency polygon. When the mid-points of all the rectangles are connected with each other by line, that is called frequency polygon. The example of frequency polygon is given in graph No. 13 below.

**Illustration 33.** Prepare a frequency polygon from the following data :

| Income (Rs.) | No. of Persons |
|---|---|
| 0- 50 | 15 |
| 50-100 | 18 |
| 100-150 | 20 |
| 150-200 | 28 |
| 200-250 | 16 |
| 250-300 | 8 |

**Solution**

FREQUENCY POLYGON

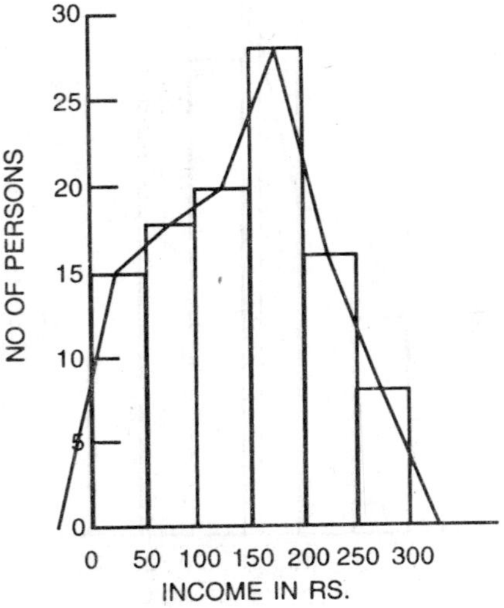


Graph 13

**3. Frequency Curve.** This is a freehand curve. When the angularities of the frequency polygon are done away with and a curve is formed, that is known as 'frequency curve'. There is no fixed scale for this kind of curve. The point to be taken into consideration in this connection is the curve be so formed that it shows the same area as are shown by histogram or frequency polygon of the concerned statistical series. In order to form frequency curves also, the histogram have to be formed. The following example will explain frequency curves.

**Illustration 34.** Draw a frequency curve from the following data :

| Groups | Frequency |
|---|---|
| 0- 8 | 25 |
| 8-16 | 28 |
| 16-24 | 30 |
| 24-32 | 26 |
| 32-40 | 18 |

**Solution**

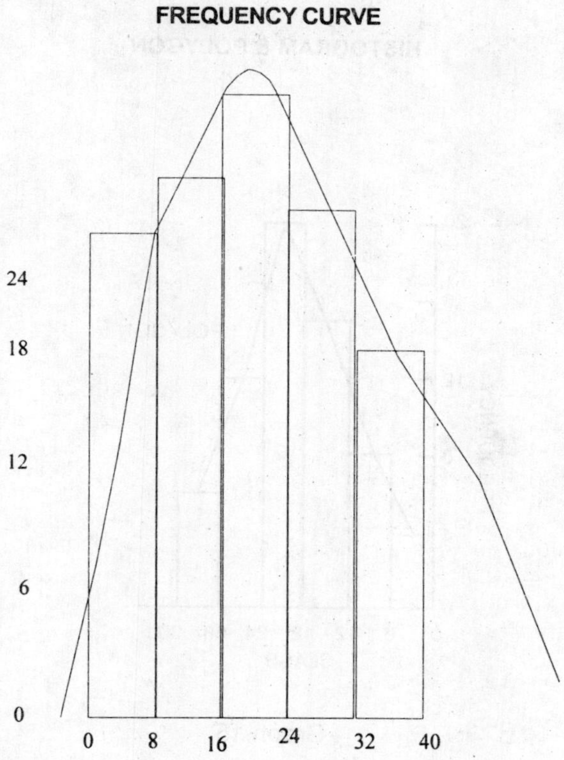


Graph 14

**Illustration 35.** Prepare a Histogram and a Frequency Polygon from the following data :

| | | | | | | |
|---|---|---|---|---|---|---|
| Class : | 0-6 | 6-12 | 12-18 | 18-24 | 24-30 | 30-36 |
| Frequency : | 4 | 8 | 15 | 20 | 12 | 6 |

[*B. Com.* (*Pass*), *Delhi*]

**Solution**

HISTOGRAM & POLYGON

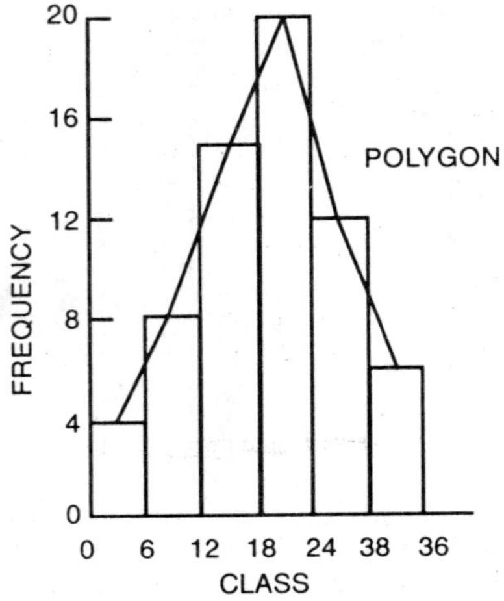


Graph 15

**Illustration 36.** Draw a Histogram from the following figures :

| | | | | | | |
|---|---|---|---|---|---|---|
| Class Intervals : | 0-20 | 20-40 | 40-60 | 60-80 | 80-100 | 100-120 |
| Frequency : | 5 | 8 | 12 | 18 | 20 | 25 |

**Solution**

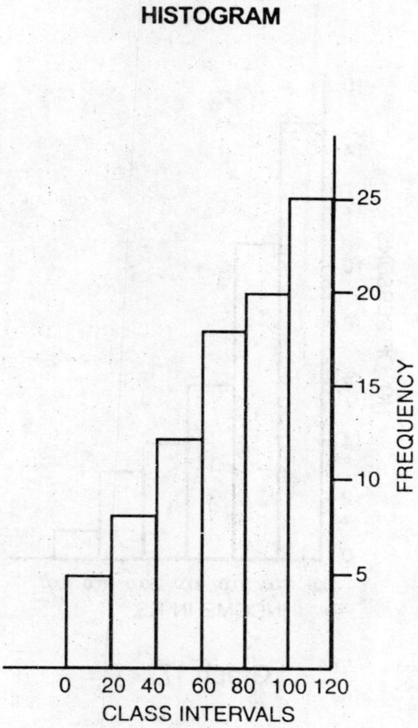


Graph 16

**Illustration 37.** Draw a Histogram from the following data :

| | | | |
|---|---|---|---|
| Income in Rs. : | 1,000-2,000 | 2,000-3,000 | 3,000-4,000 |
| No. of Persons : | 15 | 11 | 6 |
| Income in Rs. : | 4,000-5,000 | 5,000-6,000 | 6,000-7,000 |
| No. of Persons : | 4 | 3 | 1 |

**Solution**

HISTOGRAM

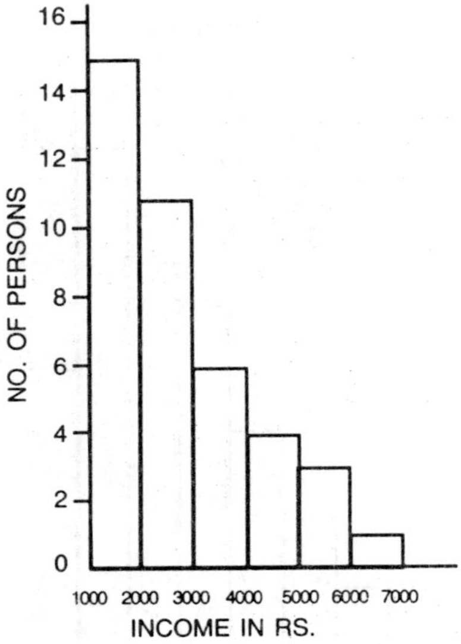


Graph 17

**Histogram for unequal class intervals**

**Illustration 38.** Construct a Histogram for the following data :

| | | | | | | | | |
|---|---|---|---|---|---|---|---|---|
| Class | : | 0-10 | 10-20 | 20-40 | 40-50 | 50-60 | 60-70 |
| Frequency | : | 4 | 6 | 14 | 16 | 14 | 8 |
| Class | : | 70-90 | 90-100 | | | | |
| Frequency | : | 16 | 5 | | | | |

[*B. Com.* (*Pass*), *Delhi*]

**Solution**

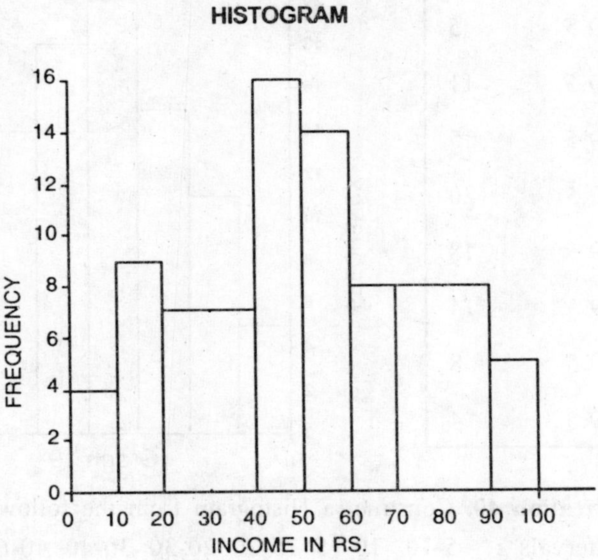


Graph 18

**Histogram for inclusive series**

**Illustration 39.** Draw a Histogram from the following data :

| | | | | | | |
|---|---|---|---|---|---|---|
| Class Intervals : | 10-19 | 20-29 | 30-39 | 40-49 | 50-59 | 60-69 |
| Frequency : | 5 | 11 | 15 | 20 | 18 | 14 |
| Class Intervals : | 70-79 | 80-89 | | | | |
| Frequency : | 8 | 4 | | | | |

**Solution**

The above statistical series is an inclusive continuous series. In order to form frequency curve this has to be changed first into exclusive continuous series in the manner given below and thereafter this will be formed into Histogram in the usual way :

| C.I. | F |
|---|---|
| 9.5-19.5 | 5 |
| 19.5-29.5 | 11 |
| 29.5-39.5 | 15 |
| 39.5-49.5 | 20 |
| 49.5-59.5 | 18 |
| 59.5-69.5 | 14 |
| 69.5-79.5 | 8 |
| 79.5-89.5 | 4 |

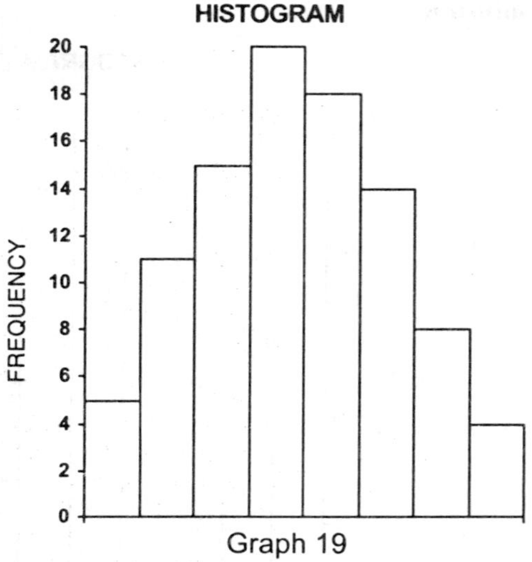

Graph 19

**Illustration 40.** Construct a Histogram from the following data :

| | | | | | | | |
|---|---|---|---|---|---|---|---|
| Class Intervals : | 5-10 | 10-15 | 15-20 | 20-30 | 30-40 | 40-60 | 60-100 |
| Frequency : | 6 | 10 | 16 | 30 | 24 | 32 | 40 |

[*C.A.* (*Old Couse*)]

**Solution**

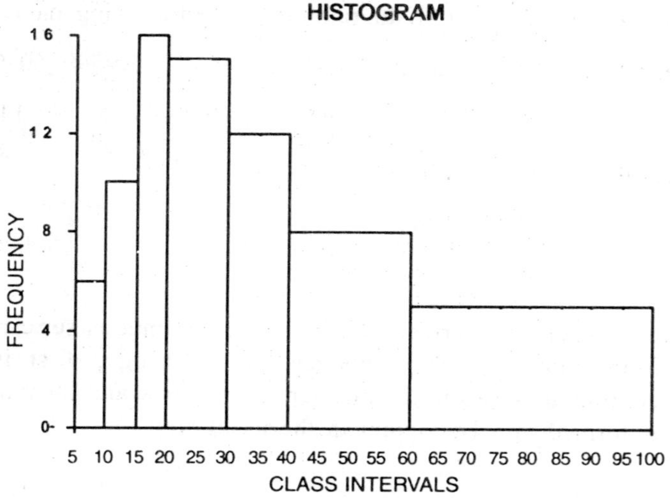

Graph 20

**4. Cumulative Frequency Curve or Ogive.** When cumulative frequencies are marked on the graph-paper, curves formed in relation thereof are called cumulative frequency curve. In order to form this graph first of all the cumulative frequencies are formed and marked on the graph-paper. Generally cumulative frequency curves are made to know the median and the values of quartiles etc. which are related to median.

From the following examples the method of forming cumulative frequency curve and the method of finding median and quartiles from that will be explained.

**Illustration 41.** Draw a cumulative frequency curve and find median from the following :

| Class intervals : | 0-10 | 10-20 | 20-30 | 30-40 | 40-50 | 50-60 |
|---|---|---|---|---|---|---|
| Frequency : | 13 | 8 | 6 | 25 | 12 | 26 |

**Solution**

| Class Intervals | Frequency | Cumulative frequency Distribution (Less than order) | |
|---|---|---|---|
| | | Cf. | |
| 0-10 | 13 | Below 10 | 13 |
| 10-20 | 8 | " 20 | 21 |
| 20-30 | 16 | " 30 | 37 |
| 30-40 | 25 | " 40 | 62 |
| 40-50 | 12 | " 50 | 74 |
| 50-60 | 26 | " 60 | 100 |

Middle Value $= \text{Value of } \frac{n}{2} \text{th item}$

$= \text{Value of } \frac{100}{2} \text{th item}$

$=$ Value of 50th item

**CUMULATIVE FREQUENCY CURVE OR OGIVE & MEDIAN**

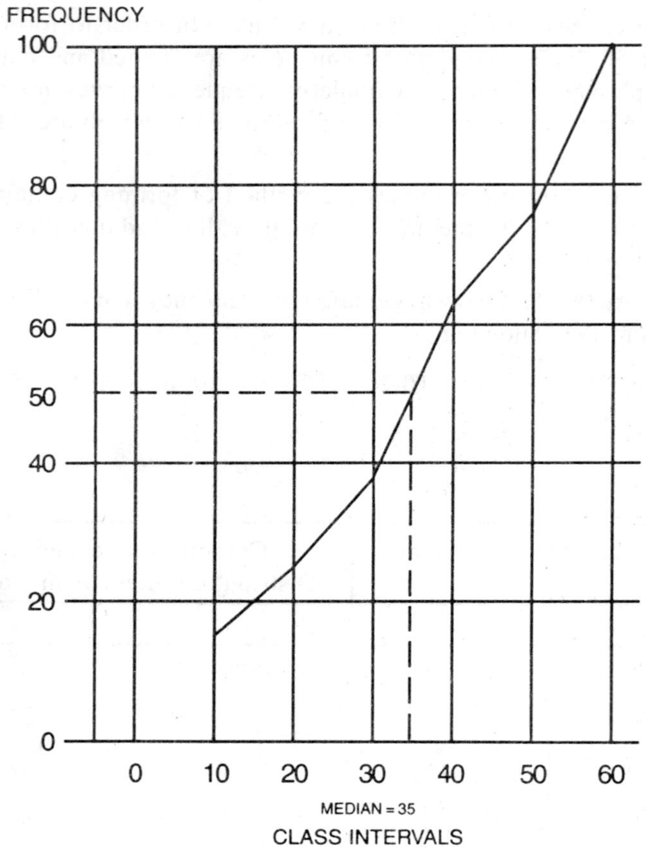


Graph 21

**Illustration 42.** Draw 'More Than' and 'Less Than' ogives from the following figures :

| | | | | | | | | |
|---|---|---|---|---|---|---|---|---|
| Marks | : | 0-10 | 10-20 | 20-30 | 30-40 | 40-50 | 50-60 | 60-70 |
| No. of Students | : | 5 | 12 | 17 | 32 | 17 | 11 | 6 |

**Solution**

First of all the above series will be changed into 'Less Than' or 'More Than' Cumulative frequency distribution as follows :

| 'Less Than' Cumulative Frequency Distribution | | 'More Than' Cumulative Frequency Distribution | |
|---|---|---|---|
| Marks | No. of Students | Marks | No. of Students |
| Less than 10 | 5 | More than 0 | 100 |
| Less than 20 | 17 | More than 10 | 95 |
| Less than 30 | 34 | More than 20 | 83 |
| Less than 40 | 66 | More than 30 | 66 |
| Less than 50 | 83 | More than 40 | 34 |
| Less than 60 | 94 | More than 50 | 17 |
| Less than 70 | 100 | More than 60 | 6 |

The 'Less Than' and 'More Than' curve from the above cumulative frequency distribution will be formed in the manner given below :

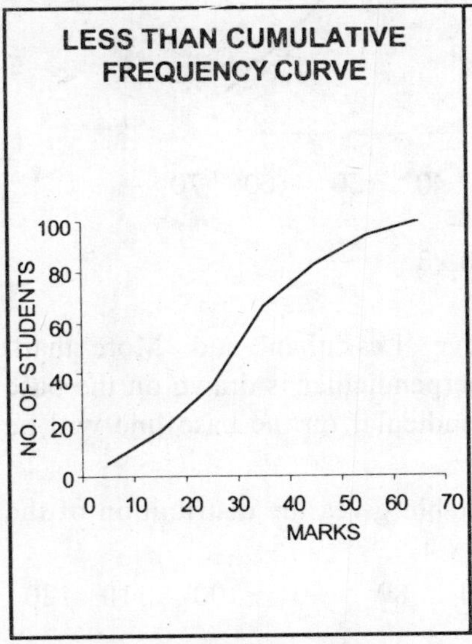


Graph 22 (a)

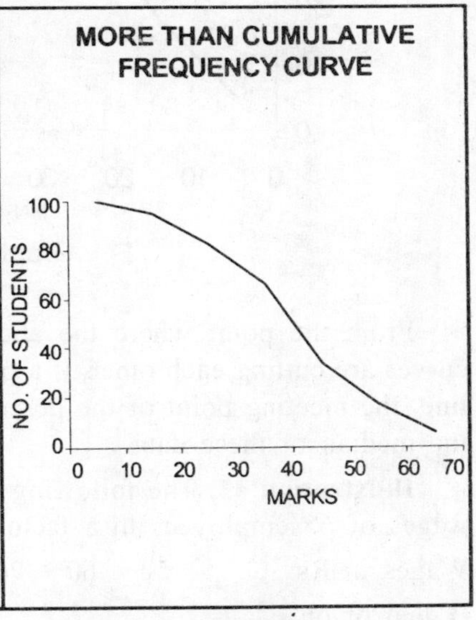


Graph 22 (b)

Both the above curves can be formed on a single graph-paper in the following way :

**CUMULATIVE FREQUENCY CURVES**

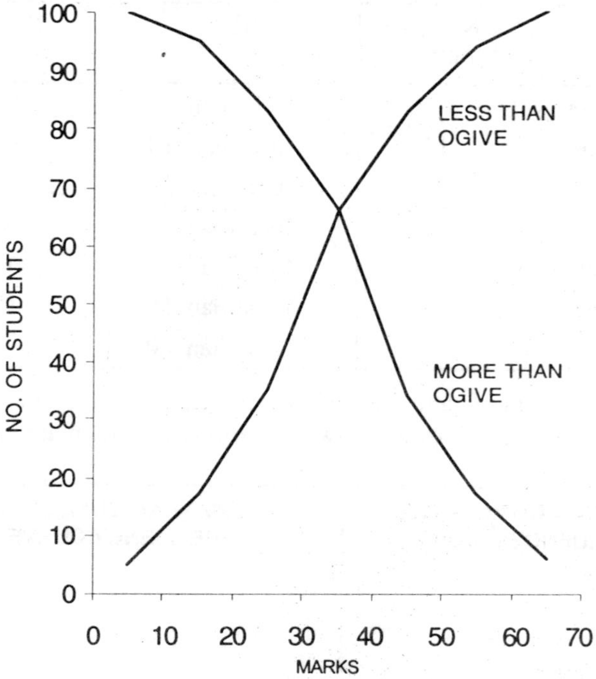


Graph 23

From the point where the above 'Less than' and 'More than' curves are cutting each other, if a perpendicular is drawn on the base line, the meeting point of the perpendicular on the base line will be the median of these data.

**Illustration 43.** The following table gives the distribution of the wages of 65 employees in a factory :

| | | | | | | | | |
|---|---|---|---|---|---|---|---|---|
| Wages in Rs. (Equal of or more than) : | 50 | 60 | 70 | 80 | 90 | 100 | 110 | 120 |
| No. of employees : | 65 | 57 | 47 | 31 | 17 | 7 | 2 | 0 |

Draw a 'less than' curve from the above data.

[*B. Com.* (*Pass*) *Delhi*]

**Solution**

The above data have first to be changed into ordinary continuous series in the following way :

| Wages in Rs. | Number of Employees |
|---|---|
| 50-60 | 8 |
| 60-70 | 10 |
| 70-80 | 16 |
| 80-90 | 14 |
| 90-100 | 10 |
| 100-110 | 5 |
| 110-120 | 2 |
| 120-130 | 0 |
| Total | 65 |

The above figures will be converted in 'less than cumulative frequency distribution' and following graph will be drawn from these values :

Less Than Cumulative Frequency Distribution

| Wages in Rs. | No. of Employees |
|---|---|
| Less than 60 | 8 |
| Less than 70 | 18 |
| Less than 80 | 34 |
| Less than 90 | 48 |
| Less than 100 | 58 |
| Less than 110 | 63 |
| Less than 120 | 65 |
| Less than 130 | 65 |

LESS THAN CUMULATIVE FREQUENCY CURVE

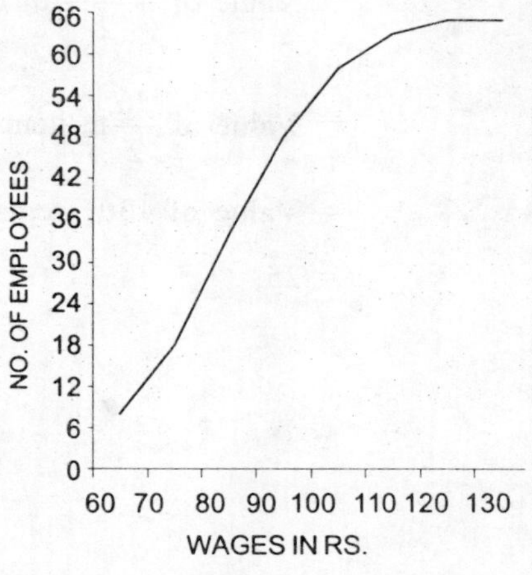


Graph 24

**5. Galton Curve.** This method was propounded by the French scholar Galton. He has mentioned the method of finding median on the graph-paper without using cumulative frequencies by this curve. Under this method, frequencies related to various variables are shown by dots. The number of frequencies of a variable are marked with the same number of dots on the Y-axis and the points for the frequencies of the next variable are marked after the points of the first variable. Then between these points a simple line is drawn which is called 'Galton-Curve' and with the help of this curve the value of the median is found.

Galton-curve is presented by the following example :

**Illustration 44.** Draw a Galton curve from the following and find the median.

| | | | | | | | | | |
|---|---|---|---|---|---|---|---|---|---|
| Size of items | : | 5 | 10 | 15 | 20 | 25 | 30 | 35 | 40 |
| Frequency | : | 2 | 1 | 3 | 4 | 5 | 3 | 5 | 2 |

**Solution**

$$\text{Median} = \text{Value of } \frac{n+1}{2} \text{th item}$$

$$= \text{Value of } \frac{25+1}{2} \text{th item}$$

$$= \text{Value of } \frac{26}{2} \text{th item}$$

$$= \text{Value of 13th items}$$

$$= 25$$

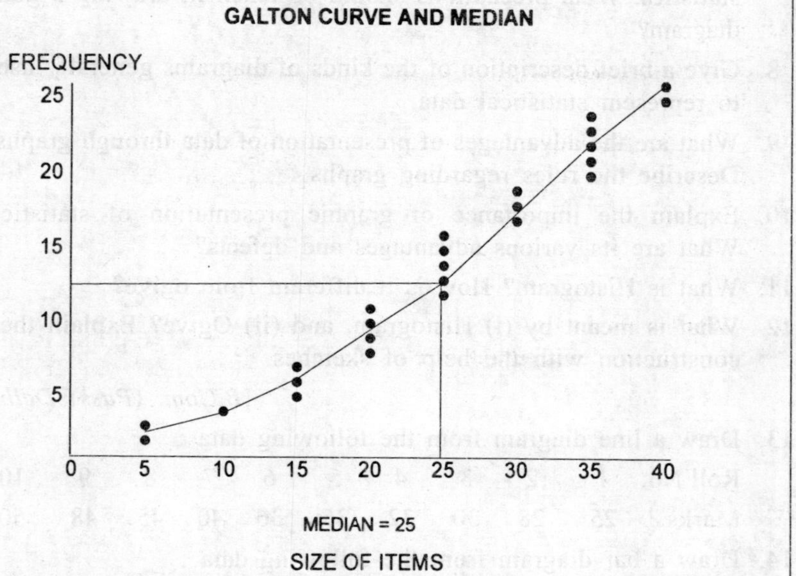


Graph 25

## QUESTIONS

1. What are the advantages of presentation of data through diagrams? What are the types of diagrams?
2. What are the different types of diagrams which are used in statistics to show the salient characteristics of groups and series? Illustrate your answer.
3. Explain briefly various types of diagrams.
4. What are the general principles of graphic presentation of data.

   (*C.S. Dec. 1998*)
5. State advantages and limitations of a graph.

   (*C.S. June 1997*)
6. What do you mean by dimensional diagram? What are the different types of dimensional diagram?

7. Show clearly the necessity and importance of diagrams in statistics. What precautions should be taken in drawing a good diagram?
8. Give a brief description of the kinds of diagrams generally used to represent statistical data.
9. What are the advantages of presentation of data through graphs? Describe the rules regarding graphs.
10. Explain the importance of graphic presentation of statistics. What are its various advantages and defects?
11. What is Histogram? How is it different from ogive?
12. What is meant by (i) Histogram, and (ii) Ogive? Explain their construction with the help of sketches.

[*B.Com.* (*Pass*) *Delhi*]

13. Draw a line diagram from the following data :

| | | | | | | | | | | |
|---|---|---|---|---|---|---|---|---|---|---|
| Roll No. | 1 | 2 | 3 | 4 | 5 | 6 | 7 | 8 | 9 | 10 |
| Marks | 25 | 28 | 30 | 32 | 35 | 36 | 40 | 45 | 48 | 50 |

14. Draw a bar diagram from the following data :

| | | | | | |
|---|---|---|---|---|---|
| Years | Ist | IInd | IIIrd | IVth | Vth |
| Income (Rs.) | 100 | 120 | 125 | 140 | 150 |

15. From the following figures prepare a multi-bar diagram :

| | College A | College B | College C |
|---|---|---|---|
| Art | 400 | 300 | 250 |
| Science | 150 | 100 | 75 |
| Commerce | 200 | 200 | 175 |

16. Prepare a sub-divided multi-bar diagram.

| | Cost of Production (Rs.) | |
|---|---|---|
| | Article A | Article B |
| Material | 500 | 600 |
| Labour | 400 | 450 |
| Factory Expenses | 250 | 350 |
| Other Expenses | 150 | 200 |
| Total Cost | 1,300 | 1,600 |

17. Prepare a rectangle for the following data :

| | | |
|---|---|---|
| (i) | Cost of Raw Materials | Rs. 6,000 |
| (ii) | Wages | Rs. 8,000 |
| (iii) | Other Costs | Rs. 4,000 |
| (iv) | Number of Units Produced | 9,000 |

[*B.Com.* (*Pass*), *Delhi*]

18. Draw a percentage sub-divided bar diagram from the following items :

| | Expenditure | |
|---|---|---|
| | Family A Rs. | Family B Rs. |
| Food | 200 | 230 |
| House Rent | 80 | 90 |
| Clothes | 50 | 60 |
| Fuel & Lighting | 30 | 30 |
| Education | 20 | 40 |
| Miscellaneous | 20 | 50 |
| Total | 400 | 500 |

19. Represent the following data pertaining to Indian Railways by suitable sub-divided bar-diagram.

(In crores of rupees)

| | 1998-99 | 1999-2000 | 2000-2001 |
|---|---|---|---|
| 1. Gross Income | 390 | 424 | 468 |
| 2. Gross Expenditure | 331 | 355 | 389 |
| 3. Net Income | 59 | 69 | 79 |

20. Prepare a rectangular diagram from the following particulars relating to the production of a commodity in a factory :

| | | |
|---|---|---|
| (i) | Units Produced | 1,000 |
| (ii) | Cost of Raw Materials | Rs. 5,000 |
| (iii) | Direct Expenses | Rs. 2,000 |
| (iv) | Indirect Expenses | Rs. 1,000 |
| (v) | Profit | Rs. 1,000 |

[*B.Com.* (*Pass*), *Delhi*]

21. Construct a pie diagram with the following data :

| Consumers : | State Electricity Board | TISCO | CESC Railway | Coal Mines | Others |
|---|---|---|---|---|---|
| Power consummed : (in KWt. hours) | 750,000 | 360,000 | 180,000 | 450,000 | 660,000 |

(*ICWA, Dec. 1996*)

22. Draw a histogram and a frequency polygon for the following data :

| (nearest to the pound) : | 102-113 | 113-124 | 124-135 | 135-146 | 146-157 | 157-168 | 168-179 | Total |
|---|---|---|---|---|---|---|---|---|
| No. of men : | 1 | 1 | 4 | 14 | 12 | 5 | 3 | 40 |

(*ICWA, Dec. 1996*)

23. The table below gives the ages of drivers of cars involved in total accidents during a certain year. Draw a pie-chart to represent the data :

| Age of drivers : | Under 20 | 20-40 | 40-60 | Over 60 | Total |
|---|---|---|---|---|---|
| Per cent of totals : | 15 | 60 | 20 | 5 | 100 |

(*ICWA, June 1997*)

24. Draw a histogram and a frequency polygon of the distribution of marks :

| Weekly wages (in Rs.) : | 1-10 | 11-20 | 21-30 | 31-40 | 41-50 |
|---|---|---|---|---|---|
| No. of workers : | 14 | 28 | 36 | 12 | 10 |

(*ICWA, June 1997*)

25. Draw a histogram of the following frequency distribution showing the number of boys on the registerof primary schools in a certain state :

| Age (in years) : | 2-5 | 5-11 | 11-12 | 12-13 | 13-14 | 14-15 | 15-17 |
|---|---|---|---|---|---|---|---|
| No. of boys (in '000) : | 150 | 3066 | 497 | 477 | 496 | 143 | 162 |

(*ICWA, Dec. 1997*)

26. Draw a suitable diagram to represent the following :

| Factory | Wages Rs. | Materials Rs. | Other Costs Rs. | Profit Rs. |
|---|---|---|---|---|
| A | 3,000 | 5,000 | 1,000 | 1,000 |
| B | 2,000 | 3,000 | 800 | 500 |

The number of units produced by A and B were 1,000 and 700 respectively, show also cost and profit per unit.

27. Represent the following data in percentages by bar diagram :

| Years | Public Co. | Private Co. | Total |
|---|---|---|---|
| 1992 | 5,000 | 20,000 | 25,000 |
| 1993 | 4,000 | 16,000 | 20,000 |
| 1994 | 6,000 | 18,000 | 24,000 |
| 1995 | 7,000 | 21,000 | 28,000 |
| 1996 | 5,000 | 15,000 | 20,000 |

[*B.Com., Jadhpur*]

28. Represent the following data of the family budget of two families with different incomes by a suitable diagram.

| Items of Expenditure | First Family Income Rs. 400 P.M. | Second Family Income Rs. 600 P.M. |
|---|---|---|
| Food | 120 | 160 |
| Clothing | 80 | 100 |
| House Rent | 60 | 120 |
| Education | 40 | 80 |
| Fuel | 20 | 40 |
| Miscellaneous | 40 | 60 |

29. Draw circular diagram from the following data :

| Type of Commodity | Expenditure in Rs. | |
|---|---|---|
| | Family A | Family B |
| Food | 300 | 500 |
| Rent | 200 | 350 |
| Clothing | 125 | 250 |
| Education | 110 | 225 |
| Miscellaneous | 75 | 125 |
| Savings | 90 | 150 |

(*B.Com., Sardar Patel*)

30. Draw a histogram and a frequency polygon from the following frequency distribution table of marks in English :

| Class boundaries: | 12.5-17.5 | 17.5-22.5 | 22.5-27.5 | 27.5-32.5 | 32.5-37.5 | 37.5-42.5 | 42.5-47.5 |
|---|---|---|---|---|---|---|---|
| Frequency : | 3 | 4 | 6 | 15 | 19 | 29 | 19 |

| | 47.5-52.5 | 52.5-57.5 | 57.5-62.5 | 62.5-67.5 | 67.5-72.5 |
|---|---|---|---|---|---|
| | 15 | 6 | 3 | 0 | 1 |

(*ICWA, Dec. 1998*)

31. Marks obtained by 50 students of a class are given below :

| | | | | | | | | | |
|---|---|---|---|---|---|---|---|---|---|
| 34 | 54 | 21 | 52 | 43 | 36 | 10 | 51 | 12 | 48 |
| 48 | 22 | 26 | 19 | 17 | 38 | 30 | 43 | 7 | 53 |
| 13 | 30 | 60 | 15 | 18 | 25 | 55 | 41 | 30 | 25 |
| 40 | 51 | 32 | 22 | 35 | 49 | 39 | 59 | 17 | 40 |
| 14 | 18 | 40 | 4 | 45 | 43 | 19 | 34 | 10 | 47 |

Construct a frequency table with class-intervals 1-10, 11-20, 21-30 and so on. Draw the histogram.

(*ICWA, Dec. 1999*)

32. Draw an appropriate diagram to represent the information given below :

Rs. 10,800 is the total profit of a business in which there are five partners A, B, C, D and E. A's share of profit is Rs. 2,700, B's share is Rs. 3,600, C's share is Rs. 2,100 D's share is Rs. 1,800 and E's share is Rs. 600.

33. A rupee spent of 'Khadi' is distributed as follows :

| | |
|---|---|
| Farmer | 19 Paise |
| Carder and Spinner | 35 Paise |
| Weaver | 28 Paise |
| Washerman, dyer & printer | 8 Paise |
| Administrative Agency | 10 Paise |
| Total | 100 Paise |

Present the above data in the form of a pie diagram.

34. The following is the table of crime figures (excluding petty cases) reported with the number of detections by the Police Dept., Govt. of Madhya Pradesh for June 2000.

| Type of Crime | Number Reported | Number Detected |
|---|---|---|
| Murder | 25 | 22 |
| Dacoity and robbery | 34 | 19 |
| House breaking (by day) | 114 | 35 |
| House breaking (by night) | 137 | 43 |
| Shooting and Stabbings | 162 | 117 |
| Total | 472 | 236 |

Prepare diagram to exhibit the incidence of each type of crime and to compute the same with the measure of efficiency of the police department as depicted by the relative figures of detection.

35. The following table gives the details of cost of construction of a house in Allahabad.

| | Rs. | | Rs. |
|---|---|---|---|
| Land | 4,500 | Cement | 800 |
| Labour | 2,500 | Lime | 800 |
| Bricks | 2,000 | Stone | 600 |
| Iron | 1,800 | Sand | 200 |
| Timber | 1,500 | Other things | 1,300 |

Represent the above figures by a suitable diagram.

36. Represent the following data by a suitable diagram :

| Year | Men | Women | Children | Total |
|---|---|---|---|---|
| 1990 | 1,80,000 | 1,10,000 | 70,000 | 3,60,000 |
| 2000 | 3,50,000 | 2,10,000 | 1,60,000 | 7,20,000 |

37. Represent the following by sub-divided bars drawn on percentage basis :

Cost, sale proceeds and Profit and Loss per table.

| Particulars : | 1995 | 2000 |
|---|---|---|
| Cost per table : | Rs. | Rs. |
| (a) Wages | 21 | 9 |
| (b) Other costs | 14 | 6 |
| (c) Polishing | 7 | 3 |
| Total Cost | 42 | 18 |
| Proceeds per table | 40 | 20 |
| Profit (+), Loss (–) | –2 | +2 |

38. Represent the following by sub-divided bars drawn on the percentage basis :

Cost, proceeds, profit or loss per chair during 1998, 1999 and 2000.

| | 1998 | 1999 | 2000 |
|---|---|---|---|
| Cost per chair : | | | |
| (a) Wage | 4.5 | 7.5 | 10.5 |
| (b) Other costs | 3.0 | 5.1 | 7.5 |
| (c) Polishing | 1.5 | 2.4 | 3.0 |
| Total Cost | 9.0 | 15.0 | 21.0 |
| Proceeds per chair | 10.00 | 15.00 | 20.00 |
| Profit (+), Loss (–) per chair | (+)1.00 | — | (–)1.00 |

39. Represent the following by sub-divided bars on percentage basis. The elements of cost, sale proceeds and profit or loss per steel chair for 1998 and 2000 are given below :

| | 1998 (Rs.) | 2000 (Rs.) |
|---|---|---|
| Wages | 16 | 22 |
| Painting and finishing | 8 | 10 |
| Materials | 16 | 32 |
| Total | 40 | 64 |
| Sale Price | 48 | 60 |
| Profit and Loss | +8 | –4 |

(*B. Com., Madras*)

40. Represent the following diagrammatically :

| | 1999 Rs. | 2000 Rs. |
|---|---|---|
| Sale Price per Heater | 30 | 50 |
| Cost per Heater : | | |
| Wages | 15 | 20 |
| Material | 10 | 12 |
| Other Cost | 10 | 13 |
| Profit (+) or Loss (–) | Rs. –5 | Rs. +5 |

[*B.Com., Garhwal*]

41. In the following table information regarding Indian National Income for 1990-91 and 1995-96 is given. Represent this information by a suitable diagram :

| | Net National Production of India (In Crores Rupees) 1990-91 | 1995-96 |
|---|---|---|
| A. Agriculture | 4,340 | 4,980 |
| B. Mines & Industry | 1,480 | 1,750 |
| C. Trade and Transport | 1,660 | 1,970 |
| D. Other Services | 1,390 | 1,720 |
| E. Total Net Production | 8,870 | 10,420 |

(*Hint*—Sub-divided Circular Diagram)

(*M.A., Agra*)

42. Represent by a suitable diagram :

Weekly consumption of milk per head in England during the year 2000.

| Income per head per week | Fresh milk | Condensed milk |
|---|---|---|
| Up to 10 shillings | 1.0 | 0.6 |
| 10 shillings tc 15 | 2.0 | 0.5 |
| 15 shillings to 20 | 2.4 | 0.5 |
| 20 shillings to 30 | 2.8 | 0.4 |
| 30 shillings to 40 | 4.0 | 0.4 |
| Above 40 shillings | 5.0 | 0.2 |

43. Show by means of squares the production of wheat in some countries given in the following table. The scale should be 1 sq. inch = 100 crore tons.

| Countries | A | B | C | D |
|---|---|---|---|---|
| Quantity in crore tons | 3,600 | 2,000 | 1,200 | 800 |

44. Diagrammatically represent the following data relating to India's foreign trade :

(in crores of Rs.)

| Year | Imports | Exports |
|---|---|---|
| 1996-97 | 961 | 640 |
| 1997-98 | 1,087 | 643 |
| 1998-99 | 958 | 677 |
| 1999-2000 | 981 | 709 |

45. Draw a graph from the following :

| Years | Production (Lakh tons) |
|---|---|
| 1995 | 50 |
| 1996 | 45 |
| 1997 | 55 |
| 1998 | 60 |
| 1999 | 30 |
| 2000 | 20 |

46. Show the following data graphically :

(Crores of Rs.)

| Years | Exports | Imports | Balance of trade |
|---|---|---|---|
| 1995 | 120 | 150 | –30 |
| 1996 | 160 | 180 | –20 |
| 1997 | 170 | 170 | 0 |
| 1998 | 200 | 180 | +20 |
| 1999 | 190 | 160 | +30 |
| 2000 | 220 | 200 | +20 |

47. The following are the share price quotations of a firm for five consecutive weeks. Present the data by an appropriate diagram.

| Week | High | Low |
|---|---|---|
| 1 | 102 | 100 |
| 2 | 103 | 101 |
| 3 | 107 | 103 |
| 4 | 106 | 105 |
| 5 | 105 | 104 |

(*M.B.A., Himachal*)

48. From the index numbers given below draw a graph :

| Months | Index No. of Prices in Calcutta | Index No. of Prices in Bombay |
|---|---|---|
| May | 169 | 204 |
| June | 182 | 222 |
| July | 182 | 225 |
| August | 192 | 228 |
| September | 198 | 231 |
| October | 211 | 233 |
| November | 227 | 249 |
| December | 238 | 266 |
| January | 250 | 255 |
| February | 253 | 255 |

49. The following table relates to loans and small savings in India during 1991-2000.

(Rs. Lakhs)

| Year | Loans | Small Savings |
|---|---|---|
| 1991 | 200 | 100 |
| 1992 | 222 | 95 |
| 1993 | 240 | 105 |
| 1994 | 220 | 110 |
| 1995 | 212 | 90 |
| 1996 | 220 | 95 |
| 1997 | 226 | 100 |
| 1998 | 240 | 80 |
| 1999 | 236 | 75 |
| 2000 | 244 | 76 |

Represent the above data by means of an index histogram.

50. Represent the following data by means of a time series graph.

| Year | Imports (Rs. '000 | Exports (Rs. '000) |
|---|---|---|
| 1990 | 267 | 307 |
| 1991 | 269 | 310 |
| 1992 | 263 | 280 |
| 1993 | 275 | 260 |
| 1994 | 270 | 275 |
| 1995 | 280 | 271 |
| 1996 | 282 | 280 |
| 1997 | 272 | 280 |
| 1998 | 265 | 260 |
| 1999 | 266 | 265 |

Show also the balance of trade.

51. From the following table draw histogram, frequency polygo annd two ogives for the following data of 100 families inn a locality :

| Mothly earning per family (Rs.) | Number of families |
|---|---|
| 800-900 | 10 |
| 900-1000 | 15 |
| 1000-1100 | 20 |
| 1100-1200 | 25 |
| 1200-1300 | 15 |
| 1300-1400 | 10 |
| 1400-1500 | 5 |

(*C.S. June 1995*)

52. Draw a histogram for the following data :

| Age in years | No. of persons |
|---|---|
| 0-10 | 5 |
| 10-20 | 15 |
| 20-30 | 18 |
| 30-40 | 22 |
| 40-50 | 35 |
| 50-70 | 30 |
| 70-100 | 15 |

(*C.S. Dec. 1995*)

53. Present the following graphically :

**Exports of Iron Ore**

| Year | Quantity (Million tons) | Value (Rs. Crores) |
|---|---|---|
| 1996 | 10.5 | 36.0 |
| 1997 | 11.0 | 40.5 |
| 1998 | 12.5 | 50.0 |
| 1999 | 14.0 | 65.5 |
| 2000 | 15.0 | 80.0 |

[*B.Com.* (*Hons.*), *Delhi*]

54. Plot a graph to represent the following data in a suitable manner.

| Year : | 1992 | 1993 | 1994 | 1995 | 1996 | 1997 | 1998 | 1999 |
|---|---|---|---|---|---|---|---|---|
| Quantity Imported (in '000 Qtts.) | 400 | 450 | 560 | 620 | 580 | 460 | 500 | 540 |
| Value of Imported quantities (in '000 Rupees) | 220 | 235 | 385 | 420 | 420 | 380 | 360 | 400 |

55. Draw a histogram and frequency polygon on the graph-paper from the data given below and read the value of mode :

| Production (in tons) | 0-10 | 10-20 | 20-30 | 30-40 | 40-50 | 50-60 | 60-70 | 70-80 |
|---|---|---|---|---|---|---|---|---|
| No. of Labours | 8 | 18 | 23 | 37 | 47 | 26 | 16 | 5 |

56. Construct :

(a) Histogram, (b) Frequency polygon, and (c) Cumulative frequency curve from the following data :

| Marks : | 1-5 | 6-10 | 11-15 | 16-20 | 21-25 | 26-30 | 31-35 | 36-40 | 41-45 |
|---|---|---|---|---|---|---|---|---|---|
| Frequency : | 7 | 10 | 16 | 32 | 24 | 18 | 10 | 5 | 1 |

57. (a) Draw an ogive curve from the following frequency distribution :

| Age in years | Under | 5 | 10 | 15 | 20 | 25 | 30 | 3540 |
|---|---|---|---|---|---|---|---|---|
| No.of persons | 4 | 10 | 20 | 30 | 55 | 77 | 95 | 100 |

(*C.S. Dec. 1996*)

58. Represent the following data by means of the histogram and frequecy polygon :

| Wages (Rs.) | No. of workers |
|---|---|
| 10-20 | 7 |
| 20-30 | 13 |
| 30-40 | 20 |
| 40-60 | 30 |
| 60-80 | 20 |
| 80-110 | 18 |

(*C.S. Dec. 1997*)

59. (a) Following figures relate to the weekly wages of workers in a factory :

Wages (in Rs.)

| | | | | | | | | | |
|---|---|---|---|---|---|---|---|---|---|
| 100 | 100 | 101 | 102 | 106 | 86 | 82 | 87 | 109 | 104 |
| 75 | 89 | 99 | 96 | 94 | 93 | 92 | 90 | 86 | 78 |
| 79 | 84 | 83 | 87 | 88 | 89 | 75 | 76 | 76 | 79 |
| 80 | 81 | 89 | 99 | 104 | 100 | 103 | 104 | 107 | 110 |
| 110 | 106 | 102 | 107 | 103 | 101 | 101 | 101 | 86 | 94 |
| 93 | 96 | 97 | 99 | 100 | 102 | 103 | 107 | 107 | 108 |
| 109 | 94 | 93 | 97 | 98 | 99 | 100 | 97 | 88 | 86 |
| 84 | 83 | 82 | 80 | 84 | 86 | 88 | 91 | 93 | 95 |
| 95 | 95 | 97 | 98 | 100 | 105 | 106 | 103 | 85 | 84 |
| 77 | 78 | 80 | 93 | 96 | 97 | 98 | 98 | 98 | 87 |

Prepare a frequency table by taking a class interval of 5.

(b) Prepare a suitable diagram with the help of the frequency table prepared in part (a) of the question.

[*B.Com.* (*Pass*) *Delhi*]

60. We are given the following frequency distribution of monthly expenditure on food incurred by a sample of 100 families in a town :

| Expenditure | Frequency |
|---|---|
| 0-50 | 7 |
| 50-150 | 24 |
| 150-250 | 30 |
| 250-400 | 27 |
| 400-600 | 8 |
| 600-300 | 4 |

Draw the frequency polygon and the histogram for this distribution.

[*B.A.* (*Hon.*), *Delhi*]

61. Draw two ogive curves from the following data :

| Class-interval | Frequency | Class-interval | Frequency |
|---|---|---|---|
| 0-5 | 7 | 20-25 | 17 |
| 5-10 | 10 | 25-30 | 10 |
| 10-15 | 20 | 30-35 | 14 |
| 15-20 | 13 | 35-40 | 9 |

[*B.Com.*, *Guru Nanak*]

62. Draw a 'less than' and 'more than' ogive curves from the following data :

| Weekly Wages (in Rs.) | No. of Workers |
|---|---|
| 100-200 | 7 |
| 200-300 | 13 |
| 300-400 | 20 |
| 400-600 | 30 |
| 600-800 | 20 |
| 800-1100 | 18 |

(*C.S. June 1998*)

63. Represent the following data by means of a suitable graph, using false base line :

| Year | Output of foodgrains (Million Tonnes) |
|---|---|
| 1993-94 | 151.3 |
| 1994-95 | 181.2 |
| 1995-96 | 187.0 |
| 1996-97 | 195.0 |
| 1997-98 | 193.0 |

(*C.S. Dec.* 1998)

64. Draw a OGIVE from the following data :

| Size of items | Frequency | Size of items | Frequency |
|---|---|---|---|
| 6 | 12 | 30 | 13 |
| 12 | 16 | 36 | 20 |
| 18 | 15 | 42 | 22 |
| 24 | 14 | 48 | 18 |

Also find the value of median and quartile.

65. What do you mean by Galton Curve? Draw this curve from the following :

| | | | | | | | | |
|---|---|---|---|---|---|---|---|---|
| Size of items : | 2 | 4 | 6 | 8 | 10 | 12 | 14 | 16 |
| Frequency : | 5 | 3 | 4 | 6 | 7 | 2 | 3 | 2 |

66. Draw of histogram from the following figures :

| Class Intervals : | 1-10 | 10-20 | 20-40 | 40-60 | 60-70 | 70-80 | 80-100 |
|---|---|---|---|---|---|---|---|
| Frequencies : | 5 | 8 | 22 | 30 | 12 | 10 | 12 |

67. Draw a histogram from the following figures :

| Income in Rs. : | 100-200 | 200-300 | 300-400 | 400-500 | 500-600 | 600-700 |
|---|---|---|---|---|---|---|
| No. of Persons : | 5 | 8 | 12 | 18 | 20 | 22 |

68. Draw a histogram from the following figures :

| Marks : | 0-10 | 10-20 | 20-30 | 30-40 | 40-50 | 50-60 |
|---|---|---|---|---|---|---|
| No. of Students : | 16 | 11 | 8 | 5 | 4 | 3 |

69. Draw a 'more than' and 'less than' ogive from the following figures :

| Class : | 0-10 | 10-20 | 20-30 | 30-40 | 40-50 | 50-60 | 60-70 | 70-80 |
|---|---|---|---|---|---|---|---|---|
| Frequency : | 6 | 8 | 12 | 14 | 9 | 6 | 5 | 2 |

70. Draw a histogram from the following figures :

| Class-Intervals : | 100-199 | 200-299 | 300-399 | 400-499 |
|---|---|---|---|---|
| Frequency : | 12 | 22 | 35 | 48 |
| Class-Intervals : | 500-599 | 600-699 | 700-799 | |
| Frequency : | 26 | 14 | 8 | |

71. Show the details of monthly expenditure of two families as given below by means of suitable diagrams :

| Items of Expenditure | Family—A Expenditure Rs. 2,000 per month Rs. | Family—B Expenditure Rs. 3,000 per month Rs. |
|---|---|---|
| Food | 800 | 1,000 |
| Clothing | 300 | 500 |
| Rent | 300 | 400 |
| Fuel and light | 100 | 150 |
| Miscellaneous | 500 | 950 |

(*C.S. June 1999*)

72. Marks obtained by 100 students in Econnomics are given below. Draw an appropriate graph to represent them :

| Marks | Males | Females | Total |
|---|---|---|---|
| 30-40 | 8 | 6 | 14 |
| 40-50 | 6 | 10 | 16 |
| 50-60 | 14 | 6 | 20 |
| 60-70 | 13 | 12 | 25 |
| 70-80 | 13 | 12 | 25 |
| 70-80 | 12 | 13 | 25 |
| Total | 53 | 47 | 100 |

(*C.S. Dec. 1999*)

# 9

# Measures of Central Tendency-Averages

"Statistics may rightly be called the science of averages." From the above statement the significance of this measures in statistics is highlighted. In statistics, data are collected and on their basis conclusions are drawn. In order to do so, the collected data are analysed through statistical methods. Measures of central tendency are turned to for help for analysing data. Central tendency which is also called average or mean presents the vast data in a precise form. That is, that unit of the vast universe is known by the 'average' which represents all the units of the universe. Many subjects are such that it is useful to describe them in terms of averages. For example it is more useful to give the average height of Indian people instead of describing their individual heights separately.

**Meaning of Averages.** Generally speaking the meaning of average or mean is taken to be representative value itself. That is, such unit as represents other units is called mean. The representative unit imbibes the qualities of the units that it represents. From amongst the definitions of average given by various scholars the following are worth looking at :

1. "*An average is a single value within the range of the data used to represent all the values in the series. Since an average is somewhere within the range of the data, it is sometimes called measure of central value.*"

— *Croxton and Cowden*

2. "*An average is purely a mathematical conception, such as the average length of life in a varied population which does not correspond to any particular group, but is only a short way of expressing an arithmetical result.*"

— *Dr. Bowley*

3. "*Measures of the location or position of a frequency distribution are called averages.*"

— *Yule and Kendall*

It is clear from the above definitions also that mean is a representative value only.

**Utility of Averages.** As stated that average is such a value as represents several units, the user gets a lot of advantages of this value. The utility and advantages of averages are the following :

**1. Precise Presentation of Vast and Complex Facts.** Many facts which are vast and difficult can be presented in a precise manner with the help of averages. Such facts as are difficult to comprehend and remember can be easily known with the help of averages. For example, it is very difficult to separately remember the statistics of income of 500 persons, but their income can be easily estimated by knowing their average income and it can be easily remembered also.

**2. Helpful comparing various facts.** The or more facts can be compared among them by using averages which is not possible otherwise. For instance, it will be difficult on the basis of individual data to know in respect of the citizens of two nationalities as to which citizen has more income than the other. But this can be easily known by finding out the average incomes of the individuals of both the countries.

**3. Making facts easy and comprehensible.** Fact are easily understood from averages because only one unit is to be remembered under it.

**Characteristics of a good Average.** The following characteristics should be there under a good average :

**1. Representative unit.** The average should be able to reveal the nature and characteristics of units that it represents.

**2. Simple.** The average should be easy to be determined and trace.

**3. Test through Mathematical Operation.** A good average has the characteristics of being found correct when subjected to mathematical operation.

**4. Unaffected by marginal units.** If there are too small or two big units in the universe, they should not affect the average and only then can it represent most of the units.

**5. Definite Calculation.** It is necessary for a good average that it should have a definite method of calculation so that the same figure is obtained as average whosoever uses that method.

## KINDS OF AVERAGES

Averages can be divided into the following from different points of view :

**Types of Averages**

**1. Mathematical Averages**

(a) Arithmetic Mean

(b) Geometric Mean

(c) Harmonic Mean

**2. Positional Averages**

(a) Median

(b) Mode

**3. Business Averages**

(a) Moving Average

(b) Progressive Average

(c) Composite Average

Various types of averages can be shown with the help of the following chart :

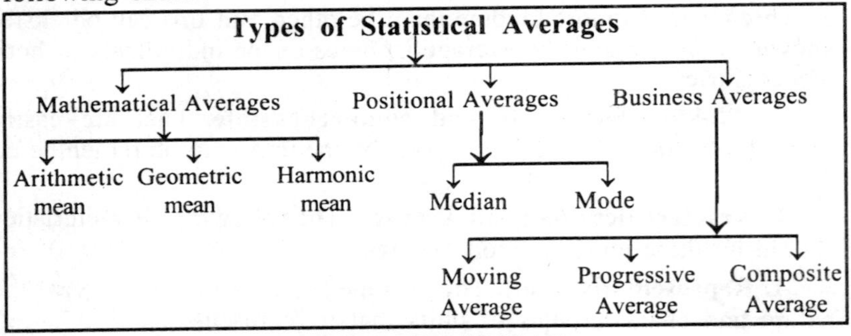


## ARITHMETIC MEAN

It is a prevalent and popular mean, for it is easy to calculate and comprehend. The estimate of its popularity can be had by the fact that generally, when the word 'mean' is used, it is taken in the sense of arithmetic mean. "*When the total of items is divided by the number of items, the quotient is the arithmetic mean.*"

Following are the merits and demerits of arithmetic mean :

**Merits**

1. It is easy to calculate.
2. It is found out on the basis of all the items of the series, and no item is left out while finding it out.
3. Further algebraic operations can be performed by this. The number of items or value can be known on the basis of this mean.

4. It is definite, therefore whosoever is calculating arithmetic mean of the given figures, everybody will have the same value of it.

**Demerits**

1. Too small or too big items greatly affect this mean. In case there are greater inequalities among the values of items, this mean cannot be the representative value of the series.
2. It is not easy also to calculate in comparison to median.
3. Under this generally such value emerges as the representative value which is not given in that series.
4. If the value of one or two items of the series is not known, this mean cannot be determined, while other averages such as median can be determined.
5. Sometimes, by this average such results are obtained as only disfigure the matter of fact. For example, in firms A, B and C 10, 12 and 9 persons are working respectively and their average or mean will be $\frac{10+12+9}{3} = \frac{31}{3} = 10.33$. which will be apparently incongruous since persons can not be cut into parts.

## TYPES OF ARITHMETIC MEAN

Arithmetic mean are of the following two types :

(i) Simple Arithmetic Mean and

(ii) Weighted Arithmetic Mean.

**(1) Simple Mean.** This type of mean is very simple in calculation. This is known by dividing the total of all the units of the universe by the number of units. The calculation method of this type of mean in various statistical series is done in the following manner :

**Method of Calculation of Simple Mean**

**(a) Individual Series.** In individual series, the calculation is done by following two methods :

**1. Direct Method.** According to this method, first of all, all the units are added and then their total is divided by the numbers of items and the quotient becomes the simple mean. The following formula is used under this method to calculate it.

$$\overline{X} = \frac{X_1 + X_2 + .... X_n}{N} \quad \text{or} \quad \overline{X} = \frac{\sum X}{N}$$

The above signs are used in the following senses :

$\overline{X}$ = Arithmetic Average; $\Sigma$ = Total or summation,

$N$ = Number of items $X$ = Variables.

**Illustration 1.** Find out the arithmetic mean from the following data :

| S. No. | 1 | 2 | 3 | 4 | 5 | 6 | 7 | 8 | 9 | 10 |
|---|---|---|---|---|---|---|---|---|---|---|
| Marks obtained | 60 | 62 | 53 | 48 | 72 | 45 | 80 | 40 | 35 | 68 |

**Solution**

| Sl. No. | Marks obtained ($X$) |
|---|---|
| 1 | 60 |
| 2 | 62 |
| 3 | 53 |
| 4 | 48 |
| 5 | 72 |
| 6 | 45 |
| 7 | 80 |
| 8 | 40 |
| 9 | 35 |
| 10 | 68 |
| $N$ = 10 | $\Sigma X$ = 563 |

$$\overline{X} = \frac{\Sigma X}{N}$$

By putting the value in the formula we get :

$$\overline{X} = \frac{563}{10}$$

$$= 56.3 \text{ Marks}$$

**2. Short-cut Method.** In case of data being too big, their totalling involves possibilities of error and operation too is cumbersome. In such cases, short-cut method is more appropriate. In calculating under this method, any value is taken as an assumed mean. And from that value difference of all the values is determined. The total of differences is divided by the number of units. The quotient is added with the assumed mean and the value after adjustment becomes the 'average'. The following formula is used for calculating the average :

$$\overline{X} = AM + \frac{\sum d}{N}$$

$AM$ = Assumed mean

$d$ = Deviation taken from assumed mean.

**Illustration 2.** Following is a list of incomes of 15 persons earned during a month.

| | | | | | | | | | | |
|---|---|---|---|---|---|---|---|---|---|---|
| S. No. | 1 | 2 | 3 | 4 | 5 | 6 | 7 | 8 | 9 | 10 |
| Income (Rs.) | 290 | 288 | 362 | 320 | 312 | 313 | 318 | 316 | 320 | 295 |
| S. No. | 11 | 12 | 13 | 14 | 15 | | | | | |
| Income (Rs.) | 300 | 310 | 280 | 293 | 310 | | | | | |

Calculate the simple mean from the above figures.

**Solution**

| S. No. | Income (Rs.) ($X$) | $d$ $AM = (310)$ |
|---|---|---|
| 1 | 290 | –20 |
| 2 | 288 | –22 |
| 3 | 362 | +52 |
| 4 | 320 | +10 |
| 5 | 312 | +02 |
| 6 | 313 | +03 |
| 7 | 318 | +08 |
| 8 | 316 | +06 |
| 9 | 320 | +10 |
| 10 | 295 | –15 |
| 11 | 300 | –10 |
| 12 | 310 | 0 |
| 13 | 280 | –30 |
| 14 | 293 | –17 |
| 15 | 310 | 0 |
| $N = 15$ | | $\Sigma d = -23$ |

Formula : $$\overline{X} = AM + \frac{\sum d}{N}$$

By putting the value, we get :

$$\overline{X} = 310 + \frac{-23}{15}$$
$$= 310 - 1.53$$
$$= \text{Rs. } 308.47 .$$

**(b) Discrete Series.** In respect of these series also the following methods are used :

(i) *Direct Method.* According to this method, each value of series is multiplied by its frequency and then the total of all the product of multiplications is divided by the total of frequencies. The quotient becomes the 'average'. The following formula is used in this respect :

$$\overline{X} = \frac{\Sigma fX}{N}$$

$f$ = frequency, $N$ = Number of items (total of frequency)

**Illustration 3.** Compute the mean from the following :

| | | | | | | | | | | |
|---|---|---|---|---|---|---|---|---|---|---|
| Height in inches | 48 | 50 | 52 | 54 | 56 | 58 | 60 | 62 | 64 | 66 |
| No. of persons | 13 | 15 | 20 | 10 | 10 | 12 | 9 | 2 | 5 | 4 |

**Solution**

| Height in inches ($X$) | No. of Persons ($f$) | $fX$ |
|---|---|---|
| 48 | 13 | 624 |
| 50 | 15 | 750 |
| 52 | 20 | 1,040 |
| 54 | 10 | 540 |
| 56 | 10 | 560 |
| 58 | 12 | 696 |
| 60 | 9 | 540 |
| 62 | 2 | 124 |
| 64 | 5 | 320 |
| 66 | 4 | 264 |
| | $N = 100$ | $fX = 5{,}458$ |

$$\overline{X} = \frac{\Sigma fX}{N}$$

By putting the values in formula we get :

$$X = \frac{5{,}458}{100}$$

$$= 54.58 \text{ inches.}$$

(ii) *Short-cut Method*. According to this method, first of all any value from among the variables is taken as an assumed mean and from that value deviation of all the variables is found. Deviations are multiplied by their frequencies. The total of the product of multiplications is divided by the number of units and the quotient is added in the assumed mean. The emerging value becomes the 'average'. The following formula is used for calculation by this method :

$$\overline{X} = AM + \frac{\sum fd}{N}$$

The signs represent the same meaning as explained earlier.

**Illustration 4.** You are given a frequency distribution of ages 150 persons of a certain locality as follows :

| | | | | | | | | | | |
|---|---|---|---|---|---|---|---|---|---|---|
| Age in years | 5 | 10 | 15 | 20 | 25 | 30 | 35 | 40 | 45 | 50 |
| No. of persons | 15 | 12 | 8 | 16 | 20 | 23 | 21 | 18 | 12 | 5 |

Find out the arithmetic average from the above data.

**Solution**

| Age in Years ($X$) | No. of Persons ($f$) | $d$ ($AM = 25$) | $fd$ |
|---|---|---|---|
| 5 | 15 | –20 | –300 |
| 10 | 12 | –15 | –180 |
| 15 | 8 | –10 | –80 |
| 20 | 16 | –5 | –80 |
| 25 | 20 | 0 | 0 |
| 30 | 23 | +5 | +115 |
| 35 | 21 | +10 | +210 |
| 40 | 18 | +15 | +270 |
| 45 | 12 | +20 | +240 |
| 50 | 5 | +25 | +125 |
| | $N = 150$ | | $\Sigma fd = +320$ |

$$\overline{X} = AM + \frac{\Sigma fd}{N}$$

$$= 25 + \frac{320}{150}$$

$$= 25 + 2.13$$

$$= 27.13 \text{ years.}$$

(iii) *Step Deviation Method.* On looking at the above series it appears that in all the values of the series there is a definite difference of 5. Therefore, while taking deviation and also taking into view the above common value, we can divide all the deviations by 5 and make the operation still more simple. This is what is called step-deviation. Put differently, the numbers resulting from dividing the deviations by common value are called step-deviation. The following formula is used for using step-deviation method :

$$\overline{X} = AM + \frac{\Sigma fd'}{N} \times i$$

$d'$ = Step Deviation $\left(\frac{d}{i}\right)$;

$i$ = Common value.

**Illustration 5.** By using step-deviation, illustration No. 4 will be solved in the following way :

**Solution**

| Age in years | No. of persons | d (AM = 25) | d′ (i = 5) | fd′ |
|---|---|---|---|---|
| 5 | 15 | –20 | –4 | –60 |
| 10 | 12 | -15 | –3 | –36 |
| 15 | 8 | –10 | –2 | –16 |
| 20 | 16 | –5 | –1 | –16 |
| 25 | 20 | 0 | 0 | 0 |
| 30 | 23 | +5 | +1 | 23 |
| 35 | 21 | +10 | +2 | 42 |
| 40 | 18 | +15 | +3 | 54 |
| 45 | 12 | +20 | +4 | 48 |
| 50 | 5 | +25 | +5 | 25 |
| | N = 150 | | | Xfd′ = +64 |

$$\overline{X} = AM + \frac{\Sigma fd'}{N} \times i$$

$$= 25 + \frac{64}{150} \times 5$$

$$= 25 + 2.13$$

$$= 27.13 \text{ years.}$$

**(C) Continuous series.** Following methods are used in continuous series.

(i) *Direct Method.* In case of continuous series, first of all, the mid-values of class intervals are found. Thereafter the mid-values are multiplied by the frequencies and the total of the product of multiplications is divided by the total of frequencies. That is to say, after finding the mid-value, the same process is adopted as is used for the discrete series. This can be known by the following formula :

$$\overline{X} = \frac{\Sigma fX}{N}$$

$X$ = Mid-values.

**Illustration 6.** Calculate mean from the following :

| | | | | | | |
|---|---|---|---|---|---|---|
| Marks obtained | 0-10 | 10-20 | 20-30 | 30-40 | 40-50 | 50-60 |
| No. of Students | 25 | 7 | 18 | 11 | 6 | 3 |

**Solution**

| Marks obtained | Mid value ($X$) | No. of students ($f$) | ($fX$) |
|---|---|---|---|
| 0-10 | 5 | 25 | 125 |
| 10-20 | 15 | 7 | 105 |
| 20-30 | 25 | 18 | 450 |
| 30-40 | 35 | 11 | 385 |
| 40-50 | 45 | 6 | 270 |
| 50-60 | 55 | 3 | 165 |
| | | $N$ = 70 | $\Sigma fX$ = 1,500 |

$$\overline{X} = \frac{\Sigma fX}{N}$$

$$= \frac{1{,}500}{70}$$

$$= 21.43 \text{ Marks.}$$

**(ii) Shortcut Method.** After finding out the mid-value of class-intervals, the same process operates as in the discrete series. The following formula will be used in this case to calculate arithmetic mean :

$$\overline{X} = AM + \frac{\Sigma fd}{N}$$

$d$ = difference between mid-value and assumed mean.

**Illustration 7.** Calculate arithmetic mean from the following figures :

| | | | | | | | | |
|---|---|---|---|---|---|---|---|---|
| C.I. | : | 0-15 | 15-30 | 30-45 | 45-60 | 60-75 | 75-90 | 90-105 |
| f | : | 3 | 8 | 12 | 16 | 11 | 6 | 4 |

**Solution**

| C.I. | M.V. | *f* | *d* ($AM$ = 52.5) | *fd* |
|---|---|---|---|---|
| 0-15 | 7.5 | 3 | –45 | –135 |
| 15-30 | 22.5 | 8 | –30 | –240 |
| 30-45 | 37.5 | 12 | –15 | –180 |
| 45-60 | 52.5 | 16 | 0 | 0 |
| 60-75 | 67.5 | 11 | 15 | 165 |
| 75-90 | 82.5 | 6 | 30 | 180 |
| 90-105 | 97.5 | 4 | 45 | 180 |
| | | $N$ = 60 | | $\Sigma fd$ = –30 |

$$\overline{X} = AM + \frac{\Sigma fd}{N}$$

$$= 52.5 + \frac{-30}{60}$$

$$= 52.5 - .5$$

$$= 52$$

(iii) *Step-deviation Method.* In continuous series, mean can be found by step-deviation method also. The following formula is used for it :

$$\overline{X} = AM + \frac{\Sigma fd'}{N} \times i$$

The same process will be applied to calculate arithmetic mean in such series by this method as described in case of discrete series.

**Illustration 8.** Calculate the average earnings of the 500 firms :

| Earnings (Rs.) | Number of firms |
|---|---|
| —10,000 to —8,000 | 20 |
| —8,000 to —6,000 | 80 |
| —6,000 to —4,000 | 95 |
| —4,000 to —2,000 | 10 |
| —2,000 to 0 | 50 |
| 0 to 2,000 | 15 |
| 2,000 to 4,000 | 80 |
| 4,000 to 6,000 | 72 |
| 6,000 to 8,000 | 20 |
| 8,000 to 10,000 | 58 |
| | 500 |

**Solution**

| Earnings (Rs.) | Mid-value (*X*) | No. of firms (*f*) | (*d*) (*AM*=1,000) | *d'* (*i*=2,000) | *fd'* |
|---|---|---|---|---|---|
| −10,000 to −8,000 | −9,000 | 20 | −10,000 | −5 | −100 |
| −8,000 to −6,000 | −7,000 | 80 | −8,000 | −4 | −320 |
| −6,000 to −4,000 | −5,000 | 95 | −6,000 | −3 | −285 |
| −4,000 to −2,000 | −3,000 | 10 | −4,000 | −2 | −20 |
| −2,000 to 0 | −1,000 | 50 | −2,000 | −1 | −50 |
| 0 to 2,000 | 1,000 | 15 | 0 | 0 | 0 |
| 2,000 to 4,000 | 3,000 | 80 | 2,000 | 1 | 80 |
| 4,000 to 6,000 | 5,000 | 72 | 4,000 | 2 | 144 |
| 6,000 to 8,000 | 7,000 | 20 | 6,000 | 3 | 60 |
| 8,000 to 10,000 | 9,000 | 58 | 8,000 | 4 | 232 |
| | | *N*=500 | | | $\Sigma fd'$=−259 |

$$\overline{X} = AM + \frac{\Sigma fd'}{N} \times i$$

$$= 1{,}000 + \frac{-259}{500} \times 2{,}000$$

$$= 1{,}000 - 1{,}036$$

$$= \text{Rs. } -36.$$

**Calculation of Arithmetic Mean in Cumulative Frequency Distribution.** In order to know the arithmetic mean in cumulative frequency distribution, first of all, the series is changed into ordinary continuous series. The method to change such distribution into continuous series will be the same as explained in 'Chapter 7'. After changing it into continuous series, arithmetic mean can be calculated by using any of the related formula. The method of calculating the arithmetic mean in such series can be made clear by the following examples.

**Illustration 9.** The following table gives the marks obtained by 70 students in Mathematics. Calculate the simple mean of the series.

| | | | | | | |
|---|---|---|---|---|---|---|
| Marks more than | 70 | 60 | 50 | 40 | 30 | 20 |
| No. of Students | 7 | 18 | 40 | 40 | 63 | 70 |

**Solution**

First of all the above cumulative frequency distribution should be converted into ordinary frequency distribution as follows :

| Marks | Mid-value ($X$) | No. of students ($f$) | $d$ ($AM$=45) | $d'$ ($i$=10) | $fd'$ |
|---|---|---|---|---|---|
| 70-80 | 75 | 7 | +30 | +3 | +21 |
| 60-70 | 65 | 11 | +20 | +2 | +22 |
| 50-60 | 55 | 22 | +10 | +1 | +22 |
| 40-50 | 45 | 0 | 0 | 0 | 0 |
| 30-40 | 35 | 23 | −10 | −1 | −23 |
| 20-30 | 25 | 7 | −20 | −2 | −14 |
| | | $N$=70 | | | $\Sigma fd'$=28 |

$$\overline{X} = AM + \frac{\sum fd'}{N} \times i$$

$$= 45 + \frac{28}{70} \times 10$$

$$= 45 + \frac{4}{10} \times 10$$

$$= 45 + 4$$

$$= 49 \text{ Marks}$$

**Illustration 10.** Find the average marks of a student from the following table :

| | | | | | | | | |
|---|---|---|---|---|---|---|---|---|
| Marks below | 10 | 20 | 30 | 40 | 50 | 60 | 70 | 80 |
| No. of students | 25 | 40 | 60 | 75 | 95 | 125 | 190 | 240 |

**Solution**

| Marks | Mid-values ($X$) | No. of Students ($f$) | $d$ ($AM$=35) | $d'$ ($i$=10) | $fd'$ |
|---|---|---|---|---|---|
| 0-10 | 5 | 25 | –30 | –3 | –75 |
| 10-20 | 15 | 15 | –20 | –2 | –30 |
| 20-30 | 25 | 20 | –10 | –1 | –20 |
| 30-40 | 35 | 15 | 0 | 0 | 0 |
| 40-50 | 45 | 20 | 10 | 1 | 20 |
| 50-60 | 55 | 30 | 20 | 2 | 60 |
| 60-70 | 65 | 65 | 30 | 3 | 195 |
| 70-80 | 75 | 50 | 40 | 4 | 200 |
| | | $N$=240 | | | $\Sigma fd'$=350 |

$$\overline{X} = AM + \frac{\sum fd'}{N} \times i$$

$$= 35 + \frac{350}{240} \times 10$$

$$= 35 + 14.58$$

$$= 49.58 \text{ marks}$$

**Calculation of Arithmetic Mean in Inclusive Continuous Series.** The calculation of average in this type of series can be done exactly in the manner stated earlier. That is to say, first the mid-values of class intervals are found and thereafter the mean is known by using any of the related formulae :

**Illustration 11.** Find out arithmetic mean from the following data :

| | | | | | | | |
|---|---|---|---|---|---|---|---|
| Marks : | 0-9 | 10-19 | 20-29 | 30-39 | 40-49 | 50-59 | 60-69 |
| No. of students : | 18 | 20 | 25 | 30 | 16 | 8 | 3 |

**Solution**

| Marks | Mid values ($X$) | No. of students | $d$ ($AM$=34.5) | $d'$ ($i$=10) | $fd'$ |
|---|---|---|---|---|---|
| 0-9 | 4.5 | 18 | –30 | –3 | –54 |
| 10-19 | 14.5 | 20 | –20 | –2 | –40 |
| 20-29 | 24.5 | 25 | –10 | –1 | –25 |
| 30-39 | 34.5 | 30 | 0 | 0 | 0 |
| 40-49 | 44.5 | 16 | 10 | 1 | 16 |
| 50-59 | 54.5 | 8 | 20 | 2 | 16 |
| 60-69 | 64.5 | 3 | 30 | 3 | 9 |
| | | $N$=120 | | | $\Sigma fd'$=–78 |

$$\overline{X} = AM + \frac{\Sigma fd'}{N} \times i$$

$$= 34.5 + \frac{-78}{120} \times 10$$

$$= 34.5 + \frac{-78}{12}$$

$$= 34.5 - 6.5$$

$$= 28 \text{ marks.}$$

***Note.*** The above series is an inclusive continuous series. The arithmetic mean of this series may be computed without converting it into exclusive form.

**Calculation of Arithmetic mean in Open-end distributions.** In order to calculate arithmetic mean in such series, first, open-end values should be known by the method explained in 'chapter 7'. After this mean can be calculated by using any method of calculation in case of continuous series.

**Illustration 12.** Find out Simple Arithmetic Average of weight from the following figures :

| | | | | | |
|---|---|---|---|---|---|
| Weights in Kgs. : | Below 20 | 20-40 | 40-60 | 60-80 | 80 and above |
| No. of persons : | 56 | 65 | 73 | 42 | 14 |

**Solution**

The lower limit of first group and upper limit of last group may be found out by deducting 20 from the upper limit of first group and by adding 20 in lower limit of last group as follows :

| Weight in Kgs. | Mid-values ($X$) | No. of persons ($f$) | $d$ ($AM$=50) | $fd$ |
|---|---|---|---|---|
| 0-20 | 10 | 56 | −40 | −2,240 |
| 20-40 | 30 | 65 | −20 | −1,300 |
| 40-60 | 50 | 73 | 0 | 0 |
| 60-80 | 70 | 42 | +20 | +840 |
| 80-100 | 90 | 14 | +40 | +560 |
| | | $N = 250$ | | $\Sigma fd = -2,140$ |

$$\overline{X} = AM + \frac{\Sigma fd}{N}$$

$$= 50 + \frac{-2,140}{250}$$

$$= 50 - 8.56$$

$$= 41.44 \text{ Kgms.}$$

**Illustration 13.** Find out the value of arithmetic mean from the following frequency distribution :

| | | | | | | |
|---|---|---|---|---|---|---|
| Class Intervals : | Below 10 | 10-20 | 20-50 | 50-100 | 100-200 | 200-500 |
| Frequencies : | 8 | 12 | 20 | 36 | 10 | 8 |

| | |
|---|---|
| Class Interval : | 500 and above |
| Frequencies : | 6 |

**Solution**

| Class Intervals | Mid-values ($X$) | Frequencies ($f$) | $d$ ($AM$=75) | $fd$ |
|---|---|---|---|---|
| 0-10 | 5 | 8 | −70 | −560 |
| 10-20 | 15 | 12 | −60 | −720 |
| 20-50 | 35 | 20 | −40 | −800 |
| 50-100 | 75 | 36 | 0 | 0 |
| 100-200 | 150 | 10 | 75 | 750 |
| 200-500 | 350 | 8 | 275 | 2,200 |
| 500-800 | 650 | 6 | 575 | 3,450 |
| | | $N$=100 | | $\Sigma fd$ = 4,320 |

$$\overline{X} = A + \frac{\Sigma fd}{N}$$

$$= 75 + \frac{4320}{100}$$

$$=75+43.20$$

$$=118.20$$

**MATHEMATICAL PROPERTIES OF ARITHMETIC MEAN**

The following mathematical properties are found in the arithmetic mean :

1. **The sum of deviations taken from arithmetic mean is always zero :** This is due to the reason that the sum of positive and negative deviations taken from the arithmetic mean is equal and therefore, the sum of deviations is zero.

This can be explained in the following manner :

$$\overline{X} = AM + \frac{\Sigma d}{N}$$

There, $AM$ is that value from which deviations are taken. And when deviations will be taken from the arithmetic mean, the value of $X$ and $AM$ will be the same and $AM$ will be equal to $X$ only when $\Sigma d$ is zero. Therefore, it is correct to say that the sum of deviations taken from arithmetic mean will always be zero.

**Example**

Variables : 15, 18, 22, 28, 37

$$\overline{X} = \frac{15 + 18 + 22 + 28 + 37}{5} = \frac{120}{5} = 24$$

If deviations are taken from 24, the positive and negative deviations will be equal and their sum will be zero as is clear from the following calculation :

| $X$ | $(\overline{X}^{d} = 24)$ | |
|---|---|---|
| 15 | −9 | |
| 18 | −6 | −17 |
| 22 | −2 | |
| 28 | +4 | |
| 37 | +13 | +17 |
| | | $\Sigma d = 0$ |

2. The sum of the squares of deviations derived from arithmetic mean will be lesser than the sum of deviations derived from any other value. This will become clear from the following example :

| | $\overline{X} = 24$ | | $AM = 15$ | | $AM = 18$ | | $AM = 22$ | | $AM = 28$ | | $AM = 37$ | |
|---|---|---|---|---|---|---|---|---|---|---|---|---|
| $X$ | $d$ | $d^2$ | $d$ | $d^2$ | $d$ | $d^2$ | $d$ | $d^2$ | $d$ | $d^2$ | $d$ | $d^2$ |
| 15 | −9 | 81 | 0 | 0 | −3 | 9 | −7 | 49 | −13 | 169 | −22 | 484 |
| 18 | −6 | 36 | 3 | 9 | 0 | 0 | −4 | 16 | −10 | 100 | −19 | 361 |
| 22 | −2 | 4 | 7 | 49 | 4 | 16 | 0 | 0 | −6 | 36 | −15 | 225 |
| 28 | 4 | 16 | 13 | 169 | 10 | 100 | 6 | 36 | 0 | 0 | −9 | 81 |
| 37 | 13 | 169 | 22 | 484 | 19 | 361 | 15 | 225 | 9 | 81 | 0 | 0 |
| $\Sigma X = 120$<br>$N = 5$ | 0 | 306 | 45 | 711 | 30 | 486 | 10 | 326 | −20 | 386 | −65 | 1,151 |

$$\therefore \overline{X} = \frac{120}{5} = 24$$

Thus it becomes clear that the sum of squares of deviations taken from arithmetic mean is the minimum (306) whereas the sum of squares of deviations taken from other values 15, 18, 22, 28 and 37 is 711, 486, 326, 386 and 1,151 respectively, which are more than 306. Therefore, it is absolutely correct to say that the sum of squares of deviations taken from arithmetic will be minimal.

3. If the value of any item, from among the items whose arithmetic mean has found, is not known, it can be easily known by the following formula :

$$\overline{X} = \frac{X_1 + X_2 + X_3 + \ldots\ldots X_n}{N}$$

For instance, if the arithmetic mean of 5 items is 15 and the values of the first four items are 8, 12, 18 and 9 respectively, then the value of the 5th item can be easily found by the above formula :

$$15 = \frac{8+12+18+9+X_5}{5}$$

$$\text{or} \quad 75 = 47 + X_5$$

$$\therefore \quad X_5 = 75 - 47 = 28$$

Thus the value of the 5th item will be 28.

**Illustration 14.** Goals scored by a football team in successive matches are 5, 2, 4, 3, 6, 0, 4, 6. What is the number of goals the team must score in the next match in order that the average comes to 4 goals per match?

[*B.Com.* (*Pass*) *Delhi*]

**Solution**

$$\overline{X} = \frac{X_1 + X_2 + X_3 + X_4 + X_5 + X_6 + X_7 + X_8 + X_9}{N}$$

$$4 = \frac{5+2+4+3+6+0+4+6+X_9}{9}$$

$$4 = \frac{30+X_9}{9}$$

$$36 - 30 = X_9$$

$$X_9 = 6.$$

$\therefore$ The team should score 6 goals in next (ninth) match.

4. When the arithmetic mean and numbers of two or more than two facts are given, their collective combined mean can easily be determined. The following formula is used for this purpose.

$$\overline{X}_{12} \ldots n \text{ (combined Mean)} = \frac{\overline{X}_1 N_1 + \overline{X}_2 N_2 + \overline{X}_n N_n}{N_1 + N_2 + N_n}$$

**Example.** If the arithmetic mean of two series are 20 and 25 respectively and the number of their items be 30 and 70 then the combined mean of both the series will be the following :

$$\overline{X}_{12} = \frac{20(30) + 25(70)}{30+70}$$

$$= \frac{600 + 1{,}750}{100}$$

$$= \frac{2{,}350}{100}$$

$$= 23.50$$

5. If the values of two series are added and deducted respectively, then the mean of these additions and deductions will be equal to sums and differences of the mean of that series. The following example will make this clear :

**Example**

| Roll No. | Marks in Accountancy | Marks in Statistics | | |
|---|---|---|---|---|
| | $(X)$ | $(Y)$ | $(X–Y)$ | $(X + Y)$ |
| 1 | 19 | 18 | + 1 | 37 |
| 2 | 21 | 22 | –1 | 43 |
| 3 | 25 | 29 | –4 | 54 |
| 4 | 30 | 25 | + 5 | 55 |
| 5 | 35 | 26 | + 9 | 61 |
| Total | 130 | 120 | 10 | 250 |
| Average | $\frac{130}{5} = 26$ | $\frac{120}{5} = 24$ | $\frac{10}{5} = 2$ | $\frac{250}{5} = 50$ |
| | | (26–24 = 2); | | (26 + 24 = 50) |

This has become clear from the above example.

6. If the values of any series are changed, the changed (right) arithmetic mean can be calculated. The old value (wrong value) of the items will be deducted from the old sum of the items; the revised or new value will be added. The revised sum will be divided by the number of items and the quotient will be the correct revised arithmetic mean.

**Example.** The average marks of 5 students is 48, but it was found later on that one of the students had got 55 marks, and while taking out mean in respect of his marks 5 were added by mistake. The revised mean in this case will be the following :

$$\Sigma X \text{ (old)} = \overline{X} \text{ (old) } N$$

$$= 48 \times 5$$

$$= 240 \text{ marks}$$

$$\Sigma X \text{ (New/correct)} = \Sigma X \text{ (old)} + \text{Correct value} - \text{Incorrect value}$$

$$= 240 + 55 - 5$$

$$= 290 \text{ marks}$$

$$\overline{X} \text{ (correct)} = \frac{\sum X \text{(Correct)}}{N}$$

$$= \frac{290}{5}$$

$$= 58 \text{ marks.}$$

7. If from all the items of a series a certain number is deducted or added to it, the arithmetic mean of that series also gets decreased or increased by the same number. In the same way if all the items of a series are multiplied or divided by a certain number, then the arithmetic mean also gets multiplied or divided in the same proportion. The following example will explain this fact :

**Example.** Variables : 18, 12, 30, 24, 21 are given

If these variables are multiplied or divided by three or 3 is added to or deducted from them, the following changes will occur in the arithmetic mean :

| | $X$ | $(X+3)$ | $(X-3)$ | $[X(3)]$ | $(X \div 3)$ |
|---|---|---|---|---|---|
| | 18 | 21 | 15 | 54 | 6 |
| | 12 | 15 | 9 | 36 | 4 |
| | 30 | 33 | 27 | 90 | 10 |
| | 24 | 27 | 21 | 72 | 8 |
| | 21 | 24 | 18 | 63 | 7 |
| Total | 105 | 120 | 90 | 315 | 35 |
| Average = | $\frac{105}{5}$ X=21 | $\frac{120}{5}$ = 24 | $\frac{90}{5}$ = 18 | $\frac{315}{5}$ = 63 | $\frac{35}{5}$ = 7 |

Thus it is proved that if any value is added, the arithmetic mean will increase by the same number, as an adding 3 the arithmetic mean has increased from 21 to 21 + 3 = 24; if any value is deducted, the arithmetic mean will increase by the same number as the above has become 21–3 = 18; the arithmetic mean will get multiplied on multiplying it by any value such as the above as become 21 × 3 = 63 and on being divided by any value, the arithmetic mean will get reduced by the same degree as in the above 21/3=7.

**Illustration 15.** The following are the monthly salaries of 30 employees of a firm :

| | | | | | | | | | |
|---|---|---|---|---|---|---|---|---|---|
| 139 | 126 | 114 | 100 | 88 | 62 | 77 | 91 | 103 | 108 |
| 129 | 144 | 148 | 63 | 69 | 148 | 132 | 118 | 142 | 116 |
| 123 | 104 | 95 | 80 | 85 | 106 | 123 | 133 | 140 | 134 |

The firm gave bonuses of Rs. 10, 15, 20, 25, 30 and 35 for the individuals in the respective salary groups : exceeding 60 but not exceeding 75, exceeding 75 but not exceeding 90 and so on up to exceeding 135 but not exceeding 150.

Find the average bonus paid per employee.

**Solution**

**Calculation of Average Bonus**

| Class Intervals | Alternative method of writing class Intervals | Tally bars | Freq. $f$ | Bonus $X$ Rs. | Total Bonus $fX$ |
|---|---|---|---|---|---|
| Exceeding 60 but not 75 | 61—75 | III | 3 | 10 | 30 |
| " 75 " 90 | 76—90 | IIII | 4 | 15 | 60 |
| " 90 " 105 | 91—105 | ~~IIII~~ | 5 | 20 | 100 |
| " 105 " 120 | 106—120 | ~~IIII~~ | 5 | 25 | 125 |
| " 120 " 135 | 121—135 | ~~IIII~~ II | 7 | 30 | 210 |
| " 135 " 150 | 136-150 | ~~IIII~~ I | 6 | 35 | 210 |
| | | | $N = 30$ | | $\Sigma fX = 735$ |

$$\overline{X} = \frac{\Sigma fX}{N}$$

$$= \frac{735}{30}$$

$$= \text{Rs. } 24.50$$

**Charlier's check for checking the accuracy of computation of arithmetic mean.** Charlier has evolved a formula to check the accuracy of arithmetic mean which is used to determine whether the mean has been correctly calculated. The following is the formula :

$$\Sigma fd = \Sigma[f(d + 1)] - \Sigma f$$

or $$\Sigma fd' = \Sigma[f(d' + 1)] - \Sigma f$$

**Illustration 16.** Calculate arithmetic mean from the following series and check your calculation by using Charlier's check method :

| | | | | |
|---|---|---|---|---|
| Class Intervals : | 100-200 | 200-300 | 300-400 | 400-500 |
| Frequencies : | 15 | 18 | 22 | 10 |
| Class Intervals : | 500-500 | 600-700 | | |
| Frequencies : | 6 | 9 | | |

**Solution**

| Class Intervals | Mid-values | Fre-quencies | $d$ ($AM$=350) | $d'$ ($i$=100) | $fd'$ | $(d' + 1)$ | $f(d' + 1)$ |
|---|---|---|---|---|---|---|---|
| 100-200 | 150 | 15 | –200 | –2 | –30 | –1 | –15 |
| 200-300 | 250 | 18 | –100 | –1 | –18 | 0 | 0 |
| 300-400 | 350 | 22 | 0 | 0 | 0 | 1 | 22 |
| 400-500 | 450 | 10 | 100 | 1 | 10 | 2 | 20 |
| 500-600 | 550 | 6 | 200 | 2 | 12 | 3 | 18 |
| 600-700 | 650 | 9 | 300 | 3 | 27 | 4 | 36 |
| | | $N$ = 80 | | | $\Sigma fd'$ = 1 | $\Sigma[f(d'+1)]$ = 81 | |

$$\overline{X} = AM + \frac{\sum fd'}{N} \times i$$

$$= 350 + \frac{1}{80} \times 100$$

$$= 350 + 1.25$$

$$= 351.25$$

**Charlier's Check Formula**

$$\Sigma fd' = \Sigma[f(d' + 1)] - \Sigma f$$

$$1 = 81 - 80$$

$$1 = 1$$

Therefore the above calculation of arithmetic mean is correct.

**Finding the value of Missing Frequency.** If the arithmetic mean of a series is given and the frequency of any one of its items is not given, the missing frequency can be traced with the help of the formula of arithmetic mean. This will be made clear from the following illustrations.

**Illustration 17.** You are given the following data of marks :

| | | | | | | | |
|---|---|---|---|---|---|---|---|
| Marks : | 0-10 | 10-20 | 20-30 | 30-40 | 40-50 | 50-60 | 60-70 |
| No. of Students : | 14 | 22 | 30 | ? | 5 | 4 | 1 |

The average marks of the students are 25. Find the number of students who obtained marks 30-40.

**Solution**

| Marks | Mid-values | No. of students | $d$ ($AM$ = 35) | $d'$ ($i$ = 10) | $fd'$ |
|---|---|---|---|---|---|
| 0-10 | 5 | 14 | –30 | –3 | –42 |
| 10-20 | 15 | 22 | –20 | –2 | –44 |
| 20-30 | 25 | 30 | –10 | –1 | –30 |
| 30-40 | 35 | $fX$ | 0 | 0 | 0 |
| 40-50 | 45 | 5 | 10 | 1 | 5 |
| 50-60 | 55 | 4 | 20 | 2 | 8 |
| 60-70 | 65 | 1 | 30 | 3 | 3 |
| | | $N$=76+$fX$ | | $\Sigma fd'$ = –100 | |

$$\overline{X} = AM + \frac{\sum fd'}{N} \times i$$

$$25 = 35 + \frac{-100}{76 + fX} \times 10$$

or $1,900 + 25fX = 2,660 + 35fX - 1000$

or $25fX - 35fX = 2,660 - 1,000 - 1,900$

or $-10fX = -240$

or $fX = 24$

∴ The number of students who obtained marks 30 – 40 is 24.

**Combined Mean.** When the averages of two or more than two universe of components are given and on that basis single mean is to be found for all, then that is called combined mean. To find out this type of mean, following is the formula :

$$\overline{X}_{12} \ldots. n \text{ (Combined Mean)} = \frac{\overline{X}_1 N_1 + \overline{X}_2 N_2 + \ldots \overline{X}_n \overline{X}_n}{N_1 + N_2 + N_n}$$

$\overline{X}_1$, $\overline{X}_2$, $\overline{X}_n$ stand for arithmetic averages in various series or components.

$N_1$, $N_2$, $N_n$ stand for number of items in various series.

**Illustration 18.** Calculate combined mean from the following series :

| | A | B | C |
|---|---|---|---|
| Arithmetic Mean | 10 | 8 | 12 |
| No. of items | 250 | 300 | 400 |

**Solution**

$$X_{123} = \frac{\overline{X}_1 N_1 + \overline{X}_2 N_2 + \overline{X}_3 N_3}{N_1 + N_2 + N_3}$$

$$= \frac{10 \times 250 + 8 \times 300 + 12 \times 400}{250 + 300 + 400}$$

$$= \frac{2{,}500 + 2{,}400 + 4{,}800}{950}$$

$$= \frac{9{,}700}{950}$$

$$= 10.21$$

**Illustration 19.** The monthly average earnings of workers in factory A was Rs. 150 and in factory B it was Rs. 200; 500 and 350 workers were employed in Factory A and B respectively. Find average earnings of the workers of both factories altogether.

**Solution**

$$\overline{X}_{12} = \frac{\overline{X}_1 N_1 + \overline{X}_2 N_2}{N_1 + N_2}$$

$$= \frac{150 \times 500 + 200 \times 350}{500 + 300}$$

$$= \frac{75{,}000 + 70{,}000}{850}$$

$$= \frac{1{,}45{,}000}{850}$$

$$= \text{Rs. } 170.6$$

**Illustration 20.** There were three sections of a class namely A, B and C. The number of students in these classes were 50, 30 and 20 respectively. The average marks of students of section A were 50

and of section C were 40. The average marks of the students of all three sections were 60. Find the average marks obtained by the students of section B.

**Solution**

$$\overline{X}_{123} = \frac{\overline{X}_1 N_1 + \overline{X}_2 N_2 + \overline{X}_3 N_3}{N_1 + N_2 + N_3}$$

$$60 = \frac{50 \times 50 + \overline{X}_2 (30) + 40(20)}{50 + 30 + 20}$$

$$\text{or} \quad 60 = \frac{2,500 + 30\overline{X}_2 + 800}{100}$$

$$\text{or} \quad 6,000 = 2,500 + 30\overline{X}_2 + 800$$

$$\text{or} \quad -30\overline{X}_2 = 2,500 + 800 - 6,000$$

$$\text{or} \quad -30\overline{X}_2 = -2,700$$

$$\text{or} \quad \overline{X}_2 = 90$$

∴ The average marks of the students of section B were 90.

**Illustration 21.** The average height of three groups is found out which were 60″, 65″ and 70″ of first, second and third group respectively. The average height of the persons of all three groups was 63.5″. The number of persons in first and second groups were 25 and 15 respectively. Find out the number of persons in third group.

**Solution**

$$\overline{X}_{123} = \frac{\overline{X}_1 N_1 + \overline{X}_2 N_2 + \overline{X}_3 N_3}{N_1 + N_2 + N_3}$$

$$63.5 = \frac{60(25) + 65(15) + 70(N_3)}{25 + 15 + N_3}$$

$$\text{or} \quad 63.5 = \frac{15,00 + 975 + 70N_3}{40 + N_3}$$

$$\text{or} \quad 2,540 + 63.5\,N_3 = 1,500 + 975 + 70N_3$$

$$\text{or} \quad 63.5\,N_3 - 70\,N_3 = 1,500 + 975 - 2,540$$

$$\text{or} \quad -6.5\,N_3 = -65$$

$$\text{or} \quad N_3 = 10$$

∴ The number of persons in third group was 10.

**Illustration 22.** The mean age of all the students of a class of 50 students is 17 years. If the mean age of 30 of them is 18 years, determine the mean age of the remaining 20 students.

[*B.Com.* (*Pass*), *Delhi*]

**Solution**

$$\bar{X}_{12} = \frac{\bar{X}_1 N_1 + \bar{X}_2 N_2}{N_1 + N_2}$$

$$17 = \frac{18(30) + \bar{X}_2(20)}{30 + 20}$$

$$850 = 540 + 20\,\bar{X}_2$$

$$20\,\bar{X}_2 = 850 - 540$$

$$20\,\bar{X}_2 = 310$$

$$\bar{X}_2 = 15.5 \text{ years}$$

∴ The mean age of another group of 20 students is 15.5 years.

**Corrected Mean.** Sometimes, while calculating the arithmetic mean, the value of some is wrongly included and the mean found out in such cases will be wrong. But after knowing the mistake, it is necessary to find the correct mean. In order to do so, the wrong item should be deducted from the sum of total items and the correct items should be added thereto and then using the formula, the revised mean should be known. The following example will highlight this fact.

**Illustration 23.** The arithmetic average of 100 students is given 45. But later on it was found that the marks of a student which were '64' was wrongly included as '46'. Now you are required to calculate the correct mean.

**Solution**

$$\bar{X} = \frac{\Sigma X}{N}$$

Given $\bar{X} = 45$

$N = 100$

∴ $\Sigma X = 45 \times 100$

$= 4{,}500$

As one variable 64 wrongly being read as 46, therefore correct $X$ will 4,500 − 46 + 64.

$$= 4{,}518$$

$$\therefore \quad \text{Correct} \quad \overline{X} = \frac{\Sigma X}{N}$$

$$= \frac{4{,}518}{100}$$

$$= 45.18 \text{ marks}$$

**Illustration 24.** The monthly average income of a group of 20 persons is being calculated as Rs. 500. But later on it was discovered that a person whose income was Rs. 350 per month wrongly included as Rs. 530 and the income of another person was Rs. 630 but it was recorded as 360 while calculating the average income. Find out correct monthly average income of these persons on the basis of these information.

**Solution**

$$\overline{X} = \frac{\Sigma X}{N}$$

Given $\quad \overline{X} = \text{Rs. } 500$

$$N = 20$$

$$\therefore \Sigma X \text{ (Wrong)} = 500 \times 20$$

$$= 10{,}000$$

As two correct items 350 and 630 wrongly included as 530 and 360, therefore, correct sum of variables will be :

$$10{,}000 + 350 + 630 - 530 - 360 = 10{,}090$$

$$\therefore \quad \text{Correct} \quad \overline{X} = \frac{10{,}090}{20}$$

$$= \text{Rs. } 504.5$$

**Illustration 25.** The marks of some students were collected and were placed in a discrete series. The arithmetic mean of this series was calculated as 16 taking 50 items. But after this calculation it was discovered that frequencies of an item 6 marks was 12 which was wrongly noted as 22 from the original, while calculating the arithmetic means. Find out correct mean of this series.

**Solution**

Given $\overline{X} = 16$

$N = 50$

$\therefore \quad \Sigma fX = 16 \times 50$

$= 800$ (wrong)

The correct $\Sigma fX$ will be $800 + (6 \times 12) - (6 \times 22)$

$= 800 + 72 - 132$

$= 740$

The correct number of items will be $50 + 12 - 22 = 40$

$$\therefore \text{The correct mean} = \frac{740}{40}$$

$= 18.5$ marks

**Illustration 26.** The marks of 100 students are shown in a continuous series having groups 0-10, 10-20....and so on. The average marks were calculated as 40 of this series. But after this it was found that a student who secured 24 marks wrongly read as 42 while computing arithmetic mean. Now you are required to compute correct mean of this series.

**Solution**

Given $\overline{X} = 40$

$N = 100$

$\therefore \quad \Sigma fX = 40 \times 100$

$= 4,000$ (wrong)

The correct value of $\Sigma fX$ will be

$4,000 + 25 - 45 = 3,980$

$$\therefore \text{Correct Mean} = \frac{3,980}{100}$$

$= 39.80$ marks

The correct number in this question is 24 which will be included in 20-30 class and its mid-value will be 25; for correction this has been included in wrong $\Sigma fX$ and the wrong number is 42 which has already been included in the class of 40-45 and the mid-value 45 of the class 40-50 has been deducted from $\Sigma fX$.

**Weighted Mean.** When various items are given weight according to their importance for the purpose of relative comparison and then the mean is found, that is called weighted mean. The following formula is applied for calculating the weighted mean :

1. Direct method :

$$\bar{X}_w \text{ (Weighted mean)} = \frac{\sum WX}{WX}$$

$W$ = Weight

2. Short-cut method :

$$\bar{X}_w \text{ (Weighted mean)} = AM + \frac{\sum Wd}{\sum W}$$

**Illustration 27.** What will be weighted mean in the following sums?

| | | | | | | |
|---|---|---|---|---|---|---|
| Variables | 1 | 2 | 3 | 4 | 5 | 6 |
| Weight | 10 | 15 | 18 | 16 | 12 | 29 |

**Solution**

| Variables ($X$) | Weight ($W$) | $WX$ |
|---|---|---|
| 1 | 10 | 10 |
| 2 | 15 | 30 |
| 3 | 18 | 54 |
| 4 | 16 | 64 |
| 5 | 12 | 60 |
| 6 | 29 | 174 |
| | $\Sigma_w=100$ | $\Sigma WX=392$ |

$$\bar{X}_w \text{(Weighted mean)} = \frac{\sum WX}{\sum W}$$

$$= \frac{392}{100}$$

$$=3.92$$

In the above example, the calculation of weighted mean may be done in the following manner also :

| Variables ($X$) | Weight ($W$) | $d$ ($AM = 3$) | $wd$ |
|---|---|---|---|
| 1 | 10 | –2 | –20 |
| 2 | 15 | –1 | –15 |
| 3 | 18 | 0 | 0 |
| 4 | 16 | 1 | 16 |
| 5 | 12 | 2 | 24 |
| 6 | 29 | 3 | 87 |
| | $\Sigma W = 100$ | | $\Sigma Wd = 92$ |

$$\overline{X}_w \text{ (Weighted mean)} = AM + \frac{\sum Wd}{\sum W}$$

$$= 3 + \frac{92}{100}$$

$$= 3.92$$

**Illustration 28.** From the following data, calculate the weighted and simple average and account for the difference :

| Value | Weight |
|---|---|
| 15 | 8 |
| 20 | 6 |
| 25 | 4 |
| 30 | 4 |
| 35 | 3 |

(*C.A., May*)

**Solution**

| Value ($X$) | Weight ($W$) | $WX$ |
|---|---|---|
| 15 | 8 | 120 |
| 20 | 6 | 120 |
| 25 | 4 | 100 |
| 30 | 4 | 120 |
| 35 | 3 | 105 |
| $\Sigma X$=125<br>$N$ = 5 | $\Sigma W$=25 | $\Sigma WX$=565 |

$$\overline{X} = \frac{\sum X}{N} \qquad \overline{X}_w = \frac{\sum WX}{\sum W}$$

$$= \frac{125}{5} \qquad = \frac{565}{25}$$

$$=25 \qquad =22.6$$

The difference in simple mean and weighted mean is due to difference in weights of various values.

**Illustration 29.** Compare the results of two colleges from the following data and comment which college gives the better result?

| Faculty | College A | | College B | |
|---|---|---|---|---|
| | No. of students appeared | No. of students passed | No. of students appeared | No. of students passed |
| Arts | 600 | 480 | 100 | 70 |
| Science | 150 | 135 | 30 | 24 |
| Commerce | 250 | 200 | 70 | 56 |
| Total | 1,000 | 815 | 200 | 150 |

**Solution**

| Faculty | College A | | | | College B | | | |
|---|---|---|---|---|---|---|---|---|
| | No. of students ($W$) | No. of students passed | Percentage ($X$) | $WX$ | No. of students appeared | No. of students passed | Percentage ($X$) | $WX$ |
| Arts | 600 | 480 | 80 | 48,000 | 100 | 70 | 70 | 7,000 |
| Science | 150 | 135 | 90 | 13,500 | 30 | 24 | 80 | 2,400 |
| Commerce | 250 | 200 | 80 | 20,000 | 70 | 56 | 80 | 5,600 |
| | 1,000 | | | 81,500 | 200 | | | 15,000 |

College A :

$$\overline{X}_w \text{ (Weighted Average)} = \frac{\Sigma WX}{\Sigma W}$$

$$= \frac{81{,}500}{1{,}000}$$

$$= 81.50\%$$

College B :

$$\overline{X}_w \text{ (Weighted Average)} = \frac{\Sigma WX}{\Sigma W}$$

$$= \frac{15{,}000}{200}$$

$$= 75\%$$

Therefore, College A gives better result.

**Standardized Death Rate.** In order to compare the death rate of the population of two places, standardized death rate is found. 'Weighted mean' method is used to find out the standardized death rate. In order to find it out the population of any of the places is taken to be standard. Assuming that to be giving weight to that, the death rate of a local population is found out or determined. That is known as the standardized death rate. The comparison of the standardized death rate of local population is made with the general death rate or crude death rate of the standardized population. The following formula is applied to find the general death rate and the standardized death rate :

General Death Rate or Crude Death Rate

$$= \frac{\text{Total Deaths}}{\text{Total Population}} \times 1{,}000$$

Standardised Death Rate

$$= \frac{\Sigma WX}{\Sigma W}$$

$W$ = Population of standard town or standard population;

$X$ = Rate of death of local town or standard population.

**Illustration 30.** Find the Crude Death Rate and Standardised Death Rate of town A and B assuming the population of town A as standard population.

| Age Group (years) | Town A | | Town B | |
|---|---|---|---|---|
| | Population | Deaths | Population | Deaths |
| Below 10 | 20,000 | 1,000 | 25,000 | 2,000 |
| 10-30 | 60,000 | 300 | 55,000 | 220 |
| 30-50 | 40,000 | 420 | 50,000 | 300 |
| 50 and above | 30,000 | 4,500 | 20,000 | 3,700 |
| | 1,50,000 | 6,220 | 1,50,000 | 6,220 |

**Solution**

| Age Group (years) | Town A (Standard) | | Town B (Local | | | |
|---|---|---|---|---|---|---|
| | Population ($W$) | Deaths | Population | Deaths | Rate ($X$) | $WX$ |
| Below 10 | 20,000 | 1,000 | 25,000 | 2,000 | 80 | 16,00,000 |
| 10-30 | 60,000 | 300 | 55,000 | 220 | 4 | 2,40,000 |
| 30-50 | 40,000 | 420 | 50,000 | 300 | 6 | 2,40,000 |
| 50 & above | 30,000 | 4,500 | 20,000 | 3,700 | 18.5 | 55,50,000 |
| | 1,50,000 | 6,220 | 1,50,000 | 6,220 | | 76,30,000 |

General Death Rate of town A :

$$= \frac{\text{Total Deaths}}{\text{Total Population}} \times 1{,}000$$

$$= \frac{6{,}220}{1{,}50{,}000} \times 1{,}000$$

$$= \frac{622}{15}$$

$$= 41.47$$

General Death Rate of Town B :

$$= \frac{\text{Total Deaths}}{\text{Total Population}} \times 1{,}000$$

$$= \frac{6{,}220}{1{,}50{,}000} \times 1{,}000$$

$$= \frac{622}{15}$$

$$= 41.47$$

Standardised Death Rate of Town B :

$$= \frac{\sum WX}{\sum W}$$

$$= \frac{76{,}30{,}000}{1{,}50{,}000}$$

$$= 50.87$$

**Illustration 31.** You are given population and deaths of two towns as follows :

| Age in years | Standard Town | | Local Town | |
|---|---|---|---|---|
| | Population | Deaths | Population | Deaths |
| Below 15 | 15,000 | 180 | 10,000 | 130 |
| 15-25 | 25,000 | 200 | 20,000 | 180 |
| 25-40 | 30,000 | 150 | 40,000 | 220 |
| 40-60 | 20,000 | 200 | 22,000 | 176 |
| 60 and above | 10,000 | 200 | 8,000 | 240 |
| | 1,00,000 | 930 | 1,00,000 | 946 |

Find which town is healthier.

**Solution**

| Age Group (years) | Town A (Standard) | | Town B (Local | | | |
|---|---|---|---|---|---|---|
| | Population ($W$) | Deaths | Population | Deaths | Rate ($X$) | $WX$ |
| Below 15 | 15,000 | 180 | 10,000 | 130 | 13 | 1,95,000 |
| 15-25 | 25,000 | 200 | 20,000 | 180 | 9 | 2,25,000 |
| 25-40 | 30,000 | 150 | 40,000 | 220 | 5.5 | 1,65,000 |
| 40-60 | 20,000 | 200 | 22,000 | 176 | 8 | 1,60,000 |
| 60 & above | 10,000 | 200 | 8,000 | 240 | 30 | 3,00,000 |
| | 1,00,000 | 930 | 1,00,000 | 946 | | 10,45,000 |

General Death Rate of standard town

$$= \frac{\text{Total Deaths}}{\text{Total Population}} \times 1,000$$

$$= \frac{930}{1,00,000} \times 1,000$$

$$= 9.3$$

Standardised Death Rate of local town :

$$= \frac{\Sigma WX}{\Sigma W}$$

$$= \frac{10,45,000}{1,00,000}$$

$$= 10.45$$

Therefore, standard town is healthier than the local town.

## GEOMETRIC MEAN

Geometric mean is also a mathematical mean. This type of mean is that root of the products of the values of the series which is the number of items. That is to say, first, all the units of the series are multiplied with each other and then as many roots are found as there are units in that.

**Method of calculation.** The following formula is applied to calculate the geometric mean :

$$G.M. = \sqrt[n]{a \times b \times ... n}$$

*G.M.* = Geometric mean and *a, b, n* = different variables.

**Illustration 32.** Find out the Geometric mean from the following : 16, 25

**Solution**

$$G.M. = \sqrt[n]{a \times b}$$

$$= \sqrt{16 \times 25}$$

$$= \sqrt{400}$$

$$= 20.$$

But in case where the number of items is more than two, then it is difficult to find out the 3rd, 4th and 5th root etc. In that case the following formula used in individual series.

Individual Series

$$GM = \text{Anti-log of } \frac{\sum Logs\ of\ X}{N}$$

To find the logarithms and antilogarithms, their tables are used.

The following method is adopted to see the logarithmic and anti-logarithmic tables :

**Method of finding Logarithm.** To find logarithm, two things — Characteristic and Mantissa have to be known.

**Method to Find Characteristics**

(A) If the variables are one or more than one, the following formula is applied :

$N - 1$ = Characteristic

$N$ = Number of digits.

**Example.** The Characteristic of the following values will be as follows :

| Values | Characteristic | Clarification |
|---|---|---|
| 4325 | 3 | (4 − 1 = 3) |
| 435 | 2 | (3 − 1 = 2) |
| 35.09 | 1 | (2 − 1 = 1) |
| 5.86 | 0 | (1 − 1 = 0) |

In the above example, there are 4 digits in 4325, therefore its characteristic will be 3.

(B) *If the value is less than 1.* In case the value is less than 1, characteristic are negative and they will be calculated by the following formula :

Characteristic = $N + 1$

$N$ = Number of Zero after decimal point.

**Example.** The Characteristic of values in the following will be thus :

| Values | Characteristic | Clarification |
|---|---|---|
| .35 | $\bar{1}$ | 0 + 1 = 1 |
| .0362 | $\bar{2}$ | 1 + 1 = 2 |
| .00482 | $\bar{3}$ | 2 + 1 = 3 |
| .000532 | $\bar{4}$ | 3 + 1 = 4 |
| .0000506 | $\bar{5}$ | 4 + 1 = 5 |

The characteristics of the items which are less than one will be negative and their mantissa will be positive, therefore a bar is drawn on such characteristics.

**Method of finding Mantissa.** To find Mantissa, logarithmic table are used. Mantissa are all positive. All the values are approximated. Upto 4 figures and then looked at the vertical column of 2 figures in table and the 3rd figure is seen in the horizontal column. The 4th figure is seen in the mean difference of the horizontal column itself and then it is added to the value found before.

**Example.** After approximating the given figure 53289. Its mantissa may upto figures 5329 will be obtained, by looking 53 in the vertical side of the log-table, 2 in the horizontal side and 9 in the mean difference. This will be 7266. The characteristic of this number is 4, therefore, its absolute log will be 4.7266.

**Anti-log.** To find it out anti-log table is used.

While looking for it, first, a value is known on the basis of mantissa which can be known by looking at the table. In order to see the table, two digits (after the decimal point) are seen on the vertical side and one digit is seen on the horizontal side. In order to add decimal to the value thus found, the following formula is applied :

(a) If the value is bigger than 1, then,

N + 1 is applied.

N = Characteristic.

On the basis of N + 1 the number of digits is known after which decimal is to be added.

**Example.** From the following logarithms the anti-logs will be like this :

| Logs | Anti-logs |
|---|---|
| 3.625 | 4217.00 |
| 2.625 | 421.7 |
| 1.625 | 42.17 |
| 0.625 | 4.217 |

In the above example, 5 on .62 will be seen in the anti-log table which comes out to be 4217 and in order to add decimal to it, there will be 3 + 1 = 4 digits, in the 2nd there will be 2 + 1 = 3 digits etc.

(b) If the value is smaller than 1. If the characteristic is negative, it will be assumed that the original value is smaller than one. To add decimal to that, the following formula will be applied :

N – 1 = Number of Zero after decimal point.

N = Characteristic.

**Example**

| Logs | Anti-logs |
|---|---|
| $\bar{1}.625$ | .4217 |
| $\bar{2}.625$ | .04217 |
| $\bar{3}.625$ | .004217 |
| $\bar{4}.625$ | .0004217 |

**Illustration 33.** Calculate geometric mean from the following data :

6.5 169.0 11.0 113.0 14.2 75.5 35.5 215.0

**Solution**

| X | Logs |
|---|---|
| 6.5 | 0.8129 |
| 169.0 | 2.2279 |
| 11.0 | 1.0414 |
| 113.0 | 2.0531 |
| 14.2 | 1.1523 |
| 75.5 | 1.8779 |
| 35.5 | 1.5502 |
| 215.0 | 2.3324 |
| | ΣLogs = 13.0481 |

$$\text{G.M.} = \text{Anti-log of } \frac{\sum Logs}{N}$$

$$= \text{ " " } \frac{13.0481}{8}$$

$$= \text{ " " } 1.6310$$

$$= 42.76$$

**Illustration 34.** Compute Geometric Mean from the following .62, .0783, .005467, 1.234, 54.65, 674.82, 3,403.21, 54,302.10, .000823, .0000602.

**Solution**

| X | Logs |
|---|---|
| .62 | $\bar{1}.7924$ |
| .0783 | $\bar{2}.8938$ |
| .005467 | $\bar{3}.7378$ |
| 1.234 | 0.0913 |
| 54.65 | 1.7376 |
| 674.82 | 2.8292 |
| 3,403.21 | 3.5319 |
| 54,302.10 | 4.7348 |
| .000823 | $\bar{4}.9154$ |
| .0000602 | $\bar{5}.7796$ |
| $N$ = 10 | ΣLogs = 2.0438 |

$$\text{G.M.} = \text{Anti-log of } \frac{\sum Logs}{N}$$

$$= \text{ " " } \frac{2.0438}{10}$$

$$= \text{ " " } .20438$$

$$= 1.601$$

*Discrete Series :* The following formula will be used to calculate Geometric mean in such series.

$$\text{G.M.} = \text{Anti-log of } \frac{\Sigma fLogs}{N}$$

**Illustration 35.** Find Geometric Mean from the following frequency distribution :

| | | | | | |
|---|---|---|---|---|---|
| X | 2 | 4 | 6 | 8 | 10 |
| f | 5 | 7 | 8 | 3 | 2 |

**Solution**

| *X* | *f* | Logs | *f* Logs |
|---|---|---|---|
| 2 | 5 | .3010 | 1.5050 |
| 4 | 7 | .6021 | 4.2147 |
| 6 | 8 | .7782 | 6.2256 |
| 8 | 3 | .9031 | 2.7093 |
| 10 | 2 | 1.0000 | 2.0000 |
| | *N*=25 | | Σ*f* logs=16.6546 |

$$\text{G.M.} = \text{Anti-log of } \frac{\Sigma Logs}{N}$$

$$= \text{"} \quad \text{"} \quad \frac{16.6546}{25}$$

$$= \text{"} \quad \text{"} \quad .6662$$

$$= 4.636$$

**Continuous sums**

Find the logarithms of the mid-values of the class-intervals and the following formula will be applied to find geometeric mean.

$$\text{G.M.} = \text{Anti-log of } \frac{\Sigma fLogs}{N}$$

**Illustration 36.** Compute Geometric Mean from the following series :

| | | | | | |
|---|---|---|---|---|---|
| Classes | 0-6 | 6-12 | 12-18 | 18-24 | 24-30 |
| Frequency | 3 | 8 | 2 | 7 | 1 |

**Solution**

| Classes | Mid-values ($X$) | Frequency ($f$) | Logs | $f$ Logs |
|---|---|---|---|---|
| 0-6 | 3 | 3 | .4771 | 1.4313 |
| 6-12 | 9 | 8 | .9542 | 7.6336 |
| 12-18 | 15 | 2 | 1.1761 | 2.3522 |
| 18-24 | 21 | 7 | 1.3222 | 9.2554 |
| 24-30 | 27 | 1 | 1.4314 | 1.4314 |
| | | $N = 21$ | | $\Sigma$f Logs=22.1039 |

$$G.M. = \text{Anti-log of } \frac{\Sigma f \; Logs}{N}$$

$$= \quad " \quad " \quad \frac{22.1039}{21}$$

$$= \quad " \quad " \quad 1.0526$$

$$= 11.29$$

**Weighted Geometric Mean.** To find the weighted geometric mean, first, the logs of values are known. After this they are multiplied by their weights and the product of multiplication is divided by the sum of weights and the anti-log of the quotient is known. That is the weighted geometric mean. Weighted geometric mean can be known by the following formula :

$$\text{G.M.} = \text{Anti-log of } \frac{\Sigma W \; Logs}{\Sigma W}$$

$W$ = Weight

**Illustration 37.** From the following data compute Weighted Geometric Mean :

| | | | | | | |
|---|---|---|---|---|---|---|
| Measurements | 5 | 10 | 15 | 20 | 25 | 30 |
| Weights | 8 | 12 | 10 | 11 | 6 | 3 |

**Solution**

| Measurements ($X$) | Weights $W$ | Logs | $W$ Logs |
|---|---|---|---|
| 5 | 8 | .6990 | 5.5920 |
| 10 | 12 | 1.0000 | 12.0000 |
| 15 | 10 | 1.1761 | 11.7610 |
| 20 | 11 | 1.3010 | 14.3110 |
| 25 | 6 | 1.3979 | 8.3874 |
| 30 | 3 | 1.4771 | 4.4313 |
| | $\Sigma W = 50$ | | 56.4827 |

$$\text{Weighted G.M.} = \text{Anti-log of } \frac{\sum W\ Logs}{\sum W}$$

$$= \text{" "} \quad \frac{56.4827}{50}$$

$$= \text{" "} \quad 1.129654$$

$$= 13.48$$

**Some other examples of Geometric Mean**

**Illustration 38.** The annual rate of growth of output of a factory in five years are 5.0, 7.5, 2.5, 5.0 and 10.0 per cent respectively. What is the compound rate of growth of output per annum for the period?

**Solution**

| Values | Logs |
|---|---|
| 105.0 | 2.0212 |
| 107.5 | 2.0314 |
| 102.5 | 2.0106 |
| 105.0 | 2.0212 |
| 110.0 | 2.0414 |
| | $\Sigma$Logs = 10.1258 |

$$\text{G.M.} = \text{Anti-log of } \frac{\sum Logs}{N}$$

$$= \text{" "} \quad \frac{10.1258}{5}$$

$$= \text{" "} \quad 2.02516$$

$$= 105.9$$

Rate of growth = 105.9 − 100 = 5.9%

**Illustration 39.** The population of a town was 10 lakhs in 1990 which increased to 20 lakhs in 2000. Find out the rate of growth of population per year.

**Solution**

$$R = \sqrt[n]{\frac{P_n}{P_0}} - 1$$

$R$ = Rate of growth,
$n$ = Number of years,
$P_n$ = Population at the end of the period,
$P_0$ = Population at the beginning of the period.

Putting values in the above formula, we get :

$$R = \sqrt[10]{\frac{20}{10}} - 1$$

$$= \left(\sqrt[10]{2}\right) - 1$$

$$= \text{Anti log of } \left[\frac{Log^2}{10}\right] - 1$$

$$= \text{Anti log of } \left[\frac{0.30103}{10}\right] - 1$$

$$= [\text{Anti log of } (0.030103)] - 1$$

$$= 1.0718 - 1$$

$$= 0.0718$$

Therefore, the rate of increase per thousand will be 0.0718 (1000) = 71.8.

**Illustration 40.** A machine was purchased for Rs. 1,000 in 1995. Depreciation of the diminishing balance method was charged 40% in the first year, 25% in the second year and 10% p.a. during the next three years. What is the average rate of depreciations charged during the whole period.

**Solution**

| Year | Depreciated Value (for value of Rs. 100) ($X$) | log of $X$ |
|---|---|---|
| 1995 | 100 — 40 = 60 | 1.7782 |
| 1996 | 100 — 25 = 75 | 1.8751 |
| 1997 | 100 — 10 = 90 | 1.9542 |
| 1998 | 100 — 10 = 90 | 1.9542 |
| 1999 | 100 — 10 = 90 | 1.9542 |
| $N = 5$ | | $\Sigma \text{Log } X = 9.5159$ |

$$\text{G.M.} = \text{Anti-log of } \frac{\Sigma \text{Log } X}{N}$$

$$= \text{'' \quad ''} \frac{9.5159}{5}$$

$$= \text{'' \quad ''} 1.9032$$

$$= 80$$

∴ The average rate of depreciation during last 5 years will be 100 – 80 = 20%.

**Illustration 41.** The price of a commodity increased 5% from 1996 to 1997, by 8% from 1997 to 1998 and by 77% from 1998 to 1999. The average increase from 1996 to 1999 is quoted as 26% and not 30%. State whether it is correct or not?

**Solution**

If the arithmetic mean of increase of prices in various years will be calculated it will be 30% as follows :

| Years | Increase in prices (%) |
|---|---|
| 1996 to 1997 | 5 |
| 1997 to 1998 | 8 |
| 1998 to 1999 | 77 |
| $N = 3$ | $\Sigma X = 90$ |

$$\bar{X} = \frac{\Sigma X}{N}$$

$$= \frac{90}{3}$$

$$= 30\%$$

But it is not correct as the increase in prices has compound effect. Therefore, geometric mean of these increases should be calculated as follows :

$$\text{G.M.} = \text{Anti-log of } \frac{\Sigma \log \text{of items}}{N}$$

$$= \text{''} \quad \text{''} \quad \frac{\log 105 + \log 108 + \log 177}{3}$$

$$= \text{''} \quad \text{''} \quad \frac{2.0212 + 2.0334 + 2.2480}{3}$$

$$= \text{''} \quad \text{''} \quad \frac{6.3026}{3}$$

$$= \text{''} \quad \text{''} \quad 2.1009$$

$$= \text{''} \quad \text{''} \quad 126.2$$

$\therefore$ Increase is 126.2 – 100 = 26.2%

Thus it is true that the increase in price in given years is 26% not 30%.

**Illustration 42.** If there are $n$ measurements $X_1, X_2, X_3 \ldots.. X_n$ in all prove that the product of the ratios of each of these $n$ measures to their geometric mean is equal to unity.

**Solution**

Suppose the following are the measurements :

4, 5, 6 and 7

Their Geometric mean

$$= \text{A.L.} \frac{\log 4 + \log 5 + \log 6 + \log 7}{4}$$

$$= \text{A.L.} \left[\frac{.6021 + .6990 + .7782 + .8451}{4}\right]$$

$$= \text{A.L.} \left[\frac{2.9244}{4}\right]$$

$$= \text{A.L. } .7311 = 5.384$$

The ratio of the four measurements to their

$$\text{G.M.} = \frac{4}{5.384}, \frac{5}{5.384}, \frac{6}{5.384}, \frac{7}{5.384}$$

Their product

$$= \frac{840}{\text{A.L. } 4 \log 5.384} = \frac{840}{\text{A.L. } (4 \times .7311)}$$

$$= \frac{840}{\text{A.L.} (2.9244)}$$

$$= \frac{840}{840.3} = 1$$

We can prove the given propositions by taking any other items.

**Combined Geometric Mean**

When geometric mean of two or more series are given and later on when one geometric mean of all of them is to be found, then that is called combined geometric mean. To find combined geometric mean, the following formula is applied :

$$GM_{12 \cdots n} = \text{Anti-log of } \frac{N_1(\log GM_1) + N_2(\log GM_2) + \dots N_n(\log GM_n)}{N_1 + N_2 + N_3 + \dots N_n}$$

Here : $GM_{12 \dots n}$ = Combined geometric mean of given series.

$GM_1, GM_2, GM_3, \dots GM_n$ = Geometric mean in first, second and $n$ series.

$N_1, N_2, N_n$ = Number of figures in sets of which geometric mean is being calculated.

**Illustration 43.** If the geometric mean of two sets of two figures each are 8 and 5 respectively. Find out the combined geometric mean.

**Solution**

$$GM_{12} = \text{Anti-log of } \frac{N_1(\log GM_1) + N_2(\log GM_2)}{N_1 + N_2}$$

$$= \text{Anti-log of } \frac{2(\log 8) + 2(\log 5)}{2+2}$$

$$= \text{Anti-log of } \frac{2(.9031) + 2(.6990)}{4} = \frac{1.8062 + 1.3980}{4}$$

$$= \text{Anti-log of } \frac{3.2042}{4}$$

$$= \text{Anti-log of } .801$$

$$= 6.324$$

**Merits and Demerits of Geometric Mean**

**Merits.** 1. Geometric mean is found on the basis of all the values, therefore, it has a good representative value.

2. Too big or two small numbers hardly affect it.

3. Its algebraic evaluation is possible.

4. This an excellent method of finding the average of information increasing at compound rate.

**Demerit.** Calculative complexity is its biggest demerit. It is not easy for every one to calculate it.

## HARMONIC MEAN

This mean is the reciprocal of the arithmetic mean of the reciprocals of values. This mean is used to find out the rate of movement or speed. Like geometric mean, this is also difficult. Its calculation is done in the following way :

**Individual Series.** The following formula is applied in this :

$$H.M. = \frac{N}{\frac{1}{a} + \frac{1}{b} + \ldots \frac{1}{n}}$$

$N$ = Number of items

$a, b, n$ = Various variables

**Illustration 44.** Find harmonic mean from the following :

10 8 5 2 3

**Solution**

$$H.M. = \frac{N}{\frac{1}{a} + \frac{1}{b} + \frac{1}{c} + \frac{1}{d} + \frac{1}{e}}$$

$$= \frac{5}{\frac{1}{10} + \frac{1}{8} + \frac{1}{5} + \frac{1}{2} + \frac{1}{3}}$$

$$= \frac{5}{\frac{151}{120}}$$

$$= 5 \times \frac{120}{151}$$

$$= 3.97$$

The above formula is good to be applied for knowing smaller values, but when the values are too big, applying the following formula is more appropriate :

$$\text{H.M.} = \text{Reciprocal of } \frac{\Sigma \text{ Reciprocals}}{N}$$

To see reciprocals, 'Reciprocal Tables' are used, the method of seeing which is as below :

**Method of finding Reciprocal.** The given item is approximated upto 4 digits. Then the first two digits are looked on the vertical side, the 3rd on the horizontal side and looking for the 4th in the Mean difference, a number is known. After that, to add decimal point to that number, the following formula is applied :

(a) If the number is more than 1, the formula below will be used :

$N - 1$ = Number of zeros after decimal point

$N$ = Number of digits in item.

(b) If the number is less than 1, the formula given below will be used :

$N + 1$ = Number of digits before decimal point

$N$ = Number of zeros after decimal point in item.

The method of finding reciprocals will become clear from the following example :

**Example**

| Values | Reciprocals |
|---|---|
| 625.00 | .001600 |
| 25.82 | .04000 |
| 8.21 | .1218 |
| .832 | 1.202 |
| .636 | 1.572 |
| .0025 | 400.0 |

**Illustration 45.** Compute harmonic mean from the following data :

800 78.3 9.45 .676 .07834 .004656 .0003425 .00002853

**Solution**

| Variables | Reciprocals |
|---|---|
| 800.0 | .001250 |
| 78.3 | .012770 |
| 9.45 | .105800 |
| .676 | 1.479000 |
| .07834 | 12.764800 |
| .004656 | 214.770000 |
| .0003425 | 2919.708000 |
| .00002853 | 35047.719000 |
| $N = 8$ | Σ=Reciprocals=38196.560620 |

$$\text{H.M.} = \text{Reciprocal of } \frac{\Sigma \text{ Reciprocals}}{N}$$

$$= \text{ '' '' } = \frac{38196.560620}{8}$$

$$= \text{ '' '' } 4774.5700775$$

$$= .0002094$$

**Discrete Series.** For this type of series following formula will be used :

$$\text{H.M.} = \text{Reciprocal of } \frac{\Sigma f \text{ Reciprocals}}{N}$$

**Illustration 46.** From the following figures find the harmonic mean.

| | | | | | | |
|---|---|---|---|---|---|---|
| Size of items | 6 | 12 | 18 | 24 | 30 | 36 |
| Frequency | 8 | 9 | 6 | 10 | 2 | 5 |

**Solution**

| Size of items ($X$) | frequency ($f$) | Reciprocals | $f$ reciprocals |
|---|---|---|---|
| 6 | 8 | .16667 | 1.33336 |
| 12 | 9 | .08333 | 0.74997 |
| 18 | 6 | .05556 | 0.33336 |
| 24 | 10 | .04167 | 0.41670 |
| 30 | 2 | .03333 | 0.06666 |
| 36 | 5 | .02778 | 0.13890 |
| | $N = 40$ | | 3.03895 |

$$\text{H.M.} = \text{Reciprocal of } \frac{\Sigma f \text{ Reciprocals}}{N}$$

$$= \text{"} \quad \text{"} \quad \frac{3.03895}{40}$$

$$= \text{"} \quad \text{"} \quad .07597375$$

$$= 13.23$$

**Continuous Series.** To find out harmonic mean in this series, first the mid-values of class-intervals are found. After taking the reciprocals of those mid-values, the same operation is repeated as in the discrete series and the formula which is given below is applied :

$$\text{H.M.} = \text{Reciprocal of } \frac{\Sigma f \text{ Reciprocals}}{N}$$

**Illustration 47.** Calculate Harmonic Mean from the following series :

| Measurements | Frequency |
|---|---|
| 0-8 | 12 |
| 8-16 | 16 |
| 16-24 | 13 |
| 24-32 | 10 |
| 32-40 | 8 |
| 40-48 | 11 |

**Solution**

| Measurements | Mid-values ($X$) | Frequency ($f$) | Reciprocals | $f$ reciprocals |
|---|---|---|---|---|
| 0-8 | 4 | 12 | .25000 | 3.00000 |
| 8-16 | 12 | 16 | .08333 | 1.33328 |
| 16-24 | 20 | 13 | .05000 | 0.65000 |
| 24-32 | 28 | 10 | .03571 | 0.35710 |
| 32-40 | 36 | 8 | .02778 | 0.22224 |
| 40-48 | 44 | 11 | .02273 | 0.25003 |
| | | $N = 70$ | $\Sigma f$ Reciprocals=5.81265 | |

$$\text{H.M.} = \text{Reciprocal of } \frac{\sum f \text{ Reciprocals}}{N}$$

$$= \text{,, ,, } \frac{5.81265}{70}$$

$$= \text{,, ,, } .083038$$

$$= 12.04$$

**Weighted Harmonic Mean.** In order to find out weighted harmonic mean, the reciprocals of values are multiplied by weights and the product of multiplications is divided by the sum of weights. The further reciprocal of the quotient is found which shows the weighted harmonic mean. The following formula is applied for the weighted harmonic mean :

$$\text{Weighted H.M.} = \text{Reciprocal of } \frac{W \text{ Reciprocals}}{\sum W}$$

**Illustration 48.** Calculate harmonic mean from the following information :

| | | | | | | | |
|---|---|---|---|---|---|---|---|
| Indices | 100 | 110 | 105 | 120 | 95 | 80 | 130 |
| Weights | 5 | 6 | 8 | 9 | 2 | 4 | 6 |

**Solution**

| Indices | Weights | Reciprocals | $W$ Reciprocals |
|---|---|---|---|
| 100 | 5 | .010000 | .050000 |
| 110 | 6 | .009091 | .054546 |
| 105 | 8 | .009524 | .076192 |
| 120 | 9 | .008333 | .074997 |
| 95 | 2 | .010530 | .021060 |
| 80 | 4 | .012500 | .050000 |
| 130 | 6 | .007692 | .046152 |
| | $\Sigma W = 40$ | | .372947 |

$$\text{H.M.}_w = \text{Reciprocal of } \frac{\sum W \text{ Reciprocals}}{\sum W}$$

$$= \text{,, ,, } \frac{.372947}{40}$$

$$= \text{,, ,, } .009323675$$

$$= 107.23$$

**Illustration 49.** A man travels 60 miles with train which runs at the speed of 40 miles per hour, 60 miles with motor car which runs at the speed of 30 miles per hour, 20 miles with cycle at the speed of 8 miles per hour and 10 miles on foot at the speed of 5 miles per hour. Calculate the average speed per hour of whole journey,

**Solution**

| Speed in miles per hour ($X$) | Distance covered in miles ($W$) | Reciprocal $X$ | $W$ Reciprocal $X$ |
|---|---|---|---|
| 40 | 60 | .0250 | 1.50000 |
| 30 | 60 | .0333 | 1.99800 |
| 8 | 20 | .1250 | 2.50000 |
| 5 | 10 | .2000 | 2.00000 |
| | $W$=150 | | $\Sigma$($W$ Reciprocal $X$)=7.99800 |

$$HM_w = \text{Reciprocal of } \frac{\Sigma(W \text{ Reciprocal } X)}{\Sigma W}$$

$$HM_w = \text{Reciprocal of } \frac{7.99800}{150}$$

$$= \text{Reciprocal of } .053320$$

$$= 18.75 \text{ miles per hour}$$

**Verification**

| Speed in miles per hour | Miles travelled | Time taken (hours) |
|---|---|---|
| 40 | 60 | 1.50 |
| 30 | 60 | 2.00 |
| 8 | 20 | 2.50 |
| 5 | 10 | 2.00 |
| | 150 | 8.00 |

Thus he travelled 150 miles in 8 hours, therefore, his average speed per hour is as follows :

$$\frac{150}{8} = 18.75 \text{ miles per hour}$$

**Illustration 50.** A taxi car drives from a plain town to a hill station, 60 miles distant at a mileage rate of 10 miles per gallon of petrol and on the return trip at 15 miles per gallon. Find harmonic mean rate of mileage per gallon. Verify that this is the proper average in this particular case.

**Solution**

| Mileage Rate per gallon ($X$) | Distance covered ($W$) | Reciprocal | $W$ Reciprocal |
|---|---|---|---|
| 10 | 60 | .1000 | 6.000 |
| 15 | 60 | .0667 | 4.002 |
| | $\Sigma W = 120$ | | $\Sigma W$ Reciprocal = 10.002 |

$$\text{Weighted H.M.} = \text{Reciprocal of } \frac{\sum W \text{ Reciprocal}}{\sum W}$$

$$= \text{Reciprocal of } \frac{10.002}{120}$$

$$= \text{Reciprocal of } .08335$$

$$= 12 \text{ miles per gallon.}$$

**Merits and Demerits of Harmonic Mean.** This mean is based on all the numbers and is best to find out the average of speed. Even marginal items do not greatly affect this mean. The greatest demerit of this mean is the difficulty involved in its calculation. Moreover, it cannot be used by all persons.

## POSITIONAL AVERAGE

Positionally, there are two following types of averages :

1. Median
2. Mode.

## MEDIAN

Median is that value which divides the given values of series in two equal parts. In other words, median shows the middle item of the series. In a series, the number of items bigger and smaller than the median will be equal. While explaining median, *Prof. Secrist* has said, "*Median of a series is the value of that item-actual or estimated when a series is arranged in order of magnitude which divides the distribution into two parts.*"

In order to find out median, the data are arranged in ascending or descending order and then the value of middle item is determined. That is called median.

In various series, the median will be calculated in the following manner :

**Individual Series.** In order to calculate median in individual series, first of all the data are arranged in ascending order. Thereafter, applying the following formula, the value of middle item is determined. That becomes the value of median.

Formula : $M$ = Value of $\frac{N+1}{2}$ th item

$M$ = Median

$N$ = Number of items.

**Illustration 51.** The frequency table given below gives data of incomes of 15 labourers. Find the median from these data.

| S.N. | 1 | 2 | 3 | 4 | 5 | 6 | 7 | 8 | 9 | 10 | 11 | 12 | 13 | 14 | 15 |
|---|---|---|---|---|---|---|---|---|---|---|---|---|---|---|---|
| Incomes (Rs.) | 200 | 180 | 250 | 160 | 300 | 225 | 210 | 192 | 205 | 165 | 170 | 180 | 182 | 190 | 170 |

**Solution**

First of all the given figures should be arranged either in ascending order or in descending order. If the figures are being arranged in ascending order the median will be as follows :

| S. No. | Income (Rs.) |
|---|---|
| 1 | 160 |
| 2 | 165 |
| 3 | 170 |
| 4 | 170 |
| 5 | 180 |
| 6 | 180 |
| 7 | 182 |
| 8 | 190 |
| 9 | 192 |
| 10 | 200 |
| 11 | 205 |
| 12 | 210 |
| 13 | 225 |
| 14 | 250 |
| 15 | 300 |

$M$ = Value of $\frac{N+1}{2}$ th item

= Value of $\frac{15+1}{2}$ th item

= Value of 8th item

= Rs. 190

If the given figures are arranged in descending order the same result will be obtained as the value of median, as shown below :

| S. No. | Income (Rs.) |
|---|---|
| 1 | 300 |
| 2 | 250 |
| 3 | 225 |
| 4 | 210 |
| 5 | 205 |
| 6 | 200 |
| 7 | 192 |
| 8 | 190 |
| 9 | 182 |
| 10 | 180 |
| 11 | 180 |
| 12 | 170 |
| 13 | 170 |
| 14 | 165 |
| 15 | 160 |

$$M = \text{Value of } \frac{N+1}{2} \text{ th item}$$

$$= \text{Value of } \frac{15+1}{2} \text{ th item}$$

$$= \text{Value of 8 th item}$$

$$= \text{Rs. } 190$$

In the above example, the number of items was odd which could be divided by adding one. But in case the number of items is even, then by adding one it will not be fully divided and the value of the item will be in decimal. In questions like this, the operation to find out median will become clear by the following example :

**Example.** If 8 items are given in a series then in order to find the value of $\frac{8+1}{2} = 4.5$th item, we should take the average of values of 4th and 5th item and this will be the value of median.

**Illustration 52.** Find median from the following figures :

12 16 17 13 9 15 35 8 18 22

**Solution**

| $X$ |
|---|
| 8 |
| 9 |
| 12 |
| 13 |
| 15 |
| 16 |
| 17 |
| 18 |
| 22 |
| 35 |
| $N$ = 10 |

$$M = \text{Value of } \frac{N+1}{2} \text{th item}$$

$$= \text{Value of } \frac{10+1}{2} \text{th item}$$

$$= \text{Value of 5.5th item}$$

$$= \frac{15+16}{2}$$

$$= 15.5$$

**Discrete Series.** In order to find median in discrete series, the value are first arranged in ascending order and then the cumulative frequency of values is known. After this, by applying the following formula the value of the median is found :

$$\text{M} = \text{Value of } \frac{N+1}{2} \text{th item.}$$

**Illustration 53.** Eight coins were tossed together and number of heads resulting was observed. The operation was performed 256 times and the frequency that were obtained for different values of $X$, the number of heads are shown as the following table. Calculate median of the distribution $X$.

| $X$ | 0 | 1 | 2 | 3 | 4 | 5 | 6 | 7 | 8 |
|---|---|---|---|---|---|---|---|---|---|
| Frequency | 1 | 9 | 26 | 59 | 72 | 52 | 29 | 7 | 1 |

**Solution**

| $X$ | Frequency ($f$) | Cumulative frequency ($cf$) |
|---|---|---|
| 0 | 1 | 1 |
| 1 | 9 | 10 |
| 2 | 26 | 36 |
| 3 | 59 | 95 |
| 4 | 72 | 167 |
| 5 | 52 | 219 |
| 6 | 29 | 248 |
| 7 | 7 | 255 |
| 8 | 1 | 256 |

$$M = \text{Value of } \frac{N+1}{2}\text{th item}$$

$$= \text{,, ,, } \frac{256+1}{2}\text{th item}$$

$$= \text{,, ,, } 128.5\text{th item}$$

$$= 4$$

**Continuous Series.** The following points should be borne in mind while finding median in continuous series :

1. The given series should be arranged either in ascending or descending order.

2. The series should be in exclusive form. If inclusive series is given, that should be changed into exclusive series.

3. If the mid-values of classes are given, then the class-intervals should be determined from them.

4. If the distribution of cumulative frequency is given, that should be changed into simple continuous series.

After taking into account the above points, the following procedure will be adopted to find out the median :

**(a) To find median group.** The following operations will be done in this regard :

1. To find out the cumulative frequencies of classes.

2. To apply the following formula to find out the middle-item and its group.

M = N/2th item

M = Middle item.

In order to find median in continuous series N/2 is applied, not $\left(\frac{N+1}{2}\right)$ as has been told in cases of individual and discrete series. As definite value was known in individual and discrete series therefore, $\left(\frac{N+1}{2}\right)$ was used. But in continuous series that point is found out one side of which half of the items are centered and to the other side the rest of the half items after located. Therefore, in this context N/2 will be used.

3. After finding the middle-item with the help of N/2, it is seen in the cumulative frequencies. Cumulative frequencies less than middle-item are left out and this item is centered in the group of cumulative frequency exactly equal to it or just next higher to this. Therefore, this itself is called median class.

**(b) To know the value of median.** After knowing the median-group, the following Interpolation formula is applied :

$$M = l_1 + \frac{i}{f}(m - c)$$

or

$$M = l_1 + \frac{N/2 - c}{f} \times i$$

M = Median; $l_1$ = Lower limit of the middle group; $i$ = Magnitude of middle group; $f$ = frequency of middle group; $m$ = middle item. $c$ = cumulative frequency of previous group of middle group.

If the upper boundary of the middle group is used for calculating the median, then the median value will be known with the help of the following formula :

$$M = l_2 - \frac{i}{f}(c_1 - m)$$

$l_2$ = upper limit of the middle group.

$C_1$ = Cumulative frequency of middle group

The above formula will be applied only when the series is in the ascending order; if the series is in the descending order, the following formula will be applied :

$$M = l_1 - \frac{i}{f}(m - c)$$

Generally in practice the first formula is used to calculate median.

**Illustration 54.** From the following table calculate median.

| Class | Frequency |
|---|---|
| 0-7 | 7 |
| 7-14 | 18 |
| 14-21 | 24 |
| 21-28 | 32 |
| 28-35 | 10 |
| 35-42 | 6 |
| 42-49 | 5 |

**Solution**

| Class | Frequency | Cumulative frequency |
|---|---|---|
| 0-7 | 7 | 7 |
| 7-14 | 18 | 25 |
| 14-21 | 24 | 49 |
| 21-28 | 32 | 81 |
| 28-35 | 10 | 91 |
| 35-42 | 6 | 97 |
| 42-49 | 5 | 102 |

$$m = \frac{N}{2}\text{th item}$$

$$= \frac{102}{2}\text{th item}$$

$$= 51\text{th item}$$

Therefore, middle group is (21-28) because 51 lies in it.

By applying the interpolation formula, we get median :

$$M = l_1 + \frac{i}{f}(m - c)$$

$$= 21 + \frac{7}{32}(51 - 49)$$

$$= 21 + \frac{7 \times 2}{32}$$

$$= 21 + .44$$

$$= 21.44$$

The same value of median will be obtained if upper limit of middle group is used to calculate median :

$$M = l_2 - \frac{i}{f}(c_1 - m)$$

$$= 28 - \frac{7}{32} \times (81 - 51)$$

$$= 28 - \frac{7}{32} \times 30 = 28 - 6.56 = 21.44$$

If the above series is written in descending order in the following manner, the median will be calculated as following :

**Illustration 55.** Calculate median if the figures of previous illustration are given in descending order.

**Solution**

| Classes | Frequencies | Cumulative frequencies |
|---|---|---|
| 42-49 | 5 | 5 |
| 35-42 | 6 | 11 |
| 28-35 | 10 | 21 |
| 21-28 | 32 | 53 |
| 14-21 | 24 | 77 |
| 7-14 | 18 | 95 |
| 0-7 | 7 | 102 |

$$m = \frac{N}{2} \text{th item}$$

$$= \frac{102}{2} \text{th item}$$

$$= 51\text{th item}$$

$\therefore$ Middle group is 21-28

$$M = l_2 - \frac{i}{f}(m - c)$$

$$= 28 - \frac{7}{32}(51 - 21)$$

$$= 28 - \frac{7}{32} \times 30$$

$$= 28 - 6.56$$

$$= 21.44$$

**Illustration 56.** Calculate median from the following frequencies distribution :

| Income (in Rs.) | 200-300 | 300-400 | 400-500 | 500-600 | 600-700 | 700-800 |
|---|---|---|---|---|---|---|
| No. of persons | 10 | 12 | 18 | 30 | 21 | 9 |

**Solution**

| Income in Rs. | No. of persons ($f$) | Cumulative frequencies ($cf$) |
|---|---|---|
| 200-300 | 10 | 10 |
| 300-400 | 12 | 22 |
| 400-500 | 18 | 40 |
| 500-600 | 30 | 70 |
| 600-700 | 21 | 91 |
| 700-800 | 9 | 100 |

$$m = \frac{N}{2} \text{th item}$$

$$= \frac{100}{2} \text{th item}$$

$$= 50\text{th item}$$

$\therefore$ Middle group is 500-600

By interpolation the value of median will be :

$$M = l_1 + \frac{i}{f}(m - c)$$

$$= 500 + \frac{100}{30}(50 - 40)$$

$$= 500 + \frac{100}{30} \times 10$$

$$= 500 + 33.33$$

$$= \text{Rs. } 533.33$$

**Calculation of Median in Inclusive Series**

In order to calculate median in such series, the series will be changed into exclusive series.

**Illustration 57.** Given the following frequency distribution calculate the median :

| Marks | 0-9 | 10-19 | 20-29 | 30-39 | 40-49 | 50-59 |
|---|---|---|---|---|---|---|
| No. of students | 3 | 12 | 16 | 19 | 22 | 18 |

**Solution**

Above series is given in its inclusive form, therefore, it should converted in exclusive form to find out the value of median as follows :

| Marks | No. of students ($f$) | Cumulative frequency ($cf$) |
|---|---|---|
| 0-9.5 | 3 | 3 |
| 9.5-19.5 | 12 | 15 |
| 19.5-29.5 | 16 | 31 |
| 29.5-39.5 | 19 | 50 |
| 39.5-49.5 | 22 | 72 |
| 49.5-59.5 | 18 | 90 |

$$m = \frac{N}{2} \text{th item}$$

$$= \frac{90}{2} \text{th item}$$

$$= 45\text{th item}$$

∴ Median group is 29.5 – 39.5.

By interpolation :

$$M = l_1 + \frac{i}{f}(m - c)$$

$$= 29.5 + \frac{10}{19}(45 - 31)$$

$$= 29.5 + \frac{10 \times 14}{19}$$

$$= 29.5 + 7.4$$

$$= 36.9 \text{ Marks}$$

**Illustration 58.** Find out the value of median for the following data :

| Weight in lbs. | No. of Students |
|---|---|
| 60-64 | 10 |
| 65-74 | 39 |
| 75-79 | 35 |
| 80-84 | 20 |
| 85-94 | 26 |
| 95-99 | 9 |
| 100-104 | 6 |

[*B. Com.* (*Pass*), *Delhi*]

**Solution**

In order to know the median in the above inclusive series, it will be changed into enclusive series in the following manner :

| Weight in lbs. (C.I.) | No. of Students ($f$) | Cumulative Frequency ($cf$) |
|---|---|---|
| 59.5-64.5 | 10 | 10 |
| 64.5-74.5 | 39 | 49 |
| 74.5-79.5 | 35 | 84 |
| 79.5-84.5 | 20 | 104 |
| 84.5-94.5 | 26 | 130 |
| 94.5-99.5 | 9 | 139 |
| 99.5-104.5 | 6 | 145 |

$$m = \frac{N}{2}\text{th item}$$

$$= \frac{145}{2}\text{th item}$$

$$= 72.5\text{th item}$$

∴ Median group is 74.5-79.5

$$M = l_1 + \frac{i}{f}(m - c)$$

$$= 74.5 + \frac{5}{35}(72.5 - 49)$$

$$= 74.5 + \frac{1}{7}(23.5)$$

$$= 74.5 + 3.36$$

$$= 77.86 \text{ lbs.}$$

**Calculation of Median in cumulative frequency distribution.** In order to know median from such distributions, the given frequency distribution will be changed into simple continuous series and after this the same procedure will be followed as described in case of continuous series earlier.

**Illustration 59.** Calculate median from the following frequency distribution :

| | | | | | | | |
|---|---|---|---|---|---|---|---|
| Marks (less than) : | 10 | 20 | 30 | 40 | 50 | 60 | 70 |
| No. of Students : | 8 | 22 | 40 | 65 | 82 | 90 | 100 |

**Solution**

The above cumulative frequency distribution will be converted in ordinary frequency distribution as follows :

| | | | | | | | |
|---|---|---|---|---|---|---|---|
| Marks : | 0-10 | 10-20 | 20-30 | 30-40 | 40-50 | 50-60 | 60-70 |
| No. of Students : | 8 | 14 | 18 | 25 | 17 | 8 | 10 |

After converting the series into ordinary frequencies distribution the median will be calculated as follows :

| Marks (C.I.) | No. of students ($f$) | Cumulative Frequencies ($cf$) |
|---|---|---|
| 0-10 | 8 | 8 |
| 10-20 | 14 | 22 |
| 20-30 | 18 | 40 |
| 30-40 | 25 | 65 |
| 40-50 | 17 | 82 |
| 50-60 | 8 | 90 |
| 60-70 | 10 | 100 |

$$m = \frac{N}{2} \text{th item}$$

$$= \frac{100}{2} \text{th item}$$

$$= 50\text{th item.}$$

Median group is 30-40

By interpolation :

$$M = l_1 + \frac{i}{f}(m - c)$$

$$= 30 + \frac{10}{25}(50 - 40)$$

$$= 30 + \frac{10 \times 10}{25}$$

$$= 30 + 4$$

$$= 34 \text{ marks.}$$

**Illustration 60.** Compute median from the following frequency distribution :

| Income in Rs. (More than) | 100 | 200 | 300 | 400 | 500 | 600 | 700 | 800 | 900 |
|---|---|---|---|---|---|---|---|---|---|
| No. of Persons | 200 | 180 | 150 | 90 | 65 | 30 | 20 | 12 | 5 |

**Solution**

The above cumulative frequency distribution will be converted into ordinary continuous series as follows :

| Income in Rs. | 100-200 | 200-300 | 300-400 | 400-500 | 500-600 |
|---|---|---|---|---|---|
| No. of Persons | 20 | 30 | 60 | 25 | 35 |

| Income in Rs. | 600-700 | 700-800 | 800-900 | 900-1000 |
|---|---|---|---|---|
| No. of Persons | 10 | 8 | 7 | 5 |

The median of above series will be calculated as follows :

| Income in Rs. (C.I.) | No. of Persons ($f$) | Cumulative Frequency ($cf$) |
|---|---|---|
| 100-200 | 20 | 20 |
| 200-300 | 30 | 50 |
| 300-400 | 60 | 110 |
| 400-500 | 25 | 135 |
| 500-600 | 35 | 170 |
| 600-700 | 10 | 180 |
| 700-800 | 8 | 188 |
| 800-900 | 7 | 195 |
| 900-1000 | 5 | 200 |

$$m = \frac{N}{2} \text{th item}$$

$$= \frac{200}{2} \text{th item}$$

$$= 100\text{th item}$$

Middle group is 300-400

By interpolation :

$$M = l_1 + \frac{i}{f}(m - c)$$

$$= 300 + \frac{100}{60}(100 - 50)$$

$$= 300 + \frac{100 \times 50}{60}$$

$$= 300 + 83.33 = \text{Rs. } 383.33$$

**Calculation of median in open-end distribution.** In order to know median in such series, it is not necessary to know the certain value of open-ends, but if the ends of that class in which the median is centered is open, then, in such a case, the definite value of open-end should be known.

**Illustration 61.** Compute median from the following data :

| Class intervals | Below 5 | 5-10 | 10-15 | 15-20 | 20-25 | 25 & above |
|---|---|---|---|---|---|---|
| Frequency : | 10 | 12 | 20 | 16 | 19 | 3 |

**Solution**

| Class intervals (C.I.) | Frequencies ($f$) | Cumulative frequencies ($cf$) |
|---|---|---|
| Below 5 | 10 | 10 |
| 5-10 | 12 | 22 |
| 10-15 | 20 | 42 |
| 15-20 | 16 | 58 |
| 20-25 | 19 | 77 |
| 25 & above | 3 | 80 |

$$m = \frac{N}{2}\text{th item}$$

$$= \frac{80}{2}\text{th item}$$

$$= 40\text{th item.}$$

Middle group is 10-15

By interpolation :

$$M = l_1 + \frac{i}{f}(m - c)$$

$$= 10 + \frac{5}{20}(40 - 22)$$

$$= 10 + \frac{5}{20} \times 18$$

$$= 10 + 4.5$$

$$= 14.5$$

***Note.*** There is no need to find the value of open-ends of the series in order to find the value of median.

**Calculation of Median in the Distribution having Mid-values.** In such a case, the class boundaries should be found with the help of mid-points.

**Illustration 62.** Compute median from the following figures :

| | | | | | | | | |
|---|---|---|---|---|---|---|---|---|
| Mid-values : | 10 | 20 | 30 | 40 | 50 | 60 | 70 | 80 |
| Frequencies : | 5 | 12 | 16 | 25 | 18 | 13 | 6 | 5 |

**Solution**

First of all various classes should be found out with the given mid-values. The same procedure will be adopted in this regard as being described in chapter 7. The converted series will be as follows :

| | | | | | | |
|---|---|---|---|---|---|---|
| Class intervals : | 5-15 | 15-25 | 25-35 | 35-45 | 45-55 | 55-65 |
| Frequencies : | 5 | 12 | 16 | 25 | 18 | 13 |
| Class intervals : | 65-75 | 75-85 | | | | |
| Frequencies : | 6 | 5 | | | | |

| Class intervals (C.I.) | Frequencies (*f*) | Cumulative Frequencies (*cf*) |
|---|---|---|
| 5-15 | 5 | 5 |
| 15-25 | 12 | 17 |
| 25-35 | 16 | 33 |
| 35-45 | 25 | 58 |
| 45-55 | 18 | 76 |
| 55-65 | 13 | 89 |
| 65-75 | 6 | 95 |
| 75-85 | 5 | 100 |

$$m = \frac{N}{2} \text{th item}$$

$$= \frac{100}{2} \text{th item}$$

$$= 50\text{th item.}$$

∴ Middle group is 35-45

By interpolation :

$$M = l_1 + \frac{i}{f}(m - c)$$

$$= 35 + \frac{10}{25}(50 - 33)$$

$$= 35 + 6.8$$

$$= 41.8$$

**Finding out the value of missing frequencies.** Putting the given data in the formula of median, the values of missing frequency can be known.

**Illustration 63.** You are given the following incomplete frequency distribution. It is known that the total frequency is 200 and that the median is 84, find out the value of missing frequencies.

| Class intervals : | 0-20 | 20-40 | 40-60 | 60-80 | 80-100 | 100-120 |
|---|---|---|---|---|---|---|
| Frequencies : | 20 | 22 | ? | 27 | 30 | 24 |

| Class intervals : | 120-140 | 140-160 | 160-180 |
|---|---|---|---|
| Frequencies : | ? | 18 | 14 |

**Solution**

Given M = 84, N = 200 and the following distribution :

| Class Intervals (C.I.) | Frequencies ($f$) | Cumulative Frequencies ($cf$) |
|---|---|---|
| 0-20 | 20 | 20 |
| 20-40 | 22 | 42 |
| 40-60 | $f_1$ | $42 + f_1$ |
| 60-80 | 27 | $69 + f_1$ |
| 80-100 | 30 | $99 + f_1$ |
| 100-120 | 24 | $123 + f_1$ |
| 120-140 | $f_2$ | $123 + f_1 + f_2$ |
| 140-160 | 18 | $141 + f_1 + f_2$ |
| 160-180 | 14 | $155 + f_1 + f_2$ |
| | $N = 200$ | |

$$m = \frac{N}{2}\text{th item}$$

$$= \frac{200}{2}\text{th item}$$

$$= 100\text{th item}$$

Median group is 80-100 as median is 84 which will fall in this group.

$$M = l_1 + \frac{i}{f}(m-c)$$

$$84 = 80 + \frac{20}{30}[100-(69+f_1)]$$

or $$84 = 80+\frac{2}{3}(31-f_1)$$

or $$4 = \frac{2}{3}(31-f_1)$$

or $$12 = 62 - 2f_1$$

or $$2f_1 = 62 - 12$$

or $$2f_1 = 50$$

$$f_1 = 25$$

$$N = 155 + f_1 + f_2$$

$$200 = 155 + 25 + f_2$$

$$\therefore \quad f_2 = 200 - 180$$

$$= 20$$

Thus the value of missing frequencies of group 40–60 and 120-140 are 25 and 20 respectively.

**Calculation of Median by Graphic Method**

To calculate median by this method, cumulative frequency curve or ogive have to be made. On this curve, a perpendicular is drawn from the mid-item. The point on the base line where the perpendicular meets is the value of median. The following example will make this method clear :

**Illustration 64.** Find the value of median graphically from the following figures :

| | | | | | |
|---|---|---|---|---|---|
| Income in Rs. : | 0-100 | 100-200 | 200-300 | 300-400 | 400-500 |
| No. of persons : | 70 | 48 | 52 | 56 | 60 |
| Income in Rs. : | 500-600 | 600-700 | 700-800 | 800-900 | |
| No. of persons : | 55 | 49 | 45 | 65 | |

Verify it by calculating mathematically.

**Solution**

In order to know the median by graphic method from the above series, this series will be changed into cumulative frequency distribution in the following manner :

| 'Less than' Cumulative frequencies distribution | | 'More than' Cumulative frequencies distribution | |
|---|---|---|---|
| Income in Rs. | No. of persons | Income in Rs. | No. of persons |
| Less than 100 | 70 | More than 0 | 500 |
| Less than 200 | 118 | More than 100 | 430 |
| Less than 300 | 170 | More than 200 | 382 |
| Less than 400 | 226 | More than 300 | 330 |
| Less than 500 | 286 | More than 400 | 274 |
| Less than 600 | 341 | More than 500 | 214 |
| Less than 700 | 390 | More than 600 | 159 |
| Less than 800 | 435 | More than 700 | 110 |
| Less than 900 | 500 | More than 800 | 65 |

The above cumulative distributions will be marked on the graph and cumulative frequency curves will be formed. The cumulative frequency curve will be connected with 250 frequency by a horizontal line. From the point of curve where this line cuts it, a perpendicular will be drawn on the base. This will be clearly explained by the following graphs :

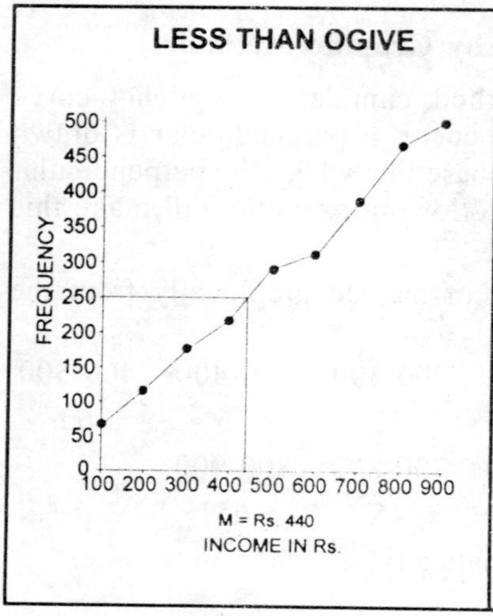


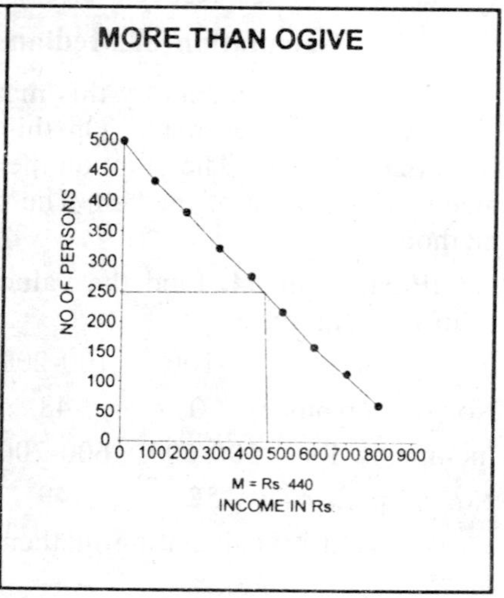

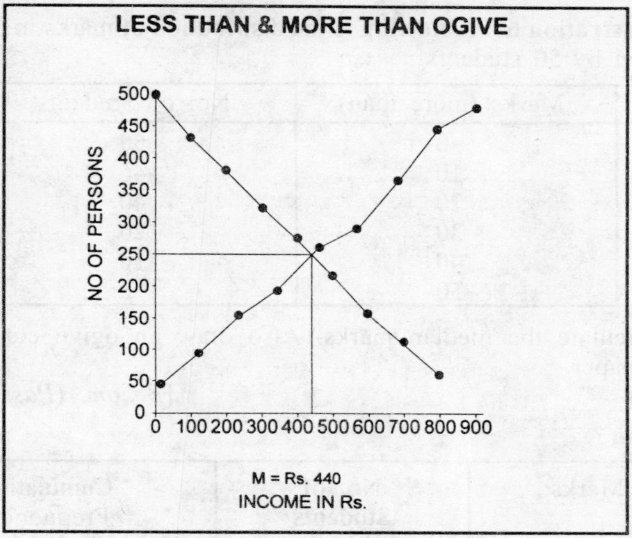


The median may be determined by drawing any one of the cumulative frequencies curve 'less than' or 'more than' or both on one graph.

**Verification**

$$\text{Median} = \text{Value of } \frac{N}{2}\text{th item}$$

$$= \text{Value of } \frac{500}{2}\text{th item}$$

$$= \text{Value of 250th item.}$$

$\therefore$ Median lies on 400-500 group

$$M = l_1 + \frac{i}{f}(m - c)$$

$$= 400 + \frac{100}{60}(250 - 226)$$

$$= 400 + \frac{100 \times 24}{60}$$

$$= 400 + 40$$

$$= \text{Rs. } 440$$

**Illustration 65.** Following is the distribution of marks in Statistics obtained by 50 students :

| Marks (more than) | No. of Students |
|---|---|
| 0 | 50 |
| 10 | 46 |
| 20 | 40 |
| 30 | 20 |
| 40 | 10 |
| 50 | 3 |

Calculate the median marks. Also draw an ogive curve on a graph paper.

[*B.Com.* (*Pass*) *Delhi*]

**Solution**

| Marks (C.I.) | No. of Students ($f$) | Cumulative Frequency ($cf$) |
|---|---|---|
| 0-10 | 4 | 4 |
| 10-20 | 6 | 10 |
| 20-30 | 20 | 30 |
| 30-40 | 10 | 40 |
| 40-50 | 7 | 47 |
| 50-60 | 3 | 50 |

$$m = \frac{N}{2}\text{th item}$$

$$= \frac{50}{2}\text{th item}$$

$$= 25\text{th item}$$

$\therefore$ Median group is 20-30

$$M = l_1 + \frac{i}{f}(m - c)$$

$$= 20 + \frac{10}{20}(25 - 10)$$

$$= 20 + \frac{10 \times 15}{20}$$

$$= 20 + 7.5$$

$$= 27.5 \text{ marks}$$

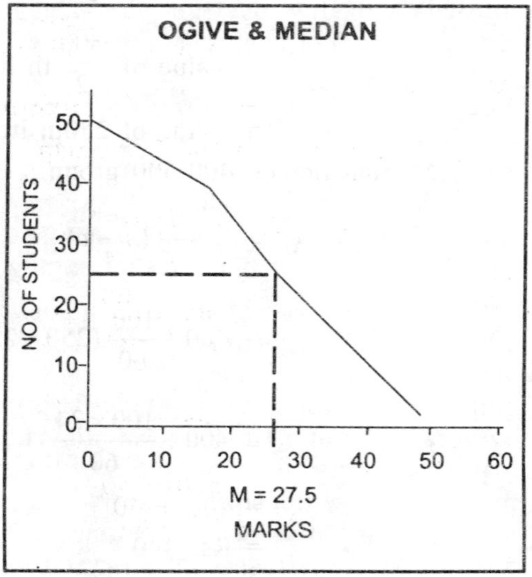

**Illustration 66.** Draw the less-than Ogive and estimate the value of the median on the basis of the data given below :

| Mid-Point | Frequency |
|---|---|
| 18 | 10 |
| 25 | 15 |
| 32 | 32 |
| 39 | 42 |
| 46 | 26 |
| 53 | 12 |
| 60 | 9 |
| | $N = 146$ |

Verify the results by calculation.

**Solution**

First, the above series will be transformed into simple continuous series. Then, this series will be changed into 'less than cumulative frequency distribution'. After marking these values on the graph, ogive will be made and from it the value of the median will be determined. These operations will be done in the following manner :

| Continuous Series | | Cumulative Frequency Distribution 'less than order' | |
|---|---|---|---|
| C.I. | Frequency | Less than | Cumulative frequency |
| 14.5-21.5 | 10 | 21.5 | 10 |
| 21.5-28.5 | 15 | 28.5 | 25 |
| 28.5-35.5 | 32 | 35.5 | 57 |
| 35.5-42.5 | 42 | 42.5 | 99 |
| 42.5-49.5 | 26 | 49.5 | 125 |
| 49.5-56.5 | 12 | 55.6 | 137 |
| 56.5-63.5 | 9 | 63.5 | 146 |

**LESS THAN OGIVE & MEDIAN**

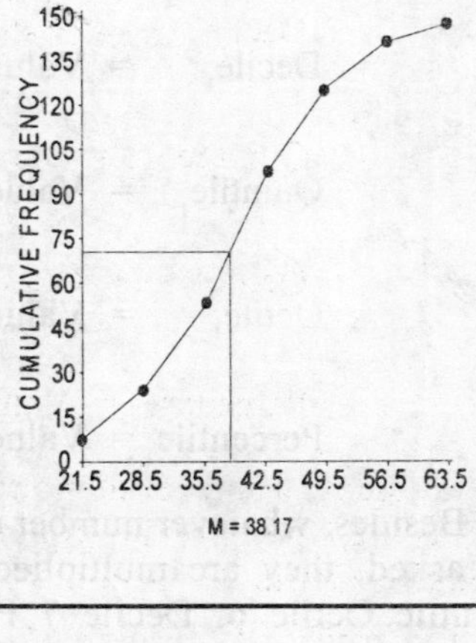


$$m = \frac{N}{2} = \frac{146}{2} = 73$$

Median Group will be 35.5-42.5

$$M = l_1 + \frac{i}{f}(m-c)$$

$$= 35.5 + \frac{7}{42}(73-57)$$

$$= 35.5 + \frac{7}{42} \times 16$$

$$= 35.5 + 2.67$$

$$= 38.17$$

**Other Measurements Depending on Median**

The way the given values can be divided into two equal parts with the help of median, in the same way, with the help of some other measurements, the series can be divided into four, five, eight, ten and hundred equal parts. The calculation of these measurements is done exactly in the same way as that for median. For this, slight change is done in the median-formula. The measurements dividing the series into four, five, eight, ten and hundred are respectively called Quartile, Quintile, Octile, Decile and Percentile. For the above various measurements, the following formulae are used :

$$\text{Quartile}_1 = \text{Value of } \frac{N+1}{4} \text{th item}$$

$$\text{Quartile}_3 = \text{Value of } \frac{3(N+1)}{4} \text{th item}$$

$$\text{Decile}_1 = \text{Value of } \frac{N+1}{10} \text{th item}$$

$$\text{Quintile}_1 = \text{Value of } \frac{N+1}{5} \text{th item}$$

$$\text{Octile}_1 = \text{Value of } \frac{N+1}{8} \text{th item}$$

$$\text{Percentile}_1 = \text{Value of } \frac{N+1}{100} \text{th item}$$

Besides, whatever number of quintile, octile, decile and percentile are asked, they are multiplied in the above formula. For example Quintile Octile 6, Decile 7 Percentile 77 will have the following formula respectively.

$$\text{Quintile}_4 = \text{Value of } \frac{4\,(N+1)}{5} \text{ th item}$$

$$\text{Octile}_6 = \text{Value of } \frac{6\,(N+1)}{8} \text{ th item}$$

$$\text{Decile}_7 = \text{Value of } \frac{7\,(N+1)}{10} \text{ th item}$$

$$\text{Percentile}_{77} = \text{Value of } \frac{77\,(N+1)}{100} \text{ th item}$$

In order to find the values of above measurements from among the class-intervals of continuous series, the following formulae will be used :

$$\text{Quartile}_1 = l_1 + \frac{i}{f}(q_1 - c)$$

$$\text{Quartile}_3 = l_1 + \frac{i}{f}(q_3 - c)$$

$$\text{Quintile}_1 = l_1 + \frac{i}{f}(qt_1 - c)$$

$$\text{Octile}_1 = l_1 + \frac{i}{f}(o_1 - c)$$

$$\text{Decile}_1 = l_1 + \frac{i}{f}(d_1 - c)$$

$$\text{Percentile}_1 = l_1 + \frac{i}{f}(p_1 - c)$$

In the above formulae $q_1$, $q_3$, $qt_1$, $O_1$, $d_1$ and $p_1$ are for the values of Quartile 1, Quartile 3, Quintile 1, Octile 1, Decile 1 and Percentile 1 respectively. All the other signs have the same meaning which has been given in the median.

The calculation of the above measurements will be clarified by the following examples :

**Illustration 67.** Calculate the Quartiles, Quintile 2, Octile 5, Decile 8 and Percentile 16 from the following data :

| | | | | | | | | |
|---|---|---|---|---|---|---|---|---|
| Roll No. : | 1 | 2 | 3 | 4 | 5 | 6 | 7 | 8 |
| Marks : | 8 | 10 | 25 | 20 | 6 | 9 | 15 | 21 |
| Roll No. : | 9 | 10 | 11 | 12 | 13 | 14 | 15 | 16 |
| Marks : | 32 | 28 | 20 | 34 | 10 | 13 | 16 | 25 |

**Solution**

| Marks |
|---|
| 6 |
| 8 |
| 9 |
| 10 |
| 10 |
| 13 |
| 15 |
| 16 |
| 20 |
| 20 |
| 21 |
| 25 |
| 25 |
| 28 |
| 32 |
| 34 |
| N = 16 |

$$\text{Quartile}_1\ (Q_1) = \text{Value of } \frac{N+1}{4} \text{th item}$$

$$= \text{Value of } \frac{16+1}{4} \text{th item}$$

$$= \text{Value of } 4.25\text{th item}$$

$$= \text{Value of } 4th + \frac{5th - 4th}{4} \text{ th item}$$

$$= 10 + 0$$

$$= 20 \text{ Marks.}$$

$$\text{Quartile}_3\ (Q_3) = \text{Value of } \frac{3\,(N+1)}{4} \text{th item}$$

$$= \text{Value of } \frac{3\,(16+1)}{4} \text{th item}$$

$$= \text{Value of } \frac{51}{4} \text{th item}$$

$$= \text{Value of } 12.75\text{th item}$$

$$= 25 \text{ Marks}$$

$$\text{Quintile}_2 = \text{Value of } \frac{2\,(N+1)}{5} \text{th item}$$

$$= \text{Value of } \frac{2\,(16+1)}{5} \text{th item}$$

$$= \text{Value of } \frac{34}{5} \text{th item}$$

$$= \text{Value of } 6.8\text{th item}$$

$$= 14.6 \text{ Marks.}$$

$$\text{Octile}_5 = \text{Value of } \frac{5(N+1)}{8} \text{ th item}$$

$$= \text{Value of } \frac{5(16+1)}{8} \text{ th item}$$

$$= \text{Value of } \frac{85}{8} \text{ th item}$$

$$= \text{Value of 10.625th item}$$

$$= 20.625 \text{ Marks.}$$

$$\text{Decile}_8 = \text{Value of } \frac{8(N+1)}{10} \text{ th item}$$

$$= \text{Value of } \frac{8(16+1)}{10} \text{ th item}$$

$$= \text{Value of } \frac{136}{10} \text{ th item}$$

$$= \text{Value of 13.6th item}$$

$$= 26.8 \text{ Marks.}$$

$$\text{Percentile}_{16} = \text{Value of } \frac{16(N+1)}{100} \text{ th item}$$

$$= \text{Value of } \frac{16(16+1)}{100} \text{ th item}$$

$$= \text{Value of } \frac{272}{100} \text{ th item}$$

$$= \text{Value of 2.72th item}$$

$$= 8.72 \text{ Marks.}$$

**Illustration 68.** Compute Quartiles, Quintile$_3$, Octile$_6$, Decile$_2$ and Percentile$_{25}$ from the following :

| | | | | | | | |
|---|---|---|---|---|---|---|---|
| Size of item : | 3 | 6 | 9 | 12 | 15 | 18 | 21 |
| Frequency : | 9 | 15 | 6 | 2 | 21 | 18 | 5 |

**Solution**

| Size of item | Frequency | Cumulative Frequency |
|---|---|---|
| 3 | 9 | 9 |
| 6 | 15 | 24 |
| 9 | 6 | 30 |
| 12 | 2 | 32 |
| 15 | 21 | 53 |
| 18 | 18 | 71 |
| 21 | 5 | 76 |

$$\text{Quartile}_1 = \text{Value of } \frac{N+1}{4}\text{th item}$$
$$= \text{Value of } \frac{76+1}{4}\text{th item}$$
$$= \text{Value of } 19.25\text{th item}$$
$$= 6$$

$$\text{Quartile}_3 = \text{Value of } \frac{3(N+1)}{4}\text{th item}$$
$$= \text{Value of } \frac{3(76+1)}{4}\text{th item}$$
$$= \text{Value of } 57.75\text{th item}$$
$$= 18.$$

$$\text{Quintile}_3. = \text{Value of } \frac{3(N+1)}{5}\text{th item}$$
$$= \text{Value of } \frac{3(76+1)}{5}\text{th item}$$
$$= \text{Value of } \frac{231}{5}\text{th item}$$
$$= \text{Value of } 46.2\text{th item}$$
$$= 15.$$

$$\text{Octile}_6 = \text{Value of } \frac{6(N+1)}{8}\text{th item}$$
$$= \text{Value of } \frac{6(76+1)}{8}\text{th item}$$
$$= \text{Value of } \frac{462}{8}\text{th item}$$
$$= \text{Value of } 57.75\text{th item}$$
$$= 18.$$

$$\text{Decile}_2 = \text{Value of } \frac{2(N+1)}{10} \text{th item}$$

$$= \text{Value of } \frac{2(76+1)}{10} \text{th item}$$

$$= \text{Value of } \frac{154}{10} \text{th item}$$

$$= \text{Value of } 15.4\text{th item}$$

$$= 6.$$

$$\text{Percentile}_{25} = \text{Value of } \frac{25(N+1)}{100} \text{th item}$$

$$= \text{Value of } \frac{25(76+1)}{100} \text{th item}$$

$$= \text{Value of } \frac{1925}{100} \text{th item}$$

$$= \text{Value of } 19.25\text{th item}$$

$$= 6.$$

**Illustration 69.** Find Quartile$_1$, Quartile$_3$, Quintile$_3$, Octile$_4$, Decile$_6$ and Percentile$_{12}$ from the following figures :

| | | | | | | | | |
|---|---|---|---|---|---|---|---|---|
| Mid-value : | 7 | 21 | 35 | 49 | 63 | 77 | 91 | 105 |
| Frequency : | 8 | 2 | 12 | 27 | 32 | 17 | 19 | 9 |

**Solution**

First of all the above series will be changed into simple continuous series in the following manner. After this applying the relevant formulae, the above measurements will be calculated.

| Groups | Frequency | Cumulative Frequency |
|---|---|---|
| 0-14 | 8 | 8 |
| 14-28 | 2 | 10 |
| 28-42 | 12 | 22 |
| 42-56 | 27 | 49 |
| 56-70 | 32 | 81 |
| 70-84 | 17 | 98 |
| 84-98 | 19 | 117 |
| 98-112 | 9 | 126 |

$$q_1 = \frac{N}{4}\text{th item}$$

$$= \frac{126}{4}\text{th item}$$

$$= 31.5\text{th item}$$

Quartile$_1$ group is 42 – 56

By interpolation :

$$Q_1 = l_1 + \frac{i}{f}(q_1 - c)$$

$$= 42 + \frac{14}{27}(31.5 - 22)$$

$$= 42 + \frac{14}{27} \times 9.5$$

$$= 42 + 4.93$$

$$= 46.93$$

$$q_3 = \frac{3\,(N)}{4}\text{th item}$$

$$= \frac{3\,(126)}{4}\text{th item}$$

$$= \frac{378}{4}\text{th item}$$

$$= 94.5\text{th item}$$

Quartile$_3$ group is 70-84

By interpolation :

$$Q_3 = l_1 + \frac{i}{f}(q_3 - c)$$

$$= 70 + \frac{14}{17}(94.5 - 81)$$

$$= 70 + \frac{14}{17} \times 13.5$$

$$= 70 + 11.12$$

$$= 81.12$$

$$qt_3 = \frac{3\,(n)}{5} \text{ th item}$$

$$= \frac{3\,(126)}{5} \text{ th item}$$

$$= \frac{378}{5} \text{ th item}$$

$$= 75.6\text{th item}$$

Quintile$_3$ group is 56-70.

By interpolation :

$$\text{Quintile}_3 = l_1 + \frac{i}{f}\,(qt_3 - c)$$

$$= 56 + \frac{14}{32}\,(75.6 - 49)$$

$$= 56 + \frac{14}{32} \times 26.6$$

$$= 56 + \frac{372.4}{32}$$

$$= 56 + 11.64$$

$$= 67.64$$

$$Q_4 = \frac{4\,(N)}{8} \text{ th item}$$

$$= \frac{4\,(126)}{8} \text{ th item}$$

$$= \frac{504}{8} \text{ th item}$$

$$= 63\text{th item}$$

Octile$_4$ group is 56-70

$$\text{Octile}_4 = l_1 + \frac{i}{f}\,(o_4 - c)$$

$$= 56 + \frac{14}{32}\,(63 - 49)$$

$$= 56 + \frac{14}{32} \times 14$$
$$= 56 + 6.125$$
$$= 62.125$$

$$d_6 = \frac{6\,(N)}{10} \text{th item}$$
$$= \frac{6\,(126)}{10} \text{th item}$$
$$= \frac{756}{10} \text{th item}$$
$$= 75.6\text{th item}$$

$\text{Decile}_6$ group is 56-70

$$\text{Decile}_6 = l_1 + \frac{i}{f}\,(d_6 - c)$$
$$= 56 + \frac{14}{32}\,(75.6 - 49)$$
$$= 56 + \frac{14}{32} \times 26.6$$
$$= 56 + 11.64$$
$$= 67.64$$

$$p_{12} = \frac{12\,(N)}{100} \text{th item}$$
$$= \frac{12\,(126)}{100} \text{th item}$$
$$= \frac{1512}{100} \text{th item}$$
$$= 15.12\text{th item}$$

$Percentile_{12}$ Group is 28-42

By interpolation :

$$\text{Percentile}_{12} = l_1 + \frac{i}{f}(p_{12} - c)$$

$$= 28 + \frac{14}{12}(15.12 - 10)$$

$$= 28 + \frac{14}{12} \times 5.12$$

$$= 28 + 5.97$$

$$= 33.97$$

**Illustration 70.** From the following calculate quartiles :

| | | | | | | | | | |
|---|---|---|---|---|---|---|---|---|---|
| X : | 5-15 | 15-25 | 25-35 | 35-45 | 45-55 | 55-65 | 65-75 | 75-85 | 85-95 |
| f : | 5 | 8 | 12 | 16 | 29 | 14 | 9 | 4 | 3 |

**Solution**

| *X* | *f* | *cf* |
|---|---|---|
| 5-15 | 5 | 5 |
| 15-25 | 8 | 13 |
| 25-35 | 12 | 25 |
| 35-45 | 16 | 41 |
| 45-55 | 29 | 70 |
| 55-65 | 14 | 84 |
| 65-75 | 9 | 93 |
| 75-85 | 4 | 97 |
| 85-95 | 3 | 100 |
| | $N = 100$ | |

$$q_1 = \frac{N}{4} \text{th item}$$

$$= \frac{100}{4} \text{th item}$$

$$= 25\text{th item}$$

Therefore, quartile first group is 25-35

$$Q_1 = l_1 + \frac{i}{f}(q_1 - c)$$

$$= 25 + \frac{10}{12}(25 - 13)$$

$$= 25 + \frac{10}{12} \times 12$$

$$= 25 + 10$$

$$= 35$$

$$q_3 = \frac{3N}{4} \text{th item}$$

$$= \frac{3 \times 100}{4} \text{th item}$$

$$= 75\text{th item}$$

Therefore, quartiles third group is 55-65

$$Q_3 = l_1 + \frac{i}{f}(q_3 - c)$$

$$= 55 + \frac{10}{14}(75 - 70)$$

$$= 55 + \frac{10}{14} \times 5$$

$$= 55 + 3.57$$

$$= 58.57$$

**Illustration 71.** Calculate median and quartiles from the following data :

| | | | | | | | | |
|---|---|---|---|---|---|---|---|---|
| $X$ : | 1-3 | 3-5 | 5-7 | 7-9 | 9-11 | 11-13 | 13-15 | 15-17 |
| $f$ : | 3 | 26 | 44 | 28 | 10 | 3 | 4 | 2 |

**Solution**

| $X$ | $f$ | $cf$ |
|---|---|---|
| 1-3 | 3 | 3 |
| 3-5 | 26 | 29 |
| 5-7 | 44 | 73 |
| 7-9 | 28 | 101 |
| 9-11 | 10 | 111 |
| 11-13 | 3 | 114 |
| 13-15 | 4 | 118 |
| 15-17 | 2 | 120 |
| | $N = 120$ | |

$$m = \frac{n}{2} \text{ th item}$$

$$= \frac{120}{2} \text{ th item}$$

$$= 60 \text{ th item}$$

$\therefore$ Median group is 5-7

$$m = l_1 + \frac{i}{f}(m - c)$$

$$= 5 + \frac{2}{44}(60 - 29)$$

$$= 5 + \frac{2}{44} \times 31$$

$$= 5 + 1{:}41$$

$$= 6.41$$

$$q_1 = \frac{N}{4} \text{ th item}$$

$$= \frac{120}{4} \text{ th item}$$

$$= 30\text{th item}$$

Therefore, the first quartile group is 5-7.

$$Q_1 = l_1 + \frac{i}{f} + (q_1 - c)$$

$$= 5 + \frac{2}{44} \times (30 - 29)$$

$$= 5 + \frac{2}{44} \times 1$$

$$= 5 + 0.05 = 5.05$$

$$q_3 = \frac{3N}{4} \text{th item}$$

$$= \frac{3\,(120)}{4} \text{th item}$$

$$= 90\text{th item}$$

Therefore, third quartiles group is 7-9.

$$Q_3 = l_1 + \frac{i}{f}(q_3 - c)$$

$$= 7 + \frac{2}{28}(90 - 73)$$

$$= 7 + \frac{2}{28} \times 17$$

$$= 7 + 1.21$$

$$= 8.21$$

**Illustration 72.** You are given the following incomplete distribution. It is known that total frequency is 250 and that median is 360. Estimate by calculation the missing frequencies.

| | | | | | |
|---|---|---|---|---|---|
| Value : | 200-250 | 250-300 | 300-350 | 350-400 | 400-450 |
| Frequency : | 35 | ? | 44 | 40 | 28 |
| Value : | 450-500 | 500-550 | 550-600 | | |
| Frequency : | ? | 25 | 13 | | |

**Solution**

| Value (C.I.) | Frequencies ($f$) | Cumulative Frequencies ($cf$) |
|---|---|---|
| 200-250 | 35 | 35 |
| 250-300 | $f_1$ | $35+f_1$ |
| 300-350 | 44 | $79+f_1$ |
| 350-400 | 40 | $119+f_1$ |
| 400-450 | 28 | $147+f_1$ |
| 450-500 | $f_2$ | $147+f_1+f_2$ |
| 500-550 | 25 | $172+f_1+f_2$ |
| 550-600 | 13 | $185+f_1+f_2$ |

$$m = \frac{N}{2}\text{th item}$$

$$= \frac{250}{2}\text{th item}$$

$$= 125\text{th item}$$

Median group is 350–400 as median value 360 will lie in this group.

$$M = l_1 + \frac{i}{f}(m - c)$$

$$360 = 350 + \frac{50}{40}[125 - (79 + f_1)]$$

$$360 = 350 + \frac{5}{4}(125 - 79 - f_1)$$

$$360 = 350 + \frac{5}{4}(46 - f_1)$$

$$1440 = 1400 + 230 - 5f_1$$

$$5f_1 = 1400 + 230 - 1440$$

$$5f_1 = 190$$

$$f_1 = 38$$

$$N = 185 + f_1 + f_2$$

$$250 = 185 + 38 + f_2$$

$$\text{or } f_2 = 250 - 185 - 38$$

$$= 27$$

**Illustration 73.** From the following data, find out the value of median and quartiles graphically and verify your results using formula :

| | | | | |
|---|---|---|---|---|
| Salary in Rs. : | 100-200 | 200-300 | 300-400 | 400-500 |
| No. of Employees : | 86 | 80 | 88 | 115 |
| Salary in Rs. : | 500-600 | 600-700 | 700-800 | |
| No. of Employees : | 75 | 60 | 96 | |

**Solution**

To find median and quartile by graph, first the above series is changed into cumulative frequency distribution in the following manner :

| Cumulative Frequency Distribution | | | |
|---|---|---|---|
| C.I. | *f* | Salary in Rs. | No. of Employees (*cf*) |
| 100-200 | 86 | Less than 200 | 86 |
| 200-300 | 80 | Less than 300 | 166 |
| 300-400 | 88 | Less than 400 | 254 |
| 400-500 | 115 | Less than 500 | 369 |
| 500-600 | 75 | Less than 600 | 444 |
| 600-700 | 60 | Less than 700 | 504 |
| 700-800 | 96 | Less than 800 | 600 |

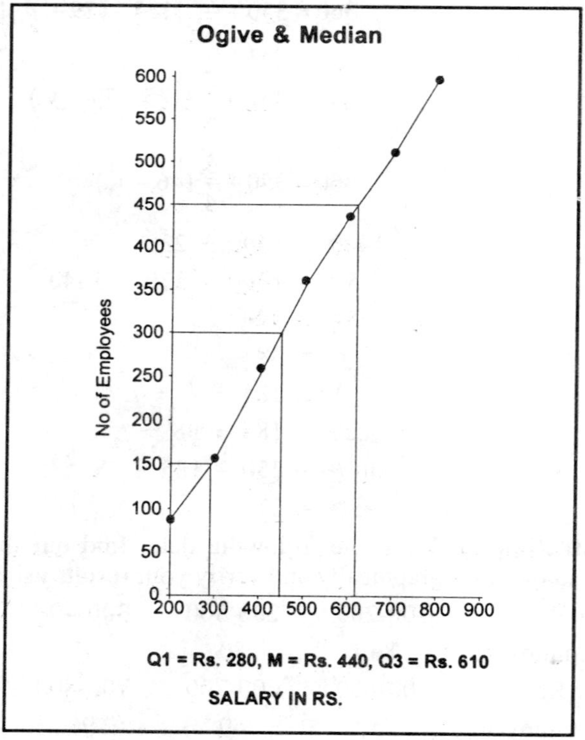


$$m = \frac{N}{2}\text{th item} = \frac{600}{2} = 300\text{th item}$$

(Median Group is 400-500)

$$q_1 = \frac{N}{4}\text{th item} = \frac{600}{4} = 150\text{th item}$$

(Quartile First Group is 200-300)

$$q_3 = \frac{3N}{4}\text{th item} = \frac{3\times 600}{4} = 450\text{th item}$$

(Quartile Third Group is 600-700)

**Verification**

$$M = l_1 + \frac{i}{f}(m-c)$$

$$= 400 + \frac{100}{115}(300-254)$$

$$= 400 + \frac{100}{115}(46)$$

$$= 400 + 40$$

$$= \text{Rs. } 440$$

$$Q_1 = l_1 + \frac{i}{f}(q_1 - c)$$

$$= 200 + \frac{100}{80}(150-86)$$

$$= 200 + \frac{100}{80}\times 64$$

$$= \text{Rs. } 280$$

$$Q_3 = l_1 + \frac{i}{f}(q_3 - c)$$

$$= 600 + \frac{100}{60}(450-444)$$

$$= 600 + \frac{100}{60}\times 6$$

$$= \text{Rs. } 610$$

**Illustration 74.** Draw the more-than Ogive from the following data and obtain the values of median :

| Mid value | Frequency |
|---|---|
| 15 | 6 |
| 25 | 18 |
| 35 | 32 |
| 45 | 46 |
| 55 | 54 |
| 65 | 38 |
| 75 | 22 |
| 85 | 16 |
| 95 | 10 |

(*C. A. 1975*)

**Solution**

From the above data, first, simple continuous series will be formed; then it will be changed into more than cumulative frequency distribution and thereafter the values of median will be found by graph. These calculations will be in the following way :

| | Continuous Series | | More than Cumulative Frequency Distribution | |
|---|---|---|---|---|
| C.I. | *f* | *cf* | More than | *cf* |
| 10-20 | 6 | 6 | 10 | 242 |
| 20-30 | 18 | 24 | 20 | 236 |
| 30-40 | 32 | 56 | 30 | 218 |
| 40-50 | 46 | 102 | 40 | 186 |
| 50-60 | 54 | 156 | 50 | 140 |
| 60-70 | 38 | 194 | 60 | 86 |
| 70-80 | 22 | 216 | 70 | 48 |
| 80-90 | 16 | 232 | 80 | 26 |
| 90-100 | 10 | 242 | 90 | 10 |
| Total | 242 | | | |

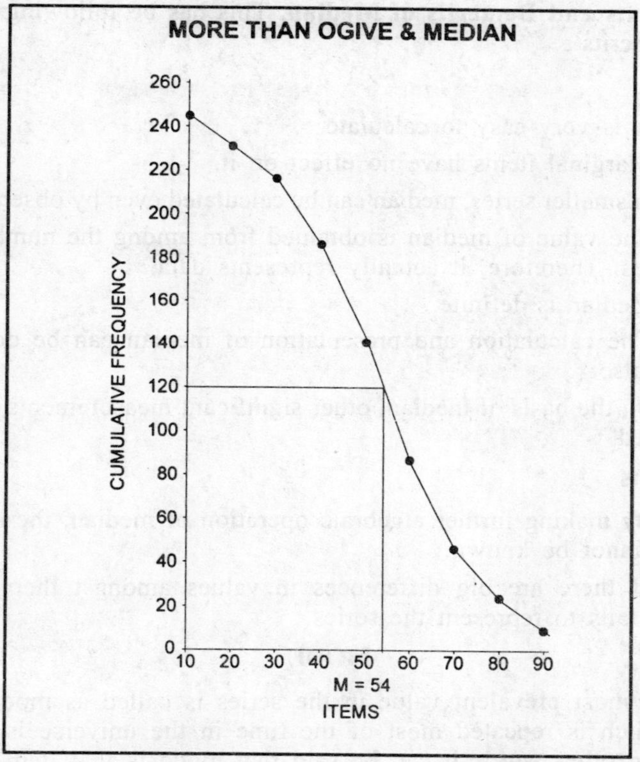


**Verification**

$$m = \frac{N}{2}\text{th item} = \frac{242}{2}\text{th item}$$

$$= 121\text{th item}$$

$\therefore$ Median group is 50–60.

$$M_{12} = l_1 + \frac{i}{f}(m-c)$$

$$= 50 + \frac{10}{54}(121-102)$$

$$= 50 + \frac{10}{54} \times 19$$

$$= 50 + 3.52 = 53.52$$

**Merits and Demerits of Median.** This has be following merits and demerits :

**Merits**

1. It is very easy to calculate.

2. Marginal items have no effect on it.

3. In smaller series, median can be calculated even by observation.

4. The value of median is obtained from among the numbers of the series. Therefore, it actually represents data.

5. Median is definite.

6. The calculation and presentation of median can be done by graphs also.

7. On the basis of median, other significant measurements can be calculated.

**Demerits**

1. By making further algebraic operation of median, the sum of items cannot be known.

2. If there are big differences in values amongst themselves, median fails to represent the series.

## MODE

The most prevalent value in the series is called as mode. The item which is repeated most of the time in the universe is called mode. In other words it can be said that mode is that item which frequently occurs. Through mode is known the prevalence or fashion of any fact, article or unit in the universe. Various scholars have defined mode in the following ways :

1. *"The value of the graded quantity in a statistical group (or wages, heights, or some other measurable quantity) at which the numbers registered are most numerous, is called the mode, or the position of greatest density or the predominant value."*

   — *Dr. A.L. Bowley*

2. *"Mode may be defined as the predominant kind, type or size or item or the position of greatest density."*

   — *Boddington*

3. *"The mode of a distribution is the value at the point around which the items tend to be most heavily concentrated. It may be regarded as the most typical of a series of values."*

   — *Croxton & Cowden*

The presentation of mode through graph may be shown by following diagram :

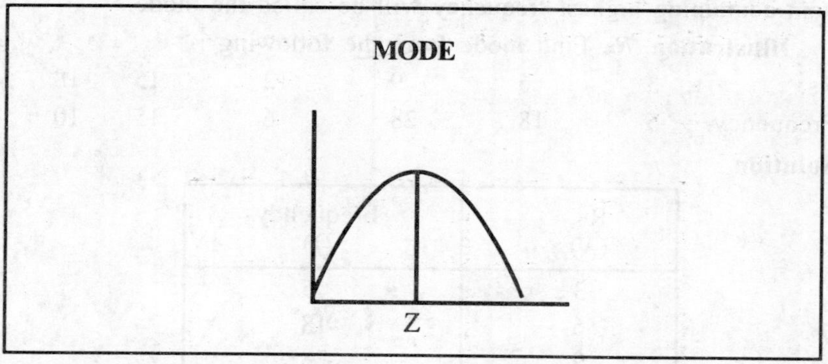


### Method of Calculation of Mode

In different series there are the following methods of calculation of mode :

**Individual Series.** Generally, there is no mode in individual series because in such series each item mostly occurs only once. But if any item has repeatedly appeared in the same series then that item does become the mode. In order to know the mode in that series, first, that series have to be changed into discrete or continuous series and thereafter either by observation or by formula the mode is found. This will become clear from the following example :

**Illustration 75.** Calculate the mode from the following figures : 50, 55 80, 79, 62, 82, 55, 65, 55, 73, 81, 76, 81, 63, 50, 80, 79, 55, 71, 55.

**Solution**

First of all the above individual series will be changed in discrete series in the following way :

| | | | | | | | | | | | | |
|---|---|---|---|---|---|---|---|---|---|---|---|---|
| Variables : | 50 | 55 | 62 | 63 | 65 | 71 | 73 | 76 | 79 | 80 | 81 | 82 |
| Frequency : | 2 | 5 | 1 | 1 | 1 | 1 | 1 | 1 | 2 | 2 | 2 | 1 |

Thus 55 is mode because it has highest frequency in the series.

(*By observation*)

**Discrete Series.** The mode in this series can be found by the following two methods :

(a) By observation; or

(b) By grouping.

**(a) By observation.** If the frequency of an item is much more than other items, than mode can be known by observation and the item containing highest frequency will be called the mode.

**Illustration 76.** Find mode from the following :

| | | | | | | |
|---|---|---|---|---|---|---|
| Rs. | : 3 | 6 | 9 | 12 | 15 | 18 |
| Frequency | : 5 | 18 | 28 | 6 | 15 | 10 |

**Solution**

| Rs. ($X$) | Frequency ($f$) |
|---|---|
| 3 | 5 |
| 6 | 18 |
| 9 | 28 |
| 12 | 6 |
| 15 | 15 |
| 18 | 10 |

As 28 is the highest frequency in the above series, therefore, the item Rs. 9 which contains this frequency is mode. (*By observation*)

**(b) By grouping.** If there are many items in the series which occur more frequently than other items, but their frequency among themselves is equal or nearly equal, then the mode in such cases should be known by grouping of frequencies.

The following two tables are made to know the mode by this method :

1. Grouping Table
2. Analysis Table.

**1. Grouping Table.** For grouping, a frequency-table is made prepared. In this table there are six columns made for frequency. In the first column the frequencies are put as they are given in the questions. In the second column pairs of two are formed starting from the first. In the third column are put the pairs of two leaving out the first frequency. In the fourth column are put the pairs of three each starting from the first frequency. In the fifth column pairs of three leaving out the first one frequency and in the sixth column pairs of three leaving out the first two frequencies are placed.

**2. Analysis Table.** After preparing a grouping table, an analysis table is prepared. In this table, those items are shown whose frequencies are the maximum in various columns of the grouping table.

**Illustration 77.** Find mode from the following data :

| | | | | | | | | | |
|---|---|---|---|---|---|---|---|---|---|
| Size of item : | 0 | 5 | 10 | 15 | 20 | 25 | 30 | 35 | 40 |
| Frequency : | 8 | 2 | 10 | 15 | 12 | 6 | 8 | 16 | 3 |

**Solution**

**Grouping Table**

| Size of item | Frequencies | | | | | |
|---|---|---|---|---|---|---|
| | 1 | 2 | 3 | 4 | 5 | 6 |
| 0 | 8 | 10 | | | | |
| 5 | 2 | | 12 | 20 | | |
| 10 | 10 | **25** | | | **27** | |
| 15 | 15 | | **27** | | | 37 |
| 20 | 12 | 18 | | **33** | | |
| 25 | 6 | | 14 | | 26 | |
| 30 | 8 | 24 | | | | 30 |
| 35 | **16** | | 19 | 27 | | |
| 40 | 3 | | | | | |

**Analysis Table**

| Column No. | Items containing maximum frequencies | | | | | |
|---|---|---|---|---|---|---|
| 1 | | | | | | 35 |
| 2 | | 10 | 15 | | | |
| 3 | | | 15 | 20 | | |
| 4 | | | 15 | 20 | 25 | |
| 5 | 5 | 10 | 15 | | | |
| 6 | | 10 | 15 | 20 | | |
| | 1 | 3 | 5 | 3 | 1 | 1 |

Thus item 15 contains the maximum frequency more times, therefore, it is a mode of this series.

### When mode is Ill-defined

When it is known by observation or grouping method that frequencies are maximum of more than one items, in that case, mode is ill-defined. In such a situation, the probable value of mode can be known with the help of arithmetic mean and median applying the following formula :

$$Z = 3M - 2\overline{X}$$

$$Z = \text{Mode.}$$

**Illustration 78.** Compute mode from the following figures :

| | | | | | | | |
|---|---|---|---|---|---|---|---|
| Size : | 8 | 16 | 24 | 32 | 40 | 48 | 56 |
| Frequency : | 6 | 12 | 18 | 15 | 17 | 18 | 6 |

**Solution**

| Size | Frequencies | | | | | |
|---|---|---|---|---|---|---|
| | 1 | 2 | 3 | 4 | 5 | 6 |
| 8 | 6 | 18 (8–16) | | | | |
| 16 | 12 | | 30 (16–24) | 36 (8–24) | | |
| 24 | **18** | **33** (24–32) | | | **45** (16–32) | |
| 32 | 15 | | **32** (32–40) | | | **50** (24–40) |
| 40 | 17 | **35** (40–48) | | **50** (32–48) | | |
| 48 | **18** | | 24 (48–56) | | 41 (40–56) | |
| 56 | 6 | | | | | |

**Analysis Table**

| Column No. | Items containing maximum frequencies | | | | |
|---|---|---|---|---|---|
| 1 | | 24 | | | 48 |
| 2 | | | | 40 | 48 |
| 3 | | | 32 | 40 | |
| 4 | | | 32 | 40 | 48 |
| 5 | 16 | 24 | 32 | | |
| 6 | | 24 | 32 | 40 | |
| | 1 | 3 | 4 | 4 | 3 |

In the above case, the mode is ill-defined because the maximum frequency of both items 32 and 40 has appeared 4 times each in the grouping table. Therefore, the probable value of mode in this case will be found with the help of the following formula :

$$Z = 3M - 2\overline{X}$$

Thus to know the mode from the above formula, the arithmetic mean and median of the series has to be known first which will be as follows :

| Size $X$ | Frequencies $(f)$ | $(cf)$ | $d$ $(AM = 32)$ | $d'$ $(i = 8)$ | $fd'$ |
|---|---|---|---|---|---|
| 8 | 6 | 6 | –24 | –3 | –18 |
| 16 | 12 | 18 | –16 | –2 | –24 |
| 24 | 18 | 36 | –8 | –1 | –18 |
| 32 | 15 | 51 | 0 | 0 | 0 |
| 40 | 17 | 68 | 8 | 1 | 17 |
| 48 | 18 | 86 | 16 | 2 | 36 |
| 56 | 6 | 92 | 24 | 3 | 18 |
| | $N = 92$ | | | | $\Sigma fd' = 11$ |

$$m = \frac{N+1}{N} \text{th item}$$

$$= \frac{92+1}{2} \text{th item}$$

$$= 46.5\text{th item}$$

$$= 32.$$

$$\overline{X} = AM + \frac{\sum fd'}{N} \times i$$

$$= 32 + \frac{11}{92} \times 8$$

$$= 32 + \frac{88}{92}$$

$$= 32 + 0.96$$

$$= 32.96$$

$$
\begin{aligned}
Z &= 3M - 2\overline{X} \\
&= 3(32) - 2(32.96) \\
&= 96 - 65.92 \\
&= 30.08.
\end{aligned}
$$

**Calculation of Mode in continuous Series.** In this series the following method will be adopted to know mode :

**Various Factors Considered for Mode**

The following factors should be considered while calculating mode in continuous series :

1. If series is in inclusive form it should be converted in exclusive form.

2. If mid-values of groups are given, proper class-intervals should be known.

3. If cumulative frequency distribution is given it should be converted into class-intervals.

4. If various groups are having un-equal class-intervals, these should be made equal.

After considering above factors, following procedure will be adopted to calculate mode in such series :

**(a) Finding Modal Group.** That group which has the maximum frequency will be the modal group. Such a group can be found by observation or grouping method. In order to know a modal group by grouping method, the same method will be applied as has been described earlier in relation to discrete series.

**(b) Finding Value of Mode.** After finding the modal group, the value of mode can be found with the help of the following formula :

$$Z = l_1 + \frac{\Delta_1}{\Delta_1 + \Delta_2} \times i$$

or

$$= l_1 + \frac{f_1 - f_0}{(f_1 - f_0) + (f_1 - f_2)} \times i$$

$Z$ = Mode

$l_1$ = Lower limit of modal group

$\Delta_1 = f_1 - f_0$

$\Delta_2 = f_1 - f_2$

$i$ = Class interval of modal group

$f_1$ = Frequency of modal group

$f_0$ = Frequency of the class preceding the modal group.

$f_2$ = Frequency of the class succeeding the modal group.

Above formula may be written as follows :

$$Z = l_1 + \frac{f_1 - f_0}{2f_1 - f_0 - f_2} \times i$$

If the upper boundary of the modal group is used, then for calculating the mode the following formula will be applied :

$$Z = l_2 - \frac{\Delta_2}{\Delta_1 + \Delta_2} \times i$$

$$\text{or} \quad l_2 - \frac{f_1 - f_2}{2f_1 - f_0 - f_2} \times i$$

Some of the various questions and solutions of mode are given below :

**Illustration 79.** Find the modal income from the following data :

| Income in Rs. | No. of Persons |
|---|---|
| 0-100 | 48 |
| 100-200 | 62 |
| 200-300 | 100 |
| 300-400 | 72 |
| 400-500 | 64 |
| 500-600 | 30 |

**Solution**

| Income in Rs. | No. of Persons |
|---|---|
| 0-100 | 48 |
| 100-200 | 62 |
| 200-300 | 100 |
| 300-400 | 72 |
| 400-500 | 64 |
| 500-600 | 30 |

100 is the maximum frequency and 200-300 is the group which contains it, therefore, it is a modal group. (*By observation*)

By interpolation, we get mode :

$$Z = l_1 + \frac{f_1 - f_0}{2f_1 - f_0 - f_2} \times i$$

$$= 200 + \frac{100 - 62}{200 - 62 - 72} \times 100$$

$$= 200 + \frac{38}{66} \times 100$$

$$= 200 + 57.58$$

$$= \text{Rs. } 257.58.$$

**Illustration 80.** Find mode from the following figures :

| | | | | | |
|---|---|---|---|---|---|
| Class intervals : | 0-20 | 20-40 | 40-60 | 60-80 | 80-100 |
| Frequency : | 5 | 22 | 17 | 21 | 18 |
| Class intervals : | 100-120 | 120-140 | | | |
| Frequency : | 16 | 12 | | | |

**Solution**

To find modal group in the given frequencies distribution grouping method will be adopted as follows :

**Grouping Table**

| Class intervals | Frequencies 1 | 2 | 3 | 4 | 5 | 6 |
|---|---|---|---|---|---|---|
| 0–20 | 5 | 27 | | 44 | | |
| 20–40 | **22** | | **39** | | **60** | |
| 40–60 | 17 | **38** | | | | **56** |
| 60–80 | 21 | | **39** | **55** | | |
| 80–100 | 18 | 34 | | | 46 | |
| 100–120 | 16 | | 28 | | | |
| 120–140 | 12 | | | | | |

**Analysis Table**

| Column No. | Items containing maximum frequencies | | | | |
|---|---|---|---|---|---|
| 1 | 20-40 | | | | |
| 2 | | 40-60 | 60-80 | | |
| 3 | 20-40 | 40-60 | 60-80 | 80-100 | |
| 4 | | | 60-80 | 80-100 | 100-120 |
| 5 | 20-40 | 40-60 | 60-80 | | |
| 6 | | 40-60 | 60-80 | 80-100 | |
| | 3 | 4 | 5 | 3 | 1 |

Therefore 60-80 is the modal group.

By interpolation :

$$Z = l_1 + \frac{f_1 - f_0}{2f_1 - f_0 - f_2} \times i$$

$$= 60 + \frac{21 - 17}{42 - 17 - 18} \times 20$$

$$= 60 + \frac{4}{7} \times 20$$

$$= 60 + 11.43$$

$$= 71.43.$$

**Illustration 81.** Calculate the value of the mode by the usual formula (after grouping, if necessary).

| $X$ | $f$ |
|---|---|
| 10-20 | 4 |
| 20-30 | 6 |
| 30-40 | 5 |
| 40-50 | 10 |
| 50-60 | 20 |
| 60-70 | 22 |
| 70-80 | 24 |
| 80-90 | 6 |
| 90-100 | 2 |
| 100-110 | 1 |

**Solution**

**Grouping Table**

| X | Frequencies | | | | | |
|---|---|---|---|---|---|---|
| | 1 | 2 | 3 | 4 | 5 | 6 |
| 10–20 | 4 | 10 | | 15 | | |
| 20–30 | 6 | | 11 | | 21 | |
| 30–40 | 5 | 15 | | | | 35 |
| 40–50 | 10 | | 30 | 52 | | |
| 50–60 | 20 | **42** | | | **66** | |
| 60–70 | 22 | | **44** | | | **52** |
| 70–80 | **24** | 30 | | 32 | | |
| 80–90 | 6 | | 8 | | 9 | |
| 90–100 | 2 | 3 | | | | |
| 100–110 | 1 | | | | | |

**Analysis Table**

| Column No. | Groups Containing Maximum Frequencies | | | | |
|---|---|---|---|---|---|
| 1 | | | | 70-80 | |
| 2 | | 50-60 | 60-70 | | |
| 3 | | | 60-70 | 70-80 | |
| 4 | 40-50 | 50-60 | 60-70 | | |
| 5 | | 50-60 | 60-70 | 70-80 | |
| 6 | | | 60-70 | 70-80 | 80-90 |
| Total | 1 | 3 | 5 | 4 | 1 |

∴ Modal group is 60-70.

$$Z = l_1 + \frac{f_1 - f_0}{2f_1 - f_0 - f_2} \times i$$

$$= 60 + \frac{22 - 20}{2\,(22) - 20 - 24} \times 10$$

$$= 60 + \frac{2 \times 10}{44 - 44}$$

$$= 60 + \frac{20}{0}$$

$$= 60.$$

**Calculation of Mode in Inclusive Series.** To know mode in this type of series, the series should be changed into exclusive series. Then the mode should be known.

**Illustration 82.** Calculate mode from the following figures :

| | | | | | |
|---|---|---|---|---|---|
| Marks | : | 1-5 | 6-10 | 11-15 | 16-20 | 21-25 |
| No. of Candidates | : | 7 | 10 | 16 | 32 | 24 |
| Marks | : | 26-30 | 31-35 | 36-40 | 41-45 | |
| No. of Candidate | : | 18 | 10 | 5 | 1 | |

**Solution**

First, the above series will be changed into exclusive series and then the mode will be calculated by the simple method.

| Marks | No. of Students |
|---|---|
| 0.5-5.5 | 7 |
| 5.5-10.5 | 10 |
| 10.5-15.5 | 16 |
| 15.5-20.5 | 32 |
| 20.5-25.5 | 24 |
| 25.5-30.5 | 18 |
| 30.5-35.5 | 10 |
| 35.5-40.5 | 5 |
| 40.5-45.5 | 1 |

Group 15.5-20.5 contains maximum frequency, therefore, it is a modal group.

(*By observation*)

By interpolation :

$$Z = l_1 + \frac{f_1 - f_0}{2f_1 - f_0 - f_2} \times i$$

$$= 15.5 + \frac{32 - 16}{64 - 16 - 24} \times 5$$

$$= 15.5 + \frac{16}{24} \times 5$$

$$= 15.5 + 3.33$$

$$= 18.83 \text{ marks.}$$

**Calculation of Mode in the unequal class Distribution.** To know mode in such a series, first, it is changed into equal class distribution. Then the mode should be calculated by the usual method.

**Illustration 83.** Calculate mode from the following frequencies distribution :

| | | | | | | | |
|---|---|---|---|---|---|---|---|
| Class intervals : | 0-5 | 5-10 | 10-20 | 20-30 | 30-32 | 32-35 | 35-40 |
| Frequency | 6 | 9 | 22 | 25 | 12 | 8 | 10 |
| Class-intervals : | 40-43 | 43-45 | 45-50 | 50-60 | 60-65 | 65-70 | |
| Frequency | 8 | 12 | 4 | 10 | 2 | 4 | |

**Solution**

The above series is an unequal class distribution series. Therefore, the mode will be calculated after changing it into equal class distribution in the following way :

| Class-intervals | frequency |
|---|---|
| 0-10 | 15 |
| 10-20 | 22 |
| 20-30 | 25 |
| 30-40 | 30 |
| 40-50 | 24 |
| 50-60 | 10 |
| 60-70 | 6 |

Modal class in 30-40 (*by observation*).

$$Z = l_1 + \frac{f_1 - f_0}{2f_1 - f_0 - f_2} \times i$$

$$= 30 + \frac{30 - 25}{2(30) - 25 - 24} \times 10$$

$$= 30 + \frac{5}{60 - 49} \times 10$$

$$= 30 + \frac{5}{11} \times 10$$

$= 30 + 4.55$

$= 34.55.$

**Illustration 84.** Calculate Mode from the following data :

| Class-Interval | Frequency |
|---|---|
| 0-2 | 2 |
| 2-3 | 2 |
| 3-6 | 6 |
| 6-10 | 12 |
| 10-12 | 6 |
| 12-15 | 15 |
| 15-18 | 15 |
| 18-24 | 25 |
| 24-25 | 2 |
| 25-29 | 8 |
| 29-30 | 2 |
| 30-32 | 2 |
| 32-35 | 2 |
| 35-36 | 1 |

[*B.Com.* (*Pass*) *Delhi*]

**Solution**

The above series is an unequal class-interval series. Therefore, it has to be changed, first into equal class interval series. After this the mode will be calculated by the method shown below :

| Class-Intervals | Frequency |
|---|---|
| 0-6 | 10 |
| 6-12 | 18 |
| 12-18 | 30 |
| 18-24 | 25 |
| 24-30 | 12 |
| 30-36 | 5 |

Modal Group is 12–18.

$$Z = l_1 + \frac{f_1 - f_0}{2f_1 - f_0 - f_2} \times i$$

$$= 12 + \frac{30 - 18}{2(30) - 18 - 25} \times 6$$

$$= 12 + \frac{12}{60 - 43} \times 6$$

$$= 12 + \frac{72}{17}$$

$$= 12 + 4.24$$

$$= 16.24.$$

**Illustration 85.** Compute mode from the following frequencies distribution :

| | | | | | | |
|---|---|---|---|---|---|---|
| Class-intervals : | 0-40 | 40-60 | 60-80 | 80-100 | 100-120 | 120-160 |
| Frequency : | 16 | 22 | 28 | 16 | 8 | 8 |

**Solution**

The mode will be calculated after changing the above series into equal class distribution in the following manner :

| Class-intervals | Frequency |
|---|---|
| 0-20 | 8 |
| 20-40 | 8 |
| 40-60 | 22 |
| 60-80 | 28 |
| 80-100 | 16 |
| 100-120 | 8 |
| 120-140 | 4 |
| 140-160 | 4 |

Modal group is 60-80 (*By observation*)

$$Z = l_1 + \frac{f_1 - f_0}{2f_1 - f_0 - f_2} \times i$$

$$= 60 + \frac{28 - 22}{2(28) - 22 - 16} \times 20$$

$$= 60 + \frac{6}{56 - 38} \times 20$$

$$= 60 + \frac{6}{18} \times 20$$

$$= 60 + 6.67$$

$$= 66.67.$$

**Illustration 86.** Compute mode from the following distribution :

| | | | | | | | | |
|---|---|---|---|---|---|---|---|---|
| Class-Intervals : | 0-3 | 3-5 | 5-7 | 7-11 | 11-15 | 15-18 | 18-20 | 20-23 |
| Frequency | 4 | 7 | 8 | 16 | 20 | 25 | 10 | 6 |
| Class-Intervals : | 23-27 | 27-30 | 30-35 | 35-40 | | | | |
| Frequency | 12 | 9 | 5 | 2 | | | | |

**Solution**

Above frequencies distribution is of unequal class-intervals, therefore, it will be converted in equal class-intervals as follows to calculate mode :

| Class-intervals | Frequency |
|---|---|
| 0-5 | 11 |
| 5-10 | 20 |
| 10-15 | 24 |
| 15-20 | 35 |
| 20-25 | 12 |
| 25-30 | 15 |
| 30-35 | 5 |
| 35-40 | 2 |

$$Z = l_1 + \frac{f_1 - f_0}{2f_1 - f_0 - f_2} \times i$$

$$= 15 + \frac{35 - 24}{2(35) - 24 - 12} \times 5$$

$$= 15 + \frac{11}{70 - 24 - 12} \times 5$$

$$= 15 + \frac{11}{34} \times 5$$

$$= 15 + 1.62$$

$$= 16.62.$$

**Calculation of Mode in Open end Distribution.** If the class boundaries of the modal group are given and class boundaries of other groups are not given then it is not necessary to know the value of open-end for calculating mode. But if there is no boundary of the modal group then the limits will be calculated according to the method explained in 'Chapter 7' and after this mode may be found out by adopting the usual process of its calculation.

**Illustration 87.** Compute the value of mode from the following frequencies distribution :

| | | | | | | |
|---|---|---|---|---|---|---|
| Class-intervals : | Below 15 | 15-30 | 30-45 | 45-60 | 60-75 | 75-90 |
| Frequency : | 24 | 33 | 45 | 52 | 32 | 16 |
| Class-intervals : | 90-105 | 105 & above | | | | |
| Frequency : | 10 | 5 | | | | |

**Solution**

| Class-intervals | Frequency |
|---|---|
| Below 15 | 24 |
| 15-30 | 33 |
| 30-45 | 45 |
| 45-60 | 52 |
| 60-75 | 32 |
| 75-90 | 16 |
| 90-105 | 10 |
| 105 & above | 5 |

Modal group is 45-60 (*By observation*)

$$Z = l_1 + \frac{f_1 - f_0}{2f_1 - f_0 - f_2} \times i$$

$$= 45 + \frac{52-45}{2(52)-45-32} \times 15$$

$$= 45 + \frac{7}{104-45-32} \times 15$$

$$= 45 + \frac{7}{27} \times 15$$

$$= 45 + 3.89$$

$$= 48.89.$$

**Illustration 88.** Compute the value of mode from the following frequency distribution :

| Class intervals | Frequency |
|---|---|
| 0–10 | 12 |
| 10–20 | 18 |
| 20–30 | 25 |
| 30–40 | 30 |
| 40–50 | 20 |
| 50–60 | 16 |
| 60–70 | 9 |
| 70–80 | 5 |

**Solution**

After knowing the class boundaries of the above series, the mode will be calculated in the following manner :

| Class-intervals | Frequency |
|---|---|
| 0-10 | 12 |
| 10-20 | 18 |
| 20-30 | 25 |
| 30-40 | 30 |
| 40-50 | 20 |
| 50-60 | 16 |
| 60-70 | 9 |
| 70-80 | 5 |

Modal group is 30–40 (*By observation*)

$$Z = l_1 + \frac{f_1 - f_0}{2f_1 - f_0 - f_2} \times i$$

$$= 30 + \frac{30 - 25}{2(30) - 25 - 20} \times 10$$

$$= 30 + \frac{5}{60 - 45} \times 10$$

$$= 30 + \frac{5}{15} \times 10$$

$$= 30 + 3.33$$

$$= 33.33.$$

### Calculation of Mode in those Frequency Distributions in which Mode is ill-defined

In such series, the probable value of mode is known after applying arithmetic mean and median with the help of the following formula :

$$Z = 3M - 2\overline{X}$$

**Illustration 89.** Compute mode from the following frequencies distribution :

| Marks | 0-5 | 5-10 | 10-15 | 15-20 | 20-25 | 25-30 | 30-35 | 35-40 |
|---|---|---|---|---|---|---|---|---|
| No. of students | 8 | 6 | 18 | 12 | 12 | 17 | 8 | 2 |

**Solution**

**Frequency Table**

| Marks | Frequencies | | | | | |
|---|---|---|---|---|---|---|
| | 1 | 2 | 3 | 4 | 5 | 6 |
| 0–5 | 8 | 14 | | 32 | | |
| 5–10 | 6 | | 24 | | 36 | |
| 10–15 | **18** | **30** | | | | **42** |
| 15–20 | 12 | | 24 | **41** | | |
| 20–25 | 12 | 29 | | | **37** | |
| 25–30 | 17 | | **25** | | | 27 |
| 30–35 | 8 | **10** | | | | |
| 35–40 | 2 | | | | | |

**Analysis Table**

| Column No. | Groups containing maximum frequency | | | | |
|---|---|---|---|---|---|
| 1 | 10-15 | | | | |
| 2 | 10-15 | 15-20 | | | |
| 3 | | | | 25-30 | 30-35 |
| 4 | | 15-20 | 20-25 | 25-30 | |
| 5 | | | 20-25 | 25-30 | 30-35 |
| 6 | 10-15 | 15-20 | 20-25 | | |
| | 3 | 3 | 3 | 3 | 2 |

The frequencies of class 10-15, 15-20, 20-25 and 25-30 have been proved to be repeatedly maximum. Thus mode in this series is ill-defined which will be calculated with the help of arithmetic mean and median in the following manner :

| Marks (C.I.) | Mid-value ($X$) | Frequencies ($f$) | $cf$ | $d$ ($AM$=17.5) | $d'$ ($i$=5) | $fd'$ |
|---|---|---|---|---|---|---|
| 0-5 | 2.5 | 8 | 8 | –15 | –3 | –24 |
| 5-10 | 7.5 | 6 | 14 | –10 | –2 | –12 |
| 10-15 | 12.5 | 18 | 32 | –5 | –1 | –18 |
| 15-20 | 17.5 | 12 | 44 | 0 | 0 | 0 |
| 20-25 | 22.5 | 12 | 56 | 5 | 1 | 12 |
| 25-30 | 27.5 | 17 | 73 | 10 | 2 | 34 |
| 30-35 | 32.5 | 8 | 81 | 15 | 3 | 24 |
| 35-40 | 37.5 | 2 | 83 | 20 | 4 | 8 |
| | | $N$ = 83 | | | | $\Sigma fd'$=24 |

$$X = AM + \frac{\sum fd'}{N} \times i$$

$$= 17.5 + \frac{24}{83} \times 5$$

$$= 17.5 + 1.45$$

$$= 18.95 \text{ marks}$$

$$m = \frac{N}{2}\text{th item}$$

$$= \frac{83}{2}\text{ th item}$$

$$= 41.5\text{th item}$$

Therefore middle group is 15–20

$$M = l_1 + \frac{i}{f}(m-c)$$

$$= 15 + \frac{5}{12}(41.5 - 32)$$

$$= 15 + \frac{5}{12}(9.5)$$

$$= 15 + 3.96$$

$$= 18.96 \text{ marks}$$

$$Z = 3M - 2X$$

$$= 3(18.96) - 2(18.95)$$

$$= 56.88 - 37.90$$

$$= 18.98 \text{ marks.}$$

**Illustration 90.** Fifty workers of a certain factory at Naini receive the following amount as their monthly wages :

Wages in Rs.

| | | | | | | | | | | | | |
|---|---|---|---|---|---|---|---|---|---|---|---|---|
| 40 | 42 | 42 | 44 | 45 | 45 | 45 | 46 | 48 | 48 | 50 | 50 | 50 |
| 50 | 50 | 52 | 53 | 54 | 55 | 55 | 55 | 55 | 55 | 56 | 56 | 58 |
| 58 | 59 | 60 | 60 | 60 | 60 | 60 | 62 | 64 | 65 | 65 | 65 | 65 |
| 66 | 68 | 70 | 70 | 70 | 71 | 72 | 75 | 75 | 76 | 80 | | |

Arrange the above data in classes with class-intervals of five rupees each and find modal wage.

**Solution**

**Arrangement of data in classes**

| Classes | Tally Sheet | Frequency |
|---|---|---|
| 40-45 | IIII | 4 |
| 45-50 | ~~IIII~~ I | 6 |
| 50-55 | ~~IIII~~ III | 8 |
| 55-60 | ~~IIII~~ ~~IIII~~ | 10 |
| 60-65 | ~~IIII~~ II | 7 |
| 65-70 | ~~IIII~~ I | 6 |
| 70-75 | ~~IIII~~ | 5 |
| 75-80 | III | 3 |
| 80-85 | I | 1 |
| | | 50 |

Group 55-60 is the modal group, because it contains the maximum frequency.

By interpolation :

$$Z = l_1 + \frac{f_1 - f_0}{2f_1 - f_0 - f_2} \times i$$

$$= 55 + \frac{10-8}{20-8-7} \times 5$$

$$= 55 + \frac{2}{5} \times 5$$

$$= \text{Rs. } 57$$

**Calculation of Mode by using Alternative Formula**

When the frequency of modal group is less than that of the preceding group or the double frequencies of modal group are less than the sum of the frequencies of the preceding and proceeding groups, the following formula for calculating mode will not be used :

$$Z = l_1 + \frac{f_1 - f_0}{2f_1 - f_0 - f_2} \times i$$

If the above formula will be used in this sit:ation, the value of mode will come out less than the lower limit of modal group which is inconsistent, therefore in such a situation the following alternative formula will be used :

$$Z = l_1 + \frac{f_2}{f_0 + f_2} \times i$$

The use of this formula will be clear from the following illustration :

**Illustration 91.** Find mode from the following data :

| Variables | Frequencies |
|---|---|
| 0-10 | 7 |
| 10-20 | 35 |
| 20-30 | 34 |
| 30-40 | 31 |
| 40-50 | 8 |
| 50-60 | 12 |

**Solution**

**Grouping Table**

| Variables | Frequencies | | | | | |
|---|---|---|---|---|---|---|
| | 1 | 2 | 3 | 4 | 5 | 6 |
| 0–10 | 7 | 42 | | | | |
| 10–20 | **35** | | **69** | **76** | | |
| 20–30 | 34 | **65** | | | **100** | |
| 30–40 | 31 | | 39 | | | **73** |
| 40–50 | 8 | 20 | | 51 | | |
| 50–60 | 12 | | | | | |

**Analysis Table**

| Column No. | Groups containing maximum frequency | | | | |
|---|---|---|---|---|---|
| 1 | | 10-20 | | | |
| 2 | | | 20-30 | 30-40 | |
| 3 | | 10-20 | 20-30 | | |
| 4 | 0-10 | 10-20 | 20-30 | | |
| 5 | | 10-20 | 20-30 | 30-40 | |
| 6 | | | 20-30 | 30-40 | 40-50 |
| | 1 | 4 | 5 | 3 | 1 |

It is found from the analysis table that 20-30 is a modal group. The frequencies of its preceding group 10-20 are more than this group. Therefore, for calculating mode, the formula given below should not be used :

$$Z = l_1 \frac{f_1 - f_0}{2f_1 - f_0 - f_2} \times i$$

Because by using this, the value of mode will come out to be 15 which will be less than the lower boundary of the modal group and therefore, it will be irrational. This point can be clarified by placing the values given in the above formula which is as following :

$$Z = 20 + \frac{34 - 35}{2(34) - 35 - 31} \times 10$$

$$= 20 + \frac{-1}{68 - 66} \times 10$$

$$= 20 + \frac{-1}{2} \times 10$$

$$= 20 - 5$$

$$= 15$$

To say then that the mode is 15 will be wrong because the modal group is 20-30. Therefore, the mode should neither be less than 20 nor should it exceed 30. In such a situation, therefore, the following formula will be applied for calculating mode :

$$Z = l_1 + \frac{f_2}{f_0 + f_2} \times i$$

By putting the value in the above formula we get :

$$Z = 20 + \frac{31}{35+31} \times 10$$

$$= 20 + \frac{31}{66} \times 10$$

$$= 20 + 4.7$$

$$= 24.7.$$

## Finding the value of Missing Frequencies if value of Mode is given

If the value of mode is given and the frequency of any group is not given, then by placing the given value in the formula of mode the missing frequency can be known.

**Illustration 92.** Find the value of missing frequency of group 36–45 from the following figures, if the value of mode is given 48.

| Class-intervals : | 18-27 | 27-36 | 36-45 | 45-54 | 54-63 | 63-72 |
|---|---|---|---|---|---|---|
| Frequency : | 6 | 8 | ? | 18 | 12 | 9 |
| Class-intervals : | 72-81 | 81-90 | | | | |
| Frequency : | 5 | 2 | | | | |

**Solution**

As the value of mode is 48, therefore it must be situated in 45–54 group. By placing the known values in the formula of mode, the missing frequencies can be known as follows :

$$Z = l_1 + \frac{f_1 - f_0}{2f_1 - f_0 - f_2} \times i$$

$$48 = 45 + \frac{18 - f_0}{2(18) - f_0 - 12} \times 9$$

or $$48 - 45 = \frac{18 - f_0}{36 - f_0 - 12} \times 9$$

or $$3 = \frac{18 - f_0}{24 - f_0} \times 9$$

or $72 - 3f_0 = 162 - 9f_0$

or $-3f_0 + 9f_0 = 162 - 72$

or $6f_0 = 90$

or $f_0 = 15$

∴ Frequency of group 36–45 will be 15.

**Illustration 93.** Find number of persons who are getting monthly salary of Rs. 300-400 and 800-900 from the following incomplete frequency distribution.

| Monthly Salary Rs. | : | 0-100 | 100-200 | 200-300 | 300-400 | 400-500 |
|---|---|---|---|---|---|---|
| No. of persons | : | 13 | 18 | 17 | ? | 22 |
| Monthly Salary Rs. | : | 500-600 | 600-700 | 700-800 | 800-900 | 900-1000 |
| No. of persons | : | 18 | 15 | 13 | ? | 8 |

Also find total number of persons included in above distribution if the modal salaries are Rs. 460 and median salaries are Rs. 450 of the above distribution.

**Solution**

In this question, modal group and median group are 400-500 because the values of median and mode are Rs. 450 and Rs. 460 respectively. In order to find the missing frequencies the following calculations will be made to find out these frequencies :

| Monthly income in Rs. (C.I.) | No. of persons ($f$) |
|---|---|
| 0-100 | 13 |
| 100-200 | 18 |
| 200-300 | 17 |
| 300-400 | $f_0$ |
| 400-500 | 22 |
| 500-600 | 18 |
| 600-700 | 15 |
| 700-800 | 13 |
| 800-900 | ? |
| 900-1000 | 8 |

Modal group is 400–500

$$Z = l_1 + \frac{f_1 - f_0}{2f_1 - f_0 - f_2} \times i$$

$$460 = 400 + \frac{22 - f_0}{2(22) - f_0 - 18} \times 100$$

or $$460 - 400 = \frac{22 - f_0}{44 - 18 - f_0} \times 100$$

or $$60 = \frac{22 - f_0}{26 - f_0} \times 100$$

or $1560 - 60f_0 = 2200 - 100\, f_0$

or $-60f_0 + 100\, f_0 = 2200 - 1560$

or $40f_0 = 640$

or $f_0 = 16$

Thus the frequency of group 300-400 is 16, the frequency of group 800-900 will be calculated as follows :

| Monthly Salary in Rs. (C.I.) | No. of persons ($f$) | Cumulative Frequencies ($cf$) |
|---|---|---|
| 0-100 | 13 | 13 |
| 100-200 | 18 | 31 |
| 200-300 | 17 | 48 |
| 300-400 | 16 | 64 |
| 400-500 | 22 | 86 |
| 500-600 | 18 | 104 |
| 600-700 | 15 | 119 |
| 700-800 | 13 | 132 |
| 800-900 | $f_x$ | $132 + f_x$ |
| 900-1000 | 8 | $140 + f_x$ |

Median group is 400–500

$$M = l_1 + \frac{i}{f}(m - c)$$

$$450 = 400 + \frac{100}{22}(m - 64)$$

or $$50 = \frac{100}{22}(m - 64)$$

or $1100 = 100m - 6400$

or $-100m = -6400 - 1100$

or $-100m = -7500$

or $m = 75$

$$m = \frac{N}{2} \text{th item}$$

$$75 = \frac{N}{2} \text{th item}$$

$$N = 75 \times 2$$

$$= 150$$

Thus total number of persons in this distribution is 150 and the frequencies of 800–900 will be :

$$N = 140 + f_x$$

$$150 = 140 + f_x$$

or $$-f_x = 140 - 150$$

or $$f_x = 10$$

Thus the frequency of 800–900 is 10.

**Illustration 94.** The median and mode of the following wage distribution of 230 workers are known to be Rs. 33.5 and Rs. 34 respectively. Three frequency values from the table are, however, missing. You are required to find the missing frequencies :

| Wages (in Rs.) : | 0-10 | 10-20 | 20-30 | 30-40 | 40-50 | 50-60 | 60-70 |
|---|---|---|---|---|---|---|---|
| Frequency : | 4 | 16 | ? | ? | ? | 6 | 4 |

**Solution**

| Wages in Rs. | Frequency | Cumulative Frequencies |
|---|---|---|
| 0-10 | 4 | 4 |
| 10-20 | 16 | 20 |
| 20-30 | $f_0$ | $20+f_0$ |
| 30-40 | $f_1$ | $20+f_0+f_1$ |
| 40-50 | $f_2$ | $20+f_0+f_1+f_2$ |
| 50-60 | 6 | $26+f_0+f_1+f_2$ |
| 60-70 | 4 | $30+f_0+f_1+f_2$ |
| | $N = 230$ | |

$$M = \frac{N}{2} \text{th item}$$

$$= \frac{230}{2} \text{th item}$$

As median value is given 33.5, therefore middle group will be 30–40.

$$M = l_1 + \frac{i}{f}(m - c)$$

$$33.5 = 30 + \frac{10}{f_1}(115 - 20 - f_0)$$

or $$33.5 - 30 = \frac{10}{f_1}(115 - 20 - f_0)$$

or $$3.5 = \frac{10}{f_1}(95 - f_0)$$

or $$3.5f_1 = 950 - 10f_0$$

or $$10f_0 + 3.5f_1 = 950 \qquad \text{...(i)}$$

As the value of mode is 34, therefore modal group will be 30–40.

$$Z = l_1 + \frac{f_1 - f_0}{2f_1 - f_0 - f_2} \times i$$

$$34 = 30 + \frac{f_1 - f_0}{2f_1 - f_0 - f_2} \times 10$$

or $$34 - 30 = \frac{f_1 - f_0}{2f_1 - f_0 - f_2} \times 10$$

or $$4 = \frac{f_1 - f_0}{2f_1 - f_0 - f_2} \times 10$$

or $$8f_1 - 4f_0 - 4f_2 = 10f_1 - 10f_0$$

or $$6f_0 - 2f_1 - 4f_2 = 0 \qquad \text{...(ii)}$$

$$N = 30 + f_0 + f_1 + f_2$$

$$230 = 30 + f_0 + f_1 + f_2$$

or $$f_0 + f_1 + f_2 = 230 - 30$$

or $$f_0 + f_1 + f_2 = 200 \qquad \text{...(iii)}$$

If equation (iii) is multiplied by 4, the another equation will be :

$$4f_0 + 4f_1 + 4f_2 = 800 \quad ...(iv)$$
$$6f_0 - 2f_1 - 4f_2 = 0 \quad ...(ii)$$
$$10f_1 + 2f_1 = 800 \quad ...(v)$$
$$10f_0 - 3.5f_1 = 950 \quad ...(i)$$
$$- \qquad -$$
$$-1.5f_1 = -150$$
$$f_1 = 100$$

By putting the value of $f_1$ in equation (i), the value of $f_0$ may find out as follows :

$$10f_0 + 3.5f_1 = 950 \quad ...(i)$$

or $10f_0 + 3.5\ (100) = 950$

or $10f_0 = 950 - 350$

or $10f_0 = 600$

or $f_0 = 60$

Now putting the values of $f_0$ and $f_1$ in equation (iii) the value of $f_2$ may be find out as follows :

$$f_0 + f_1 + f_2 = 200$$

or $60 + 100 + f_2 = 200$

$f_2 = 200 - 100 - 60$

or $f_2 = 40$

**Locating Mode with Graphic Method**

In order to locate mode by the graph method, first, histogram will be made. The tallest rectangle will be connected with the edges of its either side rectangles by crossing it. From the point where the connecting lines cut each other a perpendicular will be drawn on the base line. The value-point where the perpendicular will join the base will be the value of mode. By this method the plotting of mode will be done in the following way :

**Illustration 95.** Locate mode graphically from the following frequency distribution :

| | | | | | | |
|---|---|---|---|---|---|---|
| Class-Intervals : | 0-10 | 10-20 | 20-30 | 30-40 | 40-50 | 50-60 |
| Frequency : | 3 | 9 | 15 | 18 | 22 | 16 |
| Class-Intervals : | 60-70 | 70-80 | 80-90 | | | |
| Frequency : | 13 | 10 | 6 | | | |

**Solution**

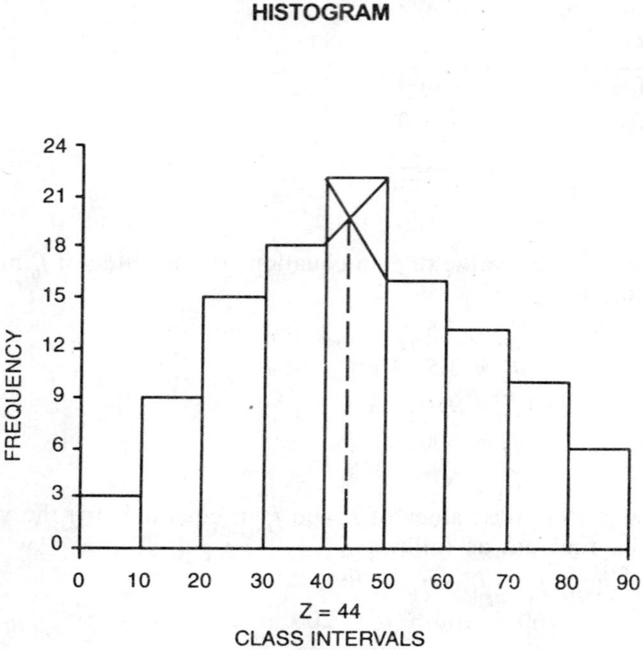


**Verification**

Modal group is 40–50 (*by observation*)

$$Z = l_1 + \frac{f_1 - f_0}{2f_1 - f_0 - f_2} \times i$$

$$= 40 + \frac{22 - 18}{2\,(22) - 18 - 16} \times 10$$

$$= 40 + \frac{4}{44 - 34} \times 10$$

$$= 40 + \frac{4}{10} \times 10$$

$$= 40 + 4$$

$$= 44$$

**Illustration 96.** Calculate mode from the following figures :

| Monthly Salary (in Rs.) | No. of Workers |
|---|---|
| 200-250 | 4 |
| 250-300 | 6 |
| 300-350 | 20 |
| 350-400 | 12 |
| 400-450 | 33 |
| 450-500 | 17 |
| 500-550 | 8 |
| 550-600 | 2 |

Also calculate mode with graphic method.

[*B.Com.* (*Pass*) *Delhi*]

**Solution**

| Monthly Salary in Rs. (C.I.) | No. of Workers ($f$) |
|---|---|
| 200-250 | 4 |
| 250-300 | 6 |
| 300-350 | 20 |
| 350-400 | 12 |
| 400-450 | 33 |
| 450-500 | 17 |
| 500-550 | 8 |
| 550-600 | 2 |

Modal Group is 400–450 (*by observation*)

$$Z = l_1 + \frac{f_1 - f_0}{2f_1 - f_0 - f_2} \times i$$

$$= 400 + \frac{33 - 12}{2(33) - 12 - 17} \times 50$$

$$= 400 + \frac{21}{66 - 29} \times 50$$

$$= 400 + \frac{1050}{37}$$

$$= 400 + 28.38$$

$$= \text{Rs. } 428.38$$

HISTOGRAM & MODE

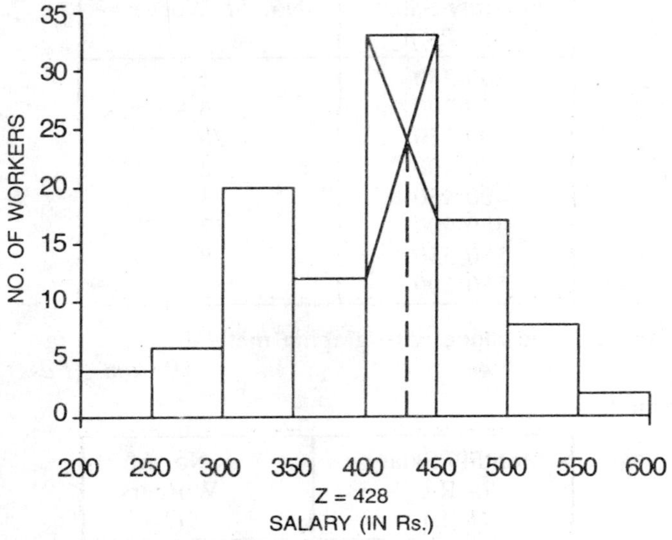


**Illustration 97.** The monthly profits in rupees of 100 shops are distributed as follows :

| Profits per Shop | No. of Shops |
|---|---|
| 0-100 | 12 |
| 100-200 | 18 |
| 200-300 | 27 |
| 300-400 | 20 |
| 400-500 | 17 |
| 500-600 | 6 |

Determine the 'modal value' of the above distribution graphically and verify the result by calculation.

[*B.Com.* (*Hons*)]

**Solution**

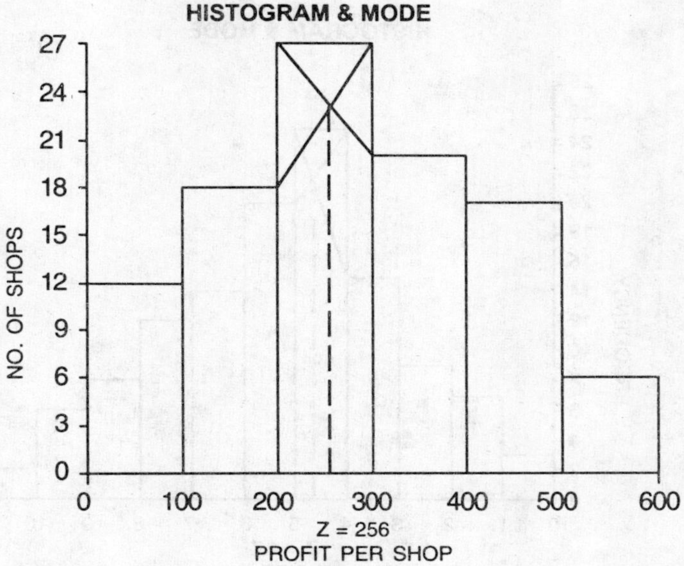


**Verification**

Modal Group is 200–300

$$Z = l_1 + \frac{f_1 - f_0}{2f_1 - f_0 - f_2} \times i$$

$$= 200 + \frac{27 - 18}{2(27) - 18 - 20} \times 100$$

$$= 200 + \frac{9}{54 - 38} \times 100$$

$$= 200 + \frac{9 \times 100}{16}$$

$$= 200 + 56.25$$

$$= 256.25$$

**Illustration 98.** Find out the mode of the following data graphically and check the result through calculation :

| | | | | | | | | | |
|---|---|---|---|---|---|---|---|---|---|
| Size : | 0-1 | 1-2 | 2-3 | 3-4 | 4-5 | 5-6 | 6-7 | 7-8 | 8-9 |
| Freq. : | 3 | 7 | 9 | 15 | 25 | 20 | 14 | 12 | 8 |
| Size : | 9-10 | 10-11 | | | | | | | |
| Freq. : | 6 | 2 | | | | | | | |

[*B.Com.* (*Pass*), *Delhi*]

**Solution**

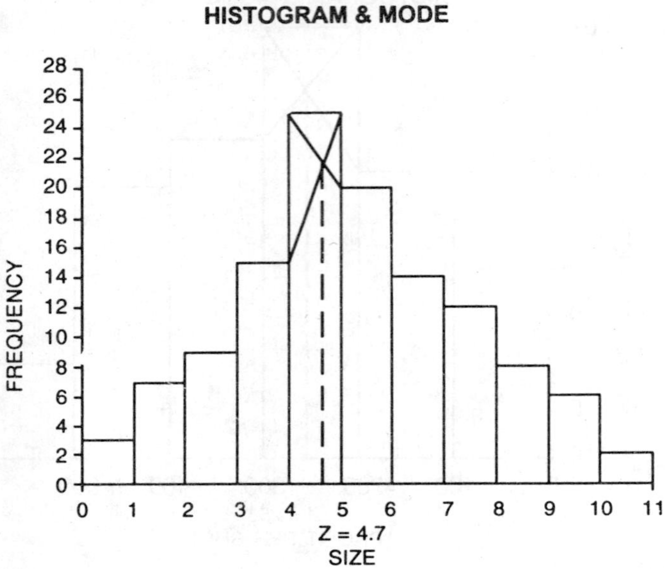


**Verification**

Modal Group is 4—5

$$Z = l_1 + \frac{f_1 - f_0}{2f_1 - f_0 - f_2} \times i$$

$$= 4 + \frac{25 - 15}{2(25) - 15 - 20} \times 1$$

$$= 4 + \frac{10}{50 - 35} \times 1$$

$$= 4 + \frac{10}{15}$$

$$= 4.67$$

**Merits and Demerits of Mode.** It has the following merits and demerits :

**Merits.** 1. Mode is easy to calculate.

2. Mode has practical utility. This is useful in know the customs, fashions and nature of society.

3. Too large or small items that is, extreme items have no effect on this mean.

4. This mean is capable of representing the maximum units of a series. Therefore, in comparison of other averages, this average has more representative value.

**Demerits.** 1. Sometimes, there are many a series in which more than one items have equal maximum frequencies value. In that case the mode cannot be determined.

2. No mathematical evaluation can be done by mode.

3. Modes to not highlight the relative significance of values.

**Illustration 99.** From the following data, calculate the Mean, Median and Mode :

| C.I. | *f* |
|---|---|
| 5–15 | 16 |
| 15–25 | 24 |
| 25–35 | 36 |
| 35–45 | 48 |
| 45–55 | 88 |
| 55–65 | 42 |
| 65–75 | 28 |
| 75–85 | 10 |
| 85–95 | 8 |
| | 300 |

(*C.A.*)

**Solution**

| C.I. | mv (*X*) | *f* | *cf* | *d* (*Am* = 50 | *f'* (*i* = 10) | *fd'* |
|---|---|---|---|---|---|---|
| 5–15 | 10 | 16 | 16 | –40 | –4 | –64 |
| 15–25 | 20 | 24 | 40 | –30 | –3 | –72 |
| 25–35 | 30 | 36 | 76 | –20 | –2 | –72 |
| 35–45 | 40 | 48 | 124 | –10 | –1 | –48 |
| 45–55 | 50 | 88 | 212 | 0 | 0 | 0 |
| 55–65 | 60 | 42 | 254 | 10 | 1 | 42 |
| 65–75 | 70 | 28 | 282 | 20 | 2 | 56 |
| 75–85 | 80 | 10 | 292 | 30 | 3 | 30 |
| 85–95 | 90 | 8 | 300 | 40 | 4 | 32 |
| | | $N = 300$ | | | | $\Sigma fd' = -96$ |

(i) $$\overline{X} = AM + \frac{\Sigma fd'}{N} \times i$$

$$= 50 + \frac{-96}{300} \times 10$$

$$= 50 + \frac{-960}{300}$$

$$= 50 - 3.20$$

$$= 46.80$$

(ii) $$m = \frac{N}{2} \text{th item}$$

$$= \frac{300}{2} \text{th item}$$

$$= 150\text{th item}$$

$\therefore$ Median group is 45–55

$$M = l_1 + \frac{i}{f}(m - c)$$

$$= 45 + \frac{10}{88}(150 - 124)$$

$$= 45 + \frac{10}{88} \times 26$$

$$= 45 + \frac{260}{88}$$

$$= 45 + 2.95$$

$$= 47.95$$

(iii) Modal group is 45–55

$$Z = l_1 + \frac{f_1 - f_0}{2f_1 - f_0 - f_2} \times i$$

$$= 45 + \frac{88 - 48}{2(88) - 48 - 42} \times 10$$

$$= 45 + \frac{40}{176 - 90} \times 10$$

$$= 45 + \frac{400}{86}$$

$$= 45 + 4.65$$

$$= 49.65$$

**Illustration 100.** Find out Mean, Median and Mode from the following data :

| | | | | | | | | |
|---|---|---|---|---|---|---|---|---|
| Marks below : | 10 | 20 | 30 | 40 | 50 | 60 | 70 | 80 |
| No. of students : | 15 | 35 | 60 | 84 | 96 | 127 | 198 | 250 |

*(B.Com., Agra)*

**Solution**

| Marks (C.I.) | Mid-value ($X$) | No. of students ($f$) | $Cf$ | $d$ ($A$ = 35) | $d'$ ($i$ = 10) | $fd'$ |
|---|---|---|---|---|---|---|
| 0-10 | 5 | 15 | 15 | –30 | –3 | –45 |
| 10-20 | 15 | 20 | 35 | –20 | –2 | –40 |
| 20-30 | 25 | 25 | 60 | –10 | –1 | –25 |
| 30-40 | 35 | 24 | 84 | 0 | 0 | 0 |
| 40-50 | 45 | 12 | 96 | 10 | 1 | 12 |
| 50-60 | 55 | 31 | 127 | 20 | 2 | 62 |
| 60-70 | 65 | 71 | 198 | 30 | 3 | 213 |
| 70-80 | 75 | 52 | 250 | 40 | 4 | 208 |
| | | $N$ = 250 | | | | $\Sigma fd'$ = 385 |

(i) $$\overline{X} = AM + \frac{\Sigma fd'}{N} \times i$$

$$= 35 + \frac{385}{250} \times 10$$

$$= 35 + 15.4$$

$$= 50.4$$

(ii) $$m = \frac{N}{2}\text{th item}$$

$$= \frac{250}{2}\text{th item}$$

$$= 125\text{th item}$$

∴ Median group is 50–60.

$$M = l_1 + \frac{i}{f}(m - c)$$

$$= 50 + \frac{10}{31}(125 - 96)$$

$$= 50 + \frac{10 \times 29}{31}$$

$$= 50 + \frac{290}{31}$$

$$= 50 + 9.35$$

$$= 59.35$$

(iii) Modal group is 60–70 (*By observation*)

$$Z = l_1 + \frac{f_1 - f_0}{2f_1 - f_0 - f_2} \times i$$

$$= 60 + \frac{71 - 31}{2(71) - 31 - 52} \times 10$$

$$= 60 + \frac{40 \times 10}{142 - 83} = 60 + \frac{400}{59}$$

$$= 60 + 6.78 = 66.78$$

**Relationship among Arithmetic Mean, Median and Mode**

There can be a definite relationship among arithmetic mean, median and mode, but the nature of relationship depends upon the nature of series. From this point of view the character of various series can be divided into the following parts :

**1. Perfectly Symmetrical Distribution.** In this type of series, there is a kind of symmetry in the fluctuations of values. The curve of this type of series is formed like that of a bell-shape. From the following curves the nature of this series will be clear :

SYMMETRICAL DISTRIBUTION

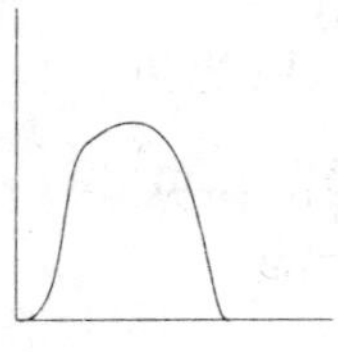

**Example 1**

| | | | | | | | |
|---|---|---|---|---|---|---|---|
| Class-Interval : | 0-10 | 10-20 | 20-30 | 30-40 | 40-50 | 50-60 | 60-70 |
| Frequency : | 5 | 8 | 12 | 18 | 12 | 8 | 5 |

In this type of series, arithmetic mean, median and mode have equal values that is, $\overline{X} = M = Z$. The following chart will make the relationship of median, arithmetic mean and mode clear in such distribution :

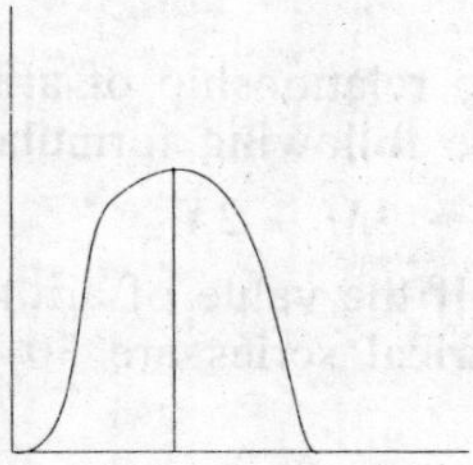

$\overline{X} = M = Z$

**Illustration 101.** If the value of arithmetic mean in a symmetrical series is 20, what will be the value of median and mode?

**Solution**

$$\overline{X} = M = Z$$

$$\overline{X} = 20$$

$\therefore$ The Value of $M$ and $Z$ will also be 20.

**2. Moderately Asymmetrical Series.** There is a definite order in the fluctuations of values in this type of series, but the ratio of fluctuation is not symmetrical. The inclination of curves in such series is either to the right or to the left. This will become clear from the following examples and curves.

**Example 2**

| | | | | | | | | |
|---|---|---|---|---|---|---|---|---|
| (A) | Class-interval : | 0-10 | 10-20 | 20-30 | 30-40 | 40-50 | 50-60 | 60-70 |
| | Frequency : | 5 | 10 | 18 | 25 | 16 | 8 | 4 |
| (B) | Class-interval : | 0-10 | 10-20 | 20-30 | 30-40 | 40-50 | 50-60 | 60-70 |
| | Frequency : | 4 | 8 | 16 | 25 | 18 | 10 | 5 |

**MODERATELY ASYMMETRICAL SERIES**

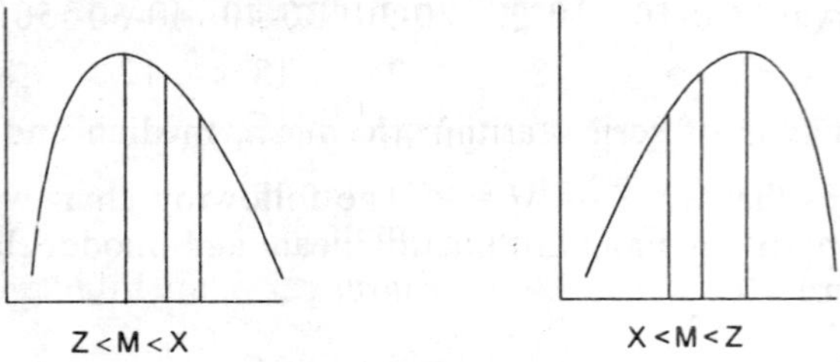


In such series, the relationship of arithmetic mean, median and mode is known by the following formula :

$$Z = 3M - 2X$$

**Illustration 102.** If the value of arithmetic mean and median in a moderately symmetrical series are 30 and 32, find the value of mode.

**Solution**

$$Z = 3M - 2\overline{X}$$

$$Z = 3(32) - 2(30)$$

$$Z = 96 - 60$$

$$Z = 36.$$

**3. Perfectly Asymmetrical Distribution.** Values in this kind of series do not have any definite order. Hence no definite relationship among arithmetic mean, median and mode is found in such series. From the following example and graph, the nature of such a series will be clear :

**Example 3**

| Class-interval : | 0-10 | 10-20 | 20-30 | 30-40 | 40-50 | 50-60 | 60-70 | 70-80 | 80-90 |
|---|---|---|---|---|---|---|---|---|---|
| Frequency : | 15 | 8 | 22 | 2 | 2 | 25 | 6 | 18 | 4 |

**PERFECTLY ASYMMETRICAL DISTRIBUTION**

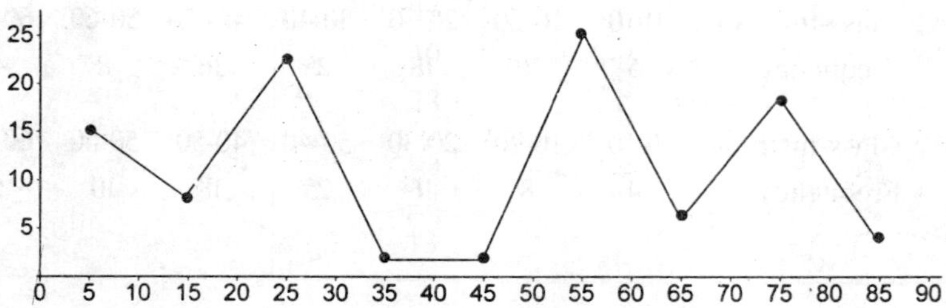

**Illustration 103**

(a) You are given the value of mean and median as 86 and 94 of a moderately asymmetrical distribution. What will be its most probable mode?

(b) Compute mean :

$$M = 20,\ Z = 25$$

(c) You are given the value of arithmetic mean and mode as follows :

$$\overline{X} = 50,\ Z = 48$$

Calculate median from the above.

(d) If the value of arithmetic mean in a perfectly symmetrical series is 32, find the value of median and mode.

(e) If the value of mean and median is a perfectly asymmetrical series is 28 and 37, what will be the value of mode.

**Solution**

(a)
$$\begin{aligned} Z &= 3M - 2\overline{X} \\ &= 3(94) - 2(86) \\ &= 282 - 172 \\ &= 110 \end{aligned}$$

(b)
$$\begin{aligned} \overline{X} &= \frac{3M - Z}{2} \\ &= \frac{3(20) - (25)}{2} \\ &= \frac{60 - 25}{2} \\ &= \frac{35}{2} = 17.5 \end{aligned}$$

(c)
$$\begin{aligned} M &= \frac{2\overline{X} + Z}{3} \\ &= \frac{2(50) + (48)}{3} \\ &= \frac{100 + 48}{3} \\ &= \frac{148}{3} \\ &= 49.33 \end{aligned}$$

(d) In perfectly symmetrical series, the values of arithmetic mean, median and mode is equal. That is,

$$\overline{X} = M = Z$$

Therefore if in a perfectly symmetrical series the value of arithmetic mean ( $\overline{X}$ ) is 32, then the value of its median and mode will also be 32.

(e) In perfectly asymmetrical series, there is no definite relationship in its arithmetic mean, median and mode, therefore, if in such a series, the value of arithmetic mean ( $\overline{X}$ ) and median (*M*) is 28 and 37 respectively, then it is not possible to find out the probable value of its mode (*Z*).

**Illustration 104.** In a moderately asymmetrical series, the value of mode and median is 20 and 24 respectively. Locate the value of mean.

[*B.Com.* (*Pass*), *Delhi*]

**Solution**

$$Z = 3\,M - 2\,\overline{X}$$

$$20 = 3(24) - 2\,\overline{X}$$

$$2\,\overline{X} = 72 - 20$$

$$2\,\overline{X} = 52$$

$$\overline{X} = 26$$

## BUSINESS AVERAGES

This type of averages are used to analyse various business activities. They are of the following types :

1. Moving Averages
2. Progressive Averages
3. Composite Averages

### (1) Moving Averages

Such averages are used to analyse facts based on time. The method of calculation of this mean is based on arithmetic mean. To calculate this average, first, the base of moving years is fixed. This can be three yearly, four yearly and five yearly etc. Then the following operation is adopted :

1. Assuming to know a three yearly average, first the values of three years will be added; then leaving out the first year, the values of next there years will be added. Likewise, the previous year will be

left out and the next year will be included and the sum of the value of each three years will be known. The sums will be placed in the middle of years of which they are sums. This process will be repeated till the last year.

2. After this, sums will be divided by 3, and the quotients will be 3 yearly moving average.

The following formula can be used to know the moving average :

$$\text{3 yearly Moving Average} = \frac{a+b+c}{3}, \frac{b+c+d}{3}, \frac{c+d+e}{3} + .... \frac{x+y+z}{3}$$

The following example will make this average clear.

**Illustration 105.** Find three yearly moving averages from the following time series and plot them on graph-paper.

| Years | Expenditure (in '000 Rs.) | Years | Expenditure (in '000 Rs.) |
|---|---|---|---|
| 1990 | 5 | 1996 | 16 |
| 1991 | 8 | 1997 | 18 |
| 1992 | 6 | 1998 | 20 |
| 1993 | 10 | 1999 | 22 |
| 1994 | 11 | 2000 | 25 |
| 1995 | 15 | 2001 | 30 |

**Solution**

| Years | Expenditure (in '000 Rs.) | Three Yearly Moving Averages |
|---|---|---|
| 1990 | 5 | |
| 1991 | 8 | $\frac{5+8+6}{3} = \frac{19}{3} = 6.33$ |
| 1992 | 6 | $\frac{8+6+10}{3} = \frac{24}{3} = 8.00$ |
| 1993 | 10 | $\frac{6+10+11}{3} = \frac{27}{3} = 9.00$ |
| 1994 | 11 | $\frac{10+11+15}{3} = \frac{36}{3} = 12.00$ |

| | | |
|---|---|---|
| 1995 | 15 | $\frac{11+15+16}{3}=\frac{42}{3}=14.00$ |
| 1996 | 16 | $\frac{15+16+18}{3}=\frac{49}{3}=16.33$ |
| 1997 | 18 | $\frac{16+18+20}{3}=\frac{54}{3}=18.00$ |
| 1998 | 20 | $\frac{18+20+22}{3}=\frac{60}{3}=20.00$ |
| 1999 | 22 | $\frac{20+22+25}{3}=\frac{67}{3}=22.33$ |
| 2000 | 25 | $\frac{22+25+30}{3}=\frac{77}{3}=25.67$ |
| 2001 | 30 | |

These moving averages have been shown by graph in the following manner :

**MOVING AVERAGES CURVE**

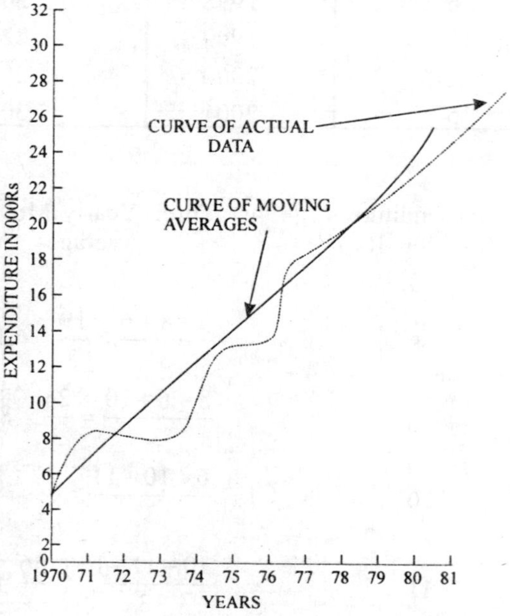

## (2) Progressive Averages

Such averages also are like arithmetic mean. The way values go on increasing the progressive averages of all of them are simultaneously obtained. Following formula may be used to calculate such averages :

$$\frac{A}{1}, \frac{A+B}{2}, \frac{A+B+C}{3}. \frac{A+B+C+D}{4}. \frac{A+B+N_n}{N}$$

**Illustration 106.** Calculate progressive mean from the following data :

| Years : | 1996 | 1997 | 1998 | 1999 | 2000 | 2001 |
|---|---|---|---|---|---|---|
| Profits in '000 Rs. : | 8 | 12 | 19 | 21 | 20 | 34 |

**Solution**

| Years | Profits in '000 | Progressive Average |
|---|---|---|
| 1996 | 8 | $\frac{8}{1}=8$ |
| 1997 | 12 | $\frac{8+12}{2}=10$ |
| 1998 | 19 | $\frac{8+12+19}{3}=13$ |
| 1999 | 21 | $\frac{8+12+19+21}{4}=15$ |
| 2000 | 20 | $\frac{8+12+19+21+20}{5}=16$ |
| 2001 | 34 | $\frac{8+12+19+21+20+34}{6}=19$ |

## (3) Composite Average

When the average of arithmetic means is found, that is called composite mean. In other words, this is the average of averages.

**Illustration 107**

| Years | Salaries of Various Quarters ('000 Rs.) | | | |
|---|---|---|---|---|
| | I Quarter | II Quarter | III Quarter | IV Quarter |
| 1998 | 18 | 20 | 25 | 21 |
| 1999 | 22 | 35 | 19 | 40 |
| 2000 | 25 | 36 | 22 | 33 |
| 2001 | 28 | 42 | 35 | 35 |

**Solution**

| Years | Sales in Quarters (in '000 Rs.) | | | | | |
|---|---|---|---|---|---|---|
| | I Quarter | II Quarter | III Quarter | IV Quarter | Total | Average |
| 1998 | 18 | 20 | 25 | 21 | 84 | 21 |
| 1999 | 22 | 35 | 19 | 40 | 116 | 29 |
| 2000 | 25 | 36 | 22 | 33 | 116 | 29 |
| 2001 | 28 | 42 | 35 | 35 | 140 | 35 |
| Total | 93 | 133 | 101 | 129 | 456 | 114 |
| Average | 23.25 | 33.25 | 25.25 | 32.25 | 114.00 | 28.5 |

Composite Average (Average of Averages)

$$= \frac{21+29+29+35}{4} = \frac{114}{4} = 28.5$$

Or

$$\frac{23.25+33.25+25.25+32.25}{4} = \frac{114}{4} = 28.5$$

## WHICH AVERAGE IS THE BEST?

On looking at the averages referred earlier, it is generally inquired as to which average is the best? Excellence of average depends upon the aim, urgencies and circumstances of investigation. One average can be suitable for one type of investigation and totally unsuitable for another type. Therefore, only this much can be said in this context that different averages may be suitable in different circumstances. There below are mentioned some points regarding which average will be taken to be better for which investigation on the basis of which this fact can be decided.

**1. Object of Inquiry.** The object of inquiry has the greatest effect on the excellence or selection of average. If the investigation is meant to inquire into economic or practical facts of a study, arithmetical mean is suitable. If the units of inquiry increase geometrically or at compound rate, geometric mean should serve better. In the same way geometric mean is suitable for preparing index numbers because from them reversibility tests come out to be correct. Harmonic mean are suitable to find out average speed or movement. If various units of universe are separately significant, using weighted average will serve the purpose. To find out the maximum repeated frequency of the universe, mode is most suitable and if the middle item of the series is to be determined, median should be used.

**2. Number of Variables.** If the number of variables is too small in the universe, then median or mode are not at all the useful averages. Only the arithmetic mean should be used.

**3. Difference in the values of various Items.** If there is too big a difference in the values of the items, arithmetic mean should not be used, geometric mean should be used.

**4. Importance of Highest and Lowest Items.** If the extreme items are not to be given any importance, median or mode is more useful.

**5. Type of Series.** In individual series or in other series if there are many items whose values are equal or near equal, in that case mode should not be used because in such series, mode is ill-defined. Arithmetic mean will be more appropriate in such a series.

**6. Easy in Calculation.** If an easy mean is to be used from the point of view of easy calculation, geometric or harmonic mean should not be used because they are difficult in calculation.

**Formulae used in this Chapter at a Glance**

**1. Arithmetic Mean**

(A) Individual series :

(i) Direct Method :

$$\overline{X} = \frac{X_1 + X_2 + X_3 + \ldots X_n}{N}$$

or $\frac{\Sigma X}{N}$

(B) Grouped Data :

(i) Direct Method :

$$\overline{X} = \frac{\Sigma fX}{N}$$

(ii) Short-Cut Method:

$$\overline{X} = AM + \frac{\sum fd}{N}$$

(ii) Short-Cut Method :

$$\overline{X} = AM + \frac{\sum fd}{N}$$

(iii) Step Deviation Method :

$$\overline{X} = AM + \frac{\sum fd'}{N} \times i$$

**2. Weighted Mean**

(i) Direct Method : $\overline{X}_w = \frac{\sum WX}{\sum W}$

(ii) Short Method : $\overline{X}_w = AM + \frac{\sum Wd}{\sum W}$

**3. Combined Mean**

$$\overline{X}_{12n} = \frac{\overline{X}_1 N_1 + \overline{X}_2 N_2 + \ldots \overline{X}_n N_n}{N_1 + N_2 + \ldots N_n}$$

**4. Geometric Mean**

(A) Individual Series :

$$Gm = \sqrt{a \times b \times \ldots n} \text{ or } G.M. = A.L. \text{ of } \frac{\sum Logs}{N}$$

(B) Discrete & Continuous Series :

$$G.M. = A.L. \text{ of } \frac{\sum f\, Logs}{N}$$

Weighted Geometric Mean :

$$\text{Weighted } G.M. = A.L. \text{ of } \frac{\sum W\, Logs}{\sum W}$$

Rate of Compound Growth : $R = \sqrt[n]{\frac{P_n}{P_0}} - 1$

**5. Harmonic Mean**

(A) Individual Series :

$$H.M. = \frac{N}{\frac{1}{a} + \frac{1}{b} + \ldots \frac{1}{n}} \text{ or Reciprocal of } \frac{\sum \text{Reciprocals}}{N}$$

(B) Discrete & Continuous Series :

$$H.M. = \text{Reciprocal of } \frac{\sum f \text{ Reciprocals}}{N}$$

Weighted Harmonic Mean :

$$\text{Weighted } H.M. = \text{Reciprocal of } \frac{\sum W \text{ Reciprocals}}{\sum W}$$

**6. Median**

(A) Individual Series :

$$M = \text{Value of } \frac{N+1}{2} \text{ th item}$$

(B) Discrete Series :

$$M = \text{Value of } \frac{N+1}{2} \text{ th item}$$

(C) Continuous Series :

(i) To find median group :

$$m = \frac{N}{2} \text{ th item}$$

(ii) To Find median group :

$$M = l_1 + \frac{i}{f}(m - c)$$

**7. Other measurement based on median**

(A) Individual and Discrete Series :

$$Q_1 = \text{Value of } \frac{N+1}{4} \text{ th item}$$

$$Q_3 = \text{Value of } \frac{3(N+1)}{4} \text{ th item}$$

$$D_1 = \text{Value of } \frac{(N+1)}{10} \text{ th item}$$

$$O_1 = \text{Value of } \frac{(N+1)}{8} \text{ th item}$$

$$P_1 = \text{Value of } \frac{(N+1)}{100} \text{ th item}$$

(B) Continuous series :

(i) To find group :

$$q_1 = \frac{N}{4} \text{ th item}$$

$$q_3 = \frac{3N}{4} \text{ th item}$$

$$d_1 = \frac{N}{10} \text{th item}$$

$$O_1 = \frac{N}{8} \text{th item}$$

$$P_1 = \frac{N}{100} \text{th item}$$

(ii) To find the value of measurement :

$$Q_1 = l_1 + \frac{i}{f}(q_1 - c)$$

$$Q_3 = l_1 + \frac{i}{f}(q_3 - c)$$

$$D_1 = l_1 + \frac{i}{f}(d_1 - c)$$

$$O_1 = l_1 + \frac{i}{f}(q_1 - c)$$

$$O_1 = l_1 + \frac{i}{f}(o_1 - c)$$

**8. Mode**

Continuous Series : $Z = l_1 + \frac{\Delta_1}{\Delta_1 + \Delta_2} \times i$ or $Z = l_1 + \frac{f_1 - f_0}{2f_1 - f_0 - f_2} \times i$

Alternative formula :

$$Z = l_1 + \frac{f_2}{f_0 + f_2} \times i$$

When mode is ill-defined :

$$Z = 3M - 2\overline{X}$$

**9. Relationship between mean, median and mode**

(i) In Perfectly Symmetrical Series :

$$\overline{X} = M = Z$$

(ii) In Moderate Asymmetrical Series :

$$Z = 3M - 2\overline{X}$$

**10. Moving Average**

$$\frac{a+b+c}{3}, \frac{b+c+d}{3}, \frac{c+d+e}{3}, \ldots$$

**11. Progressive Average**

$$\frac{a}{1}, \frac{a+b}{2}, \frac{a+b+c}{3}, \frac{a+b+c+d}{4}, \ldots$$

**12. Composite Mean**

$$\frac{\overline{X}_1 + \overline{X}_2 + \overline{X}_3 \ldots \overline{X}_n}{N}$$

## QUESTIONS

1. What do you mean by Averages? What are the kinds of Averages?
2. What are the merits and demerits of averages? What are the characteristics of an ideal average?
3. What are the desiderations of a good average? Compare the mean, the median and the mode in the light of these considerations. Why are averages called as measures of central tendency? *(B.Com., Mysore)*
4. Explain the Law of Averages and describe the objects of computing statistical averages. Also distinguish clearly between Averages of Position and Mathematical Averages.
5. What is an average? Give at least three merits and demerits of any two averages known to you. *(B.Com., Mysore)*
6. What do you mean by central tendency? Describe the measures of measuring the central tendency. Point out the usefulness and limitations of each method.
7. Discuss the essential requisites of a measure of 'Central Tendency'. Under what circumstances would a geometric mean and a harmonic mean be more useful than the arithmetic mean.
8. 'Every average has its own peculiar characteristics. It is difficult to say which averages is the best.' Explain with examples. [*B.Com., Rohtak, B.Com., (Hons.) Delhi*]
9. What are the functions of an average? Explain the desirable properties which an average should possess? What of the average possesses most of these properties?

10. What purpose is served by an Average? Discuss the relative merits and shortcomings of various types of statistical averages.
11. What are 'measures of location'? In what circumstances would you consider them as the most suitable measure for describing the central tendency of a frequency distribution?
[*B.Com.* (*Hons.*) *Delhi*]
12. "An average is a substitute for a complex group of variables, but it is not always safe to depend on the substitute alone to the exclusion of individual measurement of the group." Discuss.
13. "Each average has its own special features and it is difficult to say which one is best." Explain and illustrate.
14. Define the term 'average' and also principal types of average. Describe concrete cases in which (a) the Arithmetic Mean or (b) Median is specially appropriate.
15. Find the Arithmetic Mean from the following data :

| S. No. | Income (Rs.) | S. No. | Income (Rs.) |
|---|---|---|---|
| 1 | 120 | 11 | 96 |
| 2 | 125 | 12 | 125 |
| 3 | 118 | 13 | 150 |
| 4 | 116 | 14 | 155 |
| 5 | 130 | 15 | 160 |
| 6 | 99 | 16 | 162 |
| 7 | 200 | 17 | 167 |
| 8 | 210 | 18 | 170 |
| 9 | 180 | 19 | 153 |
| 10 | 192 | 20 | 180 |

($\overline{X}$ = Rs. 150.4)

16. Calculate Mean from the following figures :

| | | | | | | | | | | |
|---|---|---|---|---|---|---|---|---|---|---|
| Size of Items : | 11 | 12 | 13 | 14 | 15 | 16 | 17 | 18 | 19 | 20 |
| Frequency : | 26 | 28 | 18 | 19 | 22 | 25 | 30 | 32 | 40 | 45 |

($\overline{X}$ = 16.13)

17. You are given the following series :

| | | | | | | |
|---|---|---|---|---|---|---|
| Class Intervals : | 0-5 | 5-10 | 10-15 | 15-20 | 20-25 | 25-30 |
| Frequency : | 5 | 8 | 12 | 10 | 6 | 3 |

Compute the simple mean from the above data.

($\overline{X}$ = 13.98)

18. Calculate the Mean of the following frequency distribution relating to marks secured by students in Statistics :

| Marks | No. of Students | Marks | No. of Students |
|---|---|---|---|
| 0-5 | 1 | 40-45 | 20 |
| 5-10 | 6 | 45-50 | 25 |
| 10-15 | 8 | 50-55 | 12 |
| 15-20 | 7 | 55-60 | 7 |
| 20-25 | 11 | 60-65 | 6 |
| 25-30 | 10 | 65-70 | 5 |
| 30-35 | 10 | 70-75 | 4 |
| 35-30 | 17 | 75-80 | 1 |

*(Delhi B.Com.)*

($\overline{X}$ = 39.37)

19. Tabulate the following data by taking 10 as the class-interval and calculate the Arithmetic Mean :

| | | | | | | | | | |
|---|---|---|---|---|---|---|---|---|---|
| 30 | 45 | 55 | 65 | 60 | 90 | 115 | 85 | 95 | 100 |
| 95 | 65 | 75 | 85 | 125 | 110 | 87 | 65 | 100 | 115 |
| 65 | 60 | 75 | 96 | 130 | 95 | 125 | 115 | 65 | 70 |
| 95 | 85 | 65 | 60 | 80 | 85 | 75 | 95 | 55 | 45 |
| 35 | 45 | 40 | 85 | 135 | 140 | 95 | 65 | 45 | 35 |
| 115 | 90 | 80 | 125 | 130 | 35 | 90 | 100 | 95 | 85 |
| 85 | 120 | 115 | 40 | 35 | 125 | 35 | 105 | 75 | 45 |

($\overline{X}$ = 83.43)

Hint :

| C.I. : | 30-40 | 40-50 | 50-60 | 60-70 | 70-80 | 80-90 | 90-100 |
|---|---|---|---|---|---|---|---|
| f : | 6 | 7 | 2 | 10 | 5 | 10 | 11 |

| C.I. : | 100-110 | 110-120 | 120-130 | 130-140 | 140-150 |
|---|---|---|---|---|---|
| f : | 4 | 6 | 5 | 3 | 1 |

20. Find the average marks of a student from the following table :

| Below | Marks | No. of Students |
|---|---|---|
| " | 10 | 25 |
| " | 20 | 40 |
| " | 30 | 60 |
| " | 40 | 75 |
| " | 50 | 95 |
| " | 60 | 125 |
| " | 70 | 190 |
| " | 80 | 240 |

($\overline{X}$ = 49.58)

21. Calculate the arithmetic average by short-cut method from the following series :

| | | | | | |
|---|---|---|---|---|---|
| Expenditure (below) | 5 | 10 | 15 | 20 | 25 |
| No. of Students | 6 | 16 | 28 | 38 | 46 |

(*Allah., B.Com.*)

($\overline{X}$ = Rs. 12.93)

22. A factory pays workers on piece rate basis and also a bonus to each worker on the basis of individual output in each quarter. The rate of bonus payable is as follows :

| Output in Units | Bonus in Rupees |
|---|---|
| 70-74 | 40 |
| 75-79 | 45 |
| 80-84 | 50 |
| 85-89 | 60 |
| 90-94 | 70 |
| 95-99 | 80 |
| 100-104 | 100 |

The individual output of a batch of 50 workers is given below :

| | | | | | | | | | |
|---|---|---|---|---|---|---|---|---|---|
| 94 | 83 | 78 | 76 | 88 | 86 | 93 | 80 | 91 | 82 |
| 89 | 97 | 92 | 84 | 92 | 80 | 85 | 83 | 98 | 103 |
| 87 | 88 | 88 | 81 | 95 | 86 | 99 | 81 | 87 | 90 |
| 84 | 97 | 80 | 75 | 93 | 101 | 82 | 82 | 89 | 72 |
| 85 | 83 | 75 | 72 | 83 | 98 | 77 | 87 | 71 | 80 |

By suitable classification, you are required to find :

(1) Average bonus per worker for the quarter

(2) Total quarterly bonus paid to the whole batch

(3) Average output per worker. (*C.A.*)

(59.7, 2985, 86.3)

23. Find the average marks of a students from the following table :

| | | | | | | | |
|---|---|---|---|---|---|---|---|
| Marks above | 60 | 50 | 40 | 30 | 20 | 10 | 0 |
| No. of Students | 35 | 43 | 58 | 65 | 82 | 90 | 100 |

($\overline{X}$ = 42.3)

24. Compute Median from the following data :

28 29 26 35 32 45 50 52 53 56 58 59 60 62 63

(*M*=52)

25. Compute median from the following figures :

35 38 60 62 63 70 75 80 89 93 95 100

($M$=72.5)

26. Find Median from the following data :

| | | | | | | | | | | |
|---|---|---|---|---|---|---|---|---|---|---|
| Age in years : | 5 | 10 | 15 | 20 | 25 | 30 | 35 | 40 | 45 | 50 |
| No. of Persons : | 28 | 32 | 35 | 40 | 52 | 56 | 48 | 35 | 29 | 10 |

($M$ = 25 years)

27. Calculate Median from the following frequency distribution :

| Variable | Frequency |
|---|---|
| 0-20 | 12 |
| 20-40 | 15 |
| 40-60 | 18 |
| 60-80 | 13 |
| 80-100 | 20 |
| 100-120 | 16 |

($M$ = 63.08)

28. Compute the Median from the following figures :

| Production in Kgs. | No. of Producers |
|---|---|
| 1-100 | 69 |
| 101-200 | 25 |
| 201-300 | 48 |
| 301-400 | 56 |
| 401-500 | 39 |
| 501-600 | 40 |
| 601-700 | 25 |

($M$ = 316.57)

29. Determine the Quartiles and the Median for the following data :

| Income per month | Number of Persons |
|---|---|
| Below Rs. 30 | 69 |
| 30-40 | 167 |
| 40-50 | 207 |
| 50-60 | 65 |
| 60-70 | 58 |
| 70-80 | 27 |
| 80 & above | 10 |

($M$ = 43.16, $Q_1$ = 34.9, $Q_3$ = 51.4)

30. The following frequency distribution shows the marks secured by 885 students in statistics out of 100 at the B.Com. Examination of a university.

| Class intervals | Frequency | Class-intervals | Frequency |
|---|---|---|---|
| 0-10 | 18 | 50-60 | 250 |
| 10-20 | 25 | 60-70 | 160 |
| 20-30 | 41 | 70-80 | 92 |
| 30-40 | 89 | 80-90 | 63 |
| 40-50 | 127 | 90-100 | 20 |

(a) Find the median marks by drawing an 'Ogive',

(b) Check up the value of the median so found by using the standard formula for finding the median.

($M$ = 55.7)

31. Convert the following distribution into 'more than' frequency distribution :

| Weekly wages less than Rs. | No. of Workers |
|---|---|
| 20 | 41 |
| 40 | 92 |
| 60 | 156 |
| 80 | 194 |
| 100 | 201 |

For the data given above, draw an Ogive and hence find out the value of median.

[*B.Com.* (*Pass*) *Delhi*]

($M$ = Rs. 42.66)

32. Compute Median and Quartiles from the following :

| Income (Rs.) | No. of Employees |
|---|---|
| Below 10 | 4 |
| 10-20 | 14 |
| 20-30 | 18 |
| 30-40 | 30 |
| 40-50 | 17 |
| 50-60 | 12 |
| 60-70 | 10 |
| 70-80 | 8 |
| 80-90 | 5 |
| 90-100 | 2 |

Estimate the number of persons earning over Rs. 55 per day.

($M$=38, $Q_1$=26.67, $Q_3$=55.83, 31 persons are earning more than Rs. 55)

33. From the table given below find out the Median and Quartiles :

| Size : | 11-15 | 16-20 | 21-25 | 26-30 | 31-35 | 36-40 | 41-45 | 46-50 |
|---|---|---|---|---|---|---|---|---|
| Frequency : | 7 | 10 | 13 | 26 | 35 | 22 | 11 | 5 |

($M$ = 31.71, $Q_1$ = 25.93, $Q_3$ = 36.81)

34. Below are given the marks obtained by a batch of 20 students in certain class-test in History and Geography.

| Roll No. | Marks in History | Marks in Geography | Roll No. | Marks in History | Marks in Geography |
|---|---|---|---|---|---|
| 1 | 53 | 58 | 11 | 25 | 10 |
| 2 | 54 | 55 | 12 | 42 | 42 |
| 3 | 52 | 25 | 13 | 33 | 15 |
| 4 | 32 | 32 | 14 | 48 | 46 |
| 5 | 30 | 26 | 15 | 72 | 50 |
| 6 | 60 | 85 | 16 | 51 | 64 |
| 7 | 47 | 44 | 17 | 45 | 39 |
| 8 | 46 | 80 | 18 | 33 | 38 |
| 9 | 35 | 33 | 19 | 65 | 30 |
| 10 | 28 | 72 | 20 | 29 | 36 |

In which subject the level of knowledge, of the students is higher?

(Median; History = 45.5, Geography = 40.5. Therefore, the level of knowledge is higher in History than Geography.)

35. Draw an ogive for the following distribution read the median and verify the result by calculation. How many workers earn monthly wages between Rs. 60 and Rs. 72?

| Monthly wages : | 50-55 | 55-60 | 60-65 | 65-70 | 70-75 | 75-80 | 80-100 |
|---|---|---|---|---|---|---|---|
| No. Of workers : | 6 | 10 | 22 | 30 | 16 | 12 | 15 |

($M$ = 67.9, 58)

36. The following table gives the diastolic blood pressure reading of 250 proposers for life insurance in U.K.

| Diastolic blood pressure | No. of Proposers |
|---|---|
| 59.5-67.5 | 9 |
| 67.5-72.5 | 31 |
| 72.5-77.5 | 39 |
| 77.5-82.5 | 114 |
| 82.5-87.5 | 30 |
| 87.5-95.5 | 27 |

Calculate the Median, first Quartile and third Quartile.

($M$ = 79.52, $Q_1$ = 75.38, $Q_3$ = 82.26)

37. Calculate mode, $Q_1$ and $Q_3$ from the following data :

| | | | | | | | | | | |
|---|---|---|---|---|---|---|---|---|---|---|
| Roll No. : | 1 | 2 | 3 | 4 | 5 | 6 | 7 | 8 | 9 | 10 |
| Marks : | 43 | 48 | 65 | 58 | 31 | 60 | 37 | 48 | 62 | 78 |

(*B.Com., Madurai*)

(Z = 48, $Q_1$ = 41.5, $Q_3$ = 62.75)

38. According to the census of 1971 the following are the population figures in thousands of 36 cities of India :

| | | | | | |
|---|---|---|---|---|---|
| 2,488 | 391 | 203 | 178 | 360 | 176 |
| 1,490 | 131 | 777 | 258 | 213 | 147 |
| 733 | 437 | 176 | 143 | 522 | 284 |
| 193 | 181 | 672 | 302 | 160 | 153 |
| 591 | 263 | 213 | 142 | 407 | 160 |
| 169 | 92 | 387 | 239 | 204 | 151 |

Find the Mediar and the Quartiles.

($M$ = 213, $Q_1$ = 162.25, $Q_3$ = 403)

39. Find the Median and the Quartiles from the following data :

| Wages in Rs. | No. of Workers |
|---|---|
| 25 and under 30 | 10 |
| 30 and under 35 | 15 |
| 35 and under 40 | 19 |
| 40 and under 45 | 26 |
| 45 and under 50 | 18 |
| 50 and under 55 | 29 |
| 55 and under 60 | 24 |
| 60 and under 65 | 4 |
| 65 and under 70 | 8 |
| 70 and under 75 | 7 |
| Total | 160 |

($M$ = 47.78, $Q_1$ = 38.95, $Q_3$ = 55.625)

40. Compute Median and Quartiles from the following data :

| | | | | | | | |
|---|---|---|---|---|---|---|---|
| Central value : | 10 | 20 | 30 | 40 | 50 | 60 | 70 |
| Frequency : | 18 | 19 | 12 | 20 | 16 | 8 | 5 |

($M$ = 35, $Q_1$ = 18.42, $Q_3$ = 47.81)

41. Calculate Mode from the following data :

| | | | | | | | |
|---|---|---|---|---|---|---|---|
| Size of items : | 3 | 6 | 9 | 12 | 15 | 18 | 21 |
| Frequency : | 8 | 18 | 28 | 13 | 20 | 16 | 10 |

($Z$ = 9)

42. From the following figures, compute Mode :

| | | | | | | | | |
|---|---|---|---|---|---|---|---|---|
| Income (Rs.) : | 5 | 10 | 15 | 20 | 25 | 30 | 35 | 40 |
| No. of Persons : | 26 | 29 | 35 | 34 | 32 | 28 | 22 | 15 |

($Z$ = 20)

43. Compute mode from the following frequency distribution of earners by monthly income :

| | | | | |
|---|---|---|---|---|
| Income (Rs.) : | Below 200 | 200-399 | 400-599 | 600-799 |
| No. of earners : | 25 | 72 | 47 | 22 |
| Income (Rs.) : | 800-999 | 1,000-1,199 | | |
| No. of earners : | 13 | 7 | | |

[*B.A.* (*Eco. Hons.*), *Calcutta*]

(330.06)

44. Find modal marks from the following series :

| Marks obtained | No. of Students |
|---|---|
| Below 10 | 20 |
| " 20 | 30 |
| " 30 | 36 |
| " 40 | 60 |
| " 50 | 65 |
| " 60 | 82 |
| " 70 | 100 |

($Z$ = 34.86)

45. You are given the following data :

| Profits in (Rs.) | No. of Firms |
|---|---|
| Above 8,000 | 22 |
| " 7,000 | 40 |
| " 6,000 | 52 |
| " 5,000 | 100 |
| " 4,000 | 116 |
| " 3,000 | 133 |
| " 2,000 | 140 |
| " 1,000 | 150 |

($Z$ = 5470.59)

Find Mode from the above data.

46. Calculate Mode from the following table :

| | | | | | | | | |
|---|---|---|---|---|---|---|---|---|
| Central value | : | 30 | 40 | 50 | 60 | 70 | 80 | 90 |
| Frequency | : | 7 | 12 | 17 | 29 | 31 | 5 | 3 |

($Z$ = 61.46)
(*B.Com., Agra*)

47. From the following information, calculate mode :

| | |
|---|---|
| Lower limit of the modal class | ... 200 |
| Upper limit of the modal class | ... 220 |
| Frequency of the modal class | ... 40 |
| Frequency of the class succeeding the modal class | ... 30 |
| Frequency of the class preceding the modal class | ... 28 |

(210.91)
(*B.Com., Osmania*)

48. Fifty workers of a certain factory at Naini receive the following amount as their monthly wages :

| Wages in Rs. | | | | | | | | | |
|---|---|---|---|---|---|---|---|---|---|
| 40 | 42 | 42 | 44 | 45 | 45 | 45 | 46 | 48 | 48 |
| 50 | 50 | 50 | 50 | 50 | 52 | 53 | 54 | 55 | 55 |
| 55 | 55 | 55 | 56 | 56 | 58 | 58 | 59 | 60 | 60 |
| 60 | 60 | 60 | 62 | 64 | 65 | 65 | 65 | 65 | 66 |
| 68 | 70 | 70 | 70 | 71 | 72 | 75 | 75 | 76 | 80 |

Arrange the above data in classes with class-intervals of five rupees each and find the modal wage.

($Z$ = 57)

49. Following figures relate to the size of holdings of farmers :

| Size of Holdings (in Hactares) | No. of Farmers |
|---|---|
| 0-1 | 12 |
| 1-2 | 16 |
| 2-3 | 22 |
| 3-4 | 40 |
| 4-5 | 50 |
| 5-6 | 20 |
| 6-7 | 10 |
| 7-8 | 12 |
| 8-9 | 10 |
| 9-10 | 8 |

Draw the histogram of the above data and then find the modal value.

Also check the value by direct calculation.

[*B.Com.*, (*Pass*) *Delhi*]

(4.25)

50. Prepare a histogram for the following data and find out the value of mode :

| Marks | No. of candidates |
|---|---|
| 0-5 | 6 |
| 5-10 | 12 |
| 10-15 | 17 |
| 15-20 | 30 |
| 20-25 | 10 |
| 25-30 | 10 |
| 30-40 | 8 |
| 40-60 | 8 |

[*B.Com., (Pass), Delhi*]

(16.97)

51. Draw Histogram and Frequency polygon for the following data and read mode from the histogram.

| Profits per shop (in '000) | Number of shops | Profits per shop (in '000) | Number of shops |
|---|---|---|---|
| 0-100 | 12 | 300-400 | 20 |
| 100-200 | 18 | 400-500 | 17 |
| 200-300 | 27 | 500-600 | 06 |

(*B.Com., Karnataka*)

(256.25)

52. Calculate Geometric Mean from the following figures :

4328
592.35
93.62
4.328
.6789
.0532
.00556
.000632

(*G.M.* = 1.841)

53. Find Geometric Mean from the following data :

| | | | | | | | |
|---|---|---|---|---|---|---|---|
| Size of Items : | 4 | 8 | 12 | 16 | 20 | 24 | 28 |
| Frequency : | 18 | 15 | 6 | 10 | 9 | 8 | 2 |

(*G.M.* = 10.20)

54. Compute Geometric Mean from the following series :

| | | | | | | | | |
|---|---|---|---|---|---|---|---|---|
| Groups : | 0-5 | 5-10 | 10-15 | 15-20 | 20-25 | 25-30 | 30-35 | 35-40 |
| Frequency : | 12 | 8 | 13 | 11 | 9 | 6 | 3 | 5 |

(*G.M.* = 12.26)

55. Find Harmonic Mean from the following :

568
21.8
1.63
.0325
.00635
.000462
3.085
43.92

(*H.M.* = 0.003398)

56. Calculate Harmonic Mean from the following data :

| | | | | | | |
|---|---|---|---|---|---|---|
| Rs. : | 6 | 12 | 18 | 24 | 30 | 36 |
| Frequency : | 6 | 3 | 5 | 10 | 9 | 2 |

(*H.M.* = 15.23)

57. Compute Harmonic Mean from the given frequency distribution :

| | | | | | |
|---|---|---|---|---|---|
| Class-intervals : | 0-10 | 10-20 | 20-30 | 30-40 | 40-50 |
| Frequency : | 8 | 10 | 6 | 5 | 3 |

(*H.M.* = 11.78)

58. Find out the Median and the Mode in the following series :

| | | | | | | | |
|---|---|---|---|---|---|---|---|
| Size (below) : | 5 | 10 | 15 | 20 | 25 | 30 | 35 |
| Frequency : | 1 | 3 | 13 | 17 | 27 | 36 | 38 |

($M$ = 21, $Z$ = 24.29)

59. Calculate mean and mode from the following data :

| | | | | | | | | |
|---|---|---|---|---|---|---|---|---|
| Marks below : | 80 | 70 | 60 | 50 | 40 | 30 | 20 | 10 |
| No. of Students : | 50 | 45 | 40 | 30 | 16 | 10 | 7 | 3 |

(*B.Com., Banaras*)

($X$ = 44.8, $Z$ = 46.67)

60. On the basis of given frequency distribution find out (a) Median (b) Mode :

| Value in marks: | 0-5 | 5-10 | 10-15 | 15-20 | 20-25 | 25-30 | 30-35 |
|---|---|---|---|---|---|---|---|
| Frequency : | 25 | 125 | 100 | 300 | 250 | 125 | 20 |

($M$ = 18.7, $Z$ = 19)

61. The following table gives the marks obtained by 70 students in Mathematics. Calculate the simple mean and geometric mean of the series.

| Marks | No. of students |
|---|---|
| More than 70 | 7 |
| More than 60 | 18 |
| More than 50 | 40 |
| More than 40 | 50 |
| More than 30 | 63 |
| More than 20 | 70 |

($X$ = 50.43, *G.M.* = 48.09)

62. Calculate Mean, Median and Mode from the following data of the heights in inches of a group of students :

61, 62, 63, 61, 63, 64, 64, 60, 65, 63, 64, 66, 64

Now suppose that a group of students whose heights are 60, 66, 59, 68, 67 and 70 inches, is added to the original group. Find Mean, Median and Mode of combined group.

($\overline{X}$ = 63.08, M = 63.0, Z = 64 and for combined group.

$\overline{X}$ = 63.68, $M$ = 64, $Z$ = 64)

63. Find the Mean, Median and Mode from the following distribution :

| Class Intervals : | 0-15 | 15-30 | 30-45 | 45-60 | 60-75 | 75-90 |
|---|---|---|---|---|---|---|
| Frequency : | 5 | 23 | 22 | 20 | 6 | 3 |

($X$ = 39.02, $M$ = 37.84, $Z$ = 36.98)

(Hint : Use alternative formula of mode.)

64. Calculate Mean, Median, Quartiles and 4th Decile from the data given below :

| Marks Group : | 0-5 | 5-10 | 10-15 | 15-20 | 20-25 | 25-30 | 30-35 |
|---|---|---|---|---|---|---|---|
| No. of Students : | 4 | 6 | 10 | 16 | 12 | 8 | 4 |

($\overline{X}$ = 18, $M$ = 18.125, $Q_1$ = 12.5, $Q_3$ = 23.75, $D_4$ = 16.25)

65. From the figures given below find the Mode, Median and Quartiles. What information you deduce from them?

| Age (years) : | 20-25 | 25-30 | 30-35 | 35-40 | 40-45 | 45-50 | 50-55 | 55-60 |
|---|---|---|---|---|---|---|---|---|
| No. of Persons : | 50 | 70 | 100 | 180 | 150 | 120 | 70 | 59 |

($Z$ = 38.64, $M$ = 39.99, $Q_1$ = 34, $Q_3$ = 47.05)

66. Calculate Mode, Median and both Quartiles from the following table :

| Marks : | 1-5 | 6-10 | 11-15 | 16-20 | 21-25 | 26-30 | 31-35 | 36-40 |
|---|---|---|---|---|---|---|---|---|
| No. of Students : | 3 | 10 | 20 | 30 | 20 | 9 | 5 | 3 |

(*M.A., Agra*)

($Z$ = 18, $M$ = 18.33, $Q_1$ = 13.5 and $Q_3$ = 23.5)

67. For the following distribution of income groups, find mean, median and mode :

| Income (in Rs.) | No. of persons | Income (in Rs.) | No. of perons |
|---|---|---|---|
| 0-200 | 80 | 600-800 | 80 |
| 200-400 | 165 | 800-1000 | 32 |
| 400-600 | 230 | 1000-1200 | 13 |

(*B.Com., Bombay*)

($\overline{X}$ = 452.67, $M$ = 447.83, $Z$ = 460.47)

68. The marks (out of maximum of 100) obtained by candidates in an examination are shown in the following frequency table. Calculate the Arithmetic average and Mode.

| Marks | Number of Candidates |
|---|---|
| 17.5-22.5 | 2 |
| 22.5-27.5 | 8 |
| 27.5-32.5 | 33 |
| 32.5-37.5 | 80 |
| 37.5-42.5 | 170 |
| 42.5-47.5 | 243 |
| 47.5-52.5 | 213 |
| 52.5-57.5 | 145 |
| 57.5-62.5 | 67 |
| 62.5-67.5 | 35 |
| 67.5-72.5 | 4 |

($\overline{X}$ = 46.97, $Z$ = 46.04)

69. Calculate Mean, Median and Mode from the following frequency distribution :

| Age in Years | No. of Persons |
|---|---|
| Below 10 | 16 |
| 10-20 | 25 |
| 20-30 | 32 |
| 30-40 | 28 |
| 40-50 | 32 |
| 50-60 | 25 |
| 60 & above | 16 |

($\overline{X} = M = Z = 35$)

70. Calculate Mean, Median, Mode and seventh percentile of the following distribution :

| Age (years) | Observed Frequency |
|---|---|
| 0-10 | 2 |
| 10-20 | 11 |
| 20-30 | 20 |
| 30-40 | 26 |
| 40-50 | 30 |
| 50-60 | 10 |
| 60-70 | 1 |
| Total | 100 |

($\overline{X} = 35.5$, $M = 36.54$, $Z = 41.67$, $P_7 = 14.55$)

71. Find out the Median and the Mode from the following table :

| | | | | | | | | | |
|---|---|---|---|---|---|---|---|---|---|
| No. of days Absent Less than : | 5 | 10 | 15 | 20 | 25 | 30 | 35 | 40 | 45 |
| Number : | 29 | 224 | 465 | 582 | 634 | 644 | 650 | 653 | 655 |

($M = 12.15$ days and $Z = 11.35$ days)

72. Calculate mode, median and arithmetic average for the following frequency distribution :

| | | | | | | | | | | |
|---|---|---|---|---|---|---|---|---|---|---|
| Marks : | 5 | 10 | 15 | 20 | 25 | 30 | 35 | 40 | 45 | 50 |
| No. of Students : | 20 | 43 | 75 | 67 | 72 | 45 | 39 | 9 | 8 | 6 |

(*B.Com., Madras*)

($\overline{X} = 22.27$, $M = 20$, $Z = 15$)

73. Eight coins were tossed together and the number of heads resulting was observed. The operation was performed 256 times and the frequency that were obtained for the different values of $x$, the number of heads are shown in the following table. Calculate Mean, Median and Quartiles of the distribution $x$.

| $x$ : | 0 | 1 | 2 | 3 | 4 | 5 | 6 | 7 | 8 |
|---|---|---|---|---|---|---|---|---|---|
| Frequency : | 1 | 9 | 26 | 59 | 72 | 52 | 29 | 7 | 1 |

($\overline{X} = 3.97$, $M = 4$, $Q_1 = 3$, $Q_3 = 5$)

74. Calculate Mode and Arithmetic Average from the following series and account for the difference, if any :

| Size of Item | Frequency |
|---|---|
| 6-10 | 20 |
| 11-15 | 30 |
| 16-20 | 50 |
| 21-25 | 40 |
| 26-30 | 10 |

($\overline{X} = 17.67$, $Z = 18.8$)

75. Compute the Mode and Median of the following :

| Size | Frequency | Size | Frequency |
|---|---|---|---|
| 0-5 | 20 | 25-30 | 16 |
| 5-10 | 24 | 30-35 | 34 |
| 10-15 | 32 | 35-40 | 10 |
| 15-20 | 28 | 40-45 | 8 |
| 20-25 | 20 | | |

($Z = 13.33$, $M = 18.57$)

76. Convert the following into ordinary frequency table and compute Mean, Median and Mode.

| | No. of Labourers |
|---|---|
| Income more than Rs. 5 | 100 |
| Income more than Rs. 10 | 90 |
| Income more than Rs. 15 | 86 |
| Income more than Rs. 20 | 75 |
| Income more than Rs. 25 | 62 |
| Income more than Rs. 30 | 58 |
| Income more than Rs. 35 | 47 |
| Income more than Rs. 40 | 32 |
| Income more than Rs. 45 | 28 |
| Income more than Rs. 50 | 16 |

($\overline{X} = 32.2$, $M = 33.64$, $Z = 36.52$)

85. Compute the Weighted Index from the following data :

| Articles | Index | Weight |
|---|---|---|
| Food | 120 | 4 |
| Cloths | 130 | 2 |
| House Rent | 150 | 2 |
| Education | 100 | 1 |
| Miscellaneous | 160 | 1 |

(Weighted Index = 130)

86. Calculate Weighted Mean from the following :

| | | | | | | |
|---|---|---|---|---|---|---|
| Size of Items : | 6 | 12 | 18 | 24 | 30 | 36 |
| Weights : | 8 | 15 | 22 | 16 | 25 | 14 |

(Weighted Mean = 22.62)

87. Compute Weighted Geometric Mean from the following series :

| | | | | | | |
|---|---|---|---|---|---|---|
| Classes : | 0-10 | 10-20 | 20-30 | 30-40 | 40-50 | 50-60 |
| Weights : | 18 | 2 | 6 | 5 | 13 | 6 |

(Weighted Geometric Mean = 18.18)

88. Find Weighted Harmonic Mean from the following figures :

| | | | | | | |
|---|---|---|---|---|---|---|
| Rs. : | 2 | 4 | 6 | 8 | 10 | 12 |
| Weight : | 1 | 2 | 4 | 6 | 3 | 4 |

(Weighted Harmonic Mean = 6.60)

89. Find the general death rate and standardized death ratio from the following information :

| Age groups (Years) | Local Population | | Standard Population | |
|---|---|---|---|---|
| | No. of Persons | Deaths | No. of Persons | Deaths |
| Below 15 | 10,000 | 100 | 15,000 | 105 |
| 15-30 | 25,000 | 100 | 30,000 | 60 |
| 30-40 | 35,000 | 70 | 35,000 | 105 |
| 40 & above | 30,000 | 240 | 20,000 | 240 |
| | 1,00,000 | 510 | 1,00,000 | 510 |

(General Death Ratio of both populations = 5.1)

(Standard Death Ratio of local population = 5)

90. On the basis of the following data, compare which town is healthier assuming the population of town A as standard population :

| Age groups (Years) | Town A | | Town B | |
|---|---|---|---|---|
| | Population | Deaths | Population | Deaths |
| Below 10 | 8,000 | 96 | 12,000 | 120 |
| 10-30 | 12,000 | 60 | 18,000 | 36 |
| 30-50 | 20,000 | 80 | 25,000 | 50 |
| 50 & above | 10,000 | 150 | 15,000 | 180 |
| | 50,000 | 386 | 70,000 | 386 |

General Death Rate of Town A = 7.72,
General Death Rate of Town B = 5.51,
Standard Death Rate of Town B = 5.28,
Therefore, Town B is healthier than Town A.

91. (a) Convert the following into an ordinary frequency table and find out mode :

| | | | | | |
|---|---|---|---|---|---|
| 5 students | get | less | than | 3 | marks |
| 12 " | " | " | " | 6 | " |
| 25 " | " | " | " | 9 | " |
| 30 " | " | " | " | 12 | " |

(b) The population of five town, A, B, C, D, E was 20,000, 26,000, 23,000, 25,000 and 24,000 respectively. The average income of the resident for the respective towns was 280, 270, 240, 230 and 300. Find out the average income per head for all the towns combined.

[(a) $Z$ = 7.29, (b) Combined mean = 263.47]

92. (a) Compute Mean if you are given the following value :

$Z = 25 \qquad M = 28$

(b) Compute Median if you are given the values of Arithmetic Mean and Mode as 10 and 8 respectively.

(c) What will be the most appropriate value of Mode if the value of Arithmetic Averages is 40 and of Median is 48.

[(a) $\overline{X}$ = 29.5, (b) $M$ = 9.33, (c) Z = 64]

93. (a) Find the correct Mean from the following information :

| | |
|---|---|
| No. of observations | 100 |
| Arithmetic Mean | 12 |

One observation which is 15 read wrongly as 5.

(b) Find the value of missing frequency from the following data :

| Size of Items | Frequency |
|---|---|
| 5 | 10 |
| 10 | 12 |
| 15 | 16 |
| 20 | — |
| 25 | 8 |
| 30 | 5 |

You are given the value of Arithmetic Average as 16.

[(a) 12.10, (b) 14]

94. (a) The annual rates of growth of a factory in 5 years are 5.0, 7.5, 2.5, 5.0 and 10.0 per cent respectively. What is the compound rate of growth per annum for the period?

(b) Find the average rate of increase in population which in the first decade has increased 20%, in next 30% and in the third 45%.

[(a) 5.9%, (b) 30.2%]

95. (a) A man travels first quarter of a mile at the speed of 10 miles per hour, second quarter at the speed of 8 miles per hour, third quarter at the speed of 5 miles per hour and last quarter at the speed of 3 miles per hour. What is his average speed for the entire miles?

(b) A train runs first 60 kilometers at the speed of 100 km. per hour, next 40 km. at the speed of 80 km. per hour and last 100 km. at the speed of 60 km. per hour. What is the average speed of the train for the whole journey?

[(a) 5.28 miles per hour, (b) 72.20 miles per hour]

96. (a) Typist A can type a letter in five minutes, typist B in ten minutes and typist C in fifteen minutes. What is the average number of letters typed per hour per typist?

(b) A taxi ride in Delhi costs one rupee for first kilometre and sixty paise each additional kilometre. The cost for each kilometer is incurred in the beginning of the kilometer, so that the rider pays for a whole kilometre. What is the average cost for 2¾ kilometres?

(c) An investor buys Rs. 1,200 worth of shares in a company each month. During the first 5 months he bought the shares at a price of Rs. 10, Rs. 12, Rs. 15, Rs. 20 and Rs. 24 per share. After 5 months what is the average price paid for the shares by him?

[*B.Com., Pass* (*Pass*) *Delhi*]

[(a) 7.33, (b) Rs. 0.80, (c) Rs. 14.63)

97. (a) If $\overline{X} - M = 5$ and $Z = 50$ find out $\overline{X}$ and $M$.

(b) The mean of 40 items is 17. If the mean of 10 items among them is 20. Find out the mean of the rest.

(*B.Com., Sardar Patel*)

[(a) $\overline{X} = 65$, $M = 60$, (b) $\overline{X} = 16$]

98. The average rainfall for a week, excluding Sunday, was 10 cm. Due to heavy rainfall on Sunday, the average for the week rose to 15 cm. How much rainfall was there on Sunday?

[*B.Com.* (*Pass*) *Delhi*]

(45 cm.)

99. The average marks of 100 students was 40, later on it was discovered that 74 marks of a student were read 14 marks by mistake. Find out correct mean.

(*B.Com., Agra*)

[Corrected $\overline{X} = 40.6$]

100. 50 students appeared in an examination, following is the result of passed students :

| | | | | | | |
|---|---|---|---|---|---|---|
| Marks : | 4 | 5 | 6 | 7 | 8 | 9 |
| No. of students : | 8 | 10 | 9 | 6 | 4 | 3 |

If combine mean marks of all the 50 students are 5.16, find the average marks of failed students?

(*B.Com., Agra*)

($\overline{X}_2 = 2.1$)

101. In a moderately asymmetrical series mode is the difference between 3 median and 2 mean. If mean is 15.6 and median is 15.73, find the probable value of mode.

(15.99)

102. The average rainfall in a city was 0.4 (excluding Sunday). Due to heavy rains on Sunday the average of the week increased to 1.1", find the rainfall on Sunday.

(*B.Com., Agra*)

(5.3)

103. The average annual salaries of all the employees of a Co. was Rs. 3000. The average annual salaries of male and female workers of this Co. was Rs. 3,200 and Rs. 2,200 respectively. Find the percentage of male and female employees of the company.

(*B.Com., Agra*)
(80%, 20%)

104. A train runs 30 minutes at speed of 40 miles per hour. Afterwards due to repair in railway lines it runs 10 minutes at the speed of 12 miles per hour. After this it ran with its original speed for 20 minutes except 2 minutes, when it ran at the speed of 30 miles per hour due to passing on a bridge. Find the average speed of the train.

(*B.Com., Agra*)
(35 miles per hour)